A Supplement and Expansion for Mythras

Published under license in the UK by Aeon Games Publishing
games.aeonbooks.co.uk

ISBN 978-1-91147-107-3

The Design Mechanism

Credits

Luther Arkwright Created by Bryan Talbot

Developed and Written By
Chad Bowser, Pete Nash, Bryan Steele and Lawrence Whitaker

Additional Material By
Bryan Talbot, James Cast, Rodney Leary and John White

Editing
Alexandra James

Proof Reading
Gamesmyths

Design and Layout
Alexandra James

Artists
Bryan Talbot and Lee Smith

Special Thanks
John Hutchinson

Playtesters
Chad Bowser, Tim Evans, David Finch, Pete Nash,
Bryan Steele, Howard Tytherleigh and Lawrence Whitaker

Contents

Introduction

Luther Arkwright: Roleplaying Across the Parallels is based on the graphic novels of Bryan Talbot. The Characters are agents of the Valhalla Project, people aware of the existence of the multiverse and possessed of talents and qualities the Valhalla Project needs in its bid to safeguard and preserve the fundamental structure of the parallels. Other forces, principally those known as The Disruptors, seek to destabilise or control the multiverse for their own ends. The Valhalla Project's agents oppose these plans and frequently work in the shadows, frequently alone, to target Disruptors and ensure that each parallel is free to develop without a malign, external influence.

Mythras Rules

This is not a standalone game; you will need a copy of the Mythras rules. The rules contain most of the things needed for the basics of the game system *Luther Arkwright: Roleplaying Across the Parallels* uses, and this book provides everything else. The Mythras Imperative edition is available as a free PDF download from the Design Mechanism website (www.thedesignmechanism.com/products).

One thing to note is that Mythras Imperative does not contain the rules and mechanics for Mysticism. You will need the complete Mythras rules if you wish to make full use of Mysticism (see the *Mind Games* chapter) in your Arkwright campaign.

Arkwright and Bryan Talbot

Luther Arkwright appears in two sets of graphic novels by British artist and writer, Bryan Talbot. The first set, *The Adventures of Luther Arkwright*, introduces the epnoymous antihero, the multiverse, Zero-Zero, the Valhalla Project and W.O.T.A.N, and the sinister Disruptors. A synopsis of the story can be found on pages 167 to 171. The second set, *Heart of Empire*, focuses on Luther's daughter, Victoria, and her growing realisation of her true identity.

Bryan was very much influenced by the writer Michael Moorcock and his creation, Jerry Cornelius. Moorcock was writing in the 1970s and Cornelius, an urban antihero, reflects the fashions and rebellions of that decade. Bryan developed Arkwright in the early 1980s, but the Cornelius influence is more than evident, as is the concept of the multiverse, which is a common theme throughout all Moorcock's work.

Luther Arkwright's adventures are very much in the Steam Punk vein — and, in fact, predate the emergence of Steam Punk as a recognisable genre by almost a decade. They have more in common with Jules Verne and H G Wells than the Science Fiction of the time time (which was busying itself with the emerging cyberpunk movement) and channel British television shows of the late 1960s and 1970s such as *The Avengers, Adam Adamant Lives! The Mystic Hand of Tarot*, and *The Freewheelers*. Luther Arkwright is quintessential British — *English* — Science Fantasy. Bryan experiments with *fin de siecle* ideas, mixes them with Moorcockian tropes, the dystopia of Anthony Burgess's *A Clockwork Orange*, adds dashes of New Age mysticism and wraps the whole lot in the kind of aesthetic violence and eroticism found in the works of Moebius, Bilal and Druillet. Luther Arkwright is New Wave storytelling using the comic book medium. It is ambitious, visionary, ironic, brutal, sexy and fun; it is mature and challenging, but never takes itself too seriously. Michael Moorcock himself said:

> *"I think Luther Arkwright — a kind of alternate history of the British Empire and its ongoing effects — improves all the time. He remains one of my own personal favourites and one of the best examples of what a talented writer/artist can do with a form. I believe that the reason the story remains so fresh and interesting is because under all the glorious invention and wild adventure, glamorous Characters and exotic machinery, Talbot deals in fundamental realities and makes stern self-demands."*

If you have not yet read any of the Luther Arkwright stories, we urge you to do so — although it is not strictly necessary to fully enjoy this book. However, Arkwright's saga contains countless nuances that cannot be captured anywhere else save through Bryan's masterful storytelling, and so reading the saga is a worthwhile investment. Alternatively, *Big Finish Productions* have a superb audio version featuring David Tennant as Luther and this is another great way of becoming more familiar with the story.

When is this Game Set?

Luther Arkwright's saga is told in two collections; the first, *The Adventures of Luther Arkwright*, tells the story of the hunt for Fire-Frost and is spread across several parallels. The second, *Heart of Empire*, focuses on Arkwright's daughter, Victoria, and takes place some 20 years after the frst collection. This game draws most heavily on the first collection of stories and is actually set slightly earlier, in 1981 rather than 1984.

Games Masters can, of course, choose to set their campaigns wherever and whenever they wish — such is the beauty of a multiverse.

Within These Pages

Luther Arkwright: Roleplaying Across the Parallels is organised as follows:

The Arkwright Multiverse
Background to the multiverse of Luther Arkwright, an overview of the Characters' role in the game as Valhalla Project agents and a synopsis of Arkwright's own history.

Character Creation
Rules for creating Characters for *Luther Arkwright: Roleplaying Across the Parallels*. If you're eager to start, then skip straight to page 17.

Traits, Passions & Dependencies
Every character in the Luther Arkwright roleplaying game is special; this chapter deals with those special abilities, Passions and things the character relies upon to make it through the tough times.

Madness & Other Colours
The rules necessary for handling psychological trauma, including fear and insanity — recurring themes in the Arkwright saga.

Technology
Handling technology from many different variant Earths, plus standard equipment for Valhalla Agents.

Firearms & Combat
Specialised rules for combat involving all manner of weapons — from muskets through to vibro beamers.

Vehicles
Rules for creating and managing different vehicle types — from motorcycles to land iron-clads, air ships to star destroyers.

W.O.T.A.N & The Disruptors
Profiling the two forces watching the multiverse: Zero-Zero's Valhalla Nova, and the entropy-embracing Disruptors.

Parallels
Further detail on the nature of the myriad Earths, along with profiles of several different parallels ripe for adventure, and guidance for creating new parallels.

Games Master Resources
Valuable advice for running Arkwright campaigns, and game statistics for Characters appearing in the Arkwright saga — both friends and foes.

On Thin Ice
An introductory scenario on parallel 13.16.94, where a new ice age grips the planet and the Disruptors are planning destruction on a massive scale.

The Arkwright Saga
Synopses of both *The Adventures of Luther Arkwright* and *Heart of Empire*.

The Arkwright Multiverse

Ours is not the only existence — not the only timestream in which there is an Earth. There are others and, like the planets in space, there is an infinite number. But, unlike the planets, these other Earths are separated from us by imperceptible barriers and a dimension our science has yet to name. These Earths exist parallel to our own, echoes of a basic blueprint, each unique in some way. On some Earths, the Thousand Year Reich is a hard reality; some may still have dinosaurs as the dominant life form; some may just be atomic wastelands as a result of global conflict.

The Disruptors

Across the civilised parallel worlds, a secret war is being waged for their control. On one side are the mysterious organisations known collectively as *Disruptors*. Working mainly through indigenous agents, they have manipulated the course of history to their own ends on many different continua, engineering wars, *coups feu*, plagues, peace treaties, revolutions, assassinations and the like for at least fifteen centuries. Most of their agents are dupes, Pawns in a scheme far greater than they comprehend. Naming their lodges with titles such as *The People of the Truth, The Rationalists, The Cult of the Guardian Angel* and so forth, they adopt quasi-religious, political or criminal fronts with a screening system of initiation rites designed to be training grounds for fanatics. The rank and file members of these secret societies are ignorant of the higher levels of authority, which in turn blindly obey the orders they receive from the Disruptor elite power group. The location of Disruptor Command is a carefully guarded mystery — it could be on any of the myriad parallel time continua. Orders from Disruptor Central Command are directed through sophisticated communication terminals available to only the one or two key agents who are uppermost in the Disruptor hierarchy on each parallel. In return for following orders, these overlords, who are usually heads of state or religion, receive aid from the Disruptors — usually in the form of information they can convert into technology of a higher level than that of the world they inhabit — thus enabling them to maintain the dominance of their particular sphere.

The Chess Board

If the members of these secret societies are the Disruptors' *Pawns*, then the secret leaders are their *bishops*. And they also have their *Knights* and *Rooks* The Knights are rarer. These are special operatives, able to traverse and enter different timestreams by the use of interdimensional shuttlecraft — strange tubular structures powered by psionic energy sucked from the fabric of space-time by Disruptor engines. Their Rooks are super-soldiers, a powerful strike force.

Many worlds of course, are still free of Disruptor influence and it was on one of these, a stable parallel in relation to much of the multiverse, that an agency arose capable of checking their activities. On this Earth, the Middle Ages in Europe saw the rapid growth of the Holy Roman Empire. The Germanic states were united and strong and proceeded through diplomacy and war to either annex or conquer the countries of the civilised world. Dominated by the Empire, neither England, Spain nor France developed as major powers and by the end of the 17th Century, the by Emperor Frederick X and his decadent court held sway over the entire globe.

A New World's Order

But another power had been rising. The technological revolution started by Gutenberg and the Medieval Alchemists, and accelerated by the expansion of the Empire, had grown at an unprecedented rate. Science had become the new religion and the Futurist Renaissance was the movement of the people. The military coup, the execution of Frederick and the establishment of a dictatorship based on the principles of the Advancement of Science were inevitable, merciless and brief.

The effects of a world ruled by a scientific elite were dramatic. By 1800 John Dalton had perfected his Theory of Relativity. By 1820 man had landed on the moon. By 1850 world poverty and famine were abolished. Then, in 1881 Karl Marx proved the existence of parallel worlds and proposed an annotation system to designate different continua using his own parallel as a norm: 00-00-00, with 00-00.01, and 00-01-00 as the 'flanking' time streams. Over the centuries the dictatorship had mellowed into a benevolent one; in 1900 it was dissolved and the World Government established. Zero-Zero became the first technologically advanced Earth to live in harmony with itself, freed of religious and racial dogma and maintaining ecological balance.

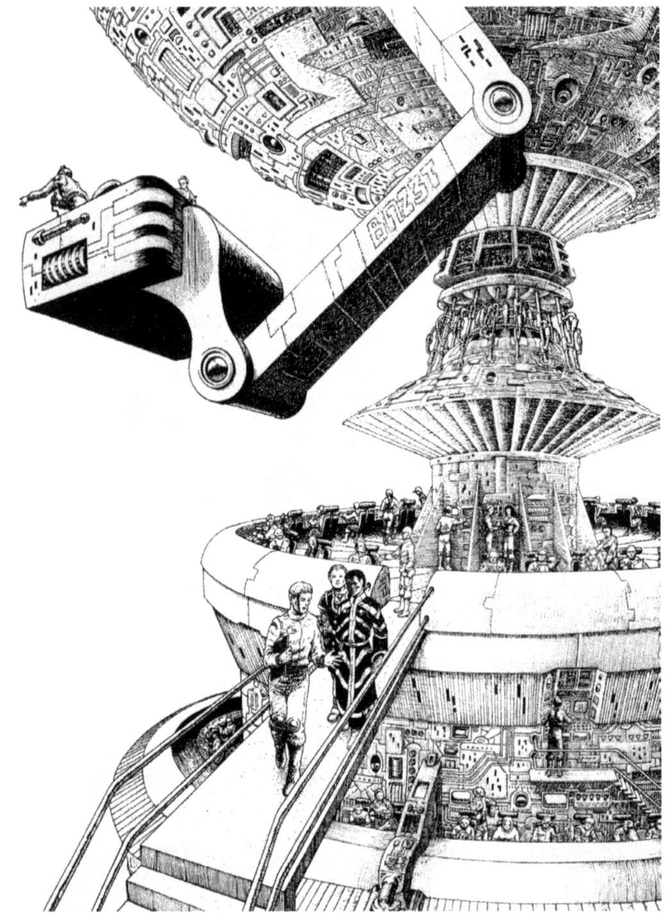

The Valhalla Project

One of the first acts of the administration was to initiate the Valhalla Programme to monitor parallel worlds and observe the effects of multiverse fluctuation on historical trends. London was chosen as the site of the giant *Valhalla Nova* complex that would house the most advanced technology of the time. The hyper computer W.O.T.A.N was an integral part of the structure — scanning the continua, correlating, analysing, displaying information, assessing probabilities and issuing directives. It was 1905 before the complex became fully operational and W.O.T.A.N extrapolated the existence of the Disruptors (as it termed them) and their activities. The government immediately authorised section leaders of Valhalla Nova to take steps to counter the Disruptor influe nce and W.O.T.A.N was given additional programming to adapt to the new situation. An agency within Valhalla Nova was established to deal with field operations. Although Zero-Zero had no means of breaching the dimensional barrier — no means of travelling across the parallels, there was another way.

Psychic research had been a science Zero-Zero for 150 years. Zero-Zero had discovered the ability of human minds to harness psionic energy and had also found methods of developing and enhancing psionic abilities. One of PSI section's most astonishing discoveries was the *Empathic Link*; those who possessed this power could, through concentration, communicate with their parallel selves on other continua. Although extremely rare, Valhalla employed these people as their Field Operatives — usually using them to set up anti-Disruptor espionage networks with their individual alternatives and report back by thought transference to their alternate selves on Zero-Zero.

FireFrost

It was several years later, in 1958, after the capture of a Disruptor lodge and its communications equipment, that W.O.T.A.N developed the quantum theory and technology necessary to enable Zero-Zero to construct audio visual communication terminals dimilar to those of the Disruptors. Since then, Zero-Zero has been fighting the Disruptors continuously, but at a safe distance, like a surgeon trying to cut a cancerous growth from a patient's body. But something was to emerge that would not only endanger their world, but also threaten devastation to every single Earth in the multiverse: *FireFrost*.

In 1913, on parallel 00.72.87, J R Montpellier, a French archaeologist, discovered an ancient Egyptian scroll in a hidden chamber beneath the Temple of Ra at Heliopolis. The professor was subsequently killed and the artifact, the FireFrost Codex, stolen from the *Musée national de Paris* by Disruptor agents. Taken out of context, this event would appear to have little significance;

however, as W.O.T.A.N had already perceived, 00.72.87 had a remarkably singular feature: a completely unique mythology, especially the Egyptian line. This centred around the Fire Opal of Set; according to the mythos the magical Fire Opal was created by Set, the god of evil, as an awesome weapon of unlimited power.

W.O.T.A.N's probability matrix calculated two disturbing possibilities: a 97% likelihood of some solid, material basis for this deviation from conventional Egyptian mythology (i.e, the existence of FireFrost) and the 55% likelihood that the location of this powerful weapon was contained in some form of cypher within the hieroglyphics of the FireFrost Codex — now in the hands of the Disruptor Elite. The Distuptors did not appear to act immediately on the information they held, but over the passing decades W.O.T.A.N was constantly alert for any movement in such a direction.

Enter Arkwright

In 1964, on parallel 00.30.22, a very similar timestream to our own, Luther Arkwright appeared from a different parallel. He was 14 years old and had escaped from a Disruptor training station. A product of advanced genetic engineering, he had been groomed from shortly after birth to be the ultimate Disruptor agent — and, like FireFrost, he is unique. Luther, has no other selves, having been conceived on only one parallel, and his escape across parallels was made without the use of machinery. Arkwright is singular in the multiverse and can shift dimensions psionically. Having rebelled against his Disruptor programming, Arkwright spontaneously and instinctively flung himself across the continua to the parallel of his birth.

Hunted by Disruptor agents, travelling and hiding, it was five years before Arkwright was tracked down, contacted and recruited to Zero-Zero by Rose Wylde, Valhalla Nova's Field Operations section leader; a psychic with a strong Empathic Link with her other selves.

Arkwright soon became Valhalla's prime agent, spearheading the fight against his former masters. In 1981 he obrained information from a dying Disruptor Knight he'd shot in a duel; FireFrost was hidden in the Great Pyramid of Cheops on parallel 00-72-87, and the Disruptors were going to get it. Shunting to 00-72-87 and teaming-up with Octobriana (a Mongolian warrior and indigenous Zero-Zero agent), Arkwright followed the Disruptor strike force, its black armoured, genetically engineered Rooks, into the pyramid through the laser-drilled tunnel they had excavated. Inside, Arkwright used his psychic ability to locate FireFrost before the Rooks. The two halves of the Fire Opal of Set were anchored to the floor, each one in the grip of a giant, stone sphinx; the legend the ancient Egyptians had assimilated into their mythology was told in bas relief around the walls of the chamber. Using psychometry, Arkwright wrenched out the residual data stored in the psychic radiation emanating from the device. In a fugue state his mind was flooded with imagery and information revealing the true origin and nature of FireFrost.

The Disruption Spiral

Arkwright saw war: a centuries-long war between two vast star systems spanning lights years and countless parallel continua. War in space and on land; huge armies of genetically engineered troops, immense war machines and whole worlds destroyed. He saw FireFrost, constructed in secrecy by the best scientists of a psychic humanoid species, and on one parallel only. Powered by psionic energy, the binding force of the multiverse, this ultimate deterrent was designed to disrupt the atomic structure of the cosmic blueprint: a *God Weapon* — destroyer of worlds, a destroyer of universes.

Inevitably, it was activated. Once brought together, the two halves could not be separated and the Disruption Spiral began. Working in geometric progression, this device accelerated entropy across every parallel. At first only random, relatively minor effects were apparent: increased nightmares, illness, sucide rates, and strange phenomena, such as showers of organic matter and speaking in tongues, were manifest. As the cycle progressed, the results of this unrestrained entropy were of greater effect and incidence. Before long, planets were subject to hurricanes, tidal waves, earthquakes, firestorms and, eventually, complete destruction. Solar systems broke down into component matter as the galaxy collapsed in on itself to become a black hole. And, its purpose fulfilled, immune from natural laws, *FireFrost* was spewed forth from the celestial grave of its mother galaxy, to drift for eons through the emptiness of intergalactic space.

Arkwright saw the apocalypse device, after an unimaginable stretch of time, entering our galaxy and being drawn into the gravitational pull of prehistoric Earth to crash in the primordial soup. He saw FireFrost split into its original halves as it sank into the depths, there to wait through the passing millennia, as land masses rose and fell and Earth's contours were formed, embedded in limestone, until its discovery by the excavations of the pyramid builders and its concealment in the Great Pyramid. With Luther within a psychometric trance, Disruptor shock troops arrived. Outnumbered, Octobriana shouldered the semi-conscious Arkwright and made to retreat, but was overcome by the Rooks. Fortunately the Rooks, being little more than human automatons, had no knowledge of who Arkwright and Octobriana were or they would have killed them. When Arkwright and Octobriana regained consciousness the soldiers were gone.

So was FireFrost...

The Role of the Characters

A million spheres... The many parallel worlds of the Luther Arkwright stories are vast and limitless, from the stable base world of Zero-Zero to the distant realms across the multiverse. It is a kaleidoscope of potential adventures and new tales within which Characters can become entwined. This chapter examines the role the Characters take in *Luther Arkwright: Roleplaying Across the Parallels* and includes full rules for character creation.

Agents of Valhalla

In *Luther Arkwright: Roleplaying Across the Parallels*, the Characters take on the role of specialist agents that have proven themselves worthy of the title through a variety of special skills. The Characters are not just run-of-the-mill operatives carrying a gun or blade for the Valhalla Project. They are the psychically gifted, the mystics, and the burgeoning experts in their fields. The Valhalla Project turns to the Characters when the worlds need their specific skills, and they answer the call accordingly.

The Valhalla Project has need of as many able bodies within its ranks as it can train effectively, but there are always those that rise to the top. These highly skilled and trained members of the agency, be they indigenous operatives or agents who shunt between the parallels, are given the duty to right what needs righting, or wrong what needs to be wronged. They fight against the constant presence and meddling of the Disruptors, joining other high profile agents such as Rose Wylde and even Luther Arkwright himself in the war against disorder and chaos.

Each character is responsible for a variety of important duties on their missions, forming a team of special agents willing and able to monitor the needs of the multiverse. Their missions may take them across the known parallels and possibly beyond, or they may remain on one parallel, focused on delivering it from Disruptor influence. Yet for the whole time they have the backing of Valhalla, and their allies by their side. The multiverse is maintained and kept in order due to the actions of these special, gifted few.

What Makes a Valhalla Agent?

To monitor and police the parallels, the Valhalla Project recruits agents from both Zero-Zero and on specific parallels where Disruptor activity is suspected or known. In the case of local agents Zero-Zero field officers are sent to scout for and recruit agents from the populace, slowly and steadily drawing them into the

secretive work of the Valhalla Project and revealing to them the secret truth of reality: that there is not one universe, but many.

Agents are chosen for their unique capabilities and train in a variety of skills, all of them essential to the battle against the Disruptors. Field Officers guide their progress and coach their development, with the help of numerous necessary technologies. Valhalla agents need to be on a different level of self-awareness and acuity than their fellow homo sapiens in order to grasp the fractious concepts that a trans-dimensional understanding brings with it. It takes a special kind of person to even qualify as a Valhalla agent, and a remarkable level of strength and tenacity to graduate from basic training to higher and more specialised roles. Valhalla agents are prime examples of what can be done with the human condition when applied properly, especially in the presence of those who have already evolved beyond normality.

Training to become a Valhalla agent is difficult for the most skilled inductees, but with the right instruction and dedication they can graduate into a world — or rather multiple worlds — of exciting adventure. With enough practice and mission work, they might just help save the future of the multiverse.

Modus Operandi

The chronicled tales of Luther Arkwright show that the multiverse is constantly threatened by the machinations of the Disruptors, but there is so much more to understand. The multiverse is always being tested and pushed to the limits beyond the heavily-monitored and maintained metaphysical walls of Zero-Zero and, if left unchecked, the parallels will fall into chaos and ruin. The calculations and predictions of the W.O.T.A.N supercomputer and its analysts show where things need to be urged, protected, ceased or even destroyed in order to protect the larger picture, the greater good.

When important events within the multiverse are judged necessary to be adjusted in some way, Valhalla gathers its experts. These experts draw up a host of possible results based on hundreds of thousands of calculations, past results and futurist theories before searching the roster of agents that can do what needs to be done. Once Valhalla believes they have the best set of agents for the best potential results for the parallel in question they arrange for the mission to begin.

The agent team is notified of its impending mission, and the orders for their assembly are broadcast across the parallels. Arrangements are made for their briefing, which may include a return to Zero-Zero, or may be performed in the field. Valhalla Command makes sure the agents are fully prepared for what they will be doing, the technology they will be using, and any special information about the missions and parallel in question. Only in dire emergency circumstances will the agents be sent directly to a mission parallel without being briefed first, but when the situation demands it, Valhalla does whatever it takes to ensure the ordered flow of the multiverse.

The Characters are these team members, agents of Valhalla, and their missions are the focus of their adventures. Some missions will be short, limited-objective, limited-time operations; others will be more elaborate and involved, requiring weeks, months or even years of preparation and execution. Roleplaying in the Luther Arkwright multiverse will see the Characters travelling between the parallels, performing a variety of different activities on behalf of the Valhalla Project and W.O.T.A.N.

Most mission scenarios will pit the agents against the dark schemes of the Disruptors. The Characters can expect to be sent into situations where the protection and stability of the parallel will be their responsibility (while maintaining the clandestine nature of their agency). The nature of the missions will determine what course of action the Characters are supposed to take on behalf of the multiverse, but rest assured that every Valhalla agent may be required to save or take lives, preserve local laws, or perhaps commit heinous crimes. The Characters will be instructed what needs to be done, what cannot be done, and where the line of duty and commitment is drawn – if there is one at all.

Some examples of Valhalla agent missions:

- Intercept a Disruptor member in a low technology parallel before it seeds a world with harmful equipment
- Planting Valhalla political specialists in the Parliament Office of a targeted parallel rife with unrest
- Ensuring the conception and protection of a potential psionic protégé for future agents to recruit
- Start a new revolution in a parallel United States to swing favour towards the British Crown
- Assassination of a corrupt leader in Communist Russia known to be in league with the Disruptors
- Aid the resistance in a Nazi-dominated world where the Third Reich emerged victorious over the Allies

The very nature of the Valhalla Project's role in the multiverse places a great deal of power in the hands of a very select few, and these agents are its eyes, ears, hands and weapons of the Valhalla Project. It is through their actions during mission deployments that they will become the tools of manipulating the parallels. It is a tough job and one that not everyone will be suited for, but a necessary one in light of the madness that would reign if the Disruptors are left unchecked.

Moral Imperatives: No Easy Solutions

In the Arkwright multiverse, the agents will face many moral dilemmas; people they come into contact with may or may not even know they are the opposition, agents of the Disruptors. It is a cut and dry choice to battle against an army of Disruptor Shock Troops – but where does the line lie when the enemy is a liberation freedom fighting force or the entire democratic process of a parallel in need of revolution? Will the Characters be able to handle the ethical complications that come up when the calculations of W.O.T.A.N call for the assassination of a room full of otherwise innocent politicians? The Characters of the Luther Arkwright setting will sometimes need to ask themselves whether pulling the trigger is the right or wrong thing to do, and deal with the consequences either way.

There are many different ways that Games Masters can create and run their Luther Arkwright campaigns. Some games will be heavy on action and excitement; including car chases, death-defying battles on floating dirigible cities, and vibrobeamer gunfights with Disruptors in dark, Victorian alleys. Other campaigns could be heavy political and ethical dramas; espionage between warring nations, counter-balancing commercial plots, and helping downtrodden peasants survive in the wake of horrible disasters. Anything is possible with the right amount of invention and planning.

New Concepts from the Multiverse...

The earliest pages of the Luther Arkwright graphic novels reveal incredible abilities, ideologies and technologies. In *Luther Arkwright: Roleplaying Across the Parallels*, all these strange and fascinating things are part of the Characters' repertoire – and also the repertoire of their enemies. Anything is technically possible in the multiverse, but some of the Arkwright mainstays are outlined with special rules of their own. These higher concepts are defined in greater detail within the pages of this book, but here are some examples of the things explored in the game.

Trans-Dimensional Travel and Multiversal Constants

The primary concern and area of expertise of the Valhalla Project is maintaining order between all the parallels, no matter how enormous and conceptually difficult a task that is. The calculations of their unimaginably powerful supercomputer at the head of the agency draw complex plans that stretch out from the stable parallel of Zero-Zero to encompass the rest of the multiverse. In order to perform their sometimes inexplicable duties, Valhalla agents need to travel between and understand the different parallels.

Agents make use of different parallel-travelling methods ranging from large, elaborate machines that open physical tunnels between parallels, sophisticated shifting points monitored constantly by expert agents, and the rare psionicist skilled in metatransportation. The Characters will see many different parallels, no matter how they move around the multiverse.

Luther Arkwright is the pinnacle agent of Valhalla. Luther displayed the unique and powerful ability to travel between parallels undetected using his unprecedented psionic mastery, and the planning masters of the Valhalla Project have tried to recreate his ability for decades without success. Nevertheless, both communication across the parallels and travel between them has become a reality (and a closely guarded secret) both for the Valhalla Project and the Disruptors.

Another major Valhalla agent, Rose Wylde, is psychically linked with her alternate selves, feeling what they feel, sensing what they sense, and experiencing what they experience: yet each alternate Rose remains an individual, despite this powerful psycho-empathic tether. Multi-parallelism is an extremely rare psionic effect, and those agents that display it are normally allocated to special roles within the Valhalla Project. Zero-Zero research scientists believe that multi-parallelism is a sign that certain fixed items – places, locations and even people – are omnipresent throughout the parallels. No matter how different they might be from one parallel to the next, these fixed points will still appear. Rose and other multi-parallel psionicists are just one example of such constants; others exist: the circle of Stone Henge, the great San Francisco earthquake of 1906, and the Royal Library of Alexandria in

Egypt. These are examples of Constants and are a sign that everything across the multiverse is connected.

Characters will need to understand the multiverse, its parallels, and how to travel between them. It is an essential and ultimately fundamental aspect of the Valhalla Project.

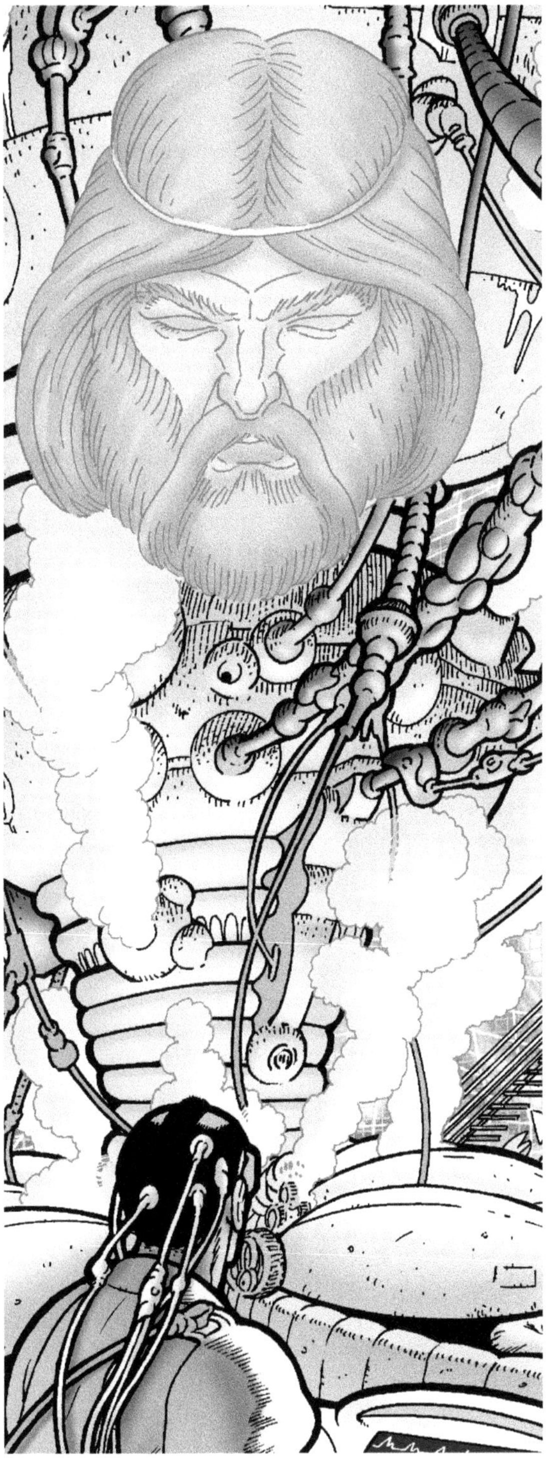

Horror From Within and Without

The push and pull of life in the Valhalla Project is hard on the mental state. Seeing so many different worlds, trying to understand how to interact with them, and performing their assigned duties eventually takes its toll on their strongest of minds. Plus, many agents display certain vulnerabilities and conditions, symptoms or side effects of their special powers and purpose in the multiverse: compulsions, addictions, neuroses and psychoses. Even Arkwright himself suffered multiple breakdowns and mental fugues while coming to terms with his destiny. There are several aspects of working for the Valhalla Project that can be difficult to deal with, and some agents may crack under the pressure.

The Valhalla Project sometimes demands a great deal from its agents, and this can weigh heavily on the psyche. Sleepless nights, nightmares, and fracturing minds are not uncommon amongst long term agents. Psychological evaluations and regular psychiatric testing are a requirement of all agents, and pharmaceutical compensators are issued alongside most mission equipment packages.

The Disruptors are aware of the taxing nature of Valhalla's work, and regularly include psychological terror tactics in their own schemes. Sowing chaos and creating the types of anarchic strife necessary to destabilise the parallels, the Disruptors have no moral constraints and will stop at nothing to achieve their goals. They are not above trying to murder Valhalla agents, induce in them nervous breakdowns, ensure they fall into harmful depressions, or become addicted to dangerous substances in order to cope. It does not matter whether an enemy agent dies at the end of a bayonet or at the end of a self-knotted rope; it is still a win for the Disruptors.

And then there is exposure to physical horrors and atrocities: the depths to which humans will sink, the punishments and tortures they are willing to inflict on their fellows. As if human monsters were not enough, agents will occasionally find themselves exposed to things utterly alien to the imagination: mutations and experiments gone awry, and even intelligences that have evolved beyond our solar system and beyond our own multiverse. Humankind is not alone. Neither is it safe. The vast majority of people, across every parallel, are oblivious to these secrets, but Valhalla's agents may glimpse them and, worse yet, be required to defeat them, or become their allies...

High Technology with a Steam Punk Attitude

Many Science Fiction tropes are to be found in Luther Arkwright's multiverse, but there is also a pervasive Steam Punk and *fin de siecle* resonance. There is inter-parallel travel, powerful weaponry capable of atomising a target at ten paces, floating war engines, and more. In order to have these amazing technological feats at their disposal without losing the feel of being in the Olde World, the Luther Arkwright setting uses different angles of mixing science and engineering.

In this roleplaying game, Characters will be exposed to mechanical devices that work in mysterious ways to achieve wondrous effects. Steam powered and clockwork machines perform amazing tasks. Alchemical experimentation and psionic enhancements turn the average into the superhuman. A recurring theme in the Arkwright serials is the evolution of humankind away from its original, natural roots; trying to reach new heights in human evolution. Transcending humanity through a number of different avenues is a challenging theory, but the results cannot be disputed: agents will be exposed to – by choice or by order – a variety of new ideas and technologies that could change their very being forever.

Technology plays a large part in every Character's career within the Valhalla Project, and they will have some very interesting tools at their disposal (as well as being used against them).

Some examples of technology the Characters will wield or be exposed to are as follows:

- Thompson "Spitfire" Napalm Pistol
- Ironcloud Dirigible War Fortress
- Tyr ICS (Injected Combat Stimulant)
- The Bifrost Parallel Bridging Apparatus

Hints of Homo Novus – Psionics

Luther Arkwright displays the single largest collection of psionic abilities in one being. Along with the heightened state of his reflexes, physique and almost preternatural level of charm and social skill, Luther became the example of a new evolution of humanity – the *homo novus*. Although there has not yet been another example of a true *homo novus* in the multiverse since the revelation of Luther's true nature, the first signs of the evolution have begun to appear throughout mankind.

The influence of the new genetic strains within the populace across the parallels has introduced a number of new abilities in some human beings. These abilities are collectively called psionics. Psionics are preternatural talents that spring from the innermost corners of the mind, allowing one to perform amazing feats and generate undeniably powerful effects. Theorists believe that the rise in psionic ability in humankind is directly due to the rise in parallel travel. It is a vicious cycle. More psionic travellers between parallels cause more psionic travellers to be born or discovered, which in turn causes more travel, and so on. Some Valhalla experts also wonder if, in alcohol-fuelled gossip circles, Luther's infamous promiscuity could be spreading the *homo novus* genetic strains as well. No matter how the presences of psionicists are increasing, the Valhalla Project is eager to keep track of them. Should it be possible, psionically-skilled individuals that are located are tagged to be ushered into agent training – eventually.

There are several different types of psionics. Most psionically-gifted individuals can call upon a few powers; perhaps three at the most and rarely master more than one. Only truly gifted psionicists develop more abilities than that, and none have shown the same ranges of power as Arkwright (although some come close).

While psionic abilities are covered in much greater detail later in this book, some good examples are as follows:

- Absorption – Siphoning Bioelectric Current from Living Nervous Systems
- Psychometry – Reading of Emotions and Thoughts
- Telekinesis – Application of Invisible Force
- Breaking the Seals of the Real – Mysticism

The idea of magic, witchcraft and sorcery has existed for centuries in nearly all parallels. It can be much more for a very rare few who understand it fully. Students of the "lost arts" collectively call these talents Mysticism. Mysticism is similar to psionics in the way that a normal human being can, with the right practices and skills, create supernatural effects beyond the scope of normal, mortal constraints.

The Valhalla Project monitors mystics just as it monitors psychics and other potential agents. Those who have learned to channel their inner energies are important to Valhalla, and so mystics of many different schools may find themselves working side by side with other agents in the defence of the multiverse.

The rules for Mysticism are covered in the Mythras rules, pages 221 to 229, and are dealt with later in the Mysticism chapter of this book.

Welcome to the Forever War

The agents of the Valhalla Project have been battling against the schemes and ploys of the Disruptors for decades, and now the Characters will be on the front lines – a thousand front lines in countless parallel worlds. This is not going to be easy for anyone, but with the right amount of training and practice the agents could do well toward winning this war for the multiverse.

With luck, the Characters might actually survive to see the end of it.

Luther Arkwright

The only son of Captain Gavin Arkwright VC and Sarah Arkwright, Luther was orphaned at birth when, on Thursday 16th February 1950, fire swept through the maternity wing of St Mary's Hospital in Paddington, London, killing his parents. Luther survived thanks to the quick thinking of Staff Nurse Vanessa Morgan.

Even as a newborn the Disruptors knew of Luther's special powers. Unlike most, Luther is unique in the multiverse: there are no alternate versions of him on any other parallel. His psychic potential was also incredibly evident, even before Luther began to develop it with any serious purpose in his early 20s. He is also able to move between parallels through sheer psychic force and leave no signature to indicate his passing or presence: another unique facet of this remarkable person. Someone of Luther Arkwright's capabilities would be invaluable to the Disruptors and they made it their mission to capture him at the earliest possible opportunity.

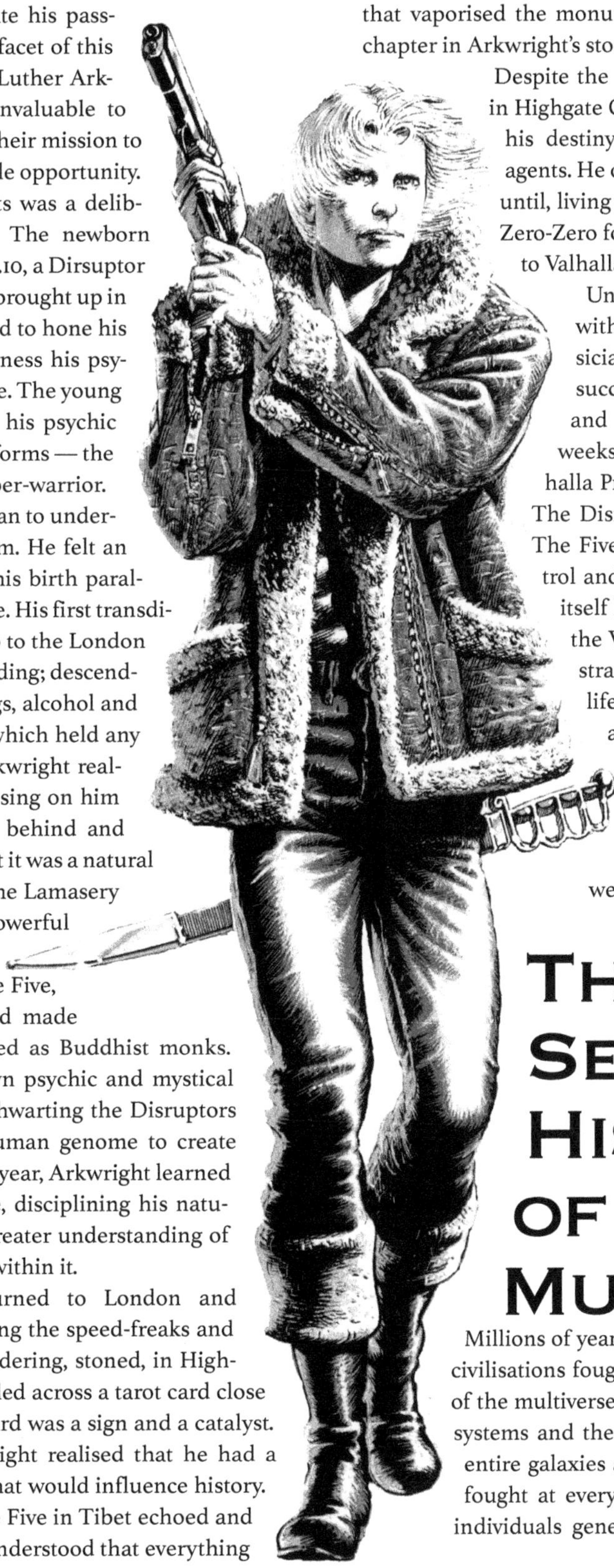

The fire that killed his parents was a deliberate attack by the Disruptors. The newborn Luther was taken to parallel 02.79.10, a Dirsuptor controlled parallel where he was brought up in an artificial environment designed to hone his nascent psionic abilities and harness his psyche entirely to the Disruptor cause. The young Luther was schooled not just in his psychic abilities but also in combat of all forms — the Disruptors' attempt to forge a super-warrior.

At the age of 14, Arkwright began to understand what was happening to him. He felt an overwhelming connection with his birth parallel and knew that he had to escape. His first transdimensional shift was from 02.79.10 to the London of his birth where he went into hiding; descending into a life of petty crime, drugs, alcohol and casual relationships — none of which held any meaning. Eventually, in 1970, Arkwright realised that the Disruptors were closing on him once again and so left London behind and made for Tibet. At first he thought it was a natural place to hide but as he reached the Lamasery he realised he was following a powerful psychic summons.

In Tibet he was trained by The Five, an advanced alien race that had made Earth their home and manifested as Buddhist monks. The Five had mastered their own psychic and mystical abilities and were dedicated to thwarting the Disruptors (in part by manipulating the human genome to create *homo novus*). Over the course of a year, Arkwright learned to control his *prana*, or life force, disciplining his natural psychic talents and gaining greater understanding of both the multiverse and his role within it.

Nevertheless Arkwright returned to London and lapsed back into his old life among the speed-freaks and acid casualties of Highgate. Wandering, stoned, in Highgate Cemetery, Arkwright stumbled across a tarot card close to the tomb of Karl Marx. The card was a sign and a catalyst. In one shocking instant, Arkwright realised that he had a destiny to fulfill, something that would influence history. Things shown to him by The Five in Tibet echoed and resonated and Arkwright understood that everything he had experienced until this point was preparation for what destiny had in store. This realisation resulted in an unleashing of Arkwright's psychic powers, an uncontrolled burst of psionic energy that vaporised the monument to Marx and signalled the latest chapter in Arkwright's story.

Despite the psychic revelation he had experienced in Highgate Cemetery, Arkwright still fought against his destiny and sought to hide from Disruptor agents. He descended further into heroin addiction until, living rough and on the very edge of survival, Zero-Zero found him and Rose Wylde brought him to Valhalla Central.

Under the watchful eye of Valhalla, and with the expert help of Zero-Zero's physicians and psychotherapists, Arkwright successfully beat his heroin dependency and regained his strength in a startling two weeks — to the shock of everyone. The Valhalla Project gave him the purpose he needed. The Disruptors had schooled him in violence. The Five of Tibet had shown him how to control and channel his life force. The multiverse itself had revealed a greater destiny; and now the Valhalla Project brought these disparate strands together. For the first time in his life, Luther Arkwright became *whole* — and not only that, he stopped hiding and chose the side of Order over the side of Entropy. In the battle for the sanctity and stability of the multiverse, Arkwright is one of destiny's eternal weapons.

The Secret History of the Multiverse

Millions of years in the past, two ideologically opposed civilisations fought a multi-dimensional war for control of the multiverse. Each civilisation controlled entire star systems and the war lasted for centuries and engulfed entire galaxies across many dimensions. This war was fought at every level: hand to hand combat between individuals genetically engineered for battle, between

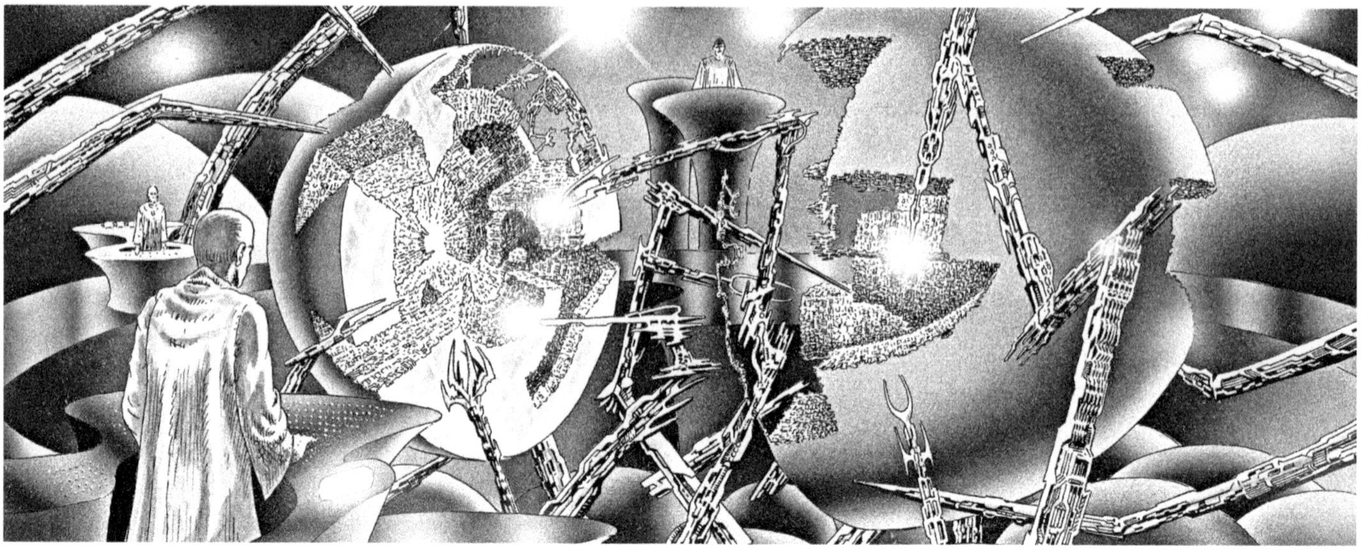

vast fleets of great starships, and in the higher dimensions on a mathematical level where quantum weaponry was employed in hyper-destructive battles that could be measured in milliseconds.

Eventually one of the civilisations, a humanoid race possessed of highly advanced psionic capabilities, forged the device known as FireFrost. FireFrost was designed as a deterrent — and it worked. The warring civilisations reached an accord and peace reigned for decades. Until, that is, FireFrost was activated. Who activated it and how is unknown, but FireFrost destroyed entire galaxies and caused the fall of whole parallels. Eventually the matter unleashed as part of FireFrost's activation collapsed in on itself, forming a neutron star. Around it was formed a Black Hole and from it FireFrost re-emerged, a source of terrifying power that drifted through galactic space for aeons. Eventually FireFrost drifted into our own solar system and was inevitably, inexorably, drawn towards Earth. It struck the nascent Earth and split into two halves, unleashing waves of psionic energy across every Earth in every parallel. This secondary activation caused amino acids to form and from there, the first stages of simple life, as FireFrost — both the taker and bringer of life — sank into the primordial ocean.

Although FireFrost is now lost, its existence resonates through every civilisation, every variation of Earth and every human psyche. The progenitor of the human race, FireFrost is ingrained into our DNA. It is the source of countless myths of birth, life, death, eternal existence and the apocalypse. FireFrost is at the heart of the mythology of every culture: the Fire Opal of Set; the Philosopher's Stone; the Holy Grail; the Hindu god Shiva. FireFrost *resonates and endures.*

But for hundreds of millions of years it has been sundered, its halves lost to each other. If reunited, FireFrost ceases to be a source of life and becomes, once again, the ultimate weapon. And FireFrost is unique — it has no counterpart on any other parallel, even though its power threads through the multiverse leaving nowhere untouched.

The Disruptor Plan

The Disruptors are the descendents of FireFrost's creators, the winners of that galactic war millions of years ago. FireFrost is their lost inheritance and their ultimate goal is to find it and make it complete. This is a search that must take place across the multiverse because the parallel of FireFrost's existence is unknown. The Disruptors have therefore become pervasive, determined, unstoppable. To possess FireFrost is to rule the multiverse, to make the whole of reality bend to their will.

There are other legacies too. FireFrost was the ultimate weapon, but that vast war created others. The Entropy Configuration, a device capable of merging parallels and harnessing the vast energy that results, is another ancient relic the Disruptors seek. With time and resources, they will find these things — unless the Valhalla Project can stop them.

The Disruptors have been at work through the multiverse for an unknown length of time, millennia, certainly, and have been in possession of trans-dimensional capabilities for far longer than Zero-Zero — yet they have kept their existence and technology secret. So secret, in fact, that Zero-Zero did not become aware of the Disruptors' existence until the 1920s, and sure of it until the late 1930s and early 1940s. Zero-Zero's scientists had posited that variations across the parallels would be vast, with each generating its own psychologies, cultures, languages and histories. Instead, W.O.T.A.N calculated and demonstrated that the socio-historic variations fell within 30% of the Marx-Oppenheimer Index, across a sample of one thousand neighbouring parallels. Such a low value of variance was astounding: the probability of parallels developing similar constants at similar times was miniscule. Valhalla Central demonstrated this through 'The Gregorian Test'. W.O.T.A.N calculated that there was a 735,000 to 1 probability against parallels developing the Gregorian Calendar. Yet of the one thousand parallels sampled only 5, or 0.005%, still used the Julian Calendar (or some other variation).

Campaign Dates for Arkwright Games

Luther Arkwright's adventures begin in 1984 and follow his search for FireFrost. It is recommended that *Luther Arkwright: Roleplaying Across the Parallels* campaigns be set in a similar time period and the scenarios in this book take 1981 as the base year.

Of course, with infinite variation across infinite Earths, actual dates are meaningless. 1984 on Zero-Zero for example, is at a technology level at least two centuries ahead of the 1984 of parallel 00.38.56, which displays a technological level akin to our own Edwardian era. What this means is that Games Masters should not be afraid of having a date exhibit wildly different characteristics in terms of technology, fashion, customs and culture to those we are most familiar with. 1981 in one parallel may have achieved faster-than-light travel owing to scientific advances made during the Enlightenment. In another, 1981 may signal the revolutionary new power called electricity, owing to the fact that the Enlightenment never took place.

The Arkwright feel though, definitely cleaves towards the Steam Punk part of the spectrum — although it is clearly only one, possible approach. *Luther Arkwright: Roleplaying Across the Parallels* is quite capable of supporting transhuman-level Science Fiction as well as Victorian-inspired Science Fantasy.

This is *your* multiverse; *your* 1981. Create as you need.

W.O.T.A.N deduced that some external force was manipulating the parallels and termed this external force *Disruption*. It was enough to galvanise the expansion of the Valhalla programme with a view towards understanding the nature of this manipulation and determining its source.

This was the true birth of the Valhalla programme's network of agents. W.O.T.A.N deduced that manipulation was locally controlled across a vast spread of parallels. This meant tiny, incremental, iterative manipulations engineered by individuals or small cells. Valhalla adopted similar tactics. Its early efforts were focused on observing, investigating and collating. Between 1910 and 1930 Valhalla established a complex and far-reaching intelligence network that began to assemble, with W.O.T.A.N's assistance, the indisputable existence of Disruptor cells actively working across western Europes, but not confined to them. The rise of National Socialism in dozens of forms helped expose active Disruptor cells and with the eruption of World Wars across so many parallels, Valhalla agents were able to operate with a certain degree of impunity in capturing and interrogating Disruptor agents.

These agents yielded little, but enough to prove the existence of another powerful, intelligent, malicious trans-dimensional agency. Valhalla had always thought itself unique; had always thought itself an agent of peace and stability. But now it had an enemy, and this enemy was just as aware of Valhalla as Valhalla was aware of the Disruptors.

A new war had begun, and it is still being waged.

Character Creation

Characters in *Luther Arkwright: Roleplaying Across the Parallels* are agents of the Valhalla Project. This chapter shows how to create an agent and draws on the basic character creation process found in Mythras and Mythras Imperative. There are some differences however, reflecting the contemporary period of the Arkwright saga, and changes have been made in the following areas..

- ***Skills***: Standard and Professional skills have been expanded to reflect the contemporary setting. The list of Standard skills has been changed slightly.
- ***Culture***: The culture section now just concerns itself with a Civilized culture, though different technologies and ideologies are reflected in the skills available to Characters.
- ***Career***: The careers have been expanded to include contemporary professions.
- ***Traits and Dependencies***: These are unique to Luther Arkwright Characters and are explained below.

Valhalla Agents

Unless the Games Master decides otherwise, all Characters are agents of the Valhalla Project, the body responsible for cataloguing and monitoring the multiverse and, to a certain extent, protecting its existence from outside intrusions, mostly by the (equally secretive) Disruptors.

The Valhalla Project has an extensive monitoring system in place across the parallels that is constantly on the look-out for people with the skills and disposition to work as field agents. Many field agents simply observe and report to a senior agent and have no direct participation in the multiverse's safety: these low-level observers occupy every echelon of society, from the homeless right through to the super rich. Some may not even know they work for Valhalla; others might suspect they work for some higher power, but may believe it to be one of many conspiracy organisations ranging from the Bilderberg Group through to the Illuminati.

Above these Observers are the Field Agents, and Field Agents are the active foot soldiers of Valhalla. Often they have spent time as Observers and have been fully appraised of who they serve and then raised to Field Agent status. Many others though, are recruited and trained as Field Agents directly. Characters in Luther Arkwright are all Field Agents although it is perfectly possible to be an Observer.

Traits

Field Agents are chosen for their special abilities. These might be astounding but mundane accomplishments, such as possessing an extremely high IQ, or having a remarkable aptitude for certain skills or disciplines. They might be special powers, such as psychic talents, particular mutations, or a unique ability — such as Arkwright's ability to pass through the multiverse undetected. Through extensive research and screening, Valhalla has found that people with such gifts are more disposed to the strange and intense work the Valhalla Project offers than 'normal' every-day humans.

Therefore every character in Luther Arkwright also has some special ability or power, known as a *Trait*, that marks him or her out from the rank and file and identifies them as a Valhalla agent. Part of character creation is determining what makes the character special.

Creating a Character

Luther Arkwright character creation follows the general steps of character creation found in Mythras, which is roughly:

1. A rough character concept for play
2. Determine Characteristics and Identify Traits
3. Derive Attributes
4. Determine Culture
5. Determine Passions
6. Decide Pre-Valhalla Career
7. Determine Background Events
8. Determine additional Background elements, such as Social Class and family
9. Determine Dependencies
10. Decide how the character came into Valhalla's service and determine final skills

Step 1: Character Concept

It is assumed that Characters in a Luther Arkwright campaign are all agents, or potential agents, of the Valhalla Project. There are many different backgrounds from where Characters might originally hail, but the overall concepts behind playing in the Luther Arkwright universe all steer toward one true end – becoming a Valhalla Project agent in service of the W.O.T.A.N supercomputer.

Here are some good examples:

- A man handpicked by recruitment for impressive natural psionic talents
- A charming politician-in-training skilled in espionage
- A silver-tongued socialite groomed for social manipulation
- A veteran soldier with great martial aptitude

> **Anna Thames' Chronicle**
>
> To illustrate character creation, we'll follow the generation of Anna Thames, a Valhalla Agent of Parallel 14.03.71, a Neo-Victorian Parallel that still embodies Victorian fashions and attitudes even a century after the Old Queen's death. Anna is a feisty, quick-witted, airship smuggler from the port city of Liverpool who has come to Valhalla's attention due to her particular psychic talents...

Dependencies

A downside of having a special talent or power is that such people tend to be susceptible to certain conditions that make them potentially more fragile than others. It's a paradoxical truth that many who are considered geniuses in their particular fields are also susceptible to depression, anxiety, addiction, irrational compulsions, paranoia, and even more extreme sexual and violent tendencies. Luther Arkwright is a good example: a powerful psychic, able to shift between the parallels, he has predispositions towards violence and has, in the past, been dependent on many highly addictive and harmful narcotics. He is not alone: all Valhalla agents display, to a lesser or greater degree, similar frailties and these are known as *Dependencies*. To a certain extent Dependencies balance-out the benefits of Traits, but they are distinct from them and there is not necessarily a direct relationship. A powerful telepath, for example, might have only a mild addiction dependence on alcohol whereas a relatively stable-looking polyglot might also harbour a deep and violent sociopathic nature. Part of character creation is determining the nature and intensity of the Dependency.

> **Assigning Skill Points — Limits**
>
> In the standard Mythras rules, Cultural and Career skills are capped: players must allocate between 5% and 15% to the skills noted for their chosen cultural background and profession. To help encourage a little more diversity and expertise, Luther Arkwright Characters have no such caps. All skills listed must receive at least 1%, but there is no restriction on how many points an individual skill receives. This applies across all instances of allocating skill points.

Anna Thames' Chronicle

Simon has just joined a Luther Arkwright campaign, along with three other players, that is being Games Mastered by Emma. The Games Master explains that the Characters all originate from Parallel 14.03.71. This Parallel has, for some some reason, remained at a level of development akin to Victorian Europe and this inspires Simon to create a character from Liverpool, Anna Thames, a young woman with some experience of piloting an airship and a not-too-respectful attitude towards the authorities who try to regulate commerce and crime.

Step 2: Characteristics & Traits

Characteristics are generated as per the Mythras standard rules for humans, no matter how the Games Master chooses to determine them. See pages 9 to 12 (pages 6 to 8 in Essentials) Despite the expectations of their extraordinary lifestyle, Valhalla Project agents are still normal human beings aside from the existence of special talents – Traits.

After the player has determined the character's Characteristics, they then make a number of rolls on the Traits table. The Valhalla Project recruits humans who exhibit certain Traits useful for policing the multiverse and opposing the Disruptors. Each character has one awakened Trait and may even have more. Traits are particular powers, capabilities or qualities that elevate the character above the mundane level. Page 40 gives details on Traits; how many a Character receives, their descriptions, and how they function.

Step 3: Attributes

Once the Characters have their base Characteristics and Trait(s) calcuated, the next step is to determine all of the special secondary Attributes important to the Mythras system. The following Attributes are calculated in all the same fashion as listed in the Mythras core rules:

- Action Points
- Damage Modifier
- Prana Points (see below)
- Experience Modifier
- Healing Rate
- Height and Weight
- Hit Points
- Initiative Bonus
- Luck Points
- Movement Rate
- Tenacity Points (see below)

Prana Points

The Attribute of Magic Points is renamed to *Prana Points*, reflecting inner resources used by certain Traits and game effects, such as Psionics and Mystical talents. Prana Points are extremely important to Characters that deal heavily with the preternatural and arcane aspects of the Arkwright multiverse. Where their interactions demand it, this inner well of strength is as important as a Character's Hit Points – perhaps more so.

Characters start with a number of Prana Points equal to their POW Characteristic. When Prana Points reach zero, the character has exhausted his or her ability to call on their powers or talents.

Tenacity Points

The new Attribute of Tenacity reflects the psychological well-being and resilience needed by Valhalla Project agents when travelling through the parallels and battling the chaos of the Disruptors. Tenacity Points are based on POW, but vary based on the activities and events during the game.

A character's Tenacity Points represent mental or psychological Hit Points. They can suffer damage and be reduced in the same way locational hit points can be reduced through physical damage. As Tenacity Points are reduced, the character becomes more vulnerable to certain Conditions (see page 51). When Tenacity Points reach a negative value, any Conditions gained through exposure to traumatic, horrifying or sanity-shaking events become permanent. When Tenacity Points reach a negative value equal to their starting value (less any modifier for Dependencies – see below) then the character is considered permanently insane or incapable of any further mental function. Just as a massive loss of Hit Points results in physical death, a massive loss of Tenacity Points results in mental instability

Characters start with a number of Tenacity Points equal to their POW Characteristic.

Standard Skills

Skills represent how Characters interact with the world around them. Skill values are determined exactly as presented in the Mythras rules, although Standard and Professional skills have been expanded to reflect the contemporary setting. The contemporary Skill range and new Skills in this game are perfect for agents of the Valhalla Project. The Standard skills in Luther Arkwright are as follows:

Revised Standard Skill List

Athletics	STR+DEX
Brawn	STR+SIZ
Conceal	DEX+POW
Customs	INT x2
Dance	DEX+CHA
Deceit	INT+CHA
Endurance	CON x2
Evade	DEX x2
First Aid	INT+DEX
Home Parallel	INT x2*
Influence	CHA x2
Insight	INT+POW
Native Tongue	INT+CHA
Perception	INT+POW
Sing	CHA+POW
Stealth	DEX+INT
Swim	STR+CON
Unarmed	STR+DEX
Willpower	POW x2

**Home Parallel is the Locale skill renamed. Most Characters are assumed to possess a general knowledge of the climate, cultures, geography, fauna and flora of their home parallel.*

Professional skills have also undergone some changes. These are dealt with later in this chapter, beginning on page 30.

Step 4: Culture

Every Character hails from some previous lifestyle and career choice; they do not grow up in a vacuum or are chosen from birth for recruitment into the Valhalla Project.

Unlike the default cultures presented in the Mythras rules (which are structured to represent historical or fantasy societies), the cultures in *Luther Arkwright: Roleplaying Across the Parallels* do not follow the same format. Parallels can be extreme in their environmental, social and technological diversity, and so the Culture use for *Arkwright* Characters reflects this. All Characters come from a Civilised Culture and should also come from the same sort of parallel unless they are directed otherwise by the Games Master whose campaign might allow for divergent home worlds.

Culture has two components:

- Parallel Type: a *broad indication* of the level of development the parallel has reached.
- Sociological Type: a *broad indication* of the prevailing style of society and government the character has grown-up with. Sociological Type will vary from country to country: for instance, one character might grow up in an Artistically inclined version of France whilst another character from the same parallel might grow up within the highly Militaristic Canadian Empire.

These two components define the Cultural skills Characters develop as part of their upbringing. The Parallel Type provides Default skills normal for that parallel, favoured (and available) Transportation skills, and a choice of Development skills. Sociological Type provides additional Standard and Professional Skills reflecting the sociological nature of the character's upbringing and education.

Players need to note the skills and applicable choices and then distribute 100 points between them, with a minimum of +5% and maximum of +15% assigned to each skill. Customs and Native Tongue gain an automatic bonus of +40%.

Parallel Type

For convenience, parallels are categorised by their level of technological and sociological development. These are broad-brush definitions and there is clearly a huge degree of individual variation and maturity within a given category. For example, Zero-Zero, home to the Valhalla Project, falls into the Nanotechnology Age category although its ability to develop an Artificial Intelligence like W.O.T.A.N gives it hallmarks of the Spacefaring Age. Similarly, a parallel falling into the Steam Age may have mastered advanced computing methods leading to the emergence of 'Steam Punk' technology. The table on page 22 shows the different Parallel Types available.

Sociological Type

Every parallel has a mix of Sociological Types although one or two may prevail amongst the dominant powers. The Sociological Type describes the kind of society a character grew-up in, rather than the dominant type for the parallel (although these might be one and the same). Again, these are broad-brush definitions with many variations, divergences and degree of maturity.

Step 5: Passions

Passions are a part of the Cultural Background for a character, but are treated here as a separate step. Every character has the following Passions (their use is explained on page 22 of Mythras, and in the next chapter: Traits, Dependencies and Passions).

- Loyalty to Town, City, Country or Society. Starting value = POW+INT+30%
- Love a friend, sibling or romantic partner. Starting value = POW+CHA+30%
- Hate — something that the character truly despises. It can be a person, an ideal, another country, or something even more exotic. Starting value = POW+INT+30%
- One extra Passion of the player's choice. Starting value = POW x5%

Anna Thames' Chronicle

Simon initially makes five 3d6 rolls and generates the following numbers: 12, 8, 12, 14, and 10. For the two 2d6+6 rolls needed for SIZ and INT he rolls a 14 and a 15.

Simon decides to allocate the results as follows: STR 10, CON 8, SIZ 14, INT 15, POW 10, DEX 14, CHA 12.

He reasons that the tall, porcelain-skinned woman suffered from a childhood illness that affected her health, a situation not helped by the smog of her home, the great port city of Liverpool in Great Britain.

The next roll is on the Trait Table. The 1d100 roll gives Simon a result of 57 which means his character is Psychic. Emma tells Simon that they'll just note Anna's powers for now, and detail them later.

Simon then uses the allocated Characteristics to calculate his agent's Attributes:

Action Points 3, Damage Modifier +0, Prana Points 10, Experience Modifier +0, Healing Rate 2, Movement 6 metres, Initiative Bonus 15, Luck Points 2, Tenacity Points 10.

Hit Points: Leg 7/Abdomen 8/Chest 9/Arms 6/Head 7.

Having figured this much about Anna, Simon moves on to her background...

Step 6: Pre-Valhalla Career

Use the following career templates as described in the Careers and Development chapter of the Mythras rules. Where the career offers a Transportation skill, the player may use it to either choose a new skill or use it as an opportunity to improve an already known Transportation skill.

ARTIST

Composer, Illustrator, Painter, Sculptor...

An individual who produces works of a creative, aesthetic nature. Some might be poor individuals living in cluttered cellars or garrets, either through lack of talent or patrons, or through eschewing easy wealth and lucrative commissions in their own personal quest to produce distinctive or experimental works. Fortunate artists can be highly successful and wealthy though their works might become unfashionable as other individuals come in vogue. Sadly, most artists' creations usually become more collectable, and thus lucrative, after their death. The creativity and outside thinking of some artists are perfect for the erratic and unexpected life of an agent.

Parallel & Social Types

Parallel's Level of Development	Example	Default Parallel Skills	Transportation Skills	Development Skills
Pre-Industrial	18th Century social and technology equivalents	Customs, Home Parallel, Survival, Native Tongue	Drive and Ride	Select one from Craft, Navigation, Track
Steam Age	Early to mid 19th Century social and technology equivalents	Customs, Home Parallel, Survival, Native Tongue	Drive and Ride	Select one from Craft, Navigation, Track
Industrial Age	Late 19th – early 20th Century social and technology equivalents	Customs, Home Parallel, Survival, Native Tongue	Drive (land vehicle) and select one of Pilot (Airship) or Ride	Select one from Craft, Commerce, Engineering, Lore, Streetwise
Electronics Age	Mid 20th Century social and technology equivalents	Customs, Home Parallel, Mechanisms, Native Tongue	Select two from Drive (Crawler), Drive (Speeder), Drive (Walker), Pilot (Flyer), Ride (Beast)	Select one from Commerce, Electronics, Engineering, Mechanisms, Probabilities
Computer Age	Late 20th – early 21st Century social and technology equivalents	Customs, Home Parallel, Computers, Native Tongue	Select two from Drive (Crawler), Drive (Speeder), Drive (Walker), Pilot (Flyer), Ride (Beast)	Select one from Computers, Commerce, Electronics, Engineering, Mechanisms, Probabilities
Nanotechnology Age	Nanotechnology is commonplace. Artificial Intelligence is in its nascent stages. Exploration of the Solar System with planetary colonisation and orbital habitats is a reality.	Customs, Home Parallel, Computers, Native Tongue	Select two from Boating (Boats), Drive (Speeder), Drive (Walker), Pilot (Flyer), Ride (Beast)	Select one from Computers, Electronics, Engineering, Mechanisms, Probabilities, Sensors
Spacefaring Age	Artificial Intelligence is commonplace. FTL travel has been established. Socio-technological development is moving towards Singularity.	Customs, Home Parallel, Computers, Native Tongue	Select two of Drive (Speeder), Drive (Walker) Boating (Boats), Pilot (Flyer), Pilot (Spaceship)	Select one from Computers, Electronics, Engineering, Mechanisms, Probabilities, Sensors

Social Type	Standard Skills	Professional Skills
Academic	Willpower	Choose four from Culture, Linguistics, Lore, Probabilities, Science, Teach
Artistic	Dance, Sing	Acting, Art, Musicianship
Bureaucratic	Influence, Insight	Bureaucracy, Oratory, Politics
Democratic	Customs, Insight	Commerce, Culture, Linguistics
Lawless	Deceit OR Stealth and one cultural Combat Style	Select two from Commerce, Disguise, Forgery, Gambling, Lockpicking, Sleight, Streetwise
Manufacturing	Brawn, Endurance	Select two from Commerce, Craft (any), Engineering, Mechanisms.
Militaristic	Endurance, Evade, Perception, and one cultural Combat Style	Lore (Strategy and Tactics) or Science

ASSASSIN

Buttonman, Cleaner, Hitman, Liquidator, Terrorist, Triggerman...

Assassination is the killing of individuals for a career or a cause. Some men are employed as agents of a nation's government or its military, others might be members of a political or religious organisation a few are merely callous freelancers. The traditional tools associated with these specialists are the dagger, the bullet and the bomb, although other means such as poison can be used. Sometimes it is advantageous for an assassin's mission to make the killing resemble an accident. After managing to eliminate their target, a good assassin will be also able to escape the situation unscathed. Needless to say, skilled assassins are vital tools of Disruptor plans to further their stratagems in the parallels where they have established a presence – but are therefore very useful for the Valhalla Project with which to counter.

BOUNTY HUNTER

Bail enforcement agent, Bounty killer, Scalp hunter, Skip tracer...

Bounty hunters are individuals who track down and arrest or execute recognised criminals for financial gain. Sometimes they might work closely with police and legal authorities, though their profession is often subjected to legal restraints and might actually be operating illegal in some countries, states or even parallels. They are usually loathed by the criminals they hunt, but also by ordinary citizens who often see them as authorised thugs and killers. They are typically persistent and ruthless, deaf to the pleas and hard luck stories from those they prey on. However, they need to be wary of would be rescuers and avengers at all times.

Anna Thames' Chronicle

Anna's Standard Skill values begin as follows:

Athletics 24%, Brawn 24%, Conceal 24%, Customs 30%, Dance 26%, Deceit 27%, Endurance 16%, Evade 28%, First Aid 29%, Home Parallel (14.03.71) 30%, Influence 24%, Insight 25%, Native Language 27%, Perception 25%, Sing 22%, Stealth 29%, Swim 18%, Unarmed 24%, Willpower20%

Simon now needs to allocate 100 points to skills selected from the Cultural background. The Games Master and Simon agree that Parallel 14.03.71 is an Industrial Age Parallel and Anna is from a Manufacturing society. She has 100 points to distribute among skills chosen from the Industrial Age's Default Parallel Skills: Customs, Home Parallel, Survival, and Native Tongue); Transportation Skills (Drive (Ground Vehicle), Pilot (Airship); and Streetwise, which is Anna's choice from the Development Skills presented. The Social Type is Manufacturing which gives Anna Brawn and Endurance, and she also takes Commerce and Mechanisms. The 100 points are distributed thus:

Brawn +10%, Commerce +15%, Customs +40% — free bonus for all Characters, Drive (Ground Vehicle) +10%, Endurance +10%, Home Parallel +10%, Mechanisms +15%, Native Tongue (English) +40% — free bonus for all Characters, Pilot (Airship) +15%, Streetwise +15%.

With these Cultural Skills allocated, her skills look like this:

Athletics 24%, Brawn 34%, Conceal 24%, Commerce 42%, Customs 70%, Dance 26%, Deceit 27%, Drive (Ground Vehicle) 34%, Endurance 26%, Evade 28%, First Aid 29%, Home Parallel (14.03.71) 40%, Influence 24%, Insight 25%, Mechanisms 44%, Native Language 67%, Pilot (Airship) 44%, Perception 25%, Sing 22%, Stealth 29%, Streetwise 37%, Swim 18%, Unarmed 24%, Willpower 20%.

Anna is therefore a pilot with a little experience at this stage, and appears to be reasonable at fixing things and tinkering with gadgets through her Mechanisms skill. Next, she'll develop her Passions and further improve her skills through her career choices.

Ironically, those who prove too ruthless and undiscriminating in whom they terminate can find themselves with a fat bounty placed on their own heads. Their moral ambiguity, investigative skill and martial ability lend well to the 'wetwork' style of missions W.O.T.A.N sometimes arranges for agent teams.

CRIMINAL

Burglar, Conman, Gangbanger, Hacker, Mafioso, Mugger, Kidnapper, Pickpocket ...

Criminals are those who have made their livelihoods through breaking the law, skirting the enforcement agencies that uphold them, and profiting from the misfortune of others. They are used to working their own way for their own goals, and they do not take well to being forced into other peoples' rules and regulations. Criminals are present in nearly every parallel; the more strictly or harshly the powers-that-be rein in the people, the more the people want to break their laws. It is dangerous to employ career criminals for agency missions due to their dislike of playing by the

Careers

Career	Standard Skills	Professional Skills
Artist	Customs, Home Parallel, Influence, Insight, Perception, Willpower, One Transportation skill	Art (any), Commerce, Craft (primary), Craft (secondary), Culture (any), Linguistics, Streetwise
Assassin	Conceal, Deceit, Evade, Insight, Perception, Stealth; Combat Style (Unarmed, Concealable Weapons or Sniper style)	Culture (any), Demolitions, Disguise, Forgery, Linguistics, Sleight, Streetwise
Bounty Hunter	Athletics, Endurance, Evade, Insight, Perception, Stealth; Combat Style (any)	Bureaucracy, Commerce, Culture (any), Linguistics, Streetwise, Survival (any), Track
Criminal	Athletics, Deceit, Evade, Insight, Perception, Stealth; Combat Style (Unarmed or Concealable Weapons Style)	Acting, Commerce, Disguise, Electronics, Lockpicking, Sleight, Streetwise
Detective	Customs, Evade, Influence, Insight, Perception, Stealth; Combat Style (Unarmed or Side Arms style)	Bureaucracy, Culture (any), Disguise, Linguistics, Lore (any), Probabilities, Sleight, Streetwise
Entertainer	Athletics, Brawn, Dance, Deceit, Influence, Insight, Sing	Acrobatics, Acting, Oratory, Musicianship, Seduction, Sleight, Streetwise
Explorer	Athletics or Swim; Endurance, First Aid, Perception, Willpower; Combat Style (any), One Transportation skill	Astrogation, Courtesy, Customs (any), Language (any), Lore (any), Navigation, Survival (any)
Farmer	Athletics, Brawn, Endurance, Home Parallel, Perception, Willpower, One Transportation skill	Commerce, Craft (any), Mechanics, Navigation, Lore (Agriculture), Survival, Track
Gambler	Conceal, Deceit, Evade, Influence, Insight, Perception; Combat Style (Unarmed or Side Arms style)	Acting, Bureaucracy, Commerce, Courtesy, Gambling, Probabilities, Sleight, Streetwise
Hunter	Athletics or Swim; Endurance, Home Parallel, Perception, Stealth; Combat Style (Hunting style)	Bureaucracy, Commerce, Craft (traps), Navigation, Lore (hunting related), Survival (any), Track
Journalist	Customs, Deceit, Home Parallel, Influence, Insight, Native Tongue, Perception	Bureaucracy, Culture (any), Linguistics, Lore (any), Oratory, Politics, Streetwise
Mechanic	Brawn, Endurance, Home Parallel Influence, Willpower, Two Transportation skills	Commerce, Craft (primary), Craft (secondary), Electronics, Gambling, Mechanisms, Streetwise
Medic	Customs, First Aid, Home Parallel, Influence, Insight, Willpower, One Transportation skill	Commerce, Culture (any), Healing, Linguistics, Lore (health related), Science (secondary), Streetwise
Merchant	Deceit, Home Parallel, Insight, Influence, Native Tongue, Two Transportation skills	Bureaucracy, Commerce, Courtesy, Culture (any), Linguistics, Navigation, Streetwise
Mystic	Athletics, Deceit or Influence, Evade, Insight, Meditation, Perception; Combat Style (Unarmed or a weapon style), One Transportation skill	Acrobatics, Culture (any), Linguistics, Meditation, Oratory, Probabilities, Survival (any), Teach
Noble	Customs, Home Parallel, Influence, Insight, Native Tongue, Perception; Combat Style (Unarmed or Side Arms style)	Art (any), Commerce, Culture (any), Courtesy, Linguistics, Oratory, Politics
Pilot	Brawn, Endurance, Home Parallel, Perception, Willpower, Pilot and one other Transportation skill	Astrogation, Customs (any), Electronics, Linguistics, Mechanisms, Sensors, Streetwise
Politician	Customs, Deceit, Home Parallel, Influence, Insight, Native Tongue, Perception	Bureaucracy, Courtesy, Culture (any), Linguistics, Lore (socio-political), Oratory, Politics
Scholar/scientist	Customs, Home Parallel, Influence, Insight, Native Tongue, Perception, Willpower	Culture (any), Engineering, Linguistics, Lore (any), Oratory, Probabilities, Science (secondary), Teach
Scout	Athletics or Swim; Endurance, First Aid, Perception, Stealth; Combat Style (any), One Transportation skill	Comms, Customs (any), Linguistics, Navigation, Sensors, Survival (any), Track
Servant/retainer	Customs, Deceit, Home Parallel, Influence, Insight, Perception, one Transportation skill	Bureaucracy, Courtesy, Craft (service related), Culture (any), Linguistics, Politics, Streetwise
Smuggler	Conceal, Deceit, Home Parallel, Influence, Insight, Willpower, One Transportation skill	Astrogation, Bureaucracy, Commerce, Customs (any), Linguistics, Navigation, Streetwise
Soldier	Athletics or Brawn, Endurance, Evade, Unarmed; Combat Style (Side Arms style), Combat Style (Heavy Weapons style), One Transportation skill	Comms, Demolitions, Electronics, Lore (Strategy and Tactics), Mechanisms, Sensors, Survival (any)
Spy	Conceal, Deceit, Evade, Insight, Perception, Stealth; Combat Style (Concealable Weapons Style)	Comms, Culture (any), Disguise, Electronics, Forgery, Linguistics, Streetwise
Technician	Endurance, Home Parallel, Influence, Perception, Willpower, two Transportation skills	Comms, Craft (any), Electronics, Gambling, Lore (any), Mechanisms, Sensors

rules, but when the Valhalla Project asks their agents to obey the law for the better of the multiverse it can be a trial of their loyalty to say the least.

DETECTIVE

Gumshoe, Policeman, Private Eye, Private Investigator, Sleuth...

The work of a detective is to investigate people of interest, crimes and bring criminals to justice. Typically this involves working within a team of police officers and specialists, getting backed in part, by the law. Private detectives work for individuals who can pay to have information and evidence gathered to assist their own goals. Frequently this can lead to the private detective's work straying into dubious legality. Private investigators have less legal power and must operate using whatever contacts and resources they can develop for themselves. Some businesses employ investigators on a permanent basis who specialise in particular fields such as insurance fraud. Good detectives have all the right skills to do W.O.T.A.N's cross-parallel work, especially if the chaotic schemes of the Disruptors have already muddied the waters.

ENTERTAINER

Actor, Dancer, Musician, Poet...

Professional entertainers have a range of useful skills with which they can charm their fellow man. Actors generally perform in films or theatre, though some technologies and cultures might enable them to take part in interactive performances as well. Dancers entertain with diverse movements ranging from the erotic to ceremonial. Musicians use their instruments to perform concerts or provide background music. Poets recite great works of literature and lyric poetry, whereas singers perform choral works, often within choirs. Entertainers sometimes learn several complimentary arts to increase their repertoire and create unique acts. In cultures where mass communication mediums exist successful entertainers can accumulate considerable fame and fortune. Agents that have entertainment backgrounds tend to excel in missions where social charm and misdirection are important, although a good distraction from the horrors of some missions is always welcome, too.

EXPLORER

Scout, Traveller, Voyager...

Explorers are those who thrive beyond the reach of their native civilisation. They may be pioneers seeking out new territory or agents of governments and mercantile corporations. Some are employed to seek out natural commodities which they sell to merchants of more settled lands. A few are scholarly explorers, high ranked men seeking to document new cultures. Others are individuals cursed with chronic wanderlust or greedy for wealth. In some parallels, nations have vast regions of uncharted interiors and borders, whilst other parallels might seek to explore the nearby moons and stars. Agents that are well-travelled are particularly good at moving through the parallels, especially in uncharted territory.

Anna Thames' Chronicle

It's clear that Anna is a competent Airship pilot with criminal connections and therefore most likely involved in smuggling. Simon now determines which three Passions motivate her. He decides that Anna is sentimentally attached to the wild revels of her leisure time and chooses Love (City Nightlife) 55%. Thinking of the threats to her activities, his next choice is Resent (Police) 55%. Finally he decides that Anna respects the ideals of the organisation she has joined and picks Loyalty (Valhalla Project) 55%.

For her career, Simon settles on Criminal and, in particular, Smuggler. Anna, he reasons, is involved in one of the contraband operations bringing in expensive, heavily taxed items from the United States of America. The Criminal Career gives her *Athletics, Deceit, Evade, Insight, Perception, Stealth* and a Combat Style (Simon chooses the *Concealable Weapons Style*). Anna also has three skills from the Professional list and chooses *Electronics, Lockpicking and Sleight*.

With 100 points to distribute among Anna's Career skills, Simon allocates thus:

Athletics +10%, Deceit +15%, Electronics +5%, Evade +10%, Insight +10%, Lockpicking +10%, Perception +5%, Sleight +10%, Stealth +10%, Concealed Weapons Combat Style +15%.

The Games Master, Emma, tells Simon that the Concealed Weapons Combat Style includes Knife and Pistol as weapons.

Next comes Anna's Background Event. and detail...

FARMER

Gardener, Estate Owner, Forager, Harvester, Ploughman...

Farmers cultivate the land, raising or harvesting crops, or growing produce in hydroponic complexes. Many are generalists in a range of skills necessary for foraging or maintaining their chattels. Usually their produce is food and other useful flora, such as medicinal herbs or plants which produce fibres for clothing or oils for chemicals. Not all agriculturalists necessarily tend a farm or plantation. Some wander through wild regions harvesting the naturally occurring vegetation, whilst others are employed to supervise formal gardens for rich patrons. Likewise, not all farmers are necessarily yokels tied to a small pasture, orchard or vineyard. Many cultures may place high status on owners of large estates who manage the running of their property. Agents with farming backgrounds are rare, but their natural grounding and 'salt of the earth' personal histories can make them perfect for missions in lower technology parallels.

GAMBLER

Bookie, Cardsharp, Hustler...

The gambler earns his money by betting on contests of chance. Legal establishments include betting shops, casinos and sporting stadiums. Some contests are seemingly random lotteries. Others, such as picking winning race horses, are best undertaken with expert or privileged knowledge. Contests like card games require a degree of skill in assessing odds and also psychological talents in reading body language and bluffing successfully. Many

Amnesiacs

As a Games Master option, individuals might be inflicted with a lack of memory of their personal history and competence in skills they once held. Reasons will vary and can include severe concussion, mental illness, drug abuse or the backlash of a major psionic manifestation. Psychic or medical procedures might have sublimated the memories in an attempt to brainwash an individual into a political ideology, remove criminal impulses or perhaps remove their knowledge of an important secret.

The Games Master can allow the player to use a restricted pool of skills and points omitting a chosen amount of points. These unspent skill points are banked and can be awarded during play by the Games Master at suitable opportunities, usually in increments. This might help with a plot of the campaign and can conceivably give a team of agents sudden access to a useful skill that was not previously known by a member of their team. Care must be taken that there is a believable rational to any reacquired skills, nor should a player assume that every dilemma will be solved by sudden recall of the appropriate skill needed.

gamblers develop personal superstitions though some take more practical measures and try to shorten the odds against them by cheating through the use of sleight of hand, technical devices or human assistance; though this risks retribution if detected. Some, through thrill seeking or desperation, end up getting involved in unlicensed games run by criminals. Many cities, countries and societies restrict most forms of gambling, sometimes totally, whilst others with liberal laws or high stake games attract gambling tourists. In parallels where psionics is a recognised talent, casinos will in all probability have means of detecting a psychic individual and will rigorously enforce bans. Many of the same skills a gambler uses in his hobbies – bluffing, statistics, reading personal cues – make them fantastic agents for the Valhalla Project.

HUNTER

Big game hunter, Scavenger, Stalker, Trapper...

Responsible for finding, tracking, and killing or capturing creatures, the hunter is knowledgeable about the land and the behaviour of animals. A hunter may hunt in a variety of ways: simple stalking, trap laying or driving creatures into pens. The purpose of the hunt depends on the culture of the hunter. Most seek out prey for the simple purpose of gathering food, others for sport. Some hunters specialise in the extermination of deadly predators or the culling of animals for valuable body parts: furs, horns or teeth for instance. Hunters often learn a supplemental craft for preserving or skinning the creatures they kill. Some huntsmen are purely sportsmen who like to pit themselves against nature. Agents that have good hunting skills are particularly good at dealing with Disruptor minions simply by changing what manner of creature they are hunting down.

JOURNALIST

Commentator, Hack, Newshound, Pressman...

Reporting and analysing events through the printed word or audio or visual broadcasting devices, these individuals propagate the views of either themselves or other groups. Some are mouthpieces of the state whilst others are free agents or dissidents. In some societies they have the potential to sway and mould public opinion, which can bring them personal fame, though often at the cost of hostility from those their activities expose and castigate. Much like any investigator, agents that began as journalists are good, perceptive team members.

MECHANIC

Engineer, Grease monkey...

Machines need skilled individuals to assemble and operate them. This could entail anything from operating a workshop lathe to being part of a team overhauling a vast starship engine. They are archetypically individuals who are not afraid to get their hands dirty and perform manual work, though in advanced technologies they might have access to mechanised assistants and remote-operated tools. There are a lot of mechanical devices in use at the Valhalla Project, making it an easy choice to find skilled mechanics to be trained fully as agents – they will be needed.

MEDIC

Doctor, Healer, Medicine Man, Plastic Surgeon, Torturer, Vivisectionist...

Physicians have detailed knowledge of how the body works, training to heal the physical wounds of the body. This is not always the case, however. Some instead offer their skills to extract information by coercion, or further the depth of their education by questionable practices. Depending on the sophistication of the culture, some doctors embellish their treatments with ceremonial theatrics, bogus medications and manipulative psychology. Surgeons in technologically advanced cultures might use techniques involving bionics, cybernetics, clockwork-technology and vat grown body parts. Agents with medical skill are of great use for several reasons, not the least of which is the healing of fellow team members when things get bloody.

MERCHANT

Commodities Dealer, Entrepreneur, Trader...

Merchants come in many forms: the street vendor, small shopkeeper, wily caravanserai, intrepid merchant-entrepreneur, stockbrokers and many more. Although their methods or merchandise are different, all have one thing in common: to trade commodities (be it goods, food, livestock, people, property or even money) for the highest profit. Merchants know a bargain and how to drive a good one; and not all trade in legal merchandise. Due to their dealings as middle men, many merchants pick up some knowledge of foreign cultures and languages, skills that could be very useful in cross-parallel missions.

MYSTIC

Guru, Hermit, Illuminate, Master...

Mystics are those who seek mastery of the world by the attainment of perfection, spiritual insight or by becoming inured to physical discomfort. Depending on the culture from which they originate, mystics may be found as anything from reclusive mountaintop hermits to respected teachers of martial or artistic schools. The path of their development is always via mastery of self, and most are sagacious as a result of their studies. The Disruptors have infiltrated various cults in order to manipulate them to their cause, which is why W.O.T.A.N flags known mystics for potential recruitment.

NOBLE

Aristocrat, Gentry, Lord, Monarch, Peer...

Traditionally, members of the gentility or aristocracy are the elite of their culture's social class, often owing their status to heredity, although some individuals may be elevated into their ranks through services to the state, marriage or bribery. Some may be in the service of a ruler or government, whilst others are content to lead lives of leisure, made comfortable by their privileged wealth and status. Nobles are often bound by customs of behaviour, performing ancient duties, some of which are long since empty of any practicality. Convention often dictates that they are seen to live expensive lifestyles, whether or not this is realistic for their actual income. In times of strife, some bloody-handed individuals may have seized titles of nobility for themselves. When dealing with the governing powers across parallels, agents that hail from nobility have a great skillset.

PILOT

Aeronaut, Astronaut, Barnstormer, Flyboy, Test Pilot...

Pilots are those who operate vehicles that travel through the air and vacuum of space. They might be employed as flyers by their nation's military or various other official organisations. In the commercial sphere, a pilot will either work for a charter company or their own business, carrying freight or passengers or performing aerobatics for entertaining crowds and performing tasks such as crop spraying or aerial photography. Some individuals are wealthy enough to own aircraft which they use solely for their own leisure purposes. There will always be places for skilled pilots within the Valhalla Project, especially when agent teams will need to travel during their missions.

POLITICIAN

Civil Servant, Mandarin, Minister, Overseer, Steward...

Politicians are those appointed or elected to an office, charged with performing certain administrative duties and are granted a degree of authority to ensure their commands are followed. Examples include senators, bureaucratic scribes and legal advocates. Depending on the size and complexity of the organisation or government, most officials control a body of men to help perform their duties. With power comes the possibility of significant corruption, so many officials might find that there are, in theory at least, systems and laws to regulate and curb their activity if necessary. The Disruptors are often meddling with the governments of the multiverse, causing W.O.T.A.N to seek out politicians to help maintain the order of things.

SCHOLAR/SCIENTIST

Archivist, Librarian, Philosopher...

The keepers and seekers of knowledge and learning, scholars and scientists are people who are fascinated by knowledge. Scholars are not necessarily confined to dusty libraries or sterile laboratories; they may be active explorers and archivists, intent on advancing their learning or collection of data through field work. Scientists and scholars are usually specialists in particular areas of knowledge, such as physics, chemistry, biology, anthropology, history and economics. The multiverse is wide and varied; the need for academics within the agency has proven to be indispensable in maintaining order within it.

SCOUT

Ranger, Tracker, Pathfinder...

Scouts are employed by military or economic bodies to be their eyes and ears in unknown territory where they reconnoitre terrain and identify threats, natural or otherwise. Hardened by their life, scouts have an instinctive level of independence and learn to set and avoid traps and ambushes; trusting to their keen wits and senses. Most can live from what the land provides, understanding the plants, animals and seasons of the wilderness they inhabit. Some parallels are wild places untamed by civilisation, making scout agents excellent assets within them.

SERVANT/RETAINER

Aide, Butler, Chauffeur, House Maid, Governess, Major Domo, Manservant, Personal Assistant, Secretary...

Many individuals without the time, skill or inclination to do various tasks have the assistance of hired employees to perform more mundane household and business tasks. Some societies will often gauge the elite of society on the size and efficiency of their domestic staff. Some servants are deferential, tradition-bound individuals with strong ties of loyalty to their employer and the social order. However, in the cut-throat world of business, some individuals aspire to rise far higher from their initial positions and can be mercenary and devious in the pursuit of their ambitions. Given their close contact with their employers and superiors, 'underlings' are often privy to important financial and personal secrets. Some might sport a token of their allegiance such as colourful livery coats or distinctive badges and tattoos. Those in personal service of others have a knack for blending in around powerful people, and an agent that can do just that is useful in many situations.

SMUGGLER

Black Marketer, Bootlegger, Gun Runner...

Smuggling involves the illegal transportation of goods or people across borders. A smuggler's cargo might comprise proscribed items or they might be avoiding taxation, quality controls or embargos against specific nations. Typically, they need to know covert ways of crossing borders and often rely on utilising corrupt guards and officials. Their contraband is often disguised as another product or hidden in special storage lockers in vehicles and vessels. Those who choose to run illegal goods are generally prepared to flee to avoid seizure and must ditch their cargos if they fear they will be overhauled. Smuggler agents take the best part of being a criminal, a merchant and a pilot and mix them into one skilful person; albeit one that might not conjure the most trust in the management of the Project.

SOLDIER

Bodyguard, Dogs of War, Footslogger, Grunt, Mercenary, Military advisor....

Professional soldiers are the individuals of a nation who fight in the military or provide muscle for various business organisations or individuals with the means to hire them. Most of their time is spent patrolling, guarding and training. They focus on the use of weapons and other military hardware, and the study of enemy styles to make the most of any future opportunities. Some are rugged combat troops suited to meeting the enemy with shoulder arms and a bayonet, whilst others represent the pinnacle of technology, operating machinery that can retrieve vital information or else sending death across long distances. Whatever their function, most are prepared to subjugate their individuality to following a chain of command in an organised military hierarchy. Others, outside the regular military, are hard-nosed individuals who hire their skills to an employer without troubling themselves too much about the ethics of their missions. Agents that were

recruited from soldiering are perfect for the war against the Disruptors, even if they might fall to their triggers a little too quickly when more even heads could prevail.

SPY

Secret agent, Spook...

The work of a spy is to report upon and operate covertly against those his employer wishes to keep an eye on. They watch, discover and act secretively. Anyone might be a spy – servants, beggars, noblemen, even children. Likewise, those that employ spies might be anybody from a jilted lover or a desperate merchant to the ruler of a nation. Governments and powerful industrialists often devote considerable resources to information gathering using both regular espionage agents and also hiring or coercing other individuals for specific tasks. Agents mostly deal with passing of information or minor acts of sabotage, although a few sometimes perform assassination if the cause (or payment), is right.Both the Disruptors and W.O.T.A.N rely heavily on agents with backgrounds in the 'spy game' they have recruited and trained to aid their cause.

TECHNICIAN

Electrician, Laboratory Assistant...

Technicians are responsible for operating complex machinery and its maintenance and repair. This might include assisting scientists or the police in their research, or the operation and care of sophisticated military hardware. Due to the advanced sciences and multiverse-technologies that the Valhalla Project finds, researches and uses in everyday missions, agents with highly technical or engineering backgrounds are extremely useful.

Step 7: Background Events

Characters did not appear out of thin air. A lot has happened in their pasts, and players should be encouraged to make their backstories full of richness and personality. In order to aid with that process, each character makes one roll (perhaps two, if the Games

Master wishes) on the Background Events table and, working with the Games Master, decides how the results fit the campaign.

The Background table can be used to give extra details of a Player Character's history. Some can be used by the Games Master to devise plot hooks and, possibly, entire campaigns. If the Background Table in the Mythras Core Rulebook is felt to be more appropriate to a Character's specific parallel or a culture this can be used instead, although care must be taken to ensure that those background events deal with items that would fit well in a Luther Arkwright campaign.

Roll 1d100 and check the result on the following tables (pages 31 to 34) to flesh out the Character's events and make a cohesive story out of its early life.

Step 8: Background Details

There are still a few more background details Characters need. These are optional, but recommended.

Starting Money

The Valhalla Project does not let its agents in the field languish in poverty. Instead it makes sure they are deployed with enough funds to survive in whatever parallel they occupy. It may or may not be a particularly flashy or extravagant lifestyle, but it will keep them clothed, fed and ready to blend with the chosen culture.

Currencies and exchange rates will vary throughout the parallels. For gaming convenience, players can assume starting currency units are usually referred to as *Crowns* although this can easily be replaced with the term Credits (or Dollars, Euros or another familiar term) if monarchies are deemed too outdated or an unknown concept for some cultures. When Valhalla Project agents and assets are discussing monetary matters, they use the collective term 'Crowns.'

To make sure their agents fit in with a particular lifestyle within the Civilised lifestyle, players should roll on the following table to get a more specific description and modifier to their social class within the boundaries of 'Civilised' as explained in the Mythras core rules. Once this is determined, the Character rolls 1d100 and multiplies the result by by 100. This is the base amount of cash in Crowns or ready credit the character has available. The result is then modified by the money modifier value from the Civilised Social Class table.

Note that this is *ready* cash. Depending on the Class Level for the character, much greater wealth may be available in the form of savings, investments, bonds, stocks, family silver, property, extended credit and so on.

Anna Thames' Chronicle

Simon rolls 1d100 to discover Anna Thames' Background Event. The result is 33: *You keep encountering a symbol, seemingly at random. You are unsure if this is coincidence, a portent, or a construct of your imagination. It has recently become more frequent or prominent and now you are driven to understand what it means.*

Simon and Emma discuss what this symbol could be and decide together that it is some kind of runic device that Anna found in her childhood home. She remembers her father doodling it abstractedly and her mother embroidering it onto Anna's petticoat. When Anna was old enough she had the design tattooed onto her right shoulder, but she has also recently seen the same design worn by others. Perhaps the time is getting close to finding out what it means. Emma tells Simon that this is something they'll discover during the campaign — she isn't going to reveal what it means to Anna just yet...

1d100	Recruitment Method
01-30	Recruited by a Field Agent on the character's home parallel
31-40	Steadily fostered and groomed over several years by an organisation that is a front for a Valhalla recruiting cell
41-50	Identified by W.O.T.A.N as a Person of Interest and brought to Zero-Zero for training
51-60	Parents or Significant Others are Valhalla Agents who co-opt the character into service
61-70	Stumbled over a Valhalla Operation accidentally, but natural talents were immediately recognised
71-80	Psychic presence (or other talents) suddenly alerted a local Valhalla Cell to the character's usefulness
81-90	Born into the Valhalla Project on Zero-Zero and placed as a sleeper agent on the current (home) parallel
91-00	Originally being groomed, unwittingly, by Disruptors and brought into Valhalla for safekeeping and operational duties.

Recruitment to the Valhalla Project: Bonus Skill Points

Characters begin their adventures as agents of the Valhalla Project. They may be new recruits embarking on their first mission, or tenured agents preparing for yet another job. This stage of character creation determines how the agent was recruited to Valhalla's service and the final batch of Bonus Skill Points are spent on skills the Valhalla Project has focused on developing.

The specifics of recruitment can be determined by the Games Master, chosen from the below table, or rolled randomly — whichever suits the campaign and play style.

Lastly, allocate the 150 Bonus Skills to skill choices as explained on page 34 of Mythras; however, Characters should think about how Valhalla may have influenced their personal development and try to fit skills to suit the method of their recruitment into the agency.

Civilised Social Class Table

1d100	Class Level	Example Title/Description	Money Modifier	Resources
01-02	Outcast	Beggar, Homeless	x0.25	Nothing but the clothes on their back and maybe some personal armaments
03-30	Poor	Prisoner, Serf, Slave, Unemployed, Workhouse	x0.5	Resides on welfare or an another's property; owns a few keepsakes
31-80	Citizen	Freeman, Citizen, Proletariat	–	Rented accommodation or farmland; might own a dwelling or be buying it through a mortgage. Possesses simple vehicle or mount. Possesses own tools or livestock; none-military weapons
81-95	Privileged	Official, Steward, Technocrat, Warden	x3	Owns property, farm or business; furniture, tools, weapons & armour, mount or vehicle, several servants or slave retainers; support from the system
96-99	Elite	Aristocrat, Magnate, Minister, Noble, Patrician,	x5	Owns several properties, extensive farmlands or multiple businesses; expensive furniture, tools, weapons& armour, vehicles or mounts, many servants or slaves; fealty from regional inhabitants
100	Leader	Czar, Dictator, Emperor, Kaiser, President, Prince	x10	As above but of priceless quality; fealty from a dominion or nation

Age

It is recommended that Characters start as Adults — around 21 or 22 years of age. They may be older if the Games Master wishes. If Characters are older, consider increasing the Bonus Skill Points as outlined on page 33 of Mythras (or increasing the pool by 50 points for every 15 years of age over the age of 30.

Starting Equipment

Characters begin with two full sets of clothes (more depending on class), the usual personal and grooming possessions someone of their social class level could expect to have, somewhere commensurate with their class to live, and one set of weapons reflecting their favoured Combat Style. Anything else must be bought with starting money or be provisioned by Valhalla as part of a mission. Games Masters can agree to let Characters have a favoured mode of transport if this will suit the campaign, but a few lines ought to be drawn. No character should expect to begin the game with a dreadnought, starship, time machine (even Doctors of Time and Space), land ironclad or other outlandish vehicle that would be either conspicuous or out of keeping with the character's background, career and social class.

Character creation is almost finished; there are two more elements to define and these are described in the next chapter, Traits, Passions and Dependencies.

Professional Skills

The list of Professional skills found in Mythras has been changed to reflect the contemporary setting of Luther Arkwright, as shown opposite and include some new skills. Skills listed in italics are new skills described later in this section.

Revised Professional Skill List

Acrobatics	STR+DEX
Acting	CHA x2
Art	POW+CHA
Astrogate	*INT x2*
Boating[1]	STR+CON
Bureaucracy	INT x2
Commerce	INT+CHA
Comms	*INT x2*
Computers	*INT x2*
Courtesy	INT+CHA
Craft	DEX+INT
Culture	INT x2
Demolitions	*INT+POW*
Disguise	INT+CHA

Background Events

1d100	Background Event
1	You are still mystified by the disappearance of a family member 1d10 years ago but you have never given up hope that they can be found again.
2	You inadvertently learn a vital secret that could gravely inconvenience the ruling power of your home nation or parallel. If they are aware of this they might be prepared to negotiate a deal; or perhaps they would rather have you incarcerated — or dealt with in a permanent manner.
3	Your family are the protectors of an old lore or secret that is handed down to you. Does this place you under an obligation or in peril?
4	Your adolescence was plagued with disturbing nightmares, some of which gave you glimpses of other worlds and individuals you instinctively realise are real people.
5	You were was adopted by a guardian, distant relatives, a foster family or an institute. Were you abandoned by your family or were you an orphan?
6	You undertook a change of identity for some reason. This could be merely adopting a new name and background, but might include features such as having plastic surgery, new retinas or gender reassignment. Perhaps you even faked your own death?
7	You are the sole survivor of a tragedy that wiped out an entire community. You live with the guilt of the tragedy and your nightmares are plagued by the cries of the dead.
8	You are the sole survivor of a tragedy that wiped out your entire family, leaving you to fend completely for yourself. Did you thrive or suffer in the wake of this catastrophe?
9	You are ostracised by your family after you opposed them over a matter of conscience. Do you seek reconciliation or do you intend to stay a pariah in their eyes?
10	You were raised amongst a criminal family or chose to spend your youth amongst lawless people. Do you still yearn for the excitement of living your life on the wrong side of the law or are you worried that your former associates might contact you?
11	Your family were heavily involved in politics. Did this agree with your own ethics?
12	Your family is heavily involved with a cult or a secret organisation. Do you aspire to be selected for membership or do you loath or dread this society?
13	Your family moved to their new home city or nation from another for economic, political or personal reasons. Perhaps there is a mystery behind their decision to leave their old home? Or perhaps you are simply dissidents still wanted by foreign powers.
14	Your family moved to their new home city or nation from another for economic, political or personal reasons. Perhaps there is a mystery behind their decision to leave their old home? Or perhaps you are simply dissidents still wanted by foreign powers.
15	Your character was cheated out of an important legacy, or so you believe.
16	You are bequeathed an outdated weapon, vehicle or piece of equipment. Although pitted, tarnished and seemingly ineffective by the current standards of your parallel, it is a cherished heirloom.
17	You learn of a secret hideout. Possibly you have already used it.
18	You were married or in a serious relationship. Has your partner died or have you drifted apart? Possibly one of you is still in love whilst the other's heart has turned into a canker of hatred? Is there danger from a rival who hates you?
19	Your family follows archaic traditions and rituals handed down through long generations. You might choose to continue them or decide to turn your back on them. Does your decision trouble you?
20	You believe that someone or something has kept you under observation for a long time. You are unaware of their identity or purpose but intend to find out.
21	You have been imprisoned. Was this legally or illegally; did you escape or where you released?
22	You are known by law enforcement as a past offender. Whether you deserved it or not, you have a criminal record and suddenly surveillance of you has begun again – or so you suspect.
23	Someone appears to have been impersonating you. Your bank account is empty, your credit rating compromised and people are turning against you. Who is this imposter? More importantly, why you?
24	Following a traumatic childhood incident you are left scarred, either emotionally, physically or both. What caused the trauma and how do you deal with its aftermath?
25	Your family or a lover is bound tightly into the service of an important, powerful individual or corporation who has a great degree of power over them. How do you help your loved one? What hold do they have over you?
26	Either your family or your lover is enmeshed in an important political alliance. Is this at odds with your own convictions?
27	A member of your family is famous, either through their good looks, talent or virtue. Perhaps your own talents and behaviour are constantly compared to them and found wanting?
28	You were the subject of a series of experiments committed by either your family or an institution. Perhaps you seek revenge on the people who used you for their research or wish to discover who engineered your selection.
29	Deservedly or otherwise, an individual seeks revenge against you.
30	You have no proper recollections of either a great deal of your earlier life or else a specific, but shorter, period. Do you desire to learn about this missing past or do you instinctively fear any possible revelations. Do others seek to probe for the truth?

Background Events

1d100	Background Event
31	A dying family member, or another individual important to you, requests that you undertake an important journey and complete a task. What is the task? Is it important? Is it dangerous?
32	A member of your own family is embittered towards you and is a rival. Why? What is the reason? How are you related?
33	You keep encountering a symbol, seemingly at random. You are unsure if this is coincidence, a portent, or a construct of your imagination. It has recently become more frequent or prominent and now you are driven to understand what it means.
34	An insane relative is kept in a secure hospital or a prison. They are believed to have an important secret locked away in a corner of their fevered brain – that or a psychic power that has been diagnosed as madness. What is the truth of their plight?
35	You have had to perform actions in the service of a government, an organisation or a powerful individual that you have grown to bitterly regret. What did you do for them? Why do you hate them so much? Do they want you back?
36	You acquired an item which incorporates a cunningly concealed compartment or a hidden weapon. What is the weapon? Is it archaic or modern – perhaps too modern?
37	Your once prosperous family have now lost their wealth to a rival. How did this fall from grace happen? Did the rival profit?
38	You used to indulge in a particular vice that would create a scandal for you if it became public knowledge. Who else knows? Can you trust them to keep the secret?
39	Someone knows enough about you to be in a position to blackmail you for money or a favour. What do they know? How close are they to carrying out the threat?
40	A member of your family or a close friend is infamous for their behaviour. Possibly your own reputation is tarnished with the public because of your ties with the scoundrel.
41	You have a skilled criminal contact that is willing to assist you in return for remuneration. What is his or her criminal activity? How much can they be trusted?
42	At some key points in your life an invisible hand seems to have shaped your destiny. You don't as yet know who and why but suspect you may owe them a debt of service.
43	A mysterious lover keeps leaving messages and tokens for you. As yet they have not declared themselves, though you are sure they would be hostile to anyone else who courted your affection or had a monopoly on your company. Is this a simple and affectionate game, or something more sinister?
44	You have witnessed an incident which has defied rational and scientific explanation. Were you victim of an elaborate hoax or have you encountered a strange power? Are you marked as the focus for another mysterious event?
45	Your family performed a great service for a wealthy noble or person of influence. As a reward you were taken into that person's service. You can count on this powerful patron as a potential ally.
46	For some reason you have shamed your family and have been cast out. What did you do? Is there hope of reconciliation? Were you to blame or were you just a scapegoat?
47	It transpires that one of your parents is, in fact, a member of a powerful family who has turned their back on their heritage to live a simple life. This does, however, mean you are heir to a large estate or title. Will you ever realise your inheritance?
48	You believe you accidentally killed a close friend or sibling. Perhaps the horror of the situation caused you to flee, remaining silent about the tragedy but trying to live with the guilt ever since. Perhaps you have been blamed and stigmatised?
49	You come from a family that is artistically adept. Their fame has spread far and wide, granting you access to high status patrons if you yourself are an artist, craftsman or performer. Conversely it is a constant source of irritation when casual acquaintances are taken aback at your lack of talent.
50	You come from a family that is famous for its scientific achievements. Their fame has spread far and wide, granting you access to high status universities and employers if you are a Scientist or scholar. Conversely it is a constant source of irritation when casual acquaintances are taken aback at your lack of talent.
51	Your family was hunted by powerful foes. Why did your family need to keep moving and hiding? What do the pursuers want? Are they still following you? Should you confront them? You are sick and tired of being on the run.
52	You are a born to a lone parent. Your mother swears your father was a man of note and station, but she herself is of a lower status and you are considered even lower than she is. Where your father is, no one knows, but you would love to meet him some day and discover the truth about him. Perhaps, if reunited with your father, the stigma of your birth might be erased.
53	A sibling committed a heinous crime that has brought shame on your family. They fled soon after, vanishing entirely, casting suspicion on you. Were you yourself falsely blamed for the crime? Or did you willingly confess, to preserve the remnants of your family's honour? Is blood truly thicker than water?
54	You are a twin. Your brother or sister has similar characteristics and skills to yourself but you are clearly different people. Are you close, as twins usually are, or estranged? You always seem to know where your sibling is, even if relations between you are not good.
55	You met a great hero at a time when he or she was unknown. You suspected, perhaps, that this person was destined for greatness, but you still became friends before you parted. Will they remember you? Will you still be friends?
56	You met a great villain at a time when he or she was unknown. You suspected, perhaps, that this person was destined for infamy, but you still became friends before you parted. Will they remember you? Will you still be friends?

Background Events

1d100	Background Event
57	Your elder brother or sister is (or was) a great hero for some reason and you live somewhat in their shadow. You are desperate to prove that you are your sibling's equal and want to outdo their deeds, proving that your family can produce more than one hero.
58	You have studied with a noted master, scholar or wise man. Whenever you meet up with the teacher, you can request personal tuition for one or more of your related Professional Skills.
59	You have had a bounty placed on your head by an unknown individual. What are you thought to have done? How have you evaded bounty hunters in the past? How can you clear your name?
60	In recent years you have attracted the attention of a journalist who finds you a useful source of information. This may be a boon as you use him to promote yourself and your ideas, or a curse if he draws unwanted publicity to you.
61	You owe a sum of money equal to ten times your starting income. This could be for any single or multiple reasons: robbery, gambling, medical care, a divorce settlement or an unwise investment. Hopefully the debt is owed a reputable establishment that can accept repayment in practical instalments rather than a criminal and violent loans operator.
62	You inherited a piece of technology that seems to defy your attempts to identify its purpose. Is it actually a piece of elaborate artwork, an executive toy or a hoax; or does it have some useful function, as yet unknown?
63	You own a diary, map, recording disc or tape which was used by another person and includes coded information that you have yet to decipher. As the item came from an intriguing source, you are sure that it is the key to an important secret.
64	You have a fond regard for a particular location. Whilst spending periods relaxing there you find your mental well-being seems to recover at a faster rate than when at your home or in a psychological institute.
65	Through either your professional or private life you are aware of an unusual location connected with strange phenomena, as yet, unexplained by rational science. You will need to consult with your Games Master, but possible 'happenings' can be determined to be rooted there: interference with scientific instrument readings, amnesia, a high rate of insanity, illness or problem births amongst locals, mysterious disappearances, lack of wildlife, ominous folk lore, uniformity of features or high intelligence amongst locally born infants.
66	You are aware of the location of a damaged vehicle with unique or scientifically advanced properties which, at cost of money and labour can be rescued from a junkyard, museum, dangerous bog or an underwater location. Potentially you could investigate and repair it, but was it destroyed for a reason? Does it still have a dangerous flaw, and does the original owner or another individual wish to recover it?
67	You know of an individual to whom dark rumours cling. Perhaps he masks his features in some fashion and, seemingly, appears and disappears in an uncanny ways. Maybe dogs always bark at him or you feel a migraine in his presence? What is his secret and, as your paths seem to cross, what is his apparent interest in you?
68	You are convinced that you are sane but constantly hear a voice in your head or suddenly view other and unfamiliar locations. You seek an explanation for these delusions, are you being drugged or influenced by hypnosis? Are you mentally ill? Is it psionic reverberations?
69	You lost a lover or a close friend in a recent tragedy. Do you blame anyone for the death?
70	Before reaching adulthood you once ran away from home. Was this prompted by the need to try and escape from a miserable childhood or was it undertaken in the spirit of an adventure? What experiences did you have?
71	An individual is obsessed with you to the point where they constantly follow you and collect memorabilia associated with you. Possibly they are a source of great embarrassment, though perhaps they have picked up some information which is of great importance to you.
72	You feel there is something hauntingly familiar about a particular object, place or individual. (e.g. The work of a particular artist, photographs of a ruined city complex, a film actress, an opera song.) Is this just recollecting something viewed earlier in your life or is it connected with another incarnation or parallel?
73	A family member has served the Valhalla Project in the past and this is how you have come to its attention. But did your relative serve loyally or with duplicity? Why did they leave?
74	Diaries belonging to a great, great grandparent hint at things that you know have come to pass many years later. How did your great, great grandparent know what was going to happen? Were they psychic? What are these predictions? How can they be averted – or embraced?
75	A period of several years is missing from your memory. You remember everything up to the start of this period with great clarity, and everything after it, but for this block of 1d6 years, it is as though you ceased to exist. More troubling, no one you know ever questions you on this 'lost' period. What period of your life does this missing block cover? What might have happened to you? What are people not telling you? Indeed — can you be sure that this is a missing period of your life?
76	During a course of hypnotherapy you accidentally regressed to a past life from 1d4 x100 years ago. Who were you? What did you do? You are driven to uncover more of this past life — and discover other lives you have inhabited.
77	Ever since adolescence you have been plagued by recurring, vivid dreams of people who, in reality, you have never met, but in your dream-world are compelling and life-like. One of them is, in your dreams, a lover, and the love you share is far stronger than anything you've experienced in the waking world. How can you be with this soul mate? How can you find them?
78	Either a family member or a close acquaintance is in the service of a secretive group that, whilst neither a criminal conspiracy or a cult, displays some disturbing elements. From what you can gather it seeks to actively disrupt society — yet it does not behave like an anarchist or similar political group. Who are they? Could they be Disruptor puppets?

Background Events

1D100	Background Event
79	Several years ago you let an individual tell your fortune. At the time you put their surprisingly accurate observations about your past and future down to luck, keen perception or trickery, and gave no special thought to their predictions. With the passing of time, however, you have become astonished at how closely events in your life have conformed to the reading. Worryingly, an ominous event has yet to occur, and you also recollect that the reader was about to tell you something else but changed their mind. Perhaps it would be worth trying to visit the fortune teller again?
80	After finishing your education you realise that one tutor seems to have imparted false facts and theories to you: they certainly do not seem to match existing history or science. The tutor is no longer at the establishment you attended. Why did he leave, and what was his purpose? Is the knowledge he gave you intended to be useful at some stage in your future?
81	To your surprise, you recently discovered that you are the parent of a child. The infant is the product of a former relationship or perhaps the result of scientists using genetic samples you donated to their stocks, voluntary or otherwise. Why was the information of the infant's birth kept from you? Is the child in jeopardy?
82	You come from a wealthy family. However the funds you own are tainted. You are either troubled by your own conscience or, failing that, an individual seeks to draw the inequity to your attention. Do you decide to try and compensate those who lost out? Do you wish to travel somewhere where scandal or retribution cannot reach you or do you determine to find a way of silencing the claimant?
83	Some time ago you found yourself asking a powerful criminal, businessman or official for a favour. The individual was able to help you in exchange for a verbal agreement to return the favour at a time of his own choosing. You realise that the favour that will be asked of you might be to commit an illegal or morally dubious act, and you know that they have the ability to apply considerable pressure on you.
84	You are required to attend regular sessions of counselling for an emotional problem or community service for a past transgression. Failure to attend them will have repercussions for you.
85	You have impaired eyesight or hearing which has led to the adoption of a minor technological device to correct the problem.
86	The character has an illness which requires regular medication to negate the debilitating effects.
87	You were once a participant in the schemes of the Disruptors. Were you an unwitting dupe or were you once keen to do their bidding so you could gain personal power? What service did you perform for your old masters and was your mission successful? Whilst some Valhalla Project members see enormous potential in using your knowledge and your newfound antagonism towards your old spymasters, others distrust you. You suspect that a few of these doubters would like to see you permanently eliminated. Can you even trust yourself?
88	You have a favoured and beloved pet which follows you everywhere. It has no abilities or special powers, but offers comfort and companionship. If you are from a parallel with the required technology, it might have notable features which have been genetically engineered. It may even be a robot or genetically engineered creature.
89	Somehow you have picked up a loyal companion or retainer. Maybe a childhood friend, or perhaps a hanger-on from some chance encounter. This does not necessarily make your companion a welcome presence, but the relationship has somehow endured over the years.
90	You were once approached to help agents of the state by giving information on a colleague, friend or relative. What happened to the person they were interested in? You are unsure if these agents will ever call on your services again, and have qualms as to how legal their methods are and whether they actually are a legitimate arm of the government.
91	At some stage in your chosen career you were an aide to the military. You are known as a professional expert in one of your Professional skills and sometimes sought out for future tutoring.
92	You have a physical deformity in a random location. You suffer no ill effects as you have learned to adapt or you use a piece of beneficial technology to overcome it.
93	You are a member of a political or religious group. Whilst it provides comradeship and support for its members, loyalty is expected in return. Is it an illegal group or unpopular amongst sections of society? Are its members active in violence or on the receiving end of it Do you still share the group's ideals?
94	You discover that your employer or patron seems to have favoured you over others equally or more worthy. Perhaps your recent work has been a mere sinecure all along? Is this due to your natural charm or is there a hidden agency or guilt motivating your benefactor? Or are you actually being set up as a fall guy for some impending scheme or disaster?
95	You have a dependant who relies on you for financial assistance or personal company. Their situation is affected by their age or poor health. Is this duty an onerous one? Is the bond one of family or friendship or guilt?
96	You begin to suffer a series of inexplicable blackouts. Upon recovery you always find yourself near to an ancient monolith, battle ground or burial site. At first you thought someone was playing practical jokes on you, but now the frequency of attacks is increasing and upon your last awakening you were almost arrested for trespass.
97	You think you are going slowly insane. When you walk at night, street lights sometimes extinguish as you pass under them. Vehicles seem to falter when you are driving or a passenger. Even clocks appear to run slower in your presence. Are you turning paranoid, or is there some explanation as to what is going on?
98	You hear voices in your head, telling you things as they are about to happen. They predicted deaths among your family and friends. They knew when war was going to break out overseas. They knew that the head of state was going to be assassinated. Now they say that policemen are coming to your house to arrest you...
99	Five years ago, you murdered someone. Self defence? Revenge? A random compulsion? You hid the body and thought you'd got away with it. Now the news reports say the body has been discovered. How long until they find out it was you...?
100	Five years ago you and a friend committed a crime together. He or she was caught and you escaped. Your friend was sentenced to 10 years in prison. Now they are out on parole and looking for you. What was the crime? Why did you go free? Do you want your friend to find you?

Drive (type)[1]	DEX+POW
Electronics	*DEX+INT*
Engineering[2]	INT x2
Forgery	DEX+INT
Gambling	INT+POW
Linguistics[3]	INT+CHA
Lockpicking	DEX x2
Lore	INT x2
Mechanisms[2]	DEX+INT
Medicine[4]	INT+POW
Meditation	INT+POW
Musicianship	DEX+CHA
Navigation	INT+POW
Oratory	POW+CHA
Pilot[1]	*DEX+INT*
Politics	*INT+CHA*
Probabilities	*INT x2*
Ride[1]	DEX+POW
Science	*INT x2*
Seamanship	INT+CON
Sensors	*INT+POW*
Seduction	INT+CHA
Sleight	DEX+CHA
Streetwise	POW+CHA
Survival	CON+POW
Teach	INT+CHA
Track	INT+CON

[1] *These are skills that have been changed dramatically for use in the Arkwright universe, each covered in their own subsections below.*

[2] *Mechanisms permits the repair and maintenance of mechanical devices, from airship engines to clockwork automatons. Engineering represents the ability to comprehend the processes behind, and architectural design of, actual mechanical devices.*

[3] *Linguistics is a renamed version of both Language and Literacy, and it performs the same functions as both. In the contemporary worlds surrounding the Valhalla Project, anyone who understands a language well enough to speak phrases is also considered to be able to read and write in that language (if possible). For each 10% of this skill, the Character may choose one Language to apply it to.*

[4] *Medicine is the Healing skill renamed, although it performs the same function as Healing. The Skill might involve the use of technological machinery such as stethoscopes and x-ray machines, hence the need for new nomenclature.*

Mechanisms Skills Redefined

The Mechanisms skill, in addition to dealing with simple traps and clockwork devices, allows the maintenance and repair of complex mechanical equipment. This can be anything from the servicing of droid actuators to fixing moisture vapourators. The skill cannot repair something completely destroyed, but could permit a brief jury-rigged fix if enough spare parts are available.

Contrary to traditional science fiction settings, this skill also includes the maintenance and repair of starship reactors and hyperdrives. The design and building of new mechanical devices is not covered by this skill, but requires the Engineering skill instead.

Anna Thames' Chronicle

What kind of background does Anna come from? Simon rolls 1d100 on the Social Class table to find out. The result, 61, shows she is a Citizen. This indicates her upbringing was nothing remarkable; Simon decides Anna's parents struggled to make ends meet and moved to Liverpool from the Yorkshire countryside where work was more plentiful. It was here Anna fell into disreputable company, but got the chance to travel on her beloved dirigibles and airships. For her ready money, Anna has 1d100 (03 is the result), multipled by a hundred — so 300 Crowns to her name. This isn't a great deal, and reinforces both her modest upbringing and need to turn to less-than-legitimate means to earn her way.

For her age, Simon simply decides that Anna is 24 — his own age.

And how did Anna find herself recruited by Valhalla? Another 1d100 roll yields 70: *Stumbled over a Valhalla Operation accidentally, but natural talents were immediately recognised.* Emma says that, 2 years ago, on a smuggling run from Dublin to Liverpool, the captain had allowed a 'special passenger' to hitch a ride. This passenger, Rose Wilde, was a sophisticated, flame-haired Irish woman that took an immediate interest in Anna. As the airship crossed the Irish Sea, Ms Wilde calmly drew a strange weapon and shot the Captain dead. Anna was forced to take over the controls, but not without challenging Ms Wilde. Rose calmly unfastened the top buttons of her silk blouse and exposed a tattoo on her left shoulder — a symbol identical to the one on Anna's right shoulder blade. "Your captain worked for people seeking to destroy everything you know and love," Ms Wilde explained. "You, on the other hand, Ms Thames, are going to help me save it..."

Anna now has a final 150 skill points to allocate among her skills as she wishes. Simon allocates 15 points to 9 skills as follows: *Athletics, Deceit, Electronics, Evade, Insight, Lockpicking, Pilot (Airship), Perception, and Stealth.* He forgoes choosing an optional Hobby Skill and asks Emma if Anna can increase her *Concealed Weapons Combat Style* with the 15 points remaining: Emma agrees.

For equipment, Simon and Emma agree that Anna owns two reasonable sets of clothes, one of which she reserves for special occasions, has a pair of concealable revolvers, a pair of knives with one concealed in her ankle boot, and a few personal possessions for hygiene, grooming and so on. Anna Thames prefers to travel light. She has a rented room above a bookstore not far from the Liverpool's airship yards and, Emma says, Rose Wilde arranged for Anna to inherit the airship owned by the deceased captain. However she has also inherited the airship's running costs too, so she needs to find inventive ways of making money to keep the *Headlong Flight* aloft.

Transportation Skills Redefined

Not every individual in the Arkwright multiverse relies on the same methods of travel. The original skills of Boating, Drive and Ride have been removed from the default Standard skill list. These are instead supplanted with a new, more detailed set of transportation skills which reflect the diverse range of vehicles found in the multiverse.

Each category covers the control of any vehicle (or creature) which matches its environmental and propulsion specifications. The categories are:
Boating (Boats) – Waterborne craft from canoes to sea liners
Boating (Submersibles) – Vessels that travel below the surface of water
Drive (Crawler) – Wheeled or tracked land vehicle
Drive (AG) – Ground hugging, repulsor lift/anti-grav vehicles
Drive (Walker) – Multi-legged vehicles
Pilot (Airship) – Atmospheric dirigibles or other non-aerobatic flying vehicles
Pilot (Flyer) – Helicopters or fixed wing aircraft
Pilot (Spaceship) – Spacecraft with personal flight crews
Ride (Beasts) – Animals of any type
For the purposes of simplicity, any transportation skill learned as part of Culture is considered a Standard skill. All others are treated as Professional skills and must be taught by entering the correct career, picked up as a character's speciality hobby, or learned after character creation by training a new skill.

New Skills

The following are new skills created to handle the higher technology of the genre, and should be applicable to any Science Fiction setting.

Astrogate (INT x2)

In parallels where space travel has become commonplace, Astrogation is equivalent to Navigation, save that it enables starship pilots to plot a course at stellar and interstellar distances. This skill is not normally rolled against in non-stressful situations, but a roll may be required in the following circumstances:

- Trying to calculate a course whilst under fire, evading pursuit or hiding the destination
- The ship's FTL engines have been damaged or are poorly maintained
- Attempting to shave off travel time by cutting close to (or through) dangerous regions

Comms (INT x2)

This skill grants the ability to use communications equipment to detect, conceal or block comms traffic. It also grants a chance of cracking encrypted messages (providing the user has access to a code-cracker). In any situation where the attempted communication (or discovery of such) is actively challenged, an opposed roll is used to determine the result.

Computers (INT x2)

In those parallels where computer use is widespread, this skill reflects the character's ability to solve complex problems or extract complex information, using computer systems – be it through programming code, detailed use of a particular piece of software, hacking, and even diagnosing/repairing software and hardware problems. General use of computers, such as searching the internet or using a word processor or spreadsheet, does not usually require a roll unless the Character is from a parallel where computers are rarer.

Demolitions (INT+POW)

This skill permits a character to safely handle and utilise explosive materials. Most demolition attempts require no skill check if performed in a non-stressful situation whilst taking time to double check everything is set up correctly. A roll should only be necessary when:

- Cutting corners to save time or being within a combat situation
- Using substandard or unknown materials
- Setting up the explosive device as a trap
- Needing to demolish something without causing collateral damage

Electronics (DEX+INT)

This skill allows the user to tinker with, bypass or repair electronic devices. It has many applications, most often to temporarily patch up damaged equipment or replace broken circuits with spares. A darker aspect of the skill is the circumventing of electronic security, providing the character can gain access to the circuitry or a convenient data port.

Designing and building new electronic devices is not covered by this skill and instead requires the Engineering skill.

Forgery (DEX+INT)

The Forgery skill permits the creation or falsification of official documentation. This is normally used to gain the following:

- False identity documentation, whether for a spacecraft or a person
- False travel documentation, so that the holder can penetrate a secure facility or region
- False cargo manifests, to enable the smuggling of prohibited substances or objects

Forgery is not simply the physical crafting of a facsimile of the original document, assuming it's not just an electronic code. Rather it requires the knowledge of passwords, encryption, names of current overseers and dozens of other aspects. It might even necessitate the hacking of local databases to plant corroborating evidence to support the forged document.

Usually the skill is tested once to initially create the forgery. The quality of the forgery depends on the roll, which can be made in secret by the Game Master if they so desire:

Fumble: some elemental mistake is made immediately revealing the bogus nature of the forgery, so that it automatically fails any inspection check.

Failure: the forgery is sufficiently shoddy so that it always prompts an inspection check.

Success: a sufficiently good enough forgery is created so that it always passes inspection checks without needing to roll, unless the checking official has reason to be suspicious.

Critical Success: the forgery is so good that it can never be discerned from the real thing. It always passes inspection checks. Only a thorough in-depth investigation of the associated person, craft or cargo will indirectly reveal it is false.

Inspection checks occur whenever an official requests to see (or be transmitted) the forged document; a guardsman requesting travel papers or an ID card for example. The check is a simple opposed roll of the crafter's Forgery skill (at the time of making the forgery) versus the viewer's Perception, Customs/Culture, or some other relevant technical skill. If the forgery wins, then it passes inspection.

Pilot (DEX+INT)

Previously mentioned as part of the Transportation section of Standard skills, the Pilot skill permits the control of flying vehicles. Despite the degree of automation available to some advanced tech, there is a significant difference between piloting an atmospheric specific flyer and an interstellar spacecraft which requires this skill to be taken twice to cover both environments.

If a character possesses only one speciality, the Games Master is at liberty to substitute one skill for the other, imposing a difficulty penalty when attempting to pilot vessels they are not familiar with. Thus a spacecraft pilot would suffer a penalty when flying a propeller driven monoplane.

As with Astrogation, the Pilot skill is not normally checked when making normal flights. However, dramatic or dangerous situations may require the skill to be tested. For example:

- When engaging in a dogfight with another aircraft or starship
- If trying to fly through difficult conditions, such as an atmospheric storm or flak-round anti-air fire
- Attempting to control the ship to pass by physical obstacles, an asteroid field or canyon
- Landing in bad terrain or with a damaged craft

Politics (INT+CHA)

Characters possessing the Politics skill understand how to navigate and negotiate the corridors of government at local and national levels. It can be used to request a personal favour, lobbying, or even voting support. It can also be used to determine who is really in charge in any given parallel if allowed to observe its media for a few hours.

The Politics skill does not only denote personal contacts, but also reflects the character's own standing in the political structure of his nation state. Due to the degree of authority and power such standing grants, Politics is often a useful skill with which to augment checks concerning negotiations, bribery, or even intimidation attempts.

As a rough guideline, Characters that are politically active are generally limited in their rank according to their Politics skill value. For example, if the Games Master treated membership in the British government of the Indian Raj with a ranking system, lower level functionaries (clerical/secretarial rank) would require a politics skill of 50%, ministers (middle management) need 70%, high ranking ministers (upper management) necessitate 90% and a Viceroy or Governor General (leadership rank) would entail a skill of at least 110%.

Probabilities (INT x2)

Characters with the Probabilities skill understand the underlying causality of the multiverse and how parallels react and adapt to local and nearby events.

When dealing with the normal inhabitants of a parallel, the character can use this skill to determine if a set of actions will cause massive turmoil within the parallel, and therefore act accordingly. For example, a Valhalla agent, working on a parallel where all governmental duties have been turned over to AIs, could use his Probabilities skill to work out the likely repercussions of installing the complete essays of Voltair into one of the AI's data processing centres and the impact it might have on this, and other parallels. Probabilities also helps Characters to locate the point where the history of a parallel diverges from parallels sharing similar characteristics. For example, in two parallels where Nazi Germany is the prevailing world force after 1945, there may be many reasons and many points of divergence, ranging from Germany simply winning the Second World War through military prowess to more subtle reasons such as Winston Churchill's death prior to 1939.

Science (INT x2)

There are dozens of scientific disciplines and the Science skill, which can be taken multiple times, is always associated with a discipline: Science (Biology) or Science (Chemistry), for example. The major disciplies are listed below, but players and Games Masters can add their own.

Anthropology

Astronomy

Astrophysics

Biology

Botany

Chemistry

Geology

Optional Rule: Home Parallels

Agents from the Valhalla Project hail from across the multiverse, and once they are recruited they may or may not ever see "home" again. The parallels are part of a detailed addressing and labelling system used by W.O.T.A.N to map the multiverse. This works by assigning a three part number to the parallel in question, with each portion of the address indicating some arranging detail to the supercomputer and its management staff.

Unless a Games Master decides to create a specific parallel for their game, players are encouraged to make a personalised parallel from which their Character originates. Parallel addresses are designed in a three section format, such as 21.3.81, 4.10.90 or Zero-Zero's own 00.00.00.

A fun and interesting way to design a Character's home parallel is to actually take the player's own date of birth and write it in numeral form in the following order: dd.mm.yy.

For example, Bryan's birth date is August 16th, 1977. His Character's home parallel address would be written as 16.08.77. Marcus' birth date is April 10th, 1989. His Character's home parallel address would be written as 10.04.89.

This does not have to be the only way players and Games Masters create addresses for their multiverse parallels, but it is a fun way to connect players with their Characters on a personal level.

Unique Historic Divergence

One of the most interesting aspects of the multiverse is the differences and divergences that appear from parallel to parallel. Some of these differences are extremely minor, like the existence of an unlikely religious figure or a subtle change in popular culture. Other parallels are struck with much larger instances of differential — such as the National Socialist Party in control over the once-free world, a British Imperial Theocracy, or even the existence of formerly extinct animals running rampant. This is called Historic Divergence.

Players and Games Masters should decide what the Historic Divergence could be for their parallels. If the player cannot come up with a unique point of Divergence on their own, one way is to tie it to the parallel address through a date configured from the address. Using the same dd.mm.yy decryption, the parallel can be linked to a specific date in our "normal" human history.

Once the address has been turned into a date, it can be linked to a specific historic event that can be specifically altered for the Luther Arkwright parallel.

Some examples:

- Parallel 4.7.76 (linked to July 4th, 1776) could have a British assassin – perhaps a Disruptor agent – kill everyone present at the signing of the Declaration of Independence, leading to America's fall to the Crown.
- Parallel 14.7.89 (linked to July 14th, 1789) could see the quashing of the French Revolution before it ever begins, at an unsuccessful siege upon the Bastille.
- Parallel 16.8.77 (linked to August 16th, 1977) might have Elvis Presley survive to become a powerful governmental figure instead of being found dead in his home.

Mathematics

Parallel Physics

Physics

Physiology

Psionics

Psychology

Zoology

A Science roll is called for whenever a character is attempting to solve a problem scientifically within a field of expertise, use science to make a deduction about a situation, or conduct an experiment (either practical or theoretical).

If a character wishes to attempt a roll in an unspecialised field of science — a chemist attempting to approach a physics problem, for example — the Games Master can impose a skill grade of Hard or Formidable if so desired, but the minimum roll is never less than the character's base chance (INT x2) n Science. This reflects the general grounding science students tend to have across a broad range of scientific fields. So, in the example above, if the chemist has INT 16 and Science (Chemistry) 54%, and is attempting to solve a physics problem where the Games Master rates the chance of success as Formidable (half the usual chance, so 27%) the chemist actually rolls against 32%, because this is his base score in the overall Science skill.

Sensors (INT+POW)

This skill allows the accurate use and analysis of sensor devices from chemical sniffers up to military long range scanners. It is most often checked when somebody or something tries to remain hidden from the sensor user. In this case, the check is an opposed roll of the Sensors skill against the most pertinent skill for that situation, be that Stealth, Piloting, Conceal, and so on. When checking for the existence of a nominally non-perceivable substance or clue, the skill check is unopposed.

Final Steps

Every character needs to determine traits, passions and dependencies; these are all described in the next chapter, and forms part of character creation.

Traits, Passions & Dependencies

Humankind has not developed without assistance. Whilst Darwinian evolution has been the prevalent method of *homo sapiens'* development, it has not been the *only* method. The Five — mystical beings of probable alien origin, but now constants in countless parallels — have tampered with the human gene pool in a bid to create an advanced human state: *homo novus*. Psychokinetically interfering with human DNA, The Five have, over centuries and many, many parallels, slowly developed physical and psychic abilities in hundreds of genealogical lines, resulting in humans who transcend the norm. Men like Arkwright, women like Rose Wilde and Octobriana: *people like the Characters* are products of The Five's eugenic experimentation.

The Five tampered in this way to counter the Disruptors. Clearly The Five have encountered the Disruptors before and may even have some relation to one of the races involved in the galactic war that lead to the creation of FireFrost; clearly The Five are the Disruptors' enemy. To some humans they manifest as Buddhist Monks but they have been also been reported to manifest as saints, angels or even creatures of pure energy — sublimed beings that have transcended the need for physical form.

Whatever their true natures and origins, The Five have been benevolent to humanity, and their experimentation, while abhorrent to some, has been with a view to preserving order, stability and life.

And the Characters — Valhalla's agents — are products of The Five. They are *homo novus*. What makes them special, gifted, and powerful are the qualities the scientists of Zero-Zero term Traits.

Traits

Mundane individuals are useful to the Valhalla Project. The missions and plans of the supercomputer use them, but in a highly limited and covert matter. Mundane humans may never know that they work for the Project, being employed through fronts or surrogate organisations. Its most important agents, the ones who are fully aware of their role, are those W.O.T.A.N has identified as being 'Special.'

These special individuals have certain qualities or powers that set them apart from the rest of humanity. Arkwright Characters fall into this category: every character has one – occasionally more

– of these powers. Traits set the Characters apart from homo sapiens and make them of special interest to W.O.T.A.N's agenda.

Characters reflect across parallels but (usually) have wildly different histories, relationships and careers. However, although a character on a different parallel will have such differences, their Trait remains constant. So, a psychic agent demonstrates the same psychic abilities across all their incarnations (although a small number may have a different Trait altogether).

Determining Traits

The Games Master has the final say as to how many Traits a Characters has. If the Games Master decides that the campaign would benefit from the agents having multiple Traits then he or she can allow each character to generate two. If the Games Master believes that certain Traits would be good for the progress of the campaign, then he or she is free to select or suggest Traits instead.

There is also the possibility that a Trait is learnt or awakened during the course of a campaign, although this should be used sparingly. Traits can be awoken as the result of some form of trauma or psychological condition, or even scientific experimentation or mysticism. Games Masters have the final say as to where and when.

Players either roll on, or the Games Master decides from, the Traits table opposite.

Anna Thames' Chronicle

Anna is *homo novus* and Emma, the Games Master, rules that Simon can roll randomly on the Traits table. The result is 57, indicating that Anna is Psionic. Simon immediately starts listing the many powers he knows Anna should have but Emma asks him to pause for a moment.

While Anna is psychic, she doesn't really know it; it is a latent talent that Valhalla will help her develop through training and coaching on Zero-Zero. Anna's precise powers will be decided later, and this is described in the Mind Games chapter.

Traits Defined

The game effects of a Trait are described in this section. Most Traits have limited effects, although some are more potent than others and some, like psionics, have their own mechanics. Every Trait offers some form of advantage. Disadvantages come in the form of Dependencies, which are explained in their own section.

Agile

The individual has superb reflexes. When calculating Initiative the character adds one tenth of his or her Athletics skill to the Initiative 1d10 roll. For example, a Valhalla agent with the Agile

1d100	Trait
01-03	Agile
04-06	Assimilation
07-09	Broadcast Pain
10-12	Brutal
13-15	Charming
16-17	Contact
18-20	Deadshot
21-23	Eidetic
24-26	Enhanced Balance
27-29	Enhanced Vision
30-32	Forgettable
33-35	Insightful
36-37	Lucky
38-40	Menacing
41-42	Natural Armour
43-45	Nerveless
46-47	Null-Psionic
48-50	Perceptive
51-53	Polyglot
54-56	Precognition
57-58	Psionic
59-61	Quick
62-64	Regenerative
65-67	Reincarnation
68-70	Resilient
71-73	Savant
74-75	Self-Awareness
76-78	Sensitive
79-81	Sixth Sense
82-84	Strong
85-87	Technical
88-90	Tenacious
91-93	Twin
94	Unique
95-97	Unshakeable
98	Vampiric
99-00	Youthful

Trait and Athletics 50% would calculate Initiative on her Initiative Bonus +1d10+5

Assimilation

The individual can read and absorb information at an astonishingly fast rate. The character can glean the important points and inferences from a piece of text at the rate of 2 seconds per page. Therefore the contents of a 300 page book can be understood in just 10 minutes of study. The character must obviously be able to read the text in the first place and this Trait is not the same as an Eidetic Memory. Instead the character is adept at gleaning the crucial facts rather than recalling specific details with precise clarity.

Broadcast Pain

Any damage inflicted on the character is felt by everybody within a number of metres radius equal to the character's POW. Although those afflicted do not suffer Hit Point damage, the pain felt is all too real, and victims must resist both Serious and Major Wounds in the same way as the character. Recipients of Broadcast Pain cannot die, but the can be rendered unconscious or incapacitated.

Brutal

The individual has a penchant for visceral violence, and is utterly unshaken by the sight of it. No matter whether the individual is the cause of a horrifying violent scene or simply stumbling upon one, the character never has to take Willpower Skill tests to avoid Tenacity Point loss from violent or brutal horror.

Charming

Highly charismatic, any skill with CHA as a base characteristic is always at one grade easier than the norm.

Contact

The individual has a psychic bond with either an individual on their home parallel or their parallel selves across the multiverse. With concentration they can communicate their thoughts to the individual despite physical and dimensional distances. Such a feat requires the spending of a point of Prana each round. If concentration difficulty is likely, then a Willpower test must also be made.

Deadshot

The individual is a true, natural marksman; using aim reduces the situational difficulty by two grades instead of one (see Mythras page 108).

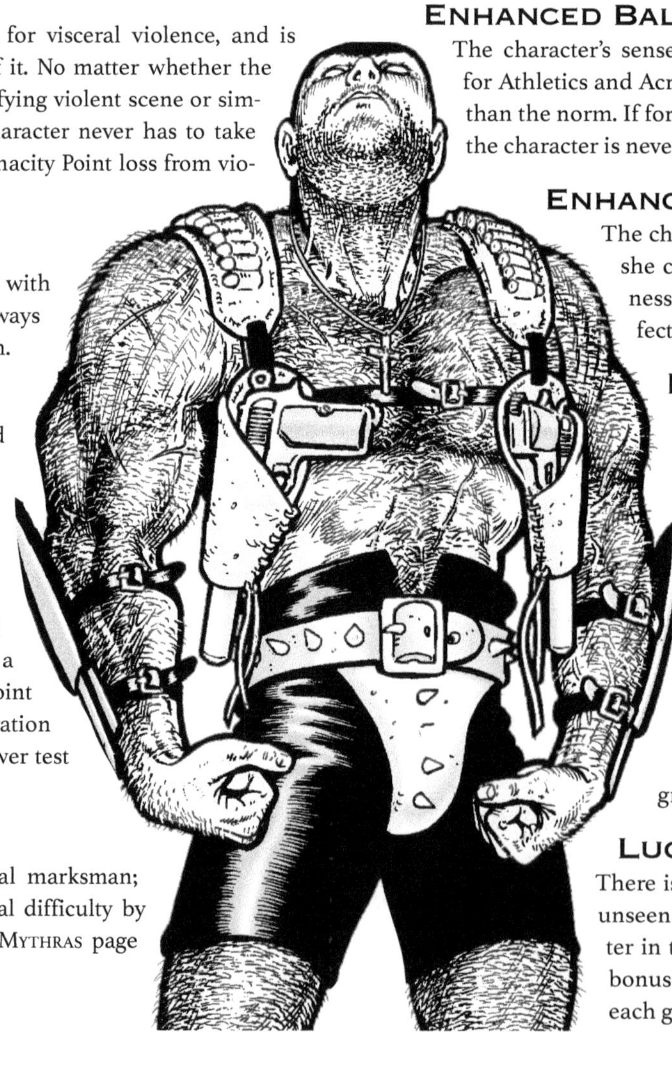

Luther Arkwright's Traits

Luther Arkwright is the culmination of The Five's efforts; the full realisation of *homo novus*. Through study with The Five, Arkwright's full potential begins to be developed, and subsequent trauma while on active service awakens several other Traits.

In game terms Arkwright is utterly unique in that he has multiple Traits: Charming, Unique, and Psionic, amongst others. While players may want to play Characters who are on a par with Arkwright, it is recommended that Games Masters dissuade such ambitions. A character like Arkwright quickly dominates (something Arkwright himself realises and is horrified by) and would become an immediate target for the most powerful Disruptor attacks.

Eidetic

The individual has an eidetic memory and can memorise an image, page of writing, scene, sound, and so forth perfectly by spending 1d6 minutes studying the subject. The character can recall or recite the precise details and nature of the subject at will. Details do not fade with age or time.

Enhanced Balance

The character's sense of balance is highly acute. Rolls for Athletics and Acrobatics are always one grade easier than the norm. If forced to use Evade to avoid an attack, the character is never left prone.

Enhanced Vision

The character's eyesight is such that he or she can see perfectly well in total darkness and suffers no modifiers or ill-effects due to the absence of light.

Forgettable

The individual's face and voice are indistinctive and cannot be remembered by most witnesses. Typically, attempts to recollect the character by strangers or casual acquaintances require a Herculean Willpower roll.

Insightful

The character is a remarkable judge of character, motive and subtext. All Insight rolls are one grade easier than the norm.

Lucky

There is no such thing as coincidence. An unseen hand seems to assist the character in their goals. The character gains a bonus Luck Point that can be used in each game session.

Menacing

The individual unconsciously radiates hostility. Opponents — or those who wish the character harm — must make an unopposed roll against Willpower to stand their ground, with a failure incating that they are forced to spend the next round backing away and placing distance between themselves and the character. If the Willpower roll is failed, the opponent flees at top speed.

Natural Armour

The individual has naturally resilient skin and subcutaneous tissue, gaining 1d2 points of natural armour.

Nerveless

The individual cannot feel pain and does not suffer the ill-effects of serious wounds, but also must roleplay the lack of general touch-sensitivity.

Null-Psionic

The Character has no Psionic powers, but his or her mind is immune to their influence. The character cannot be detected or influenced/harmed through any psychic means. The character can, however, still be injured through the physical manifestations of a psychic power (such as something hurled by telekinesis). The individual cannot be sensed by their parallel selves using the Contact and Self-Awareness Traits.

Perceptive

The character has enhanced powers of either visual, aural or olfactory perception (choose one). All Perception rolls are one grade easier than the norm. Stimuli related to the enhanced perception are that much more vivid, apparent, intricate, distinct and so forth.

Polyglot

The character is a preternatural linguist. The Character begins the game with 1d3 additional languages covered under their Linguistics skill. Communicating in an unfamilar language is always one grade easier than the norm.

Precognition

The character has a latent connection with the psi-flux which sometimes results in fits of imagery and visions in the form of lucid dreams that can relate to either the past, the present or even possible futures. The character usually requires at least six hours of sleep before attempting a Willpower roll to see if anything significant is recollected from a recent dream (within 1d6 days). If the roll is successful, the Games Master can describe what haphazard details the character recollects and intuitively knows to be of significance. The seer will not always be sure if the dreams have revealed past or future events and the Games Master may prefer to describe them in a surreal or cryptic fashion. If the roll is failed, then what is recalled of any dreams is of no importance and quickly forgotten. Fumbled rolls indicate the character has completely mistaken something inconsequential for something of value and significance.

Psionic

The individual possesses one or more psychic powers (telekinesis, telepathy, etc). See the Mind Games chapter (starting on page 56) for more details on generating Psionics and their use.

Quick

The character's Movement Rate is 9m rather than standard 6m per round.

Regenerative

The character's Healing Rate is 1d2 points higher than normal. Not only does the character heal faster, but wounds do not leave any scar tissue. The character cannot regenerate amputated body parts but if a body part suffers a Major Wound and remains attached to the body, it will regenerate given enough healing time.

Reincarnation

The Character is a reincarnation of an earlier self – and even a self from a different parallel – that possessed unique historical significance. A Character could, for instance, be a reincarnation of John F Kennedy from a different parallel. The Character can access his former memories and experiences to assist in his current life. If killed, he might also reincarnate again.

The memories of earlier incarnations may give a Character access to skills that are not widely known or used in this current incarnation. To access any useful memories requires a Willpower roll and the expenditure of a point of Prana.

Resilient

The individual is incredibly resilient to the effects of wounds. Their Hit Points are calculated using STR+CON+SIZ.

Savant

The character is adept at complex mental mathematics and deductions of probability. Any skill requiring the application of mathematics, such as Commerce, Gambling, Science (Mathematics) and so on is always at one grade easier than the norm.

Self-Awareness

The character is aware of his or her other parallel selves and their surroundings, and can perceive other parallels through their eyes. Self-Awareness does not allow for one-to-one communication, although if another self also possesses this trait then information can certainly be exchanged tacitly. The character also experiences the pain and discomfort that is felt by their other selves. Severe injury, shock or death can be traumatic. A Willpower roll is needed to resist any trauma, with death of another self imposing two grades of difficulty. Failure incapacitates the character for 2d10 minutes and also reduces their Tenacity Points by half the number of minutes of incapacitation. A Fumble renders the character unconscious for 1d3 hours and results in Tenacity Points being temporarily reduced to 1. On regaining consciousness, the psyhic trauma of experiencing the death of an alternate self results in the character losing 1d2 Tenacity Points permenantly.

Sensitive

The character is sensitive to vibrations and disruptions in the fabric of the multiverse. They can often detect cataclysmic disasters in nearby parallels or sense anomalous objects and beings from other dimensions.

The chance of sensing such phenomena is normally equal to Willpower and at times may occur involuntarily. Characters can also chose to spend time examining the stability of a known parallel using either the Meditation skill or a Hard Insight roll. This form of sensitivity can lead to psychic trauma. See the Self-Awareness Trait for a guide line as to what happens when things go wrong.

Sixth Sense

The character has an uncanny intuition of personal danger and never suffers the negative game effects for being surprised (see Mythras page 105).

Strong

The individual is skilled at landing horrifically powerful attacks on an opponent. The Damage Bonus is calculated using STR+CON+SIZ.

Technical

The character can deduce the function and operation of mechanical and electrical devices with relative ease, including devices that might be of a highly advanced nature. The character need only study a device for a maximum 21-INT minutes to understand how it works and what it does. The study time can be less at the Games Master's discretion. Note that this Trait does not confer the ability to repair or create devices; it is simply a natural empathy for form, function and purpose.

Tenacious

The character is highly resilient mentally. Tenacity Points are increased by 1d3 and there is no reduction for Dependencies (see page 49).

Twin

The Character has 1d3 identical brothers or sisters who are bonded by an empathetic link. These might be useful contacts or fellow Valhalla agents. The Games Master may elect to let a character roleplay one or more of his twin siblings for odd episodes in the campaign, particularly if the original Character dies or is incapacitated during a campaign.

Injuries and stress in a twin might result in similar side effects to their siblings as detailed in the Self-Awareness Trait.

Unique

The character is unique in the multiverse, having no alternate selves in other parallels. The character is also undetectable when travelling between parellels: certain equipment can detect the unique signatures people display when not native to a parallel; Unique Characters always show as being native.

Unshakeable

The character is known for their courage and does not panic easily. All Willpower rolls to resist fear are one grade easier.

Vampiric

The individual has a deep hunger for life energy that manifests as extreme behaviours, such as cannibalism or sexual predation. The character requires some way of achieving intimate contact with a potential victim (biting, or sexual congress for example) and must overcome the victim's Endurance with their Willpower in an Opposed Roll. If successful, the vampiric character drains the victim of either 1d3 Prana, 1d3 Hit Points, or 1d3 Tenacity per combat round, according to personal need. Drained points replenish any deficient, corresponding points the vampiric character has lost. The character cannot drain more points than have been lost, or recover more points than are needed.

Youthful

The character ages at a vastly slower rate than normal (1 year for every five that passes). This provides for a much greater life span, although the character remains mortal). The character only needs to start making aging checks once 60 is reached, and from then only needs to check every 10 years.

Passions

Introduced during the character creation chapter, a Passion is any deeply held commitment that has the capacity to influence events during play. Although they can be used as stand-alone abilities (to call them skills is to do them a disservice), passions are further expanded below to explain in more detail how they work and how they can influence Characters and Luther Arkwright campaigns.

In summary, Passions can be used thus:

- To augment another skill, reflecting the depth of one's feeling and how it drives action.
- When used in this regard the Passion adds 20% of its value to a skill being used, as long as the augmentation is thematically and dramatically important.
- As an ability in its own right to drive choices, desires and emotional actions and responses.
- When used in this way a standard roll is made against a Passion to determine how strongly the character thinks and feels about something. If a roll is a success then the character acts in-line with what the Passion would dictate. If the roll fails then the character can act freely without feeling constrained by the Passion's drives.
- To oppose other Passions – even those held by the same character. This is typically used where two Passions would conflict. For instance a personal love might dictate a course of action that would be contrary to an oath or loyalty. Use an opposed roll between the two Passions with the more successful determining how the character acts.
- As a general measure of depth of commitment, belief and loyalty to a cause. The higher the Passion's value, the more committed the character is. Characters with similar Passions can compare and contrast their ratings to determine who exhibits the deeper commitment.
- To resist some form of psychological manipulation or magical domination. In certain cases where a character is being forced into performing an act contrary to his Passions, he may substitute his Passion for the usual Willpower in the opposed roll.

During character creation, Characters establish several starting Passions; however, new Passions can be developed at any point during a game session if the circumstances warrant it. One might instantly develop 'Hate X' where someone else does something that would strongly invoke hatred to arise. Passions developed during play in this way cost no Experience Rolls and are established there and then. Of course, Characters can also choose to establish a Passion during improvement, at the cost of an Experience roll to gain a Passion at its base value (Mythras page 23)

Deepening and Waning

Passions can increase during a game independently of Experience Rolls, based on the strength of whatever occurred to trigger the increase. Also Passions can, and do, wane. A strongly held belief can be shaken by many things leading to that Passion being either reduced or, in more extreme circumstances, reversed completely. The Deepening and Waning table below shows by how much the Passion changes.

Change	+/-
Weak	1d10
Moderate	1d10+5
Strong	1d10+10

> **Anna Thames' Chronicle**
>
> Anna has the Passion Loyalty (Valhalla Project) 55%. In the course of a mission she is teamed, briefly, with Luther Arkwright. Such is Arkwright's own commitment to defeating the Disruptors, the Games Master decides that after spending several weeks in Arkwright's company, Anna's Loyalty to the Valhalla project deepens by 1d10+5%. Simon rolls 9 for a total of 14, taking Anna's Loyalty (Valhalla Project) to 69%. Her fervour is growing...

DEPENDENCIES

Although *homo novus* reflects the advancement of the human species, it is not without its downside. Those carrying the altered genomes of the *homo novus* strain are susceptible to certain frailties that can offset the distinct advantages afforded by their Traits.

These frailties are reflected in the existence of Dependencies: a need for relief and comfort which is afforded through a particular status, activity or substance. All Arkwright Characters possess at least one Dependency.

Various Characters in the Luther Arkwright stories have deep-set urges that need to be indulged to relieve the pressures of their lives. Both the Papal agent Barberini and the puritan tyrant Cromwell were compelled to engage in acts of violent lust. The Queen Empress Anne, whilst keeping aflame her love of Luther himself, needed solace for her loss and relief from the tensions of her office. She found it in opium, absinthe and the virile services of her Irish guardsmen. The US journalist Hiram Kowalsky is an intrepid reporter who chain smokes Even after managing to quit for ten years, the emotions he experiences in returning to Britain during the reign of the Empress Anne bring about a return of his habit. Arkwright himself spent several years using alcohol and drugs in an attempt to reduce his mental activity when he was being sought by the Disruptors. Eventually, he spiralled into a state of dependence on heroin and was a physical and mental wreck by the time he was rescued by W.O.T.A.N.

Whilst the indulgence of a Dependency can be a charismatic feature in the eyes of some individuals, these quirks of behaviour might lead into activity which is deemed as antisocial or an immoral vice in some cultures, and may even lead to criminal activity. Satisfying these urgings might bring about a variety of problems including social stigma, illness, chronic inactivity, incarceration or incidental physical danger. It also has the potential to place an individual in the hands of schemes devised by rivals, blackmailers, criminal organisations or enemy agents.

A starting Character starts with one or more Dependencies determined on the table below.

A Dependency begins at a value of 20% for all Characters. It is further adjusted by the following table which may increase the Dependency's score. The level of a Dependency can be allocated by a Games Master after consulting with a player about his Character's concept and background history. If required, a roll can be used to determine the initial Dependency score.

1D100	Number of Dependencies
01-75	1
76-95	2
96-00	3

1D100	Dependency Starting Value	Level and Frequency of Need
01-30	20%	Low — Occasional Indulgence
31-60	30+1d10%	Medium — Social Indulgence (Will not pass-up the chance to indulge)
61-90	40+1d10%	High — Must indulge several times a week
91-00	50+1D10%	Acute — Must indulge daily (perhaps multiple times in one day)

Dependency only becomes a significant issue when it reaches 50% and higher. At this stage the Character must find a regular 'fix' of the subject of the Dependency or begin to suffer effects akin to Fatigue as their body and/or psyche struggles with withdrawal. Dependencies can be resisted using Willpower in the same way that Endurance is used to resist physical Fatigue.

Denial of the Dependency on either a regular basis or at a critical time triggers a need for a resistance roll of Willpower against the Dependency's score %. The Willpower roll can be made more or less difficult by the Games Master according to the circumstances – such as availability of the nature of the dependency, time since the Character's last fix, and so on.

For example, Anna Thames gains a High Dependency on red wine; (Dependency (Alcohol) 44%). She drinks wine habitually;

1d100	Dependency	Effects
01-03	Activity	The individual soon feels bored or frustrated with inactivity
04-06	Alcohol	The individual is dependent on intoxicating drinks
07-08	Alternative Personae	The person needs to adopt an alternative identity or behaviour pattern in order to experience satisfaction or feel secure
09-10	Approval	Requires constant praise to avoid feelings of low self-esteem or depression
11	Arson	Igniting destructive fires provides empowerment and entertainment. Some individuals may find similar release through the use of explosives.
12-14	Authority	The individual needs to give command and leadership to others
15-17	Artistic Expression	The individual needs to find an outlet for their emotions using a favoured form of art
18-20	Collecting	The individual is always on the search to add to one of various types of collections (e.g. expensive artworks, ancient artefacts, domestic trivia or human body parts)
21-23	Communication	The individual has a need to talk, often about nothing. This might be person to person, or could be through written, wireless or internet communication
24-26	Companionship	The individual has a need for close contact with friends or the need to be in crowds, cities etc. Bonds might be with animals or artificial intelligences for some individuals
27-29	Competitive	The individual is keen to win any perceived contests and challenges
30-32	Discipline	The individual requires a fixed and orderly regime and is disdainful of disorganisation and chaos
33-35	Escapism	The individual has a need to retreat from reality. This could be through literature, cinema, roleplaying games, video games or interactive theatre
36-38	Exercise	The individual has a constant need for walking, aerobics, cycling, etc.
39-41	Fashion	The individual is a slave to contemporary fashion trends, or else favours a particular type of fashion.
42-44	Food and drink	The individual needs to intake food and non-alcoholic beverages such as tea, coffee, fizzy drinks
45-46	Gambling	The individual needs to wager on outcomes
47-48	Games	The individual finds solace in games of chance or intellect. Includes card games, board games and ones involving arcade machines and computers
49	Hunting	The individual needs to be hunting either animals or humans
50-51	Music	The individual constantly requires life to have a tune, and might even be a composer or performer

even more-so when stressed. If deprived of drink for more than a few days she must attempt to successfully resist her Dependency with her Willpower of 55% or suffer a level of Fatigue until she can drink again. In a stressful situation the Games Master rules that her Willpower roll will be one level more difficult rather than standard, meaning that her likelihood of suffering the effects of withdrawal will be that much higher.

Modifying Dependencies

Dependency scores are modified in the following circumstances:

- A Critical Success on a Dependency roll raises that Dependency score by +1d3%
- A Fumble on a Dependency roll lowers that Dependency score by -1d4%
- A Critical Success of a roll to resist a Dependency lowers that Dependency score by -1d3%
- A Fumble of a roll to resist a Dependency raises that Dependency score by +1d4%
- Prolonged denial of the Dependency without 'professional' treatment increases the Dependency score by +1d4+1% per month

Characters can also voluntarily increase a Dependency to gain a little boost from the lack of stress. A player can increase a Dependency score by 1d4+1% to receive an additional Experience Roll. This can only be done once per year.

A Dependency can also be lowered by in-game efforts that do not require skill tests. Using an Improvement Roll to decrease a Dependency score reduces it by -1d4+1%. This represents 'off camera' attempts to break the Dependency (counselling, abstinence, medical treatment, etc.), although we suggest some monetary and time expenditures to explain these instances. Characters may also undergo in-game methods of control, again such as counselling, medical treatment and so on, with the same reduction of -1d4+1%. Note, however, that undertaking in-game treatment may require several sessions to complete and may be subject to interruption or constraint due to the circumstances and nature of the scenario.

1d100	Dependency	Effects
52-54	Narcotics	The individual often feels the need for hard or soft drugs
55-56	News	The individual has a hunger for information, gossip, trivia
57-59	Nicotine	The individual needs tobacco products like cigarettes, snuff, etc.
60-62	Novelty	The individual suffers from ennui and craves new experiences
63-65	OCD	The individual has an obsessive pattern of behaviour; washing, counting, enacting a certain ritual
66-69	Pain/Abuse	The individual is masochistic and desires pain; self-inflicted, or inflicted by others
70	Pranks	The individual is a real practical joker, possibly a dangerous one at times
71	Profanity	The individual has the need to swear and profane constantly: not even aware that profanity is being used
72-73	Relationship	The individual feels like they need to develop a Passion of either Love or Hate
74	Religion	The individual has unswerving belief in a Divine Creator(s) and their doctrines, whatever they may be
75-77	Risk Taking	The individual gets excitement through staking either his life or reputation
78	Role model	The individual feels the need to mimic a figure they admire or to follow the teachings of a guru or adopt the dictates of a demagogue
79	Security Precautions	The individual needs to adopt favoured measures to insure their personal safety such as wearing bullet proof vest, circuitous journeys and locking windows and barricading doors into a room where they sleep
80-82	Sex	The individual is compelled to engage in favoured types of sexual activity
83-85	Solitude	The individual thrives on being alone. Countryside walks, mountain peaks, monastic retreats, private apartments or isolation tank
86-87	Speed	The individual has the need to attain the fastest speeds possible using vehicles, animal mounts or transportation devices
88	Sport	The individual focuses on participation in physical games
89	Stealing	The individual desires the theft of property, possibly for the challenge and adrenaline rush rather than an actual need for the item
90-92	Talisman	The individual favours wearing or carrying a particular item of jewellery or costume or a specific, trade mark weapon
93	Vandalism	The individual craves the destruction or desecration of property. Selective attacks might be on government or religious institutions, works of art or types of technology
94-96	Violence/Aggression	The individual needs to cause physical harm, fear or distress in other individuals. In some instances this can involve ritual patterns of behaviour
97	Voyeurism	The individual has a need to covertly view and possibly record the activities of others
98	Weapons	The individual only feels fulfilled or safe when carrying weaponry
99	Wisecracking	The individual has a compulsive sense of humour, often to the point of annoying everyone else
00	Vocation	The individual needs to be employed or occupied in a professional form of task

Anna Thames' Chronicle

Anna has managed to narrowly escape a violent assault at the hands of the thugs of the nefarious Doctor Bastable, a Disruptor agent and potent psychic. Her nerves are frayed, her hands shake and her pulse races. She stumbles back to her rented rooms near the airship docks and thanks God she's still alive.

The Games Master asks Simon to roll to see if Anna can resist the urge to open a bottle of wine. As she has not had a drink for a couple of days, and because the escape from Bastable was such an ordeal, the Willpower 55% roll becomes Formidable (half normal, so 28%). Anna's Willpower is matched against her Dependency 44% in an Opposed Roll. The Willpower roll is 92 — an abject failure and, although the Dependency roll is also a failure (57) the Games Master rules that Anna opens the bottle and downs a glass without even thinking about it.

There is a sudden knock at the door: Anna isn't expecting anyone and nervously creeps to the spy-hole. Outside is a messenger boy carrying an envelope. Anna tells him to push it under the door, and pushes back a Crown for his trouble. She reads the message:

We Know Where You Live...

The Games Master decides this is just too much. Her Willpower is still compromised at Formidable, but her Dependency now becomes Easy (doubled to 88%). A further Opposed Roll results in 56 for Willpower and 04 for Dependency Alcohol — a critical success. Her Dependency: Alcohol increases by 1d3% and the die roll is a 3. Anna's Dependency is now 47%.

Anna bolts the door and drains the bottle...

Luther Arkwright

ROLEPLAYING ACROSS THE PARALLELS

Characteristics

STR CON SIZ DEX INT POW CHA Luck Points

Attributes

Action Points | Damage Mod | Exp. Mod | Healing Rate | Move Rate | Prana Points | Strike Rank | Tenacity Points

Character Information

Player

Character — Parallel Designator

Sociological Type — Level of Development

Social Class — Career

Age — Gender — Handedness

Frame — Height — Weight

Description

Passions / Dependencies & Traits

%

%

% Traits:

%

Hit Locations

1d20	Location	AP / HP	Armour Type	ENC
01-03	Right Leg	/		
04-06	Left Leg	/		
07-09	Abdomen	/		
10-12	Chest	/		
13-15	Right Arm	/		
16-18	Left Arm	/		
19-20	Head	/		

Weapons

Weapon Type	Damage	Fire Rate	Range	Ammo	Traits (Size/Reach for Melee Weapons)	Load

Standard Skills

Skill	Characteristics	%
Athletics	STR+DEX	%
Brawn	STR+SIZ	%
Conceal	DEX+POW	%
Customs	INT x2	%
Dance	DEX+CHA	%
Deceit	INT+CHA	%
Drive	DEX+POW	%
Endurance	CON x2	%
Evade	DEX x2	%
First Aid	INT+DEX	%
Home Parallel	INT x2	%
Influence	CHA x2	%
Insight	INT+POW	%
Native Tongue	INT+CHA	%
Perception	INT+POW	%
Ride	DEX+POW	%
Sing	POW+CHA	%
Stealth	INT+DEX	%
Swim	STR+DEX	%
Unarmed	STR+DEX	%
Willpower	POW x2	%

Professional Skills

Skill	Characteristics	%

Fatigue

Current Level	State	Skill	Move	Strike Rank	Action Points	Recovery
○	Fresh	-	-	-	-	-
○	Winded	Hard	-	-	-	15 mins
○	Tired	Hard	-1m	-	-	3 hours
○	Wearied	Form	-2m	-1	-	6 hours
○	Exhausted	Form	Half	-4	-1	12 hours
○	Debilitated	Herc	Half	-6	-2	18 hours
○	Incapacitated	Herc	None	-8	-3	24 hours
○	Semi-Conscious	Hope	No Activity Possible			36 hours
○	Comatose		No Activity Possible			48 hours
○	Dead					Never

Sciences

INT x2 %

INT x2 %

Combat Styles

Style	%	Weapons	Traits
Unarmed	%		
	%		
	%		
	%		

Skill Grades

Grade	Modifier
Automatic	No Roll Needed
Very Easy	Double
Easy	Increase by Half
Standard	-
Hard	Reduce by 1/3
Formidable	Reduce by 1/2
Herculean	Reduce to 1/10
Hopeless	No Attempt Poss

Other Languages

Language	Characteristics	%
	INT+CHA	%
	INT+CHA	%
	INT+CHA	%
	INT+CHA	%

Equipment

Item	Enc

Money/Wealth/Property

Description

Character

Name	Career

Notes

Psionic Talents and Powers

Talent	%	Intensity	Powers

Allies, Enemies, Friends

Name	A, E or F

Valhalla History/Parallels Visited

Family

Name	Relationship

Special Events & Mental Stability

What Happened?

Madness & Other Colours

Madness and Other Colours explores psychological damage from a variety of sources. For the most part Characters are sane and mentally healthy; however, Valhalla's agents often display a certain psychological fragility or are exposed to events and circumstances that can shake their sanity, affect their mental well-being, or directly attack their grip on reality.

A character's psychological stability is measured in three ways.

Tenacity Points

A character's Tenacity Points represent mental or psychological Hit Points. They can suffer damage and be reduced in the same way locational hit points can be reduced through physical damage. Tenacity Points are equal to POW, which represents the base mental strength of the character. As Tenacity Points are reduced, the character becomes more vulnerable to certain Conditions (see below). When Tenacity Points reach a negative value, any Conditions gained through exposure to traumatic, horrifying or sanity-shaking events become permanent. When Tenacity Points reach a negative value equal to their starting value (less any modifier for Dependencies – see below) then the character is considered permanently insane or incapable of any further mental function.

Dependencies

Dependencies (see page 45) erode confidence and impact on a person's ability to rationalise and remain in mental control. Tenacity Points are reduced by Dependencies. For every 20% a character has in a Dependency, reduce Tenacity Points by 1. For example Anna Thames has the Dependency of Alcohol 44% which reduces her Tenacity points by 2.

Conditions

Conditions result from exposure to events that invoke fear, horror or may shake the sanity of an individual. They are discussed in more detail later in this chapter but they are akin to the Conditions associated with poisons and disease (see MYTHRAS page 74). Examples are phobias, mania and paranoia. Conditions are temporary while a character's Tenacity Points are positive, but when they reach a negative value, Conditions become permanent unless treated through sophisticated methods such as antipsychotic drugs and intense psychotherapy.

Losing Grip

Five things can cause an individual to lose Tenacity Points and potentially gain a Condition:

- Exposure to Fear (for example, fleeing for one's life, pursued by relentless Disruptor agents)
- Exposure to Horrific Events (for example, witnessing a gruesome murder)
- Exposure to Madness (for example, coming into contact with phenomenon that defy all rational explanation and are shocking to contemplate)
- Torture, which, despite also causing physical damage, is intended to break the will of the victim
- Psionic Trauma, caused by deliberate psionic attacks or powers.

Although these five events can be very different, they are handled in much the same way.

Intensity

Any of the five events – Fear, Horror, Madness, Torture or Psionic Trauma – are assigned an *Intensity*. Intensity is an adjective and corresponds with a skill difficulty grade, as follows:

Whenever a character is faced with a psychological event, a

Level	Intensity	Skill Grade	Typical Tenacity Loss
0	Mild	Standard	1 point
1	Unsettling	Hard	1d3
2	Disturbing	Formidable	1d6
3	Shocking	Herculean	1d10
4	Devastating	Hopeless	1d20

Willpower roll is made at the skill grade corresponding with the event Intensity. If the Willpower roll succeeds, then there are no ill-effects. If the roll fails, then Tenacity is lost, according to the Typical Tenacity Loss for the Intensity. Specific effects depend on the degree of success of the Willpower roll:

Critical

The character is unaffected by the event. Furthermore, exposure to a similar event in the future is handled at one level of Intensity less (so a potentially Shocking event would be handled as Disturbing, for example).

Success

No ill effects. No Tenacity lost – usually. The Games Master might rule that a event is still so profound that even a successful Willpower roll results in the loss of 1 Tenacity Point.

Anna Thames' Chronicle

Anna has 8 Tenacity Points and a Willpower of 55%. Normally her Tenacity Points would be 10, but her fondness for red wine has made her a borderline alcoholic and so she has the Dependency: Alcohol 44% which takes her Tenacity down by 2 points.

Investigating a suspected Disruptor safe house, Anna manages to break into the place at the dead of night. The place is dark, dingy, rat-infested and clearly has not been in use for some time. As she makes her way from room to room she stumbles across the corpse of a previous Valhalla agent who had also been sent to investigate. The corpse was clearly shot at close range with a high-powered weapon and half the head is missing. The Games Master rules that this counts as an Unsettling Horrific event. Unsettling means that Anna's Willpower roll is at Hard, or two-thirds of 55%, which is 36%. She rolls and scores 32, which means she loses no Tenacity.

However, when she finally reaches the basement of the Disruptor Safe House she finds the torture chamber used by the Disruptors to interrogate and break their prisoners, including Valhalla agents. The place is worse than a medieval dungeon; it is stocked with hooks, chains, and all manner of ghastly devices designed to inflict pain slowly and intensively. Several victims have been dumped in an antechamber and their bodies are broken in many hideous ways. The Games Master rules that this is another Horrific event, but this time at Shocking. Anna's Willpower roll is now at one tenth (Herculean), so she must roll 6 or less to avoid Tenacity loss. She rolls 94 – not bad enough for a fumble, but she loses 1d10 Tenacity. The Games Master rolls 8: Anna is reduced to 0 Tenacity: to her horror, she recognises several of the horribly mutilated victims...

Failure

Tenacity is lost at the rolled value.

Fumble

The full Tenacity Loss value is incurred. For example, undergoing a Shocking level of Torture with a fumbled Willpower roll results in the loss of the full 10 Tenacity Points.

The exception is Psionic Trauma. Some assaults, like Psychic Wrack (Sanity), inflict damage directly on Tenacity Points. In such cases the Tenacity Loss is the damage inflicted by the attack, rather than the event's intensity.

Luck Points can be used to reduce the Intensity of a event by 1.

Tenacity Loss

Losing Tenacity may result in gaining a Condition. A Condition is gained if a character loses half or more of current Tenacity points. If half or more of the Tenacity Points are lost in one go, then the Condition is Immediate. If the Condition is incurred through incremental Tenacity Point loss, then the Condition is Deferred.

Immediate Conditions take place there and then; Deferred Conditions emerge over time and after the event.

To determine the Condition's nature, the character rolls on the Immediate or Deferred Table (page 52), referring to the column corresponding with the type of event.

Where Torture is the source of the event, all Conditions are considered Deferred. The Immediate response by the victim is the physical suffering the torture inflicts; mental effects always come after the fact.

If a character's Tenacity Points fall to a negative value, Conditions are always rolled on the Deferred Table but are also treated as being permanent, requiring extensive help to cure them (see Curing Psychological Conditions on page 54). Note that even while into negative points, additional Conditions can be accrued. So, at –4 points Anna would, in our example, be subject to another Condition and any current Conditions are considered permanent until properly treated.

Conditions

Amnesia

To protect the character's sanity, the character's mind suppresses memories related to a traumatic event, although such memories may eventually be recovered.

Babbles Incoherently

The character's mind is overwhelmed, and he is unable to do anything except babble incoherently. If attacked or threatened he will flee in terror.

Catatonia

The character is stupefied and unable to take any willful actions of his own, though he may be led or forced to perform simple actions. Catatonic Characters may repeat seemingly meaningless phrases or mindlessly repeat words spoken to them.

Delusional

The character begins to believe that he is something that he is not. The character effectively assumes a new identity and possibly personality, with a corresponding distorted view of his own capabilities.

Demoralised

The character is overcome with feelings of hopelessness and helplessness; these symptoms collectively increase the difficulty of most rolls by one grade.

Disgusted

The character is revolted at the awful sights he has seen rendering him unwilling to approach or even remain within their presence. If forced to do so, the difficulty of most rolls is increased by one grade.

Disturbed

The character begins to suffer from panic attacks, insomnia and a persistent feeling of nervousness, disquiet and unease. Anxiety causes physical symptoms like dizziness, rapid pulse, sweatiness, restlessness and nervous twitches; these symptoms collectively increase the difficulty of rolls involving social interaction by one grade.

Enraged

The character flies into a murderous rage intent on utterly destroying the object of his rage (treat as Berserk — Mythras, page 183).

Faints

The character faints. Recovery is within 1d4 minutes.

Flees

The character flees in terror. Characters unable to flee, if cornered for example, may attempt to defend themselves but such actions are one difficulty grade harder.

Fugue

The character begins to experience blackouts while under stress, during which his conscious mind has no control over, or memory of, his actions. When the character is subject to extreme stress he must make a Willpower check or he will temporarily black out. During the fugue, the Games Master controls the character's actions until consciousness is regained.

Hallucinations

The character begins to see things that aren't there or to see things as they are not. The hallucinations are usually focused on a common theme, typically related to the thing that caused the derangement. Characters suffering from hallucinations are furthermore unable to deal rationally with what they are seeing;

Condition Tables

Immediate Conditions

Immediate Conditions: 1d20	Fear	Horror	Madness & Psionic Trauma
1-2	*Demoralised* for 1d8 rounds	*Babbles Incoherently* for 2d12 rounds	*Babbles Incoherently* for 2d6 rounds
3-6	*Demoralised* for 2d6 rounds	*Disgusted* for 1d6 rounds	*Babbles Incoherently* for 2d12 rounds
7-9	*Faints* for 1d6 rounds	*Enraged* for 2d6 rounds*	*Enraged* for 2d6 rounds
10-12	*Flees* in terror for 1d8 rounds	*Faints* for 1d6 rounds	*Faints* for 1d6 rounds
13-15	*Flees* in terror for 2d6 rounds	*Flees* in terror for 2d6 rounds	*Faints* for 1d8 rounds
16-17	*Paralysed* in fright for 1d2 rounds	*Paralysed* in fright for 1d4 rounds	*Flees* in terror for 2d6 rounds
18-20	*Paralysed* in fright for 1d4 rounds	*Sickened* for 1d6 rounds	*Paralysed* in fright for 1d4 rounds

Deferred Conditions

Deferred Conditions: 1d20	Fear	Horror	Madness & Psionic Trauma
1-3	*Disturbed* for 1d4 weeks	Suffers *Amnesia* for 1d12 months	Suffers *Amnesia* for 1d12 months
4-6	*Disturbed* for 1d6 months	*Disturbed* for 1d6 months	Suffers *Catatonia* for 1d12 weeks
7-8	Suffers *Nightmares* for 1d6 weeks	*Disturbed* for 1d12 months	Becomes *Delusional* for 1d6 months
9-10	Suffers *Nightmares* for 1d4 months	Suffers *Nightmares* for 1d4 months	Suffers *Fugue* for 1d12 months
11-12	Suffers *Nightmares* for 1d12 months	Suffers *Nightmares* for 1d12 months	Suffers *Hallucinations* for 1d6 weeks
13-14	Develops *Paranoia* for 1d6 weeks	*Obsessed* for 1d12 months	Suffers *Melancholia* for 1d6 months
15-16	Develops *Paranoia* for 1d4 months	*Obsessed* for 1d4 years	*Obsessed* for 1d6 years
17-18	Develops *Phobia* for 1d12 months	Develops *Phobia* for 2d12 months	Develops *Paranoia* for 2d12 months
19-20	Develops *Phobia* for 1d4 years	Develops *Phobia* for 1d4 years	Develops *Phobia* for 1d4 years

the hallucinations always elicit a strong emotional response from the character, be it terror, entrancement or obsession.

Hardened

The character's psyche is strengthened by the experience, lowering the difficulty level of future Fear, Horror or Madness checks against similar stimuli by one grade.

Melancholia

The character begins to suffer from feelings of worthlessness, hopelessness, guilt, lethargy and apathy, often leading to thoughts of suicide; these symptoms collectively increase the difficulty of most Willpower rolls by two grades.

Anna Thames' Chronicle

Anna is now reduced to 0 Tenacity and sustains a Condition. Because she lost more than half her Tenacity Points in a single go her Condition is Immediate. The 1d20 roll on the Immediate table results in 14, read on the Horror column: Flees in terror for 2d6 rounds. Unable to stand the terrible sights in the basement Anna runs in panic, seeking the relative safety of the outside street. Outside, the Games Master says that, after a little time to gather her composure, Anna can return to continue the investigation, but she has seen enough. At zero Tenacity Points her mental state is extremely fragile. The Games Master suggests that Anna make a roll against her Alcohol Dependency, with the grade set at Easy. Anna rolls 27, meaning that she *desperately* needs a drink.

Nightmares

When the character next sleeps he begins to have horrific nightmares in which he relives his traumatic experiences and worst fears. Characters suffering from nightmares soon grow weary and exhausted from lack of restful sleep.

Obsessed

The character becomes fixated upon a specific object, person, idea or activity, usually relating to his trauma. The obsession becomes the focus of the character's very existence, frequently disrupting other facets of his life.

Paralysed

The character is paralyzed in fright, completely unable to react.

Paranoia

This causes the character to be suspicious of everyone and everything. As a result of his suspicious nature, the difficulty of rolls involving social interaction are increased by one grade. Conversely paranoid Characters are frequently harder to surprise, deceive, ambush or manipulate.

Phobia

The character develops an overwhelming, unreasoning fear of something. The object of fear is typically related to the experience that caused the derangement to develop. Whenever the phobic character encounters the object of his fear, he must make a Willpower roll or be overcome by the effects of a failed Fear or Horror check.

Sickened

The character is sickened at the awful sights he has witnessed, rendering him unable to act except in self defense.

Recovering Tenacity

Tenacity Points are regained at the character's Healing Rate in Hours, if at 0 or a positive level, and in Days if negative (and until they reach 0 where the gain then changes to Hours). Recovering Tenacity requires the character to rest, avoid stress, and desist from using psionic powers. In Anna's example, she recovers her Tenacity Points at her Healing Rate of 2 in Hours, meaning that, after a decent night's sleep, she should be back to full strength.

Any deferred Conditions remain for the noted period irrespective of Tenacity Point recovery (and, if Conditions were incurred while Tenacity Points were negative, then the Conditions are permanent until treated).

Games Masters are free to adjust the rate of Tenacity Point recovery according to circumstances and other game events. For example, Anna needed a drink following the investigation of the Disruptor basement. The Games Master rules that Anna downs several large glasses of wine as a result of her Alcohol Dependency and so her Tenacity Point recovery is delayed until the following day, owing to her inebriation.

Curing Psychological Conditions

Deferred Conditions last until they have run their course or until help is sought. In the case of permanent Conditions, the only recourse is professional help, in the form of clinical treatment and psychotherapy. For the sake of simplicity it is assumed that Characters needing treatment are referred to the appropriate institutions and specialists so that Conditions can be accurately diagnosed and treated. Of course, such things might not exist on some parallels, or be difficult to find — Games Masters must use appropriate discretion. Zero-Zero does, naturally, have exceptional facilities for dealing with mental illness and emotional breakdowns and may arrange for an agent to be returned to Zero-Zero to undergo necessary treatment.

Treatment requires time and patience. Very few psychological disorders are cured swiftly; drugs and therapy might bring them under control in the short term, but proper treatment requires months and even years. For simplicity, consider that every permanent, deferred Condition requires a minimum of 4d6 months of treatment. This can be increased by 1d6 months for each level of Intensity of the event that resulted in the Condition, if the Games Master wishes, so a Phobia resulting from a Shocking event might require 7d6 months (between 7 months and 3.5 years) of treatment and therapy. Access to advanced or superior resources may reduce this time by a third; poor or inexpert facilities might double it. Again, Games Master discretion applies.

It is assumed that the early stages of the treatment – at least the first month – will be intensive, requiring either confinement or daily therapeutic sessions. This may well take a character out of active participation for this period of the treatment. Thereafter, treatment is less intensive – perhaps a couple of times per week, dropping to a couple of sessions per month over time. The character can participate actively, but remains susceptible to the Condition until treatment formally ends and he or she is cured.

If a Condition is temporary then it can run its course without treatment; however, seeking treatment halves the duration of the Condition (for example Nightmares for 1d6 weeks would last for 1d3 weeks instead).

Mind Games

The multiverse contains limitless possibilities and W.O.T.A.N tirelessly searches for special exceptions, like a collector picking through a beach for the perfect grain of sand. Of the many incredible phenomena found across the parallels, there are two families of enhanced (and to some, supernatural) abilities that appear sporadically and in rare instances – *psionics* and *mysticism*.

These two groups of powerful abilities are ways that Characters in *Luther Arkwright: Roleplaying Across the Parallels* can be set apart from the masses. They are special talents or powers that allow the wielder to tap into hidden energies, using them to manipulate their environment and those within it.

Not every Valhalla Agent must be psionically skilled or practiced in the arts of mysticism, but those who are find the uses of their special powers to be without equal in the right circumstances. Many agents are picked for recruitment solely because of these special gifts, W.O.T.A.N selecting them from the limitless multiversal populace to harness these powers for the sake of the greater good.

This chapter goes into depth on how psionics and mystical powers function in Luther Arkwright, their effects and how the Characters can use them in their own stories.

Psionics

Throughout the Luther Arkwright stories there are examples of powerful mental gifts – psionics – appearing in the populace of the multiverse. These abilities are one of the major indicators of *homo novus*, the next evolution of humankind, and the Valhalla Project knows this better than anyone else. One of W.O.T.A.N's subroutines seeks out those with such gifts and not long after they become noticed, recruitment agents are knocking at their doors.

Psychics, those who are gifted with psionic abilities, have access to families of special preternatural mental abilities. These abilities range from the linking of mental energies and manipulating objects with telekinetic force all the way to drawing energy from a living victim or controlling someone like a puppet. These powers are certainly wondrous, and may be the edge that the Valhalla Project needs over the Disruptors.

Psionic powers fall into several ability groupings called *Psionic Disciplines*, each with a number of individual talents that are based upon similar energies being manipulated. Most Psychics have access to one Discipline, with more potent Psychics having two.

Generating Psionic Ability

Psionic powers generally generally manifest during adolescence, which is represented by psionics being an available trait during character creation. Only in extremely rare instances (and Games Masters' permission) do new psionic disciplines ever spontaneously appear later in life. A character's mastery over their specific psionic discipline will grow if practiced, but the backbone of their psionic abilities will come from their initial acquisition of a Psionic Discipline.

Every Psionic Discipline has a number of Psionic Talents associated with it. These Talents are how the Discipline is used to affect the world. How to use these Talents and their effects are detailed in their respective sub-sections below.

When it is determined that a Character is a Psychic, the player may roll randomly on the Discipline table below to figure what manner of Discipline(s) the Character has access to. As always, the Games Master has final say as to the specific Discipline the Character should or can have for their chronicle.

1d100	Psionic Discipline	Talents Available
01-10	Attrition	Drain Prana, Evil Eye, Infliction, Mental Shield, Psychic Wrack, Sap Vigour
11-20	Biokinesis	Bioelectric Shock, Body Fortress, Intangibility, Mental Shield, Regenerate, Synaptic Puppetry
21-30	Clairvoyance	Mental Scan, Mental Shield, Precognition, Psychometry, Sense Danger, Sense Psi
31-40	Empathy	Empathic Link, Empathic Push, Feel Emotions, Mental Shield, Psychic Wrack, Sense Psi
41-50	Martial Mind	Body Fortress, Focus Force, Mental Shield, Psychic Wrack, Pyrokinetics
51-60	Telekinesis	Focus Force, Levitation, Mental Scan, Mental Shield, Psychokinesis, Shatter
61-70	Telepathy	Mental Scan, Mental Shield, Mind Probe, Telepathy, Thought Implant, Psychic Wrack (Sanity)
71-80	Thermokinesis	Absorb Heat, Bioelectric Shock, Cryokinetics, Mental Shield, Pyrokinetics, Sense Psi
81-90	Translocation	Intangibility, Levitation, Mental Shield, Psychic Wrack, Shift Parallel, Translocate
91-00	Dual Discipline – Roll two more times on this table, re-rolling further results of 91 or higher.	

When a Character first generates their Psionic Discipline(s), they are allowed to choose two initial Psionic Talents from those available to them.

As soon as a Character develops a Psionic Discipline, they also develop a new Professional Skill with a specialisation in that Discipline — Psionics (Discipline). This skill has a base rating of POW x2, and is calculated at its base rate for each Discipline the Character has (if multiple).

Some Talents can be found listed under multiple Disciplines. Characters should note under which Discipline they learned that Talent, as it will dictate which of their Psionic skill specialisations will be used for that Talent.

As Characters continue their lives and careers, they may acquire new Talents at the cost of three Experience Rolls per new Talent. New Disciplines are not normally acquired, but with the proper narrative reasoning a new Discipline could be opened up for the cost of five Experience Rolls.

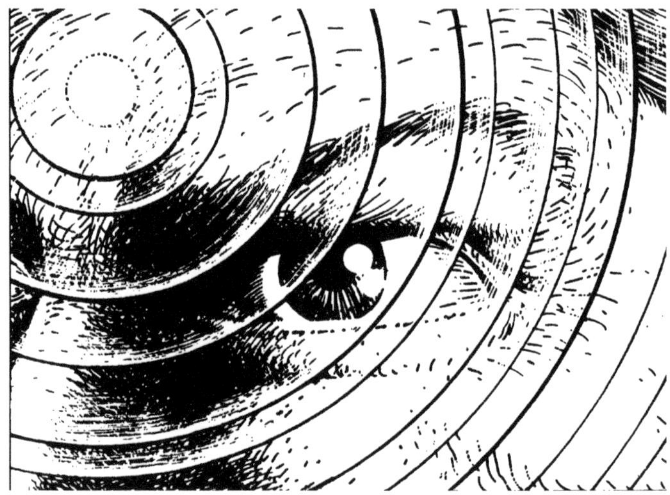

How to Use Psionics

Tapping into their internal life force, or *Prana*, a Psychic fuels their psionic powers from within and unleashes their effects upon the world. For the Psychic, it is like any other forced natural process — they will it, it happens. It can be exhausting to draw upon their powers too often, potentially even physically dangerous.

In order to activate a Psionic Talent, the Character must succeed in a Psionics skill roll (see the boxed text). If successful, the Talent functions as described. If failed, the costs are wasted. A critical success imposes two degrees of difficulty upon any resistance rolls required by the target, whereas a fumble will immediately subject the Psychic to painful mental feedback and a number of levels of Fatigue equal to the Prana spent to activate the Talent.

Psionics (POW x2)

Every Psychic has the Psionics skill roll. It is used to see if an attempt to invoke and use a psionic Talent is successful or not. It is improved in the same way as any other skill in the game, and, like any other skill, it can be augmented by another (such as a Passion) where applicable. Psionics can also be used to sense the general psychic ambience of a place — whether psionic powers are rare or common; or whether some form of psionic power has been recently employed.

Each talent in a Psionic Discipline uses the same Psionics percentage to see if it is used successfully or not. However, every Discipline requires the development of its *own* Psionics skill percentage. Therefore, a character with the Empathy Discipline at 75% is only able to invoke the talents of this discipline — the Psychic cannot try to invoke, say, Levitation. When a new discipline is learned, its Psionics score begins at the base of POWx2.

Psionic Intensity

Some talents rely on Psionic Intensity for their effects. Psionic Intensity is one twentieth of the Psionics score for the Discipline. Psionic Intensity not only dictates the effects of Talents, it also governs governs how many Talents can be kept active at any one time. A Psychic can maintain a number of Talents equal to half the Psionic Intensity of the Discipline, as long as the Talents belong to same Discipline. Talents from different Disciplines cannot be maintained simulatenously.

Recovering Prana

Prana Points are regained at the character's Healing Rate in Hours. Recovering Prana requires the character to rest, avoid stress, and desist from using psionic powers. In Anna's example, she recovers her Prana Points at her Healing Rate of 2 in Hours, meaning that, after a decent night's sleep, she should be back to full strength.

Games Masters are free to adjust the rate of Prana Point recovery according to circumstances and other game events. For example, a particular parallel might have a very high resistance to the general flow of cosmic psychic energy, meaning that Prana is recovered in days, rather than hours, or at only half its usual rate in hours.

Psionic Talents

Each Discipline is made up of distinct Talents that describe the actual powers the Psychic is capable of. There are five specific statistics for every Psionic Talent, listed in the talent's descriptions.

Range

Every Psionic Talent has a finite range in which its target can be found. These ranges are defined as:

Personal (only affects the Psychic)
Short (Touch and to within a number of metres equal to POW)
Medium (within line of sight)
Long (anywhere within the same parallel)
Multiversal (anywhere within parallels the character knows).

Duration

Psionic Talents, once active, last a specific amount of time. These durations are defined as

Instantaneous (effects take place over a few seconds)
Focus (Talent lasts for as long as the Character continues to maintain concentration, imposing one degree of difficulty on anything else performed)
Lasting (Talent lasts a specific length of time as defined in the Talent's description).

Area of Effect

Each Psionic Talent potentially affects the world in a specific way, whether it is by affecting a single target, a dimensional area, or other defining calculation. Gifted Psychics with enough control over their powers can open their minds to larger areas. The Psychic can double the area of effect by choosing to impose a level of difficulty upon their skill test and pay twice the normal costs. This can be performed multiple times, doubling the area/cost again and again, progressing with each additional level of difficulty imposed before the skill test. Thus a single target becomes two targets, becomes four targets, becomes eight targets, etc.

Cost

Every Psionic Talent has a required initial cost of at least 1 Prana Point, with some Talents requiring more to fuel them. The total cost of Prana depends on the outcome of the Psionics roll:

If the Psionics roll is a...

- *Critical Success*: the Talent's Prana Point cost is half (and if that cost would ordinarily be 1, then the cost is zero).
- *Success*: the caster spends the normal Prana Points, and the Talent works successfully.
- *Failure*: the Talent fails, but no Prana Points are expended.
- *Fumble*: the Talent fails and either 1d3, or the full Prana Point cost is expended, whichever is higher.

Resistance

Psionic Talents that target another being or object have a listed skill or derived trait used to resist the effects of the Talent. The consequences of failing these resistance tests are described in each Talent, along with any additional critical success or fumble effects that roll may have.

Absorb Heat

Range: Personal
Duration: Focus
Area of Effect: 15 Cubic Metres
Cost: 1 Prana
Resistance: N/A

The Psychic absorbs the ambient heat in the surrounding area, cooling it dramatically and potentially eliminating sources of heat. Every Round this Talent is in effect the Psychic may call upon one of three effects: lower the temperature in the Area by 5 degrees Celcius per point of Psionic Intensity, neutralise one point of Fire Intensity per point of Psionic Intensity or hold this power to be used as a Reactive Action that will eliminate one weapon attack that has the Cauterising or Incendiary weapon trait. While the power is in effect, the Psychic's exposed skin becomes flushed, sweaty and steams slightly.

Bioelectric Shock

Range: Short
Duration: Instantaneous
Area of Effect: Single Target
Cost: 1 Prana
Resistance: Endurance

The Psychic pushes psionic energy into the bio-electric currents flowing through their nervous system, causing a brilliant white arc of electric current to leap towards a target. Unless a resistance roll is made using the target's Endurance, it suffers 1 Hit Point of electrical damage per point of Psionic Intensity to the Hit Location closest to the Psychic, ignoring physical armour.

Body Fortress

Range: Personal
Duration: Focus
Area of Effect: Self
Cost: 1 Prana
Resistance: N/A

The Psychic fills his physical form with the empowering energies of his mind, greatly enhancing his musculature, reflexes and fortitude. When this Talent is activated, the Psychic gains 1 AP to all Hit Locations and increases his Damage Modifier by 1 step (see Damage Modifier table on page 9 of Mythras). This psionic power is very taxing however, and when it ends the Psychic gains one level of Fatigue.

Cryokinetics

Range: Medium
Duration: Instantaneous
Area of Effect: Single Target
Cost: 1 Prana
Resistance: Endurance/ENC x10

The Psychic rips the heat out of the air in a small area, causing a flash freeze that could solidify water, make objects brittle, and cause painful frostbite. Unless a resistance roll is made using the target's Endurance skill, all Hit Locations and objects suffer 1 point of cold damage per point of Psionic Intensity, that bypasses physical armour and item AP ratings. Targets without an Endurance skill use their ENC multiplied by 10 for their resistance test. Items specifically treated to be protected against cold and freezing are immune to this damage.

Drain Prana

Range: Short
Duration: Focus
Area of Effect: Single Target
Cost: 1 Prana
Resistance: Endurance

The Psychic can draw the existing psychic energy out of a living, sentient being just by making prolonged physical contact with it. The target must instinctively resist this Talent with their Endurance skill each Round the power is affecting them. If the Talent is successful the Psychic drains one Prana from the target to replenish his own, up to the value of Psionic Intensity. During this transference, the psionic energy takes the form of flashes of the target's thoughts, memories and fantasies visible to the draining Psychic.

As this Talent requires contact, the Psychic must be in a position to grasp the target, either passively (such as an unsuspecting handshake or embrace), or through an appropriate Combat Style (such as Unarmed) and choosing the Grip Special Effect. In a combat situation, the usual rules for breaking free of a Grip apply.

Empathic Link

Range: Multiversal
Duration: Focus
Area of Effect: All Parallel Selves
Cost: 1 Prana, 1 level of Fatigue
Resistance: N/A

The Psychic can link the thoughts, feelings and experiences of their known line of parallel selves across the parallels. This is extremely disorienting, but powerfully informative. If something painful – or fatal – were to occur to one of the linked selves while connected, all linked selves will lose 2d4 Tenacity Points instantly and likely suffer horrible mental anguish afterwards. The Psychic establishing the Empathic Link can simultaneously contact 2 additional selves per point of Psionic Intensity. If a fresh set of selves needs to be linked, a fresh Empathic Link attempt is required.

For example, Rose Wylde has been informed that Luther Arkwright has been missing for over two weeks on a mission that should have been over two days ago. Although he isn't supposed to, Luther often shifts between the parallels 'off the grid', so to speak, but not often for this long. Rose uses her Empathic Link Talent to reach out to her many selves to discover if any of them have seen him lately. She begins to connect to her parallel selves, and eventually is flooded with the unexpected feeling of intense sexual pleasure from her parallel self in Para 00.39.21. She 'looks' a little deeper into this sensation and finds Luther very much present and accounted for! He was going to have to answer for his tardiness for debriefing, but Rose would at least give her other self an hour or two first...

Empathic Push

Range: Medium
Duration: Lasting
Area of Effect: Single Target
Cost: 1 Prana
Resistance: Willpower

The Psychic with this Talent can push a particularly strong emotional reaction in a target. Unless the target resists, the Psychic may fill them with intense sadness, apathy, rage, worry, happiness, lustfulness, or other emotional states. This state lasts until the target loses consciousness for whatever reason, but cannot abate their imposed feelings while the Talent is in effect. The Psionic Intensity determines the power of the emotion felt:

- 1-2: Mild emotional feelings — enough to cause a distraction
- 3-4: Strong emotional feelings — enough to cause deep pleasure or distress
- 5+: Compelling emotional feelings — enough to consume the target's psyche

Evil Eye

Range: Medium
Duration: Lasting
Area of Effect: Single Target
Cost: 1 Prana
Resistance: Willpower

This Talent floods a target with unstable psionic energy found in the darkest parts of the Psychic's mind, effectively tainting them with unexplainably bad luck. The target may resist, but may not spend any Luck Points to reroll this test if failed. While this Talent is in effect, the target suffers two degrees of difficulty on all skill tests. The Evil Eye lasts for 10 minutes per point of Psionic Intensity. Additionally, the user's eyes each weep a single tear of blood whenever Prana is spent on this Talent.

Feel Emotions

Range: Medium
Duration: Focus
Area of Effect: Single Target (at a time)
Cost: 1 Prana
Resistance: Willpower

The Psychic can experience the exact emotional state and surface feelings of a single target each Round. Each Round this power is in effect, the target may resist again. On any Round where the power is still in effect, the Psychic may learn one additional aspect of the target's overall emotional state. This includes what is currently influencing their emotional state, and the strength or nature of any Passions or Dependencies. If a target is currently under the effects of a Mental Shield, this Talent senses nothing but an emotional void similar to a sociopath's fugue state and cannot be maintained beyond the initial Round.

Focus Force

Range: Medium
Duration: Instantaneous
Area of Effect: Single Target
Cost: 1 Prana
Resistance: Endurance

The Psychic can hurl an invisible bolt of psychokinetic force at a target like throwing a powerful unseen punch. The Focus Force bolt inflicts 1 point of damage per point of Intensity. The attack is capable of applying the Bash and Stun Location Special Effects. If successfully resisted, the Focus Force attack washes over the target causing no physical damage.

Inflict Pain

Range: Short
Duration: Focus
Area of Effect: Single Target
Cost: 1 Prana
Resistance: Endurance

The Psychic can inflict agonising paralysis upon a target with simple flesh to flesh contact. The target must resist the Talent each Round. If not, their pain receptors are flooded with psionic energy. The pain causes no physical damage, but the target loses 1 Action Point for every 2 points of Psionic Intensity. When the Talent's effects end, the target receives 1 level of Fatigue for every 2 Rounds the power was affecting them.

As this Talent requires contact, the Psychic must be a position to grasp the target, either passively (such as an unsuspecting handshake or embrace), or through an appropriate Combat Style (such as Unarmed) and choosing the Grip Special Effect. In a combat situation, the usual rules for breaking free of a Grip apply.

Intangibility

Range: Personal
Duration: Focus
Area of Effect: Self
Cost: 1 Prana
Resistance: N/A

The Psychic can phase his own atomic structure in a way that allows him to pass through solid objects unhindered. While Intangible, physical attacks inflict no damage upon the Character. Psychic and energy-based attacks inflict damage normally however. This Talent requires a great deal of concentration on the part of the Psychic. If they are successfully damaged or mentally assaulted while the power is in effect, the Psychic must pass a Willpower skill test or the power will falter. If the Psychic is partially-phased through an object when this Talent ends or is somehow disrupted, any parts of their body still inside an object immediately suffer a Major Wound.

Levitation

Range: Personal
Duration: Focus
Area of Effect: Self
Cost: 1 Prana
Resistance: N/A

The Psychic uses psionic energy to float through the air in any direction at half their normal Movement rate. This movement is totally silent and works without needing to physically move one's body — simply floating in whichever direction the Psychic wills. Floating too far away from the ground triggers the subconscious fear of falling that all sentient beings face. A Psychic can levitate a maximum number of metres equal to twice their Psionic Intensity.

Mental Scan

Range: Medium
Duration: Instantaneous
Area of Effect: 1 kilometre radius centered on Psychic
Cost: 1 Prana
Resistance: N/A

The Psychic knows the presence, distance and location of all sentient beings within range and area of effect. Hints as to the presences' nationality, culture, and the existence of any psionic ability are relayed as well. If a target with a Mental Shield is scanned, the shield is detected — but no other information from that target.

Mental Shield

Range: Personal
Duration: Lasting
Area of Effect: Self
Cost: 1 Prana
Resistance: N/A

The Psychic is immune to any form of mental scrutiny, interaction or assault, as long as the Psionic Intensity of the Mental Shield is equal to, or greater than, the Psionic Intensity of the opposing Psychic. Any attacks penetrating the Mental Shield that inflict damage to Tenacity or Prana Points have their damage reduced by the Psionic Intensity of the shield — in the same way armour reduces physical damage.

Mind Probe

Range: Short
Duration: Instantaneous
Area of Effect: Single Target
Cost: 1 Prana
Resistance: Willpower

This Talent grants the Psychic the ability to access to one piece of key information the target knows per point of Psionic Intensity. This piece of information could be a single snippet of data: a password, a name, a location, something short and simple. Whatever specific thought the Psychic pushes on, that is what rises to the surface unless the target resists.

Precognition
Range: Personal
Duration: Instantaneous
Area of Effect: Special (see below)
Cost: 2 Prana
Resistance: N/A

The Psychic opens his mind to the potential strands of fate, allowing fragmented but useful visions to flood his psyche about the near future. There are two ways this Talent can affect game play, chosen by the Games Master each time it is used. If the visions are scattered and unclear, the Psychic gains a bonus Luck Point to use over the next twenty-four hours as well as two degrees of ease toward any Probabilities skill tests taken during that time. Or, the Games Master can provide a clue relating to something important that may happen in the future (up to a number of days equal to Psionic Intensity) with the Intensity of the talent governing the accuracy of the foresight:

- 1-2: A general sense of the nature of the event (danger, illness, betrayal, and so on)
- 3-4: Reasonably Accurate but with some uncertainties
- 5+: Very accurate with clear indications of the specific nature of the event.

Psychic Wrack
Range: Medium
Duration: Focus
Area of Effect: Individual Target
Cost: 1 Prana per Point of Intensity and per Target
Resistance: Evade

Psychic Wrack enables a Psychic to harm opponents with deadly bolts or waves of psychic energy. On their turn, as a Combat Action, the psychic may launch a psionic attack against the target or targets, using his Psionics skill as the attack roll, which may be resisted with Evade. Successful attacks strike a random location, the Psionic Intensity denoting the damage inflicted. Worn armour does not protect against Psychic Wrack, but, Mind Shield functions as per that talent's description. The Psychic must concentrate to launch a Wrack attack, but can let the attack drop into dormancy to perform other actions inbetween each psychic assault. Damage inflicted depends on Psionic Intensity:

Intensity	*Damage*
1-2	1d4
3-4	1d6
5+	1d8

There are several forms of Psychic Wrack that can be developed. Each inflicts damage against a different attribute.

- Psychic Wrack (Body) — damages Hit Points
- Psychic Wrack (Sanity) — damages Tenacity Points, inflicting potential insanity and mental instability
- Psychic Wrack (Soul) — damages Prana Points, reducing psychic and mysticism capabilities.

In the case of Sanity Wrack and Soul Wrack, damage is applied to the pool rather than a specific Hit Location.

Psychokinesis
Range: Medium
Duration: Focus
Area of Effect: Single Target
Cost: 1Prana
Resistance: Special (see below)

The Psychic can mentally pick up, move, manipulate and even hurl other objects. The Character can manipulate a single object he can see with a SIZ/ENC equal to or less than his Psionic Intensity x3. If the object being manipulated is bigger, one additional Prana must be spent for every additional 5 points of SIZ/ENC. If the target does not wish to be moved, it may resist with its own Willpower. Once able to be manipulated, an object can move (unless hurled, see below) as if it had a Movement rate of 2m.

Attacking with a psychokinetically hurled object requires the object to be no larger in SIZ/ENC than the Psionic Intensity of the Talent. The object can be hurled at a similar force to that of physically hurling, say, a rock, up to a number of metres equal to the Psychic's POW. This form of attack uses Psionics (Telekinesis) as the attack skill, and inflicts damage based on its material composition (or its own weapon damage if a melee weapon is what is hurled perchance). Damage inflicted is 1d2 for soft or easily broken substances such as fruit or pottery; 1d3 for harder items that are still readily damageable such as wood and plastics, or 1d6 for items made of extremely durable materials like stone or metal. The Games Master has final say as to the damage of a given substance or item.

Psychometry

Range: Short
Duration: Focus
Area of Effect: Single Target
Cost: 1 Prana
Resistance: N/A

When the Psychic touches a single object, something of the object's past is revealed to him. This vision is viewed in real time for as long as physical contact and focus is maintained, with the Psychic watching scenes revolving around the object in some fashion — like watching a film from an omniscient viewpoint. The scenes are viewed in real time, but in no particular order or timeline.

The Intensity of the talent governs the accuracy of the revelation:

- 1-2: A general sense of the nature of the history
- 3-4: Reasonably Accurate but with some uncertainties
- 5+: Very accurate with clear indications of the specific nature of the history.

Pyrokinetics

Range: Medium
Duration: Focus
Area of Effect: 1 Cubic Metre
Cost: 2 Prana
Resistance: Special (see below)

The Psychic superheats the air in a small area, causing molecules to vibrate with energy. This creates spontaneous combustion in flammable objects and the atmosphere itself. The Intensity of the Fire is equal to the Psionic Intensity of the Talent. If a living target is caught in the area of effect, the target may either resist the Talent using Evade to escape the area, or Endurance to weather the increasing heat. Either way, resisting the power does not stop its effects on the rest of the area. There is nothing supernatural about the fire once created; it will grow, spread or be snuffed out normally.

Regenerate

Range: Short
Duration: Focus
Area of Effect: Self or Single Target
Cost: 2 Prana
Resistance: N/A

By applying the proper psionic energy to an injured Hit Location, the Psychic can heal wounded tissue. This healing knits 1 Hit Point of damage per point of Psionic Intensity of contact, with 2 Prana spent each Round. The Psychic can maintain healing at a cost of a further 2 Prana each round if he or she so wishes. While the healing is certainly potent, it cannot regenerate or reattach severed limbs.

Sap Vigour

Range: Short
Duration: Focus
Area of Effect: Single Target
Cost: 1 Prana per Round
Resistance: Endurance

The Psychic saps the health and vigour from the target, unless it resists. If this Talent is successful, the target immediately begins to suffer from a psychic form of the Bleed weapon special effect. This Bleed effect has no visual symptoms and cannot be treated with First Aid. Each Round the Talent is maintained the target must resist its effects or the 'Psychic Bleeding' continues.

Sense Danger

Range: Medium
Duration: Focus
Area of Effect: Self
Cost: 1 Prana
Resistance: N/A

The Psychic automatically knows the type, direction and number of threats actively putting him in danger while the Talent is in effect. This includes ambushes, traps, dangerous terrain and so on.

The Intensity of the talent governs the accuracy of the awareness:

- 1-2: A general sense of the nature of the danger
- 3-4: Reasonably Accurate but with some uncertainties
- 5+: Very accurate with clear indications of the specific nature of the danger.

Sense Psi

Range: Long
Duration: Focus
Area of Effect: Current Parallel
Cost: 1 Prana
Resistance: N/A

This Talent opens the Psychic's mental senses to the use of Psionic Talents elsewhere in the parallel. This power informs the user the direction and general distance of a Psychic currently using a Talent. If the Psychic being sensed is currently under the effects of Mental Shield, this Talent reveals the existence of a psionic presence but not its direction or distance.

The Intensity of the talent governs the accuracy of the awareness:

- 1-2: A general sense of the local Psionic landscape
- 3-4: Reasonably Accurate but with some uncertainties
- 5+: Very accurate with clear indications of location and strength.

Shatter

Range: Short
Duration: Instantaneous
Area of Effect: Single Object
Cost: Special
Resistance: N/A

The Psychic sends psionic energy waves into a nonliving and inorganic object, vibrating it at a molecular level in order to shatter it to pieces. The Psychic applies 1d3 points of damage per point of Prana expended to the Hit Points of the substance. The Psionic Intensity of the Talent negates twice the number of the material's Armour Points. If the AP of the object are not fully overcome, damage is reduced by the remaining amount.

For example, a psychic wants to shatter a glass door between herself and a Disruptor informant. The door has 6 AP and 20 Hit Points. The Valhalla psion's Psionics roll is 60%, giving her an Intensity of 3 which is doubled to 6 — enough to overcome the door's AP and apply damage unhindered to the glass. Had the door been made of toughened glass, with an AP of 9, the door would offer 3 points of damage reduction (9-6=3), making the task somewhat harder.

Shift Parallel

Range: Personal
Duration: Instantaneous
Area of Effect: Varies (see description)
Cost: 1 Prana
Resistance: Special (see below)

The Psychic can mentally shift between parallels. Shifting to a completely unknown parallel is always at a Formidable grade of difficulty. If the attempt fails, the Psychic remains where he is. Shifting to a known, previously visited, parallel, is at a Standard grade. For every point of Psionic Intensity, the Psychic can translocate one additional individual (so a Psychic with Psionic Intensity 3 could move himself and three others). Physical contact must be maintained during the jaunt. Unwilling passangers can resist by attempting to break physical contact or by succeeding in a Formidable Willpower roll, opposed by the shifter's Psionics skill. Mental Shield has no effect on this talent's use.

The Psychic materializes in the same spatial location on the new parallel. This may mean materializing in a building not previously there, or outdoors when a building is expected. The nature of the psionic energy permeating the multiverse adjusts the traveller's position slightly, so that he or she does not materialise within a solid substance.

Synaptic Puppetry

Range: Medium
Duration: Focus
Area of Effect: Single Target
Cost: 2 Prana
Resistance: Willpower

The Psychic uses his mental powers to link his own nervous system to that of the target's, giving him control over the target's body like a living puppet. The target may resist, but only when the power is initiated. Once in effect, the Psychic is allowed to use the target's body as if it were their own, with one degree of difficulty added to any skill tests made using the 'puppet.' The target is completely mentally aware of their surroundings during this time, they merely cannot do anything about it — they are a passenger in their own body. The puppeteer can attempt to control one extra individual for every 2 points of Psionic Intensity, but the resistance for all those being controlled becomes one grade easier.

Telepathy

Range: Medium
Duration: Focus
Area of Effect: Special
Cost: 1 Prana or Special
Resistance: Willpower

The Psychic can communicate mentally with others. There is no Prana cost when two telepaths communicate. For each point of Prana spent, one extra mind can be included in the communication. The clarity of the communication depends on the Psionic Intensity of the telepath:

- 1-2: Short sentences — up to four or five words ("Behind you!" "Disruptor Pawn in black cab.")
- 3-4: Complex sentences accompanied by a single mental image
- 5+: Complex sentences accompanied by precisely what the telepath both sees and hears

Thought Implant

Range: Short
Duration: Lasting
Area of Effect: Single Target
Cost: 1 Prana
Resistance: Willpower

The Psychic can embed a passionate compulsion into the target. The compulsion can be something as mundane as forcing someone to never refuse alcoholic beverages or to perpetually guard a location or item; or something dark and sinister like seeking one's own demise or trying to assassinate an authority figure. The target must resist normally, with a degree of ease added if the compulsion puts their life in jeopardy. The compulsion lasts a number of days equal to twice the Psionic Intensity of the Talent.

Translocate

Range: Personal
Duration: Instantaneous
Area of Effect: Varies (see description)
Cost: 3 Prana
Resistance: Special (see below)

The Psychic using this Talent vanishes into the psionic ether and reappears in the following Round up to a number of metres away from the original location equal to 3 times the Psionic Intensity of the Talent. One additional individual can be Translocated if in physical contact with the Psychic, but at a cost of 3 additional Prana.

Designing New Psionic Talents

Like with so much else in *Luther Arkwright: Roleplaying Across the Parallels*, what we have listed here is not the end of the possibilities in terms of Psionic Talents. There are examples of slight alterations to existing Talents and even the occasional appearance of a brand new psionic effect. This is how rare powers like 'hydrokinesis', 'psi-stealth' or 'chronomancy' could be developed.

Players of highly-practiced psionic Characters can even work with Games Masters to develop their own powers. It takes a great deal of time, practice, and openness to the mysteries of the mind.

In order to design a brand new Psionic Talent, a Character must first get permission from the Games Master to begin the process. Once the Games Master has given the okay to start working on this new power, several steps must be taken to potentially complete the process.

1. Link the Idea to an Existing Talent – The Psychic dreams up the potential new Talent and connects it to a Psionic Talent they already possess. For instance, a Psychic looking to create a Talent that infects others with berserker-like rage would link it to Empathic Push, or someone wanting to psionically wield water as a weapon might link it to Psychokinesis. Once the player and the Games Master have agreed this new Talent is possible, the Character spends one Experience Roll to begin the formation process.
2. Push the Limits of the Talent – Once the new Talent is imagined, the Character must practice using the aforementioned linked Talent in ways close to the intended goal as much as possible. This part of the process is the psionic equivalent of going to the gym and working out old muscles in new ways. The ultimate goal here is to achieve five critical successes using the linked Talent, after which another Experience Roll should be spent to create a theoretical new Proto-Talent.
3. Create/Test a Proto-Talent – The Games Master works directly with the player to create the exact nature of the new Psionic Talent, designing a Proto-Talent for the Character to try and wield successfully. All of the normal statistics for a Psionic Talent (Range, Area of Effect, etc.) should be determined, then the Character may begin to try and test it. During this process the Character may spend Three Experience Rolls at any time to make this Proto-Talent permanent. However, if the Proto-Talent is not what they desire just yet, a single Experience Roll can be spent before permanency to alter a single aspect of the Proto-Talent. This gives the Character a chance to make their new Talent more to their liking, but at a cost of time and effort.
4. Finalise the Talent – Once the Proto-Talent is made permanent, the Character simply has to begin using it conventionally in order to make it a final part of his psionic repertoire. This costs nothing to the Character; their new Talent is ready to unleash regularly upon the multiverse!

Games Masters will need to work very closely with their players to ensure that any new Talents that are created fit into the Arkwright multiverse and, more importantly, in their game.

Valhalla and Psychics

Valhalla greatly values those with psionic potential. Since the identification of both ambient psychic energy and *homo novus*, W.O.T.A.N has continually sought ways of harnessing psychic power. The multiverse is bound together by psychic energy: generated by all forms of life, it suffuses the parallels just as air suffuses the living world. The difficulty is in harnessing this power, especially personal reserves, and putting it to work. A few homo sapiens possess natural psychic potential, but *homo novus* is engineered to optimise it — and this is of huge interest to both W.O.T.A.N and Valhalla.

As a result, Valhalla Nova on Zero-Zero maintains dedicated laboratories for psychic research. Hooked into W.O.T.A.N's own intellect mainframe, the AI and research scientists continually seek ways of developing latent psychic potential within homo sapiens and also in fully harnessing the capabilities in *homo novus*. Psionic Characters can, if brought to Zero-Zero, take advantage of these training and research facilities. This is where new disciplines can be learned and new talents in existing disciplines unlocked. The Psi Division of the Valhalla Project is housed in the Rutherford Wing of the complex, and it can be considered a training academy where Valhalla agents can hone their powers in a safe, controlled environment. The Rutherford Wing provides training (other psychics, W.O.T.A.N-run training programs, simulations, and a battery of other, more sophisticated technological techniques) that allows for psychic development as per the training rules on page 73 of Mythras.

Anna Thames' Chronicle

Anna Thames was chosen by Valhalla for a number of different reasons, one of which was W.O.T.A.N's ironclad assurance that she possesses the genetic propensity for psionic potential. With practice and the proper tutelage, she could become one of the prized psychic agents within the project, turning her into an amazing asset.

Ms Rosemary Olivia Wilde, of the County Kerry Wildes, from Parallel 14.03.71, is this parallel's version of Agent Rose Wylde. Once it was determined that Anna had psionic potential (her Trait rolled at Character Creation turned up as Psionic Ability), Rose used the Empathic Link Psionic Talent to direct her local self to the new recruit; this just so happened to coincide with the assassination of a Disruptor Pawn — the captain of Anna's airship, *The Headlong Flight*. Despite the shocking nature of their introduction, Ms Wilde and Anna Thames have become friends, with Ms Wilde taking on the role of Anna's tutor, helping Anna to begin work on her psionic ability.

Anna's player rolls on the Psionic Discipline Table and the result is a 66 – Telepathy. Her initial skill of Psionics (Telepathy) is determined to be 20% (POW 10 x2), and she chooses Mental Shield and Thought Implant as her initial Traits.

Ms Wilde begins to use her own Empathy powers on Anna, forcing her repeatedly to eatablish her Mental Shield to try and block the psychic probes as practice for when she is deployed as a full agent. Rose initially limits her own powers to Intensity 1 so as not to overpower Anna. Anna spends 1 Prana Point and rolls her Psionics (Telepathy) skill and scores a 17 – a success, giving her an Intensity 1 Mental Shield (her Psionics skill is only 20%). This is enough to block Ms Wilde's weak *Feel Emotions* Talent.

Turnabout is fair play, and Anna decides to have some fun with her other talent, *Thought Implant*. She spends her Prana Point and rolls her Psionics (Telepathy) skill – a 10! Feeling the mental prodding, Ms Wilde steels herself and rolls her Willpower skill (rating 66%) to reject Anna's influence. Unfortunately she fails with an '82', allowing Anna to place an Intensity 1 *Thought Implant* into her tutor that will last for 2 days.

"Let's forget the stressful stuff for a little while and go to town for a few drinks, shall we?" says Ms Wilde, grabbing her purse and car keys, "My treat."

Some years later...

Anna's Psionics (Telepathy) has reached 60%, giving her a Psionic Intensity of 3. She has also developed the Telepathy and Psychic Wrack (Sanity) Talents. Anna has infiltrated a Disruptor psion training cell located in London's Isle of Dogs. Suspecting the presence of a Disruptor psychic (the ruthless Doctor Bastable), Anna invokes a Mental Shield (Intensity 3). After carefully negotiating her way through the corridors of the old warehouse she reaches the laboratory Doctor Bastable uses. Her intention is to neutralise the Doctor, and prevent other homeless youths from falling into Disruptor brainwashing programmes. Bastable is, indeed, present and has been waiting for Anna to arrive. Confronting each other across the white-walled laboratory, psychic battle is prepared. Doctor Bastable strikes first, directing *Inflict Pain* at Anna. His skill is Psionics (Disruptor Agent) 77% and his roll is 26 — a success. Anna resists with her Endurance 55% and rolls 40, successfully shrugging-off Bastable's attempts to paralyse her.

She directs her own attack: Psychic Wrack (Sanity) scoring 04 on the roll, which is a critical success. Ordinarily, a Wrack assault would cost 3 Prana but as Anna scored a critical, the cost is half (1.5 which is rounded to 2). Doctor Bastable's resistance roll against Willpower 59% must somehow better Anna's 04 critical: he rolls 47 which while successful, is not good enough to beat Anna. Her Psychic Damage is 1d6 and applied to Bastable's Tenacity Points. She rolls 5; Doctor Bastable has 10 Tenacity Points and this psionic damage is enough to inflict a Condition on the Disruptor agent. Rolling 1d20 on the Conditions Table (see page 52), the result is 17: *Flees in terror for 2d6 rounds*. Doctor Bastable is overwhelmed by images of scorpions, each with Anna's face, scuttling across the floor, worksurfaces and chairs, and he attempts to run backwards to escape them, screaming for help. He'll be like this for 5 rounds (25 seconds), which is more than enough for Anna to calmly draw her pistol, prepare a fresh cartridge, and exact some retribution for all the young lives and minds Doctor Bastable has helped to wreck.

Disruptor Psionics

Although the Valhalla Project prides itself on its nurturing of psychics, the Disruptors have also been active in the field, and for far, far longer than Zero-Zero. The Disruptors have their origins in a highly psychic, highly advanced race of beings that take part in a devastating galactic war. Although these progenitors have long since disappeared, the Disruptor organisation has always included psychics and continues to seek them out, develop their talents, and inculcate the Disruptor cause. Indeed, this was the path taken with the infant Luther Arkwright. Having identified the very first instance of *homo novus*, Disruptor agents kidnapped the new born and burned down the maternity wing of the hospital.

Arkwright was raised in a Disruptor training programme on one of the carefully hidden (and shielded) core parallels of the Disruptor high command. Here, and most likely alongside others, Arkwright was schooled psionically and taught to use his powers for violence. It is a common Disruptor tactic and potent Disruptor psychics are common in parallels where there is great need for specially skilled operatives.

Disruptor Psychics can learn any of the Psionic Disciplines described in this chapter, but there is also a specialized Disruptor Discipline. The talents are: *Disruptor Discipline: Body Fortress, Empathic Push, Evil Eye, Inflict Pain, Mental Shield, Psychic Wrack (any).*

In addition, the battle armour worn by Disruptor Rooks is technologically shielded against psionic attacks. Consider every Disruptor Rook as having the equivalent of an Intensity 2 Mental Shield in place at all times.

Mysticism

To escape the Disruptors pursuing him after he escaped from their training compound, the young Luther Arkwright undertook a mystical journey into the Himalayas where he found The Five — beings in the semblance of Buddhist monks who helped hone Arkwright's physical, mental and spiritual capabilities. Arkwright is not alone in pursuing such a path: in this game, mysticism offers very real ways of transcending the norm and those who have dedicated themselves to achieving both inner enlightenment and, consequently, certain personal powers, are of interest to Valhalla.

Mysticism functions as described in Mythras, with a few minor adjustments to fit with *Luther Arkwright: Roleplaying Across the Parallels*. The mysticism process as it is explained may work the same way, but it does define some things a little differently. The following are the key differences between Mysticism in the Mythras rules and Mysticism in the Arkwright multiverse.

- Any mention of Magic Points must be replaced with the term 'Prana Points.'
- All references to Paths of Mysticism must be replaced with the term 'Paths of Enlightenment.' (details opposite).

Learning Mysticism

Characters learn how to use Mysticism through the adherence to special Paths of Enlightenment. In something as varied and ultimately complex as the multiverse, there are numerous ways for Characters to have learned their Path of Enlightenment and achieve the arts of Mysticism.

If adding Mysticism to a Character at Character Creation, Games Masters should work with the players to determine how their Character learned how to reach their Path of Enlightenment. In these instances, where the Games Master has allowed the Character to learn Mysticism, the Character must trade one of their Traits (see Traits, Chapter 4) for the Mysticism skill at a rating of POW x2, and three initial Talents from a single Path of Enlightenment. This Path of Enlightenment can either be chosen from some of the existing ones listed in the boxed text below, or players can work with their Games Master to create their own Paths of Enlightenment. The character must also trade one Professional skill for Meditation, which is gained at its base percentage score.

If a Character wishes to learn Mysticism during the course of a campaign, the Games Master will need to decide how many Experience Rolls the Character must spend on joining a Path of Enlightenment and learning both the Mysticism Skill (at a rating of POW x2), Meditation, and one initial Talent.

Additional Talents can be learned from a Character's Path of Enlightenment as the game progresses as normal, described on page 118 of Mythras.

Alterations to Talents

Most of the Talents called upon by Mystics work in exactly the same fashion as they are described in Mythras (pages 157 – 160), but a few might have minor alterations to them in order to function seamlessly in *Luther Arkwright: Roleplaying Across the Parallels*.

Unless listed below, the Talents work exactly as published previously.

Immunity (X)

For game balance purposes, this Talent does not exist in the Arkwright multiverse. As most combat damage falls under a physical source (bullets, blades, etc.), such a Talent would be horribly imbalanced for most game play, and is replaced by Resilience (see below).

Indomitable

This Talent protects against Empathic Push and Telepathic Command, but not Synaptic Puppetry, as it is a bio-electric form of control and not a mental one.

Spirit Sense

Due to the sheer lack of a 'spirit plane' in the Arkwright multiverse, this Talent does not function. If a Games Master wishes to add the element of the spiritual and directly supernatural to their campaign, this Talent would apply normally.

Paths of Enlightenment

The nature of the multiverse allows for any number of different methods to achieve magical self-awareness, but there are a handful of known Paths of Enlightenment that players can choose from or Games Masters can use as a basis to create new ones. The following is a list of these examples, and the Mysticism Talents they teach (in addition to the ability to Enhance Attributes).

Disruptor Academy
Arrowcut, Dark Sight, Earth Sense, Formidable Natural Weapons, Indomitable, Magic Sense, Pain Control,

Focal Yoga
Adhesion, Astral Projection, Awareness, Denial (X), Heart Slow, Indomitable, Night Sight, Pain Control, Squeeze,

Shamanism
Astral Projection, Aura (X), Dark Sight, Life Sense, Squeeze,

Shaolin Monastics
Adhesion, Arrowcut, Astral Projection, Echolocation, Featherlight, Formidable Natural Weapons, Heart Slow, Pain Control,

Totemic Connection
Astral Projection, Aura (X), Awareness, Dark Sight, Life Sense, Pain Control, Squeeze,

Transcendentalist Meditation
Astral Projection, Denial (X), Indomitable, Magic (Psi) Sense

New Talents

Within a setting made up of so many parallel worlds, interacting with alternate timelines, and dealing with the traversal of the multiverse puts Characters in a unique position. The interaction with the multiverse leaves the setting open to have new and interesting Talents of Mysticism.

These new and special Talents are as follows.

Dimensional Anchor
The Mystic tethers himself to the very fabric of the parallel, ensuring that he cannot be physically moved in any fashion without allowing it to happen. Whether it is being pushed by a belligerent enemy, forced into a parallel shift, or even struck by a speeding car – the Mystic's physical form will not budge unless he desires it to happen. This does not make the Mystic immune to damage from such impacts, merely the physical repositioning.

Mind Blank
The Mystic reduces his brainwave emanations in a way that clouds any form of scanning or perception. Whether due to a telepathic Mind Scan, empathic Feel Emotions, or a technological lie detector machine, the Mystic is utterly serene and unreadable.

Parallel Sight
The Mystic can throw himself into a deep trance and look into the happenings of another parallel. If it is a parallel in which the Mystic has been before, the sight is perfectly clear and from the point of view of any being the Mystic made contact with in that parallel. Otherwise the viewing is foggy and unfocused, taken from a variety of sources chosen by the Games Master.

Resilience
The Mystic's flesh becomes infused with energy and becomes very dense, adding natural AP to all Hit Locations equal to the Intensity of the Talent.

Shift Parallel
The Mystic and a number of others in physical contact with him equal to the Intensity of the Talent are instantly shifted to another parallel. The Mystic must have already been to the target parallel, or thoroughly informed about its specifics, in order to successfully travel there.

Time Efficacy
By lengthening the moments between the passings of time, the Mystic perceives the world around him as if it were moving much slower, whereas he is actually moving much faster. This

gives the Mystic much more time with which to solve problems and perform actions. For every two points of Intensity, the Mystic gains a degree of ease on any skill test based on DEX, as well as doubling their Movement rate while this Talent is in effect. It can be a little disorienting when returning to the normal passage of time, imposing one degree of difficulty on all skill tests for the minute following this Talent's use.

Vitality

Each point of Intensity instantly removes a level of Fatigue from the Mystic and regenerates 1 HP to each Hit Location. Additionally while the Talent is in effect, the Mystic cannot gain levels of Fatigue for any amount of activity.

BRYAN TALBOT·90

Technology

The LutherArkwright saga features technological marvels of the Steampunk style, alongside those with a heavy hint of darkness rooted in horror tales. And, of course, Zero-Zero shows a parallel that has developed sapient machine intelligence, firmly rooting the Arkwright story in science fiction. This means the parallels of the multiverse could have any amount of technological advancement: with countless worlds to choose from, anything is possible.

Technology in the Luther Arkwright setting falls into several categories based on the roots of its invention and aesthetics of its native parallel, as well as the goals of its use. This chapter goes into detail concerning some of the major technologies used in Luther Arkwright, gives many examples, and even gives random generation tables for each kind of technology for Games Masters to use in a pinch. It should be noted that while their components are technological, weaponry is covered primarily in the Combat and Firearms chapter. Similarly, vehicles can be found in the Vehicles chapter.

Some Basic Assumptions

It is clearly impossible to cover every possible style and level of technology appearing across myriad Earths, many of which have developed at very different technological rates. To a large extent, Games Masters developing Luther Arkwright campaigns will need to exercise some common sense, some imagination, and also allow for a lot of leeway when dealing with the technological capabilities of different parallels.

What this chapter aims to provide are tools, ideas and play aids for employing technology of different levels and styles in Luther Arkwright scenarios. It is not, and cannot be, an exhaustive catalogue of items or a shopping list of devices. Instead, use this chapter to locate basics and then to help with on-the-spot decision-making, attaining inspiration, and for helping players and their Characters develop their own technology.

Steampunk and Clockpunk

Collectively known as 'steampunk' when it deals with hydraulics and boilers, and 'clockpunk' if it deals with springs, tension and mechanical power, this style of technology is evident throughout the Arkwright multiverse. Using science and experimentation, inventors across the parallels create amazing contraptions and mechanisms capable of wondrous effects. These sister-sciences are not all-encompassing, but the right engineer with the right tools can make these devices perform truly amazing feats.

Understanding the design behind a steampunk or clockpunk device is difficult for laymen. There is a great deal of trial-and-error in engineering something wondrous that functions through cogs, pipes, springs and tesla coils. If even a single piece of the device is off-kilter or incorrect, malfunctions are assured – from a few sparks and steam vents through to spectacular, limb-sundering explosions. Devices of these types therefore need regular maintenance by experts if they are to be trusted; even the commonly-used items Valhalla has all but perfected are treated with great care between missions.

Sample Steampunk and Clockpunk Technology

The following are items available to Valhalla agents operating in Steampunk and Clockpunk parallels.

Alarm Tetherweb

The leading room security device used by covert agents, the alarm tetherweb is a roughly 16cm diameter egg-shaped machine hub with 2d3 latched ports on the outer shell. Each port can produce up to ten metres of high-tensile wire with a magnetic or hooked end. When two or more of these wires are tethered to windows, doors, shutters, or other closed portal, and the device itself is anchored nearby, each wire strand becomes a sensitive pressure-tether like the threads of a spider's web. If the tethered portal is opened quickly, or wider than three inches, the wire unhinges automatically, retracting quickly back to the hub. This rewinding action activates a howling siren that can be heard clearly for five hundred metres in every direction. Alternatively, a wire can be pulled and rewound manually to activate the siren by hand. In case it becomes an issue, each wire has an AP value of 5 and 2 hit points.

Health Acceleration Chamber

The health acceleration chamber, often called 'Hack' for short, is a large metal contraption the shape of a decadent bathing tub with a fully enclosed metallic turtle-shell lid covered in tubes, pipes and gauges. The lid, with the aid of a pulley system or several strong individuals (combined Brawn values of 180 or more), can be removed to reveal the deep basin within. The hack is used by the old, infirm or wounded to stave off mundane ailments and accelerate physical healing. The device is filled with saline water and the subject climbs into the basin with the lid being lowered down (by outside help) and locked into place. An attendant experienced in setting the machine then adds several medical oils, salts, and chemicals into their specific receptacles. The hack pressurises the basin and healing is accelerated. For every four hours spent in a monitored and active hack, the recipient of treatment can heal injuries, poisons and diseases as if twenty-four hours had passed.

Megingjord Frame

Used to help labourers work more easily and safely, the megingjord is a steam-powered exoskeleton worn over thick clothing (to avoid chafing). Heavy metallic boots and hinged mitten-like clamps protect the feet and hands, and a heavy, loud boiler sits on the lumbar region of the lower back. While in use, the user's DEX is reduced by half (to a minimum of 1), all hit locations gain +1AP, STR is doubled and SIZ increases by half again. It takes 2d6 x2 minutes to get in and out a megingjord frame, but receiving aid from another cuts this time in half. A single boiler of fuel lasts for 1d4+2 hours and if not replenished, the suit seizes up, becoming immobile and paralyzed.

Perpetual Wakefulness Module

Worn by any agent who needs to avoid falling asleep, the perpetual wakefulness module is a bulky, five-centimetre thick wristband as wide as a man's belt made of leather strands, brass mechanisms and silver panels. When the small crank on the device is turned vigorously for 1d3+2 minutes, an internal battery is charged for the next nine hours. During that time the module emits a steady, soft clicking sound as its internal timer counts down five minute intervals. At the end of each of these intervals, the wearer receives a small-but-startling electric shock to the inside of the wrist (or ankle, if desired) to keep the wearer awake.

Svallin Heatsink Coils

These heavy copper wire coils link together to form a personal cooling device that agents can use to avoid heat exhaustion or light exposures to flame. There are four of these uncomfortable coils, one worn above each elbow and just below the knee. They clasp tightly around the wearer's limbs, and are then connected together by thin, strong wires. While worn the coils are activated when around intense heat (anything greater than 95 degrees Fahrenheit/35 degrees Celsius – but not exceeding 150F/65.5C), rapidly siphoning off heat energy and cooling the wearer. The coils condense the heat rapidly, creating rivulets of water that run off each coil. If the wearer is exposed to flame the damage is halved for the attack, but the coils stop functioning for 1d6 hours.

Mechanical Malfunction

Steampunk and clockpunk devices have many individual components and moving parts and, when they are not in perfect working order, potentially spectacular malfunctions may occur.

If using a piece of steampunk/clockpunk technology, the following instances call for a roll on the Mechanical Malfunction Table below.

- If used in concert with a Skill test and a Fumble is rolled
- If damaged in a combat or other altercation
- If used after a period of more than 60 days without appropriate maintenance/repairs (abstracted by a Mechanisms or Engineering roll)

1d100	Mechanical Malfunction
01-10	Total Destruction – Item is irreparably destroyed and bearer suffers 1d6 damage to the hit location(s) closest to the device.
11-20	Badly Wrecked – Item needs repairs before it will function again, and bearer suffers 1d3 damage to the hit location(s) closest to the device.
21-70	Broken – Item needs repairs before it will function again.
71-80	Damaged – Item only functions 50% of the time until repaired.
81-90	Timing Issues – Item ceases to function for 1d6 minutes while mechanism works out internal timing problems
91-99	Rattled – Item vibrates worriedly/painfully for 1d2 minutes, but is otherwise unharmed.
00	Spectacular Breakthrough – Something has shaken loose and falls back into place, unexpectedly creating a new and beneficial effect (Games Master's choice).

Alchemy, Biomancy and Chemistry

In *Luther Arkwright: Roleplaying Across the Parallels*, there are countless reasons to call upon the malleable sciences. Although they all generally perform similar roles, there are different subsets within this family of technologies. Alchemy is the application of certain reagents with otherwise normal items to enact change upon them.

Biomancy is the use of reagents upon living tissue to enhance its abilities or qualities beyond natural limitations, and Chemistry is the understanding of chemical processes and using them to create new compounds, and to achieve certain effects through known (and sometimes unknown) chemical reactions.

These technological sciences are used across the multiverse in as many ways as human beings can imagine, especially in the moderately advanced parallels. Whether used to further industry, society or for some other reason, the alteration of one's surroundings is a goal that most cultures share. The Valhalla Project's R&D team is consistently experimenting with chemical reagents and their uses, with some concoctions becoming time tested assets for their agents in the field.

The chemical-based technological fields have quite a few weaponised uses, making them a favorite of the Disruptors as well as enemies all over the parallels. Explosives in their most rudimentary form are actually chemical reactions, making such a wide array of deadly devices fall, at their base level, in this category of technology.

Advanced Platelet Packet

This small, perforated paper envelope contains a mixture of powerful minerals and chemical fuels for cellular growth designed to be poured directly onto an open wound. Although extremely painful, the resulting reaction chemically arrests bleeding almost instantly. The substance immediately halts the Bleed Special Effect when applied to an injury.

Sustainment Cocktail

The sustainment cocktail is an unpleasant paste that helps agents survive for many days without having to imbibe food or drink. The cocktail must be taken in heaped spoonfuls between portions of a large meal and washed down with at least a litre of water. The user must gorge himself upon the meal, water and paste for a full hour. Once done, the user will be able to survive without eating, drinking or making waste for 1d10+10 days. Their metabolism is slowed significantly; adding a degree of difficulty to any DEX related skill tests during that time. At the end of this time the user's metabolism catches up quickly, often causing hunger cramps and other intestinal distress within a few hours of wearing off.

Tyr Injected Combat Stimulant

Used by Valhalla agents immediately before entering a physically demanding combat situation, Tyr ICS is a mixture of amphetamines and adrenalizing catalysts injected directly into the vein. Almost immediately after injection the recipient's adrenaline and endorphin production goes into overdrive for 2d6 x 10 minutes. During that time, the recipient is overcome with bloodlust, causing him to disregard his own safety, in exchange for being imbued with tremendous stamina and toughness. For the duration of the drug the Damage Modifier of the recipient is increased by two steps and he is immune to all the detrimental effects of Serious Wounds and Fatigue. A Major wound will still incapacitate him.

In return, the subject may not Parry, Evade, or use Psionics or Mysticism while under the influence of Tyr. However the user automatically succeeds in resisting any Special Effect used against him.

V-17 Sobriety Regulator

The social agent's best friend, V-17 is the seventeenth version of an anti-alcohol chemical used by Valhalla agents to avoid inebriation. Formerly an injection, the V-17 is now taken in oral form before or after imbibing alcoholic beverages. A single dose of V-17 completely neutralizes any alcohol of up to 60% ABV for 1d4+2 hours. The side-effects of V-17 have more or less been worked out of the current product, although users often complain of slightly elevated body temperatures and increased (but not unnatural) sweat production. Characters using V-17 should make an Endurance roll at the end of the V-17 period, sustaining a level of Fatigue if the roll is failed.

Bad Mixtures

Most chemists are very careful when creating or using their reagents, but accidents happen and sometimes the mixtures are muddled or impure in some way. When these rare instances take place, unexpected results can occur.

When using alchemical, biological or chemical technology, the following instances call for a roll on the Unexpected Result Table.

- If the chemicals were created with a Skill test and a Fumble was rolled
- If the chemicals were polluted somehow

1d100	Unexpected Results Table
01-05	Poisonous – Chemical does not function and is instead violently toxic or gives off terrible fumes. Those in area of effect immediately begin to suffer from Asphyxiation for 2d6x5 seconds, with no chance of 'filling lungs with air.'
06-20	Sickening – Chemical does not function and is instead capable of inciting crippling nausea through contact or exposure. Those in area of effect must pass an Endurance test or vomit uncontrollably for 1d4x5 minutes.
21-70	Half-Strength – Chemical halves any and all numerical factors determined by dice rolling, rounding up.
71-90	Flush Colouration – Chemical functions as normal, but the recipient (or target) will blush deeply or pale dramatically for 2d6 hours.
91-99	Delayed Reactions – Chemical functions as normal, but does not begin to do so for 2d6x10 minutes after being 'used.'
00	The Chronos Effect – Chemical is unexpectedly long-lasting; multiplying its duration by 100 times normal.

Psionicology and Multiversal Technology

Equipment and technology that deals with inter-parallel travel, the science of the multiverse and the underlying theories of its physics are covered in this section. Psionicology is the study of psionics and how to better harness, control or tap into its potential. Multiversal theory is a collection of hypotheses and statistical analysis central to W.O.T.A.N's own programming. While examples of these technologies appear in a few parallels, the vast majority of items that are covered by this subsection will come from the shelves and storehouses of multi-parallel agencies like the Valhalla Project – or the Disruptors.

The following examples are likely to be strictly controlled, but available to assist Characters in moving and communicating between parallels.

Bifrost Bridging Apparatus

Used by W.O.T.A.N to survey the parallels remotely, the Bifrost apparatus uses the psionic connections between multiversal inhabitants. Resembling a brass-hooded chair connected to a pillar of dials, tubes and crystalline viewscreens, the Bifrost allows a skilled user to peer across the multiverse through the perceptions of one of the subject's other selves. The connection is disorienting and uncomfortable, but not painful. The subject must pass a Willpower roll to choose which parallel self the device connects with, and the connection continues until the user manages to pass a Home Parallel skill test. Disconnecting the user from the apparatus before this test is passed can leave their consciousness swirling and lost in the ether for 1d6 hours, during which time they are placed in a catatonic state of great mental duress – losing 1d3 Tenacity Points in the process.

Cerebral Amplifier/Yoke

A basket-like weave of copper straps, inward-facing silver studs, and linked golden wires connected to a single crystalline knob at one end. This unit taps into the cerebral wavelength emanations of a psionically empowered wearer. When worn, the device becomes like an antenna connected directly to the person's psionic talents. The crystalline knob can be set to either 'amplify' or 'yoke.' After which the knob can be locked into place by the turning of a removable key. While set to amplify, the device will generate and store 1 Prana Point for the wearer to use each hour (but not store more than a single point). While set to yoke however, the wearer cannot spend Prana without first suffering a single level of

Fatigue. Once locked in, the device's many studs press deeply into the forehead, temples and scalp; removing it without using the key inflicts 1 unavoidable HP of damage to the head hit location.

Parallel Anchor

The anchor is a two centimetre wide band of dull grey metal that hinges at one end and locks at the other, covered with a handful of Greek letters embossed in a bluish alloy along the side. When locked into place around the wrist or ankle of a parallel traveller, the wearer is unable to leave the current parallel, either psychically or via a machine such as The Van.

Trans Parallel Terminal

A two-way communications device incorporating a 104cm viewing monitor, the TPT allows Valhalla agents to communicate with Valhalla Nova irrespective of their current parallel. The device includes positioning systems, recording apparatus, encryption and a reasonably sophisticated computer system (equivalent to similar, early 21st Century desktop computers running graphical user interface technology). The TPT is a standard fixture and fitting in a field agent's safe house and is large enough to occupy several square metres of wall space. Every field agent disguises their TPT: false walls, elaborate screens, works of art — or sometimes, depending on the technology level of the parallel, as a general purpose home entertainment system. The device can interface with W.O.T.A.N directly, if desired, although it cannot connect directly with TPTs on other parallels; instead, relays via Zero-Zero are necessary if agents on different Earths need to communicate with each other.

Signature Sensor

With the exception of Arkwright himself (and maybe some ultra-rare exceptions in the multiverse), multiversal travellers radiate a detectable energy signature that some psionic abilities can sense in a variety of ways. This device, the Signature Sensor, allows the non-gifted to do the same. The sensor is a heavy, two-handed machine that has several dials and levers between its thick, rubber-lined handles. When used, it detects cross-parallel radiations up to a kilometre away (outside of the three-metre minimum distance bubble) with 85% accuracy. The small, illuminated screen on the face of the device points in the correct direction and uses brightness to determine proximity to the subject.

The Van

The Trans Parallel Vehicle, nicknamed 'The Van', is a prototype transport device designed for taking small teams physically across the parallels. Still being tested by select agent teams on high-priority missions, it is a large contraption of metal tubes, control panels, and complex planar interchange systems built into a large rectangular body with a pyramidal frame of energy conduits leading to the device's steerage at its apex. The Van opens a temporary travel point between two parallels entered into its navigational CPU, or entered via W.O.T.A.N itself. The Van is fully-automated and it requires a Formidable Computers roll to override its navigational settings. Usually, The Van returns to Zero-Zero between trips, but it can jump from parallel to parallel if programmed correctly. It can carry a crew of up to six and can be operated by a single occupant.

Travel between parallels takes 20+1d10 minutes to complete and the internal power systems allow up to four consecutive 'hops' before The Van needs to recharge. The Van is equipped with a Failover system that automatically returns the machine to Zero-Zero in the event of a malfunction or when it is running low on power.

The Van is equipped with an automedic, a medical device capable of stabilising Major Wounds and Serious Wounds, and healing 1d6 points of damage of Minor Wounds. It also has a locker equipped with:

6 Filter Masks
2 Artificial gills (permitting breathing underwater for up to 1 hour)
6 Short-range voice communicators (up to 10km)
4 Signature Sensors
4 Hand Computers (similar to a standard computer tablet)
1 TPT
4 Pairs of binoculars (15x magnification and 70 mm objective lens)
6 Flashlights
2 Wind-up and battery operated radio receivers
2 Multipurpose toolkits (all basic tools necessary for basic mechanical and electrical repairs)
6 Daggers
4 Vibro Beamers (see page 104)
4 Flares
6 sets of Sustainment Cocktail
1 x Mimetic Canopy that be used to cover The Van. The canopy provides general camouflage mimicking the immediate environment.

The Van does not move through space or time; it thus translocates to the same geospatial location as its origin (with local adjustments to ensure there is no materialisation within solid objects). It does have wheels and a combined STR of 50 can push the thing at a walking rate over smooth terrain.

Computers and Nanotech

High technology opens up countless opportunities. As computing becomes easier and devices shrink, what was once bulky becomes light and streamlined; what was covered in complicated controls becomes intuitive; and what once threatened danger to its users becomes safe to use. It is the collective move away from the inconvenient nature of early technologies, leaving room for invention and ingenuity to replace necessity. The further technology moves forward in a parallel, the less the people invent things because they have to – they will invent things because they *want* to.

The following items are examples of higher technology equipment from technologically sophisticated parallels:

Automated Lockpick

A small, handheld machine that fits over the keyhole/slot of any physical lock, lining up an open port of micro-tentacle wires that end in dense tumbler-pushing manipulators. With the press of a button the device unfurls the wires into the lock. The lockpick then runs hundreds of standard algorithms, moving the wires in ways to trigger the tumblers and slides of said lock. When all the moving parts are pushed into the proper position, a low-light LED glow indicates success, allowing the portal to be opened normally. The automated lockpick is nearly silent, works very quickly, and works on any tumbler-based lock (no latches or bars) that does not wholly require electronic codes. Using the automated lockpick allows the user to unlock any physical locking mechanism with 90% accuracy in 1d3 rounds.

Hologeneration Learning Annex

Also known as holodecks, these simulation devices create a virtual reality environment for recreation and training/planning purposes. Situations and scenarios ranging from a few minutes in duration up to several days are quite possible, depending on the size and sophistication of the annex and its software.

The annex has an Intensity, ranging from 1 to 5, that measures its ability to mimic reality:

1. Obviously a computer simulation with pixellated effects
2. A smoother experience but clearly a simulation
3. Realistic simulation with true depth of field and interactive graphics
4. Incorporates texture and olfactory elements for a truly immersive experience
5. Feedback technology allows for truly physical interactions within the environment; unless one is prepared the experience is as close to reality as one can get.

The Intensity of the annex is added to the INT characteristic for the purposes of improving a skill being increased by an Experience roll. This simulates the ablity to re-run scenarios and experiences to optimise learning.

However, there is a danger in spending too much time in the annex, and users can become addicted to the false reality. If a person spends more than 60 consecutive hours using a hologeneration learning annex, they must pass a Formidable Willpower test or generate a new Dependency of Escapism at 40+2d6%.

Nano-Bandage

Nanotechnology, the application of microscopic machines to perform amazingly complex tasks, is one of the highest forms of technology. One common program put into nanobots is a series of advanced first aid and emergency medical procedures, creating a metallic paste filled with thousands upon thousands of miniaturised doctors ready to treat whatever they contact. A nano-bandage is a one-gram vial of silvery fluid composed of medically-programmed nanites and a viscous, organic energy-fuel. When applied to a warm body, the nanites come to life, consuming the organic fuel to activate a rapid series of medical processes. Automatically sealing any wound in a protective shell made from the husks of nanites that have finished their work, the nano-bandage helps treat various injuries ranging from abrasions, incisions, punctures and burns. When applied, the nano-bandage heals 1d4 Hit Points to a single wounded hit location over the course of 2d6x5 minutes.

Errors in the Code

Nothing is completely infallible, and even the highest forms of technology sometimes have their own individual problems that could surface at the worst time possible. Whether it is due to damage inflicted upon the device or a simple mix up in a single line of coding, high-tech technology can falter and malfunction.

Whenever high technology is used in the following specific situations, the Games Master can make a roll on the Errors in the Code Table opposite.

- If a Fumble was rolled during a skill test while using a piece of high-technology
- If attempting to use a piece of high-technology for a purpose it was not designed for
- If using a piece of high-technology that has been corrupted from damage or foul play

1d100	Errors in the Code Table
01-15	Total Meltdown – The high-tech piece of equipment short circuits, detonates, implodes, or otherwise becomes a heap of irreparable junk
16-40	Flicker – The high-tech piece of equipment stops functioning 50% of the time until repaired
41-80	Need a Reset – The high-tech piece of equipment simply needs to be powered down and restarted in order to function again
81-99	Momentary Stall – The high-tech piece of equipment runs into some junk programming and will function as normal in 1d3+1 minutes
00	Higher Loop – The high-tech piece of equipment has a strange mixture of programs work in an unintended way, creating a fantastic new version of the same kind of equipment (Games Master determines new abilities).

Transhumanics

Technology has reached a stage where the personality, memories, emotions and experiences of a human life can be removed from the organic shell and uploaded or transposed into fabricated components — be these organic or machinelike in nature. Artificial Intelligence is as common as organic sapience and the distinction between human and machine intellect is so small as to be insignificant. Zero-Zero stands on the brink of such technology with W.O.T.A.N's evolution, and in other parallels transhumanics is the norm.

For humans, it is possible to prepare and maintain a backup copy of one's personality in some form of external storage: this form of coding is known as a matrix. When death occurs, the matrix can be loaded into a suitably prepared replacement, be it organic or otherwise, and life continues. The subject maintains all memories, personalities and skills developed beforehand and simply continues them in a new casing. Immortality is assured.

Of course such wonders may be reserved for a ruling elite, or be strictly governed to preserve only what is deemed essential to society and these rules may fuel tension and strife. But in societies that are mature enough to fully regulate the benefits, humanity advances beyond the confines of DNA and becomes a truly unfettered — nay, sublime — civilisation.

Examples of Transhumanics are as follows:

Matrix Scanner

This prized machinery connects with the entire psyche of the individual and records every aspect of the personality and capabilities of the subject, using the psionic resonance of the brain, the natural psychic energy of the multiverse and advanced brainwave and memory retrieval scanners. A perfect copy is made. The individual is effectively backed-up like any form of data, but held in the complex psionic algorithm occupying several hundred terrabytes of storage. Scanning takes 1d6+6 days, and during this time the subject is placed into a state of suspended animation while the Matrix Scanner is wired into the brain by skilled technicians. Once complete, the Matrix is stored until ready for loading into a suitable host. All physical characteristics of the host replace those of the original character, but all skills transfer over, with enhancements applied to base skill scores to reflect new phsyical capabilities such as higher STR and DEX, and so forth. Games Masters must judge the effects if this type of technology is available to Characters, but it is one way of helping to preserve Characters from otherwise certain death. If a character is killed, there is a number of minutes equal to the average of Endurance and Willpower to get the body into a Matrix Scanner so that a backup can begin. The body can be placed in suspended animation first to arrest natural death processes.

Drone

Sapient machines that tend to be human size (between SIZ 6 and 16), and are either hosts for a human Matrix or are AIs in their own right. Drones may have physical mobility, such as wheels, legs or similar; or use repulsors to float and fly. Drones can have an INT characteristic of up to 21 and be programmed with a wide range of skills as Games Masters see fit. As a base, give a drone its INT x25 in total skill points, with a cap of 100% on a skill's maximum value.

Drones have as wide a range of personalities as humans (obviously, if a drone can host a human Matrix), and are designed to optimise communications with organic, traditional humans and machine intelligence. Some parallels give drones and other AIs equal footing and rights with humans; in others, society is given over to AI regulation; and, in others, humans are considered inferior, obsolescent, and good for little more than study and amusement. Machine intelligence can be every bit as capricious as one that has emerged organically.

Xeno-Science

Over the course of the time W.O.T.A.N has been arranging missions across the multiverse, its agents have found a rare handful of parallels that have been touched by the deeply unknown. In these parallels something was introduced from the reaches of human mystery, the darkness beyond understanding, perhaps even from out of their world altogether. It is the discovery, study and utilisation of these mysterious and unknown technologies that drives the overarching field of xeno-science.

An elite team of xeno-scientists at the Valhalla Project are always ready to put a new piece of mysterious discovery under observation, into agent-testing, and potentially under lock and key. These items can hail from a number of different unknown quantities including (but not limited to) the depths of ancient Old Gods from pre-history, forgotten civilisations that survived in secret, or even from the farthest reaches of outer space.

Whenever encountering a new piece of xeno-science for the first time, the Character involved must pass an Insight skill test at a degree of difficulty set by the Games Master (based on how foreign the technology truly is) in order to understand it. Once understood, activating the technology could be easy if the Character has seen someone else use it – but not always. If the Games Master requires it, a second Insight test may be required.

The following items are suitable examples of some xeno-science technologies could bring to the Luther Arkwright roleplaying game:

Atlantean Alloy

Atlantean alloy is a golden, pearlescent metal that is lighter than steel, denser than wrought iron, and able to hold an edge sharper than a barber's razor. It was discovered in a parallel where the fabled sunken city of Atlantis raised itself from the depths to become a true superpower. When used as a construction material, armour reinforcement or edged weaponry, Atlantean alloy yields truly magnificent results. These items all have +1AP and +2HP added to their durability, and – if used as part of a weapon – will ignore half (round up) any protecting AP of anything they strike.

The Old Tongues Journals

This is a huge collection of tattered books gathered from the scrawls of what appears to be one or more madmen. Comprised of millions of words, diagrams, rough sketches and more, the journals do not resemble a cohesive collection at all. Some are printed, some are handwritten, and some are beautiful works of calligraphy in numerous languages both known and seemingly invented. The original author or authors of the journals have long since vanished in the parallel where the books were found, or any other known to the multiverse, making the true reason behind their writings lost to the unknown. The journals map out a dark idea of ancient forces more powerful than anything the Valhalla Project or the Disruptors have ever known, and show hundreds of different ways their influence can be seen across the parallels. By reading a portion of the journals, a Character can achieve a special kind of understanding of these Old Ones, and possibly glean foresight from the haphazard ramblings. This learning comes at a risk however, and reading too much into the anarchic notes could invite madness. For every 1d6x2 consecutive hours spent reading some of the Old Tongues Journals a Character may attempt to pass an Insight skill test. If successful, the character gains a strange and powerful peek into the fate of the current parallel, information that appears in the mind almost in the same way as a psychometric premonition — although no psychic power is found within the journal.

Universal Translation Matrix

A small, strange-looking device worn around and within the ear, the universal translation matrix looks like the cross between a low-tech hearing aid and a squid. Tendrils of pliable, semi-translucent plastic curl behind the ear and hold the device in place while much of the amorphous 'body' presses into the ear itself. Intelligent microprocessors attached to a multitude of sound receptors that take in hundreds of thousands of different communication wavelengths, translates them to that most commonly spoken by the wearer (it uses probability algorithms), and whispers them into the wearer's ear. The process is simple, and 98% of all forms of sound-based communication are translated perfectly – the remaining 2% will result in garbled nonsense from a very confused processing network.

Alien Incompatibility

Whenever dealing with a piece of utterly unknown xeno-science, there are numerous risks involved. The biology between user and item could be opposed, misuse could be dangerous, or it could be something as simple as the technology being too far beyond mortal understanding.

Whatever the reason, when the following instances occur, the alien nature of xeno-science rears its head and inflicts oddity upon the user:

- If a Fumble was rolled during the Insight skill test while trying to recognise the device's purpose
- If a Fumble was rolled during any skill test made to activate the device
- If using a piece of xeno-science technology after being given improper instructions

1d100	Alien Incompatibility
01-05	Implosion – The device falls apart, somehow dangerously folding in upon itself and vanishes – taking anything touching it along with it!
06-15	Multiversal Vibration – The device shifts suddenly and sends out ripples in the fabric between parallels; inflicting 1 damage to all hit locations of any parallel-travellers within 3 metres
16-20	Disintegration – The device begins to fall to ash
21-30	Mutation! – The Character touching the device undergoes 1d6 days of sporadic discomfort that ends in gaining a new random Chaos Feature (see the table on pages 275 and 276 of Mythras.)
31-40	Expedient Aging – The Character touching the device instantly and painfully ages 1d3x5 years
41-60	Incompatibility – The device will no longer function for the Character… ever
61-70	Need for Greater Understanding – The device is far more complex than first thought, and 1d6 additional Insight skill rolls will be needed to unlock the device's potential
71-80	False Use – The device is oddly not what it seems and instead reveals itself for a different and strange purpose
81-90	Illness – The Character becomes unexpectedly ill and nauseous for 1d3 hours
91-00	Psychic Evolution – The Character immediately gains 1d3 Prana Points OR rolls a random Psionic Ability

Technological Item Creation

There are a great many opportunities for new and interesting pieces of technology to be created and the Characters may make the decision to invent and build their own devices. Ingenuity and skill go hand in hand when thinking about designing and building a brand new instrument, tool, or device. A lot goes into the creation process of new technology or new applications of old technologies, but with the right planning and hard work the end results can be amazing.

Creating new technological items is handled as a specialized Task (see Mythras, page 65-67). Before construction can begin those involved must have reasonable access to:

- Suitable Funds
- Suitable Materials
- Suitable Personnel
- Suitable Workspace
- Time to Manufacture

Most of these elements require some common sense governance and are highly variable, according to what is being created. Building a hand-held radio transmitter for example, is a very different task to building an aircraft. Games Masters must make appropriate rulings and are quite within their rights to deem a project to big, complex, expensive, demanding or simply impossible for the Characters to accomplish.

Lack of, or deficiency in, one of these elements imposes one grade of difficulty to the roll used for resolving the task. Penalties are also cumulative, so lacking materials and personnel for example, makes a project two grades more difficult.

Characters need to have a clear goal for the equipment, representing what it is and what it does. This is what emerges at the end of the Task series. The singular idea behind the item being generated is what the initial Task series will invent. Modifying the original design represents another Task series that must be handled separately, but failure in additional Task series' will not necessarily ruin the original item.

Engineering Task Rounds

Building something using a Task series requires the process to be measured in Task Rounds. This variable amount of time is based primarily upon the type of item being built as well as the complexity of the device. There is a lot more effort that needs to go into building an armoured vehicle for a full agent team than a steam-powered motorcycle, just as an electromagnetic flechette launcher would be more time-intensive to construct than a clockwork harpoon gun.

The Games Master has the final say as to how long the whole process is going to take, but the table opposite shows several good examples as to what a Task Round could be for sample projects.

Engineering Enhancements

Enhancements are the best way to turn the results of a manufacturing Task Series into something bigger or better, just like any other skill-based creation in Mythras. These bonuses for exemplary work during the Task Series are calculated as normal and applied in the same fashion, but could have additional effects that are designed perfectly for Arkwright.

The second table below explains what the Enhancements from an Engineering Task Series can achieve for the new item being fabricated. Examples of various Engineering Facets that could be used in newly designed items can be found in the Engineering Facet Enhancement section, below.

Sample Tasks and Enhancements

Sample Task	Task Round Unit
Mixing an untested chemical compound solution	10 minutes – 1 hour
Repairing damaged steampunk/ clockwork technology	30 minutes – 6 hours
Building a clockwork/ steampunk sidearm	1 day – 5 days
Building a robotic life facsimile	1 month – 6 months
Constructing a land vehicle	1 month – 1 year
Erecting a heavily shielded bunker	6 months – 2 years
Building a flying war fortress	1 year – several years
Task Modifiers	***Round Unit Adjustment***
Item uses multiversal theory	Multiply time by 2
Item is based on xeno-science technology	Multiply time by 5
Item is finished and being tinkered with	10% normal time (round up)

Sample Task	Task Round Unit
Desirable	The item's estimated value in Crowns in doubled.
New Engineering Facet	The item may add a single Engineering Facet to the overall construction of the item.
Repeatable Production	Future Task Series used to create this item are performed in half the time.
User Friendly	The item is very easy to understand, adding a degree of ease to any skill test required to utilize it.

Additional Tasks for Additional Enhancements

Luther Arkwright: Roleplaying Across the Parallels allows for devices to serve much more than a single purpose, and engineers will often tinker, experiment and augment devices even long after they have come off the workbench.

To show this style of augmentative manufacturing, any item that has been successfully built using the Engineering Task System can be sent 'back to the shop' for additional tinkering. This is performed much in the same fashion as a regular Engineering Task System except the material costs should be dramatically lessened, as would the need for suitable personnel. Once the item has been put through a Task Series designed for augmentation successfully, one additional Engineering Enhancement can be added to the item.

Engineering Facet Enhancements

There are dozens of different ways for a Character to utilise the Engineering Professional skill in a Task Series to create and enhance items, and Games Masters can work with their players to come up with other uses and their effects upon the equipment built using them. The following are several regularly-used Engineering Facets that Games Masters and Characters can use as Enhancement benefits to the items they create in a Task Series.

The following are the well-known Engineering-based specialties:

Animus

Only utilised for the construction of automatons. The animated device can now be programmed with one skill (starting at base value) per 10% of the Engineering skill used in its creation. Once functional, the skills of the automaton can be improved by an engineer investing their own Improvement Rolls in fine-tuning it.

Architecture

Permits the device to be constructed at a large scale. The maximum SIZ it can reach is equal to the value of the Engineering skill used to create it, augmenting its final Hit Points.

Destruction

Utilised only for destructive automatons or weapons, the device inflicts ranged damage based upon on the value of the Engineering skill used to create it. For projectile weapons, damage is 1d6 at 01-20%, 1d8 at 21-40%, 1d10 at 41-60%, 1d12 at 61-80%, and 2d6 at 81-100%. Each Enhancement added to this increases the damage as per the Mythras Damage Modifier table. Energy weapons such as Tesla Arcs or Lightning Projectors follow the same pattern but start at 1d2 at 01-20%.

Energy/Fuel Reserve

Controls how many hours or shots the device operates for before needing a rewind, recharge or refuelling. The maximum number of charges is equal to the value of the Engineering skill used to create it.

Locomotion

Assuming a vehicle or automaton, permits the device a Movement Rate equal to one tenth of the Engineering skill used to create it. Usually the device is designed for only a single type of locomotion, either driving, sailing or lighter than air floating. If the engineer wishes to combine two or more methods, the Movement Rate must be divided between them or additional Enhancements must be used.

Metallurgy/Structuring

Adds protection to the device to make it more physically resilient. It gains a number of inherent Armour and bonus Hit Points equal to one tenth of the Engineering skill used to create it, rounding up. This physical armouring is vulnerable to the Sunder special effect in combat.

Miniaturisation

Allows the device to function at full normal ability despite being much smaller than normal. The final SIZ/ENC of the device is reduced as a percentage by the rating in the Engineering skill used to create the item.

Xeno-Biology

Permits the inclusion of an unusual Creature Ability (see Mythras pages 214 to 218) for every full 20% in the Engineering skill used to create it, subject to Games Master approval.

Transformation

Allows the device to physically switch shapes or forms from one object to another, either to hide its true use or create alternate uses for each shape. The final device can be manipulated into a number of different shapes of the same SIZ equal to the Engineering skill used to create it divided by 20.

Random Technology

There will be times during a Luther Arkwright adventure when a Games Master needs a random piece of technology. Agents could find these devices and items in the field, or perhaps Valhalla R&D has come up with a new piece of equipment for the agents to test in a specific situation or parallel. Whatever the reason, the following multi-step process of rolling on random tables creates perfect examples of strange technologies in the Luther Arkwright multiverse.

Step 1 – Basic Concept

There is a lot of interesting technologies out in the multiverse, but they tend to fall into a few specific archetypal concepts. These concepts will shape what the generated piece of technology will be as well as give the Games Master the outline of what to be building using the rest of the random rolls ahead.

Depending on the Sociological Type of the parallel in which the technology is being generated for, the Games Master should roll on the Concept Table (see page 83) choosing the column corresponding with the Sociological Type for the parallel.

The generic descriptions of the archetypal concepts are as follows:

Industrial Tool: A device or mechanism that performs some kind of function in the industrial spectrum of skills and talents. Most often this is a device used to make difficult labours easier in some fashion.

Medical Tool: A device used to heal the sick, mend wounds, monitor health or otherwise positively affect a target or targets.

Personal Equipment: A device worn or used by a single person to augment them or their skills in some fashion.

Social Interaction Device: A device used to enhance communication, understanding or other social connections between the user and others.

Travel Aid: A device that helps a person or persons get from point A to point B, whatever those points may be, quickly and safely.

Unique Device: Something designed completely outside of the norm; a strange and interesting device that does not fit into other archetypal categories.

Weapon or Armour: A device used to inflict or prevent harm to another being or target.

Step 2 – Technology Base

As described throughout this chapter, there are many different broad types of technology to be found in the multiverse. Depending on the predominant age of civilisation in the parallel in which the technology is being found, there are several leanings as to what type of technology the example could be.

Roll on the Technology Base table (page 83) to determine the general technology type of the device. Where a technology type is clearly at odds with the parellel's level of development — Transhumanism in a Steam Age parallel, for instance — this is a clear sign of Disruptor interference and the technology is likely of Disruptor origin or introduced by Disruptor agents.

Step 3 – Game Effect (Type and Efficiency)

Once the general type of technology of the device has been determined, the next step is to find the efficiency of the device in game terms. The Games Master can choose from or roll randomly on the table below to determine what the device is supposed to do, in general terms.

Step 1: Concept Table

1d100	Sociological Type					
	Academic	Artistic	Bureaucratic	Lawless	Manufacturing	Militaristic
01-10	Weapon or Armour	Industrial Tool	Travel Aid	Social Interaction Tool	Weapon or Armour	Personal Equipment
11-20	Industrial Tool	Travel Aid	Industrial Tool	Medical Tool	Travel Aid	Industrial Tool
21-40	Travel Aid	Personal Equipment	Personal Equipment	Weapon or Armour	Personal Equipment	Medical Tool
41-70	Personal Equipment	Social Interaction Tool	Medical Tool	Personal Equipment	Industrial Tool	Weapon or Armour
71-85	Social Interaction Tool	Unique Device	Social Interaction Tool	Travel Aid	Medical Tool	Travel Aid
86-95	Medical Tool	Medical Tool	Weapon or Armour	Industrial Tool	Social Interaction Tool	Social Interaction Device
96-00	Unique Device	Weapon or Armour	Unique Device	Unique Device	Unique Device	Unique Device

Step 2: Technology Base Table

<table>
<tr><th rowspan="2">1d100</th><th colspan="6">Parallel Type</th></tr>
<tr><th>Steam Age</th><th>Industrial Age</th><th>Electronics Age</th><th>Computer Age</th><th>Nanotech Age</th><th>Spacefaring Age</th></tr>
<tr><td>01-10</td><td>Psionicology and Multiversal Theory</td><td>Psionicology and Multiversal Theory</td><td rowspan="2">Psionicology and Multiversal Theory</td><td rowspan="2">Xeno Science</td><td>Xeno Science</td><td>Steampunk/ Clockpunk</td></tr>
<tr><td>11-20</td><td rowspan="2">Alchemy, Biomancy and Chemistry</td><td rowspan="5">Steampunk/ Clockpunk</td><td>Steampunk/ Clockpunk</td><td>Alchemy, Biomancy and Chemistry</td></tr>
<tr><td>21-30</td><td rowspan="2">Steampunk/ Clockpunk</td><td>Steampunk/ Clockpunk</td><td>Alchemy, Biomancy and Chemistry</td><td rowspan="4">Computers, High-Sci and Nanotech</td></tr>
<tr><td>31-40</td><td rowspan="3">Steampunk/ Clockpunk</td><td rowspan="2">Computers, High-Sci and Nanotech</td><td rowspan="5">Computers, High-Sci and Nanotech</td></tr>
<tr><td>41-50</td><td>Computers, High-Sci and Nanotech</td></tr>
<tr><td>51-60</td><td>Alchemy, Biomancy and Chemistry</td><td rowspan="2">Alchemy, Biomancy and Chemistry</td></tr>
<tr><td>61-70</td><td rowspan="2">Transhumanism</td><td rowspan="2">Alchemy, Biomancy and Chemistry</td><td rowspan="3">Transhumanism</td><td>Transhumanism</td></tr>
<tr><td>71-80</td><td>Transhumanism</td><td rowspan="2">Xeno Science</td></tr>
<tr><td>81-90</td><td>Xeno Science</td><td>Computers, High-Sci and Nanotech</td><td rowspan="2">Psionicology and Multiversal Theory</td><td>Transhumanism</td></tr>
<tr><td>91-00</td><td>Computers, High-Sci and Nanotech</td><td>Xeno Science</td><td>Xeno Science</td><td>Psionicology and Multiversal Theory</td><td>Psionicology and Multiversal Theory</td></tr>
</table>

Step 3: Effect and Efficiency Tables

1d100	Type of Effect
01-05	Nothing – The device is non-functional, or never was to begin with.
06-10	Reduces Skill – The device lowers one or more of the user's Skill ratings
11-15	Reduces Trait – The device lowers the user's Luck, Prana or Tenacity Points (choose one)
16-20	Reduces Characteristic – The device lowers one of the user's Characteristics
21-25	Heals – The device repairs damage, heals injuries or cures illness
26-30	Clairvoyance – The device allows visual perception beyond the normal scope of the user
31-35	Clairaudience – The device allows audio perception beyond the normal scope of the user
36-40	Personal Protection – The device protects the user beyond the nature of its construction
41-45	Targeted Protection – The device protects a specific target beyond the nature of its construction
46-50	Increases Skill – The device raises one or more of the user's Skill ratings
51-55	Increases Trait – The device raises the user's Luck, Prana or Tenacity Points (choose one)
56-60	Increases Characteristic – The device raises one of the user's Characteristics
61-65	Elemental Energy Generation – The device can create elemental energy (fire, cold, electricity, etc.) from seemingly nothing
66-70	Physical Element Generation – The device can create physical elements (stone, metal, ice, etc.) from seemingly nothing
71-75	Transmutation – The device can turn one substance into another
76-80	Transportation – The device can move matter through space nearly instantaneously
81-85	Inflicts Melee Damage – The device is capable of harming targets within melee range
86-90	Inflicts Ranged Damage – The device is capable of harming targets with a targeted ranged attack
91-95	Inflicts Area Damage – The device is capable of harming targets for several metres in all directions
96	Multiplicity – The device's true power is to self-replicate every 2d6x10 days
97	Bi-Purpose – Roll twice on this table; re-rolling results of 99 and 100. The device will not access both powers at once.
98	Multiple Uses – Roll two times on this table; re-rolling results of 97 and higher
99	Multiple Uses – Roll three times on this table; re-rolling results of 97 and higher
100	Multiple Uses – Roll four times on this table; re-rolling results of 97 and higher

1d100	Type of Efficiency
01-10	Feeble – +/- 2%; 1d2 damage; 1 square/cubic metre; 5 linear metres
11-20	Weak – +/- 5%; 1d3 damage; 2 square/cubic metres; 10 linear metres
21-30	Lesser – +/- 10%; 1d4 damage; 5 square/cubic metres; 25 linear metres
31-40	Minor – +/- 15%; 1d6 damage; 10 square/cubic metres; 50 linear metres
41-65	Average – +/- 20%; 1d8 damage; 20 square/cubic metres; 100 linear metres
66-80	Major – +/- 25%; 1d10 damage; 30 square/cubic metres; 500 linear metres
81-90	Greater – +/- 30%; 2d6 damage; 50 square/cubic metres; 1 linear kilometre; single parallel potential
91-99	Greatest – +/- 35%; 2d8 damage; 100 square/cubic metres; 10 linear metres; multi-parallel potentials
100	Miraculous – Something beyond description; truly unique and breathtakingly powerful

Step 4: Description

1d100	Sociological Type					
	Steam/ Clock Punk	Alchemy/Biomancy/ Chemistry	Psionicology/ Multiversal Theory	Transhumanism/ Mutagens	Computers/ High-Sci/ Nanotech	Xeno-Science
01-10	Visible fluid reservoir	Bubbles constantly	Heavy and unwieldy	Metallic construction	Seamless metal	Oily surface
11-20	Parts are leather	Separates like oil and water	Contains golden bands	Form-fitting like skin	Miniaturised size	Pulsating bulbs upon its surface
21-30	Covered in tubes	Dense and heavy	Frail-looking	Bears biohazard warnings	Shines like chrome	Cold and clammy to the touch
31-40	Hand-cranked	Looks organic	Glows slightly	Bio-degradable casing	Inscribed with instructions	Has pseudo-tentacles growing off of it
41-50	Brass and copper	Comes in two equal parts	Lightweight construction	Automated dosing injector	Illuminated controls	Has veins of exposed tubing
51-60	Numerous cogs	Held in an injector	Crystalline components	Shaped like a human organ	Contains touchscreen	Looks bio-mechanical
61-70	Scattered rivets	Smells horribly	Silvery wires	Looks organic	Sized for personal travel	Covered in unrecognizable symbols
71-80	Latched hinges that serve no purpose	Pasty and thick	Lined with LED lights	Held in plastic case	Lightweight plastic body	Somehow darker than black
81-90	Contains glass vials	Held in an aerosol sprayer	Warm to the touch	Spiky and painful-looking	Comes in multiple components	Covered in synthetic rubber flesh
91-99	Wired power source	Comes in solid, chewable form	Worn like a garment	Larger than the user	Made from translucent polymers	Totally asymmetrical
100	Roll on a different Technology Base	Roll on a different Technology Base	Roll on a different Technology Base	Roll on a different Technology Base	Roll on a different Technology Base	Roll on a different Technology Base

Once the effect(s) of the technological device has been determined, no matter if it fits with the style of the device or not (many inventors mix some strange ideas together, after all) it is time to determine how powerful the effect(s) of the device may be.

The Games Master rolls on the Effect Efficiency table (page 84) for each of the device's technological effects. The result gives a broad description of how powerful the effect is and gives several examples of what that would mean to some game effects. The Games Master has the final say on what the device actually does based on the campaign needs, but this table gives a good base to work from.

Step 4 – Description

The basic look of the device can range dramatically based on what kind of technology base it hails from, but there are some heavily repeated concepts that appear enough to form good constants for a random piece of technology.

The Games Master should roll 1d3+1 times on the Description Table (above), comparing the results to the column labelled with the base form of technology the device was made with. Each result adds another facet to the overall description of the item to create the overall look and feel for the Games Master to describe it.

Step 5: Flaws and Quirks

1d100	Flaws and Quriks
01-05	Falls apart after a single use or activation
06-10	Vibrates uncontrollably when used, making it somewhat painful to hold
11-15	Heats up uncomfortably when used; hot enough to leave welts but not truly injure
16-20	Item is cold and gives off light steam in room temperature
21-25	Functions only at day or at night
26-30	Has a limited number of uses (1d4x5, rolled secretly by the Games Master)
31-35	Item activates 1d6x30 seconds after being triggered
36-40	Changes colour mysteriously with every use
41-45	Looks much older and weathered than it really is
46-50	Can be disassembled and reassembled easily using a simple tool
51-55	User feels slightly nauseous when active
56-60	Needs to be knocked or kicked hard before it will function
61-65	Item slowly becomes heavier over time, increasing weight by 2% each week (to a maximum of 200% heavier)
66-70	Functions only when wet, but functions perfectly while underwater
71-75	Item can be set to double normal output, but has a 25% chance of becoming non-functional afterwards
76-80	Item totally self-repairs or regenerates any damage it suffers over 2d6 weeks
81-85	Bearer never feels cold or hot; always feels as if it were room temperature
86-90	Multiversal fluctuation reverberates in a three metre radius when activated
91-95	Item has 1% chance of parallel shifting with the bearer each time it is activated
96-00	Item has only one use – but the effects are seemingly permanent

Step 5 – Flaws and Quirks

In reality nothing can truly be perfect, and many technological inventions will have minor issues, flaws or quirks that appear over time. These oddities range from the comedic and easily dealt with to the bothersome and even dangerous.

Games Masters should roll once on the Flaws and Quirks table (above) to add a bit of random risk to their piece of technology.

Step 6 – Unique Narrative Trait

Sometimes a Games Master needs one last detail to make the item special – and to possibly create brand new plotlines and story arcs with nothing more than a single technological find. Nothing exists in a pure vacuum, and these narrative traits show a touch of the item's history.

Games Masters should roll once on the Unique Narrative Trait table (opposite) to add a little random interest to their piece of technology.

A fuller description of the Random Technology process and tables can be found on page 88, in Anna Thames' Chronicle.

Standard Equipment

At one point or another, Valhalla agents will need to spend some of their money on a variety of goods they need. This is normally a simple process, but things can get rather complicated depending on the level of advancement in the parallel the agent occupies.

The supply of items available in the commissary at Zero-Zero means that anything that is manufactured is purchasable there at management-set prices, but in various parallels where the age of technology is different costs vary.

The following tables show numerous useful and commonly sought after pieces of equipment Valhalla agents may have a desire to purchase during their careers. The tables show the item, its normal commissary purchase price, and the adjusted prices (if any) for different technology levels where they could be purchased from.

It should be noted that armour, weaponry and vehicles are listed with their own prices in their dedicated chapters later in this book with their own modifiers to those costs.

Step 6: Unique Narrative Trait

1d100	Type of Effect
01-05	The item's previous owner misplaced it, and is still looking to reclaim it.
06-10	The item was tagged for research by an interested party, putting the new owners in some surveillance crosshairs.
11-15	The item is one-of-a-kind, making it very difficult to repair or replace.
16-20	The item's inventor(s) are not from this parallel, and something makes it stand out as foreign.
21-25	The item has a lot of history behind it – and a lot of formerly dead owners because of it.
26-30	Someone wants to buy the item, and is willing to pay a high price for it.
31-35	There is a well-known piece of historic art in this parallel that shows the item in use.
36-40	There is a name inscribed on the underside of the item belonging to an infamous criminal.
41-45	The item's previous owner believes the item is cursed and wants to protect anyone who crosses its path from harm.
46-50	The item is revered by locals somehow, either by simple-minds as something divine or by the learned that see its potential.
51-55	The item only works because of an unexpected leap in the science behind it, making it a wonderful case study for other researchers.
56-60	There is a secret compartment in the item containing a note covered in a mysterious code.
61-65	The item is linked to an unsolved crime in the current parallel.
66-70	A powerful psionicist has his mind's eye focused upon the item from afar.
71-75	The item was part of a father-to-son inheritance chain that was broken when the Character acquired it.
76-80	The item is discovered smelling heavily of a lady's perfume unlike any the Characters have ever known.
81-85	The item is all that is left of a lost company or civilisation.
86-90	A lot of people have died trying to get their hands on the item, and it has a bad reputation for starting bloody conflicts where they otherwise were not.
91-95	The Disruptors want the item and will do anything to get their hands on it.
96-00	The item was stolen somehow from Zero-Zero's primary storage vaults.

The Standard Equipment does not contain all the possible items that agents could purchase, but gives an extensive start to the commissary supplies, showing how various parallels' technology levels alter the cost of specific things.

The following are the descriptions and some game effects of the items listed in the Standard Equipment Table (page 89).

Standard Equipment Descriptions

Alcohol (Common, Exquisite, Fine): Fermented beers, wines and liquor of various grades can be the perfect escape from the hardships of life as an agent.

Backpack/Satchel: A simple canvas, cloth or leather bag used to carry a person's goods.

Binoculars: Commonly used to magnify distant objects. Binoculars can have a visual zoom by 25, 50 or even 100 times, and more advanced examples may include night vision, HUD displays, and so on.

Clothing (Common, Fine, Luxurious): Whether in need of labourer overalls, workout wear, or even a tuxedo for special occasions, clothing is a necessity.

Communicator (Cellular Phone, Full-Wave, Radio): Personal communication is key for most Valhalla agents, and they come in older radio wavelength apparatuses, more advanced cellular telephone systems, or tiny 'comms' that use higher wavelengths to travel clearer and farther.

Computer (Desktop, Handheld, Laptop, Multi-frame): Ranging from the massive multi-tower computers of the olden days through several versions that get smaller and more powerful with each step, computers can be a great tool for a skilled agent.

Computer, Software: Used with traditional computers to gain access to a specific Professional skill, software programs can allow someone to use a skill despite their lack of training, or train at double speeds on a specific topic.

Crowbar: An ergonomic piece of steel or advanced alloy designed to wedge things open using physical strength, a crowbar makes Brawn rolls one grade easier for the purposes of opening jammed or locked items using brute strength.

Anna Thames' Chronicle

Anna has been hired to transport a mysterious cargo aboard the Headlong Flight, taking it from the air docks in Liverpool to New Carthage, largest city of the American Free Republics. The cargo arrives in a large shipping crate accompanied by the inscrutable Mr Singh, its owner/inventor. Mrs Singh has refused to divulge the nature of the cargo and he is not travelling with it, preferring to ride in the luxurious comforts of the HMS Gloriana, the largest passenger liner in the world.

On the journey across the Atlantic, Anna fends-off an attack by Icelandic Sky Pirates. One of their air grapnels manages to penetrate the cargo bay and the packing of Mr Singh's consigment is damaged. While the airship survives the attack (something the Icelandic Sky Pirates do not), Anna is concerned that the contents are damaged too, and her payment for this expensive voyage will be forfeit. Anna therefore goes to investigate. The packing is in ruins and the machine, a curious device consisting of several opaque globes attached by conduits, cables, gears and clockwork mechanisms, lies on its side. Anna starts wondering what it is and what it does. Her colleague and fellow Valhalla agent, Charles Calthrop, is a bit of a whizz with understanding gizmos and makes some deductions with a critical Engineering roll. The Games Master has to think on her feet and so uses the Random Technology tables, allowing Calthrop's character to make the various rolls while she narrates the results.

Step 1 — Concept. Using the Manufacturing column, Calthrop's roll is 79: *Medical Tool*. This weird thing has some medical application, Calthrop deduces.

Step 2 — Technology Base. Using the Industrial Age column, Calthrop's roll is 05: *Psioncology and Multiversal Theory*. Clearly this device is designed for psychics... (Calthrop winks at Anna, knowingly).

Step 3 — Effect and Efficiency. The Effect roll is 30: *Clairvoyance* and the Efficiency roll is 54: *Average*. "Well, clearly, this thing is designed to allow remote healing," Calthrop announces. With an Efficiency of 54, the device is average in terms of efficiency and can influence 1d8 damage and in a radius of 20 square metres or over 100 linear metres. "I'd hazard that a clairvoyant can amplify their own psychic energy, and tap into the psyhic energy of the subject to accelerate physical healing." The Games Master confirms that the machine, if it works, can be used to amplify a clairvoyant's powers to assist with physical healing, repairing 1d8 damage to Hit Points or Tenacity Points, either to everyone within 20 metres of the apparatus, or at a directed target up to 100 metres distant.

Step 4 — Description. Calthrop's roll on the Psioncology and Multiversal Theory column is 27: *Frail Looking*. "Mind you," Calthrop says, "I'm not so sure the bloody thing isn't completely wrecked; it looks like it's held together with duct tape." And, on closer inspection, it appears duct tape has been used in several areas...

Step 5 — Flaws and Quirks: This time Calthrop rolls 65: *Item has a 1% chance of parallel shifting with the bearer when activated*. The Games Master decides to withhold this information for now. "Hmm," Calthrop says, poking a set of gaffer-taped gears and small globes, "this looks a bit like a thingy I saw on Zero-Zero once."

Step 6 — Unique Narrative Trait. The final roll is 07: *Tagged for research by an interested party, putting any owners in some surveillance crosshairs*. "Quite ingenious really," Calthrop announces. "I can think of half a dozen groups who'd pay handsomely to get their hands on this. I know that the Royal Icelandic Paranormal Engineers commissioned some research into harnessing clairvoyant powers a few years ago, and... I say, Anna, those viking chappies who just attacked us, weren't they from...? Oh, *shit*."

Diving Suit: A plastic suit with clear faceplate and up to 1 hour of oxygen in the attached tank. Additionally, all Swim tests are made at one degree of ease due to the webbed feet and streamlined nature of the suit.

Drugs (Pharmaceutical, Recreational): Chemicals used to impose certain effects upon the user; some medical and some purely for the 'high' of their use.

Environmental Suit: A rubber or reinforced latex suit that adds 1 AP to the wearer as well as grants them a full respirator and protection from airborne substances, gasses or particulate matter.

Geiger Counter: A handheld box that clicks loudly and displays numerical values when within 30m of a source of dangerous radiation.

Goggles (Infrared, Low-Light): Special eyewear that allows the wearer to see images in little to no light. Low-light goggles require some kind of light source to function but still show detail of the view, whereas the IR goggles show gradients of heat and show very little detail despite functioning in the utter absence of light .

Lantern (Battery, Oil): A handheld light source with 30m of well-lit range (twice that in dim conditions) that either run on fuel oil or common power source batteries.

Lock picks: A set of common tumbler-shifting wires and picks that grant a +10% bonus to any skill test used to unlock a physically latched locking mechanism.

Meal (Average, Good, Excellent): Agents have to eat; some agents eat better than others it seems.

Medical Kit (First Aid, Surgical): Used to patch up wounds in a hurry as well as heal longstanding illnesses or bodily harm, these kits are also sometimes called 'doctor's bags.'

Motion Tracker: A handheld device that displays as a series of pings and clicks the nearby location of moving masses larger than a small dog within 30m.

Musical Instrument: Many agents find themselves looking for ways to pass the time between duties, and learning how to play a musical instrument can be quite helpful in the long run.

Standard Equipment Table

Item	ENC	Commisary Price	Steam/ Industrial Age	Electronics/ Computer Age	Nanotech/ Spacefaring Age
Alcohol, Common	-	3 Cr	3 Cr	2 Cr	5 Cr
Alcohol, Exquisite	-	25 Cr	100 Cr	25 Cr	20 Cr
Alcohol, Fine	-	10 Cr	25 Cr	20 Cr	10 Cr
Backpack/Satchel (holds up to 20 ENC)	1	5 Cr	8Cr	5Cr	2Cr
Binoculars	1	10 Cr	15 Cr	10 Cr	5 Cr
Clothing, Common/Fine/Luxurious	1	10/50/100 Cr	10/75/150 Cr	8/60/200 Cr	6/40/100 Cr
Communicator, Cellular Phone	-	15 Cr	100 Cr	30 Cr	30 Cr
Communicator, Full-Wave	-	50 Cr	200 Cr	100 Cr	50 Cr
Communicator, Radio	1	25 Cr	100 Cr	25 Cr	45 Cr
Computer, Desktop	2	50 Cr	N/A	100 Cr	35 Cr
Computer, Handheld	-	250 Cr	N/A	400 Cr	100 Cr
Computer, Laptop	1	100 Cr	N/A	250 Cr	50 Cr
Computer, Multi-frame	20	500 Cr	1,000 Cr	750 Cr	250 Cr
Computer, Software (per program)	-	10 Cr	N/A	50 Cr	10 Cr
Crowbar	1	25 Cr	25 Cr	20 Cr	35 Cr
Diving Suit	5	100 Cr	200 Cr	100 Cr	50 Cr
Drugs, Pharmaceutical (per dose)	-	10 Cr	50 Cr	20 Cr	5 Cr
Drugs, Recreational (per dose)	-	50 Cr	25 Cr	50 Cr	75 Cr
Environmental Suit	4	50 Cr	100 Cr	50 Cr	35 Cr
Geiger Counter	1	10 Cr	50 Cr	10 Cr	10 Cr
Goggles. Infrared/Low Light	1	25 Cr	100 Cr	25 Cr	20 Cr
Lantern, Battery	1	10 Cr	25 Cr	10 Cr	2 Cr
Lantern, Oil	1	5 Cr	5 Cr	4 Cr	8 Cr
Lock picks	-	50 Cr	100 Cr	50 Cr	75 Cr
Meal, Average/Good/Exquisite	1	6/20/50 Cr	4/35/200 Cr	5/20/100 Cr	3/15/40 Cr
Medical Kit, First Aid	2	25 Cr	50 Cr	25 Cr	20 Cr
Medical Kit, Surgical	2	75 Cr	125 Cr	75 Cr	50 Cr
Motion Tracker	1	20 Cr	N/A	25 Cr	20 Cr
Musical Instrument	2	70 Cr	70 Cr	60 Cr	50 Cr
Rope, 10m	2	10 Cr	10 Cr	8 Cr	6 Cr
Shackles	2	10 Cr	10 Cr	5 Cr	10 Cr
Tent (cost per person)	2	15 Cr	10 Cr	15 Cr	20 Cr
Tool Kit, Handyman's (hammer, screwdriver, etc.)	3	20 Cr	75 Cr	20 Cr	25 Cr
Tool Kit, Specific Career (farmer, millright, etc.)	5	40 Cr	100 Cr	40 Cr	50 Cr

Rope: A coil of hemp or nylon rope with many uses; each metre-long section of the rope has an AP of 1 and 2HP (individually, not cumulative).

Shackles: Two locking cuffs linked to less than a metre of stout chain, shackles are used to keep prisoners in line or tethered to a stationary object. Each half-metre section of the shackles has an AP of 6 and 5HP (individually, not cumulative).

Tent: A leather, canvas or nylon collapsible structure that is made in multiple sizes, colours and styles; designed to keep out the weather to a certain extent.

Tool Kit, Handyman's: A toolbox full of basic hand tools and possibly a power tool or two that can be used with the Mechanisms skill in order to make basic repairs or constructions.

Tool Kit, Specific Career: A toolbox that contains the basic needs for a specific Professional skill or sub-skill. When purchased, the Character chooses the skill the tool kit pertains to.

Lifestyle

Valhalla agents are not sent out into the parallels empty handed. They are often equipped with a few select pieces of equipment necessary for the goals at their briefing, or perhaps they receive shipments to their stationed parallel from Zero-Zero. Whatever the case may be, such equipment is nowhere near enough to serve in every instance — there is a lot more to have need for on a day-to-day basis. These additional needs are handled like any normal parallel inhabitant would; through purchasing goods via local channels.

While the Valhalla Project can provide funds for small expenses, agents do have to fend for themselves and most have some form of income, informal, legitimate or not so, from their mundane lives.

Cost of Living

The cost of living depends very much on the standard of lifestyle one wants to pursue. The table below shows base costs, in Crowns, for the various lifestyles levels. The cost of the lifestyle the character wishes to maintain should be deducted from the character's funds each month, representing the expenditure needed to maintain that lifestyle or, at the very least, its illusion. Games Masters can alter the base Cost per Month depending on how extravagantly or frugally the character wishes to live. See the Cost of Living table, below.

Valhalla Agent Stipend

Being an active agent in the Valhalla Project comes with a financial salary based on the merits of their service. At the end of each month of service, the accountants at Zero-Zero calculate what an agent's salary should be. The funds are then sent with dedicated delivery agents to where the agents are currently working or

Cost of Living

Standard of Living	Monthly Cost (in Crowns)	Lifestyle Notes
Squalor	25 Cr.	The Character has nearly nothing in his own name, sleeps in motels or by-the-hour shelters, wears the same clothes several days in a row, and eats nothing but hand-outs and junk food.
Low Class	75 Cr.	The Character has a very small apartment, a few cheap outfits to wear, and can afford takeout twice a week.
Average	100 Cr.	The Character has a large apartment or a small house, a wardrobe of average clothes and possibly one good suit or dress. The Character has access to an affordable car, and keeps a modestly stocked kitchen.
Middle Class	250 Cr.	The Character has a moderately-sized house, a few minor items of luxury, room for a family, and the amenities to keep everyone fed and entertained.
High Class	500 Cr.	The Character has a large home, multiple vehicles, a collection of fine clothing and adornments, and the additional finances to enjoy some of life's finer things.
Affluent	1,000 Cr.	The Character has a large home (possibly two), multiple vehicles, personal affectations that border on luxurious, and possibly servants helping with day-to-day life. The Character has the funds to involve himself in many eccentricities and enjoyable activities.
Insanely Rich	5,000 Cr.	The Character has a mansion, palace or other massive estate. Additionally, the Character wants for nothing. Exquisite food, art, hobbies, and general hedonism are well within their financial abilities, and they are assuredly a noticeable member of the elite society within the parallel.

deposit the funds in a holding account to be used upon returning to headquarters.

The salary amount is based upon their two highest Professional Skills. The ratings of a Character's two highest Professional Skills are added together and compared to the table below. The variable amount on the table is rolled and added to the Character's available funds at the end of each month.

Stipend

Professional Skills	Stipend (Monthly Average)
50 or less	2d6x5 (35)
51-70	2d6x10 (70)
71-90	2d6x15 (105)
91-110	2d6x20 (140)
111-130	2d6x30 (210)
131-150	2d6x50 (350)
151-170	2d6x100 (700)
171-190	2d6x250 (1,750)
191 or more	2d6x500 (3,500)

Firearms & Combat

Combat in Luther Arkwright is inevitable and, depending on the parallel and technology level, may involve everything from duelling swords to advanced energy weapons, and may even include psionic assaults. This chapter provides the rules for combat involving firearms and psionics; the basic rules for Combat are found in Mythras, and for the most part also apply here. There are, though, some considerations and differences that need to be taken into account for combat in Luther Arkwright.

Deadliness

Without superhuman conditioning, it is near impossible to avoid bullets or energy beams that travel faster than human reflexes. Using the Mythras combat rules as written, this means that unless a character tries to dive clear of the area using Evade, any hit will immediately expose the victim to one or more Special Effects. It also changes the Action Point economy; if combatants cannot use Action Points to reactively defend themselves, then most Characters will end up using all their actions to blast away, gambling on the incompetence of their foes.

Therefore both Game Masters and Players need to think carefully about how they view – and approach – gun combat. Some things to note are:

- Gun combat is dangerous!
- On the whole, people prioritise not being shot over shooting others
- The most common method of protection is to take cover
- Suppressing fire is the best way of preventing foes from shooting back
- Firearms are surprisingly inaccurate unless time is taken to brace and/or aim
- When you are shot, the consequences are dire.

Defending against gunfire largely becomes a question of body armour, using cover and trying to prevent the opponent from being able to return fire. As such, most gun battles tend to become very tactical – lots of suppressing fire, flanking movement and flushing foes from deep cover – during which Characters may pass entire combat rounds being pinned down and unable to respond until the opposition stops firing. It is perfectly possible that an entire gunfight will result in no injuries, with just one side giving up due to running out of ammunition or fleeing the battle entirely. After all, few people want to risk being riddled with a burst from a weapon on full-automatic.

The following are addendums to the existing combat rules and mesh seamlessly with them.

New Combat Actions

To reflect the gritty reality of firearms, several new types of proactive Combat Action have been created. Some of these depend on weaponry of a sufficient technological level.

Reload

As per Ready Weapon in the Mythras rules. Reloading times can vary wildly according to the type of weapon. Single shot black powder muskets are far slower to reload than changing an ammunition magazine or power source. Under combat conditions the former might take from 15 to 20 seconds (9-12 Turns) whilst the latter could be as fast as 5 seconds (3 Turns).

Sneak Peek

Sneak Peek allows somebody currently sheltering behind cover to manage a quick glance to assess the tactical situation. The action is ostensibly safe, permitting the observer a single Perception roll before ducking back into cover. If the Perception test is fumbled however, the character foolishly overextends their head or remains in sight long enough for an enemy to take a pot shot.

Steady Weapon

Allows the character to establish a firm firing posture and support an automatic weapon so that it remains stable. It requires that the character be at least partially exposed and not completely protected by cover. The primary benefit is that it reduces the recoil penalty of Burst or Full-Automatic fire by one step. This effect is similar to Brace in that its benefits continue until the character moves.

Switch Fire Mode

Switch Fire allows the user of an automatic or dual-purpose firearm to change the selector on their weapon to take advantage of other fire modes. Thus an assault rifle could be switched from semi-automatic to burst, choose different types of ammunition or a supplementary system such as an integral grenade launcher brought on line. Whilst contemporary weapons require an Action Point on the character's Turn to switch modes, sufficiently advanced high-tech firearms may permit it as a Free Action, triggered by electronic implants or psychically reading the user's mind.

Take Cover

Take Cover is a proactive action which allows a shooter to duck behind available cover in their immediate vicinity, thereby gaining some degree of protection against incoming fire. Unlike Evade it does not leave the user prone, but does rely on some form of cover being available; for example ducking back around a corner in a corridor or crouching down behind a table in a bar.

Depending on circumstances, the available cover may or may not be enough to completely protect the character. The type of cover will also determine its protective qualities. A thick steel door, for instance may prove impenetrable to bullets, whereas a thin wooden wall might only provide 4 Armour Points. For general guidelines concerning the protective qualities of certain materials, see the 'Inanimate Objects Armour and Hit Points' table on page 81 of Mythras.

New Special Effects

These new Special Effects are specifically for the use of firearms.

Circumvent Cover

Offensive, High-Tech Firearms or Certain Conditions Only

Assuming that the shooter is using some form of high-tech weaponry, they can fire around the target's cover. In most cases this will require something similar to self-guided ammunition. If used as a trick shot (for example bouncing a laser blast from a mirror, ricocheting a bullet off a wall, or bending a bullet's trajectory psychically), then the special effect should be treated as a Critical Success only with damage being reduced by one step (1d10 becoming 1d8, for example).

Drop Foe

Offensive, Firearms Only

Assuming the target suffers at least a minor wound from the shot, they are forced to make an Opposed Test of Endurance against the attacker's hit roll. Failure indicates that the target succumbs to shock and pain, becoming incapacitated and unable to continue fighting. Recovery from incapacitation can be performed with a successful First Aid check or using some form of technological, psychic or narcotic booster. Otherwise the temporary incapacitation lasts for a period equal to one hour divided by the Healing Rate of the target.

Duck Back

Offensive, Firearms Only

This special effect allows the shooter to immediately duck back into cover, without needing to wait for their next Turn to use the Take Cover action. The character must be already standing or crouching adjacent to some form of cover to use Duck Back.

Marksman

Offensive, Firearms Only

Permits the shooter to move the Hit Location struck by his shot by one step, to an immediately adjoining body area.

Overpenetration

Offensive, Critical, Firearms Only

If shooting at linearly positioned opponents or into a densely packed group, this special effect allows the shot to travel completely through the first victim to strike a second behind them, assuming that it overcomes the first target's body armour. The second victim however, only suffers half damage due to attenuation or slowing down of the shot. Overpenetration is generally of more use with high-powered weapons that inflict large amounts of

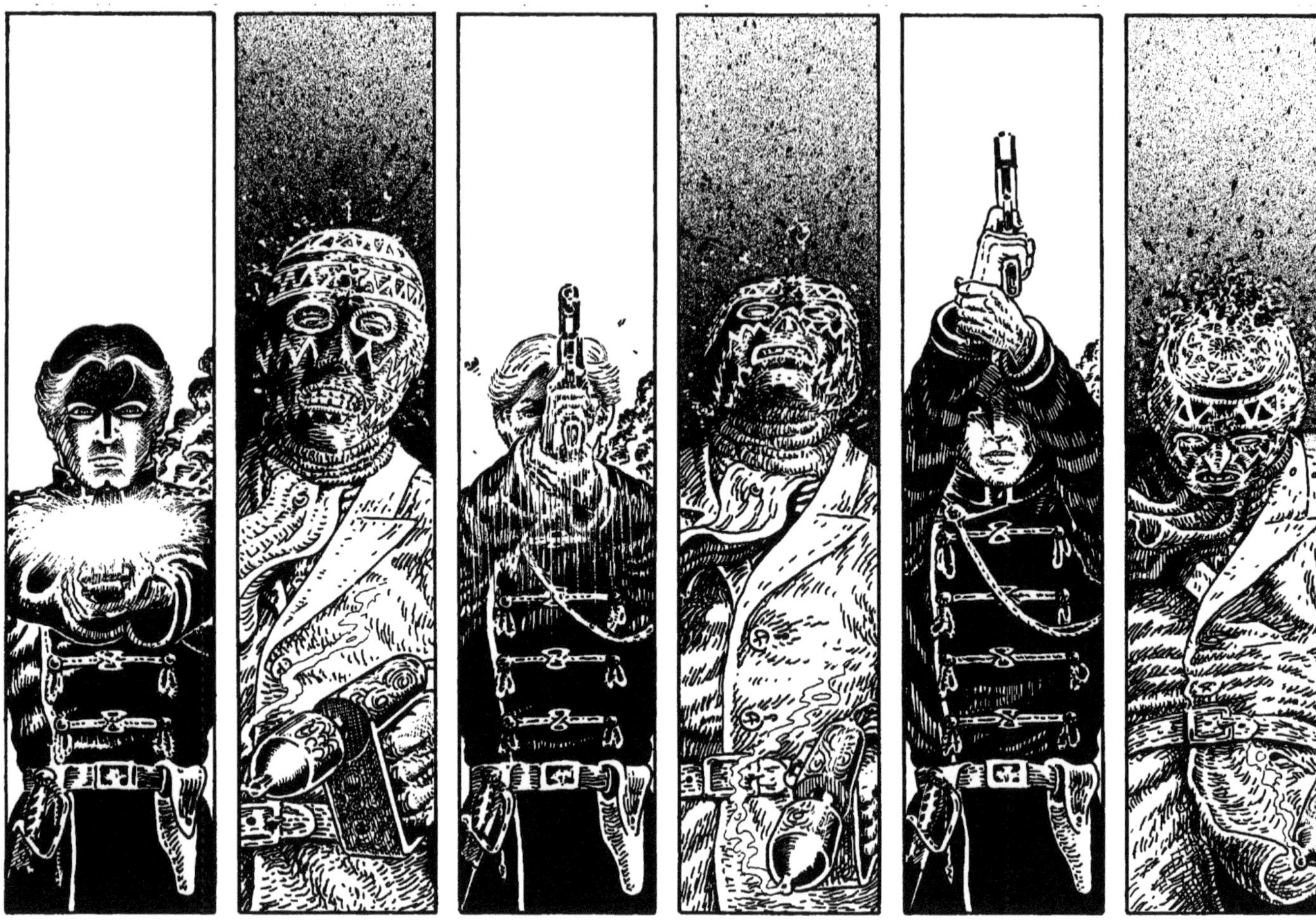

damage or those which have some sort of armour piercing ability. Any special effects inflicted on the first target are not applied to the second.

Pin Down

Offensive, Stackable, Firearms Only

Similar to Press Advantage, this special effect forces the target to make an Opposed Test of their Willpower against the attacker's hit roll. Failure means that the target hunkers down behind whatever cover is available and cannot return fire on their next Turn. Note that Pin Down works even if no actual damage is inflicted on the target (perhaps due to a successful evasion or shots striking their cover instead), as it relies on the intimidation effect of gunfire passing very close by.

Although a pinned victim is unable to fire back for the requisite time, they can perform other actions provided they do not expose themselves to fire in the process, such as crawling away to new cover, communicating with others, reloading a weapon and so on.

Weapon Malfunction

Attacker Fumbles, Firearms Only

The attacker's firearm malfunctions in such a way that it is rendered useless until time can be spent field stripping and cleaning it.

Modified Special Effects

Depending on the type of ammunition or energy projected, some Special Effects from Mythras should be slightly modified and even restricted. It is impossible to cover all types of ranged weaponry as there always be exceptions, but some general guidelines are provided for the most common effects.

Bash

Since Bash relies more on catching an opponent off balance, rather than throwing them backwards by pure force, it is perfectly reasonable for projectile ammunition to cause a target to stagger if it strikes an extremity. Energy weapons are less likely to inflict such an effect unless the physics of the beam result in some sort of surface explosion.

Bleed

Since most firearms produce very narrow wound paths, it is actually more difficult to nick or sever a major blood vessel than it is with a slicing or stabbing weapon. Due to this, Bleed should be a Critical Success only – unless the gun fires shuriken, razor fléchettes, flattened force fields or similar exotic ammunition.

Bypass Armour

Although Bypass Armour can ostensibly be used with any sort of attack, some types of ammunition might either be prevented from accessing this effect (shot gun pellets due to their spread) or built into their base performance, granting it as a bonus special effect in addition to any others gained. Much depends on how the Game Master wishes to model the weapon.

Choose Location

As per the default rules, Choose Location should be restricted to being a Critical Success only, unless the target is within close range and is either stationary or unaware of the impending attack. Telescopic scopes may extend this range (see Spot Rules).

Circumvent Parry

This is obviously of little use unless targets are using firearm resistant shields, or the defender has established some form of psychic shield.

Compel Surrender

Firearms are usually very intimidating weapons. Thus Compel Surrender need not be restricted to only those targets placed at a tactical disadvantage, and can be used at a distance.

Damage Weapon

Since striking a hand-held weapon at range is even more difficult than targeting a specific body location, this should generally be reserved for Critical Successes only. There are several exceptions however, the first being that a shield should be, by its very nature, much easier to hit. The second concerns exotic weapons that fire a cone shaped beam able to target hand-held objects within its area of affect; for instance, an induction gun that heats metal objects.

Disarm Opponent

As per Damage Weapon above. There is nothing quite as satisfying as shooting an enemy's gun right out of their hands.

Entangle

Although usually reserved for thrown weapons such as nets or bolas, entangling firearms are available on some parallels, firing either nets, bolas-like cords or even projecting a web-like resin designed to restrain a target.

Impale

The ammunition of most projectile-based firearms will be able to impale. Game Masters may wish to restrict or ban this effect for plasma or laser based energy weapons. Bullets, fléchettes and similar projectiles are too small to impose any secondary impaling effects.

Kill Silently

Obviously this cannot be selected if the weapon is inherently loud unless it possesses some sort of silencer, but it does still apply to psionic attacks and assaults. In general, any gun that fires ammunition travelling faster than the speed of sound will make significant noise, no matter what method it uses to accelerate the projectile. On the other hand, sniping with a microwave laser will be utterly inaudible.

Maximise Damage

This special effect should be available for any firearm. Remember though, that it only affects a single die.

Pin Weapon

Useful only with specialised firearms such as harpoon guns or tractor beam rifles.

Rapid Reload

Whilst useful for black powder or single round firearms, this special effect has less of an obvious application when applied to automatic weapons, where the next shot is chambered (or charged) instantly. However, Rapid Reload can be used to quickly change weapon magazines. It might also be applicable for energy weapons that possess lengthy cycle times to recharge capacitors or allow the barrel to cool.

Stun Location

Perfect for certain types of projectiles, it is an inherent bonus effect of non-lethal stun-ray weapons, where the damage roll is only used to see if it overcomes any worn protection rather than inflicting a wound.

Sunder

A somewhat unusual choice, Sunder is suitable for energy-based firearms designed to destroy ablative armours — such as that worn by Disruptor Pawns.

Trip Opponent

Assuming the firearm actually shoots ammunition with mass, there is no reason that this effect couldn't be used when shooting at the legs of an opponent, even if no damage penetrates any worn protection.

Spot Rules

The following spot rules are provided to help resolve certain features and situations caused by firearms.

Accuracy

Firearms are still subject to accuracy issues when shooting at a distance. The design of a firearm can also have a significant effect upon its accuracy. For example, due to the short barrel length and less stable firing position, handguns are typically more inaccurate than rifles.

In general use the following modifiers when using the Size and Distance Difficulty Adjustment table:

- Pistols — Increase penalty by 1 step
- Carbines/SMGs — No modifier
- Rifles — Reduce penalty by 1 step
- Sniper Rifles — Reduce penalty by 2 steps

Remember that as an exception to the normal rule, distance penalties stack with other ranged combat situational modifiers.

Automatic Fire

Some firearms automatically chamber the next shot, by using the waste gases, recoil or energy from the previous shot. With no need to recock the weapon, a range of different firing rates is available, all dependent on how much ammunition the user wishes to release.

These firing modes are Semi-Automatic, Burst and Full-Automatic. Although automatic fire can make some guns capable of dealing fearsome damage, trying to maintain accuracy with recoiling weapons is problematic. Assume that the following rules primarily apply to projectile firing automatic weapons.

Semi-Automatic

This is actually the default rate of fire for most guns, where each pull of the trigger fires a single shot and loads the next round.

Burst

Each pull on the trigger releases a limited number of rounds, usually no more than three to five, depending on the weapon. Its original purpose was to permit limited suppression fire, but restrict excessive ammunition use. It is not intended to improve the shooter's chance to hit since rapid, sequential recoil continually jerks the weapon off-line. Firing in burst mode imposes a penalty grade of Hard to the attack roll. If the attack succeeds though, the shooter rolls one die to see how many of the rounds in that burst struck home on the target. So, a three-round burst would use 1d3 and a five-round burst 1d5 (roll 1d10 and divide by 2). Roll separate location and damage for each round that hits.

Full Automatic

Normally used for full-blown suppressing fire to pin down multiple targets, full automatic can be devastating if fired into a closely grouped body of enemies. The shooter decides how many rounds of ammo to fire (up to the limit of the rate of the weapon) that are then evenly distributed across all the targets included in the arc of fire. Any spare rounds are considered lost whilst traversing aim (thus firing 15 rounds at 6 targets would be two bullets each). A separate attack roll is made for each target, but at a difficulty grade of Formidable due to the increased recoil effects of sustained fire. Roll separate location and damage for each target and each round that hits.

Only the first shot that strikes during a burst or full automatic salvo can benefit from Special Effects. Thus rolling a critical attack whilst firing in automatic mode would permit the selection of Maximise Damage, but only with the first shot, even if all the remaining rounds hit home.

Dual Firearms

Characters may use dual firearms, shooting both weapons simultaneously during their Turn to gain a more rapid rate of fire. However, this comes at a penalty to accuracy. Firing a pistol in each hand suffers a penalty of Hard to hit the target. Those trying to concurrently shoot with a carbine or SMG in each hand suffer a penalty of Formidable.

Fumbling with Firearms

Since gunfire is not normally resisted by defensive actions, a special provision should be made for when a shooter fumbles their attack roll. In this case, the intended target is allowed to select a fumble specific Special Effect, which the shooter then suffers. See also the fumble only special effect Weapon Malfunction on page 95.

Parrying Weapon Fire with Shields

As expressed earlier, it is almost impossible to deliberately parry a supersonic projectile or energy beam. Shields though, can still provide a degree of protection since they offer portable cover.

To use a shield in a fire-fight, the Passive Blocking rules on page 105 of MYTHRAS.

Game Masters may grant the shield an Armour Point value, if they wish, rather than assigning it a Size, based upon its construction material. For example, a wooden shield might be treated as 4 Armour Points, a Kevlar tactical shield 8 AP, and a Disruptor force field shield 15 AP.

Telescopic Sights

A telescopic sight improves the accuracy of a firearm over greater distances when the user takes the time to aim properly (see Accuracy on page 97). The most basic telescopic sights are simple optical magnifiers. As technology advances various advantages are introduced, such as integral rangefinders, projectile trajectory calculators, air movement sensors, atmospheric lensing compensators, IR or low light amplifiers and a host of other gadgets which improve the weapon's effective 'hit' distance.

Telescopic sights increase Close Range by a multiple according to the power of the scope. They also reduce the apparent distance (on the Size and Distance Difficulty Adjustment table) by a number of distance steps equal to the multiplier. For example a 12x scope will extend Close Range to twelve times its base distance, whilst additionally reducing the apparent distance by 12 steps, or 240m (12 x 20m) before penalties are calculated.

Creating Firearms

Given the vast capacity for technological development and variation across the parallels, it is impossible to account for every type of conceivable firearm available to Characters in Luther Arkwright. This section is therefore designed to help Games Masters design their own firearms, for situations where the firearms listed in pages 104 to 106 fail to meet a parallel's specific needs.

Purpose

The first thing to consider is what the weapon is designed to be used against. For instance, an elephant gun has ammunition calculated to take down charging big game, and thus inflicts more damage than a normal hunting rifle intended for smaller targets such as deer.

The type of damage is important too. A Rocket Propelled Grenade is manufactured to be used against armoured vehicles such as tanks. Whilst it can inflict terrible injuries, its real purpose is to destroy vehicle armour, often with the intent to follow up with a second shot to the same location which then penetrates the vehicle with greater ease (see the Ablating trait below). Therefore the base damage dice for an RPG need not be that large, allowing anyone caught in its blast radius a better chance of survival.

Other types of damage exist. Stunning or paralysis allows the creation of non-lethal weapons. Vibrobeamers rely on concentrated and directed sound waves to shatter bones and disrupt soft, internal tissue, rather than cause damage through the dispersal of kinetic energy. Disintegration, on the other hand, might inflict permanent damage on Hit Locations making it very frightening if no method of regeneration exists.

Damage

It is quite possible to be shot by small or medium calibre handgun rounds and still remain functional. At the upper end of the scale, rifle rounds can inflict terrible damage, incapacitating the victim, but still not necessarily kill them outright. Much depends on the ammunition, but the objective is generally to wound, not completely annihilate the target.

Small firearms designed for use against humans should be scaled at around 1d6 damage, able to inflict Light Wounds with a reasonable chance of a Serious Wound. Use the following calibre chart as a general guide:

Top-tier weapons designed for use against humans should not inflict any more than 20 damage maximum, but averaging just over half that, enough to regularly inflict Major Wounds. A top of the line M24 or Dragunov sniper rifle might be rated at 2d8+4 damage for instance.

Anything larger is just wasted ammunition mass or shot energy, and works against player character survivability when facing equally well-armed foes.

Projectile or Energy

The type of projectile or energy shot from a weapon will have consequences on how it works. For example, a visible Laser may be able to pass through bullet-proof glass, bounce off mirrors, and yet be utterly useless in fog or rain.

Whilst energy weapons are pretty much fixed as to their effects, projectile weapons can be quite versatile according to the ammunition type. In fact, the type and amount of damage caused depends more on the bullet, rather than the gun firing it. The latter having more influence over firing modes, range, accuracy and such like.

Ammunition Capacity

Whether a firearm shoots physical projectiles or energy beams, it will have a limited number of shots before the magazine or power source is exhausted. This is important, not because of any real world or hard science considerations, but without changing clips or recharging on a regular basis, a firefight will simply be won by whoever establishes suppressing fire first and then walks down his cowering foes.

Contemporary projectile weapons currently have magazines of about 10-30 rounds, which should be sufficient capacity to enable a decent amount of shooting until needing to change the clip. Heavier support weapons which have a much higher rate of fire, should possess larger magazines.

Overcoming Armour

Certain firearms or ammunition types, be they bullets, beams or blasts, should reduce or bypass a certain number of Armour Points according to their penetrative nature. This permits the base damage of the weapon to remain within survivable limits. Some weapons may be completely unaffected by armour entirely, like electromagnetic weapons of higher or lower frequencies; or weapons which inflict other effects, such as brain scramblers that induce unconsciousness.

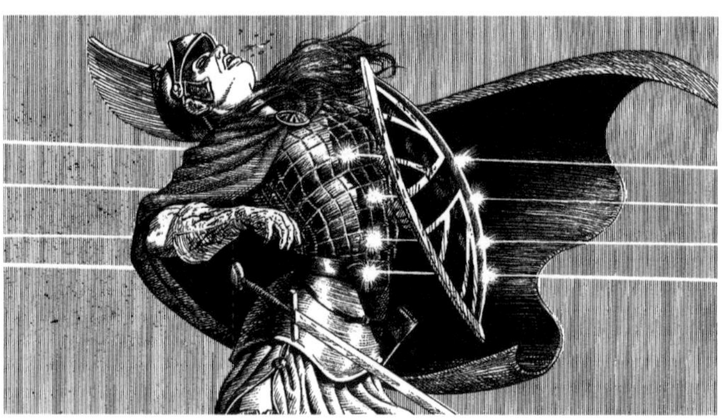

More exotic weaponry should always have some form of counter or protection available to thwart its effects. In a parallel where advanced energy weapons are available, for example, defending against an X-Ray Laser might require 1-cm thick lead-lined armour to halve its effects, or conversely 150m of air, meaning that X-Ray rifles are going to be rather poor as long range sniper weapons.

Calibre	Damage	Damage Range (Av. Damage)	Example
.22	1d4+1	2-5 (3)	Derringer
.38	1d6	1-6 (4)	Webley Service Revolver
.357 Magnum	1d8+1	2-9 (6)	Colt Python
.45/7.65 Parabellum	1d8	1-8 (5)	Browning 9mm, Luger
.44 Magnum	1d10+1	2-11 (7)	Smith & Wesson Model 29
.50	1d12	1-12 (7)	Desert Eagle

New Weapon Traits

The following list gives some new Firearm specific weapon traits. Further traits can be designed for more exotic weaponry.

Ablating

Designed to directly attack the protective armour of an object or person. Damage is done to Armour Points first. Once the armour has been reduced to zero, any remaining damage continues through to the target. Most HE (High Explosive) ammunition fits this trait.

Armour Piercing

Ignores a specific number of Armour Points equal to half the maximum damage capability of the firing weapon.

Cauterising

The bolt or beam immediately seals off any ruptured blood vessels, preventing targets from bleeding out in the event of a Major Wound. However, cauterised wounds, unless treated with the Healing skill within 1d6 days, can become infected if the victim fails a Hard Endurance roll. The infection takes the form of a poison with the following attributes (see MYTHRAS page 74):

Application: Infection
Potency: 70
Resistance: Endurance
Onset time: 1d6 days
Duration: 1 week + 1d3 days
Conditions: Exhaustion at the end of the Onset time, followed by Fever within 1d3 days, and then Maiming within 1 week
Antidote/Cure: Can be treated by the Healing skill up until the onset of Fever, at which point the infection must be treated with antibiotics in a hospital environment.

Disintegrating

Inflicts permanent Hit Point damage to the target, vaporising the area struck.

Fragmentation
The projectile violently explodes, affecting everything within its burst. The radius of this effect should be listed in parenthesis. Targets within the radius of the blast receive half damage to 1d3-1 Hit Locations (roll for each wound). Some explosive rounds (HEAP) also possess the Armour Piercing trait, so that they detonate inside an armoured object. Those that do not fully penetrate have their explosive damage reduced by double the remaining thickness of Armour Points.

Frangible
A projectile designed to disintegrate when striking a surface harder than itself. These are mainly used in fragile or dangerous environments, such as the inside of an airship or a fusion power plant, where a stray hit on equipment can have potentially catastrophic effects. They are generally ineffective against body armour.

Hollow Point
The projectile flattens inside the target, increasing the amount of damage inflicted. Roll damage twice and take the best result.

Incendiary
Designed to ignite whatever the projectile or beam hits. If the target is naturally flammable, it bursts into flame according to the Fire rules (MYTHRAS page 79). Treat as an Intensity 3 heat source for the purposes of starting a fire.

Knockout: Similar to the Paralysis trait, this energy weapon does not inflict damage, but renders the victim unconscious if the target fails in an opposed roll of Willpower against the attack roll.

Mounted
Weapons with this trait are too heavy, bulky or balanced to be utilised on a personal level. The weapon must be either mounted to a tripod, construction hard point, or upon a vehicle. Trying to fire the weapon without proper stabilisation is always a Herculean skill attempt.

Paralysing
The Hit Location struck by the energy weapon does not take any physical damage, but is instead rendered incapacitated if the target fails in an opposed roll of Endurance against the attack roll.

Scatter
The weapon or round is made of tiny shot, fléchettes or pellets which spread before they strike, reducing any range penalties by one step and inflicting damage to 1d3 adjacent Hit Locations. This comes at a cost, however. First the weapon damage roll for each location is halved; secondly any armour, natural or worn, doubles its Armour Point value against the damage.

Self-Guided
Permits the selection of the Circumvent Cover special effect.

Tracking
The munitions in this weapon have internal target-tracking mechanisms. The attacks from this weapon ignore the negative combat modifiers as a result of targeting a vehicular target moving at Moderate Speed or higher.

Tranquilising
Permits the delivery of a narcotic or medicine, either by injection from a tiny ampoule built into the projectile, or by the projectile itself dissolving directly into the bloodstream. Depending on its nature, damage might only be rolled to see if it overcomes any protection worn by the target.

Weakness
Usually applied to energy bolts or beams, the weapon suffers significant degradation to some form of environmental condition or material substance. The specific weakness is normally specified as a footnote or as part of the weapon's detailed description.

Example Weapons
This section provides a range of different example firearms, which can be used as a template to model additional weapons. Most are intended for use against humans or modest-sized animals, and

little effort is made to differentiate between specific firearms other than its form and calibre.

The weapon statistics on page 104 to 106 are merely rough approximations, representing an average weapon of that calibre and barrel length. Specific weapons may have different performance characteristics. Game Masters with a deeper interest in firearms are free to tinker with these values to represent their favoured iconic weapons.

In consideration of the nature of firearms, some of the normal statistics for ranged weapons in Mythras have been removed; such as Force, Armour Points, Hit Points. Cost has also been omitted because there are huge variations across parallels.

Other aspects have been modified somewhat. Firing Rate is now either a solitary number for single action and semi-automatic weapons, or three numbers separated by slashes, representing the rate of fire for semi-automatic, burst and automatic fire, in that order. The latter being the maximum rate of fire which can be released per Combat Action.

Likewise, reloading (depending on the weapon) assumes an easily to hand, preloaded magazine which can quickly be snapped into place by ejecting and dropping the previous one. If a spare clip or speedloader is not available, then a single bullet can be loaded per Turn.

Black Powder Weapons

Black powder is a mixture of sulphur, potassium nitrate, and powdered charcoal — 'gun powder'. The flintlock is the most recognisable black powder firearm. Flintlocks work by striking a sharpened piece of flint against a curved, hard steel *frizzen*, which is attached to a pivot; the impact of the hammer pushes the frizzen forward, and its bottom acts as a cover for a small priming pan. The sparks generated fall into the pan and ignite a small priming charge. The resulting flash travels through a touch-hole bored into the barrel to ignite the main charge.

These weapons require more maintenance than their modern counterparts. Loading any black powder firearm requires ammunition, which may come in the form of a 'cartridge' (containing a ball and the requisite amount of powder, wrapped in paper), or simply the ball and wadding without pre-measured powder; a flask of powder for pouring and priming; and a rod to ram the charge securely into the weapon's muzzle. As black powder weapons are muzzle-loading, it takes time to prepare each round.

Contemporary Weapons

Most modern firearms lack any inherent traits, but defer their effects to their ammunition. By default, standard bullets possess none, merely inflicting the weapon's basic damage. Special ammunition, however, can be purchased for most modern weapons, permitting rounds with either the Armour Piercing, Frangible, Hollow Point or Incendiary traits.

Combat Shotguns possess a versatile range of different ammunition. Other than a plain slug, shotguns may fire the following types of round: Anti-personnel grenades (Fragmentation with 2m radius), Baton rounds (Stun Location, temporary damage), Breaching rounds (Frangible), and Buckshot (Scatter).

Energy Weapons

Some parallels have achieved staggering advancements in weapon technology while others have remained relatively backward. Zero-Zero for instance, experienced many scientific breakthroughs while other parallels were still embracing steam power and the advent of the electric light. Advanced energy weapons can therefore exhibit many exotic traits and natures. These traits vary from the predictable to the more versatile.

Typical energy weapons emit a beam or bolt of energy rather than a physical projectile. The power source is usually a battery or power pack held within the weapon or carried separately and attached to the weapon via a cable. External power packs provide a far greater capacity. Laser weapons are silent, projecting a lased beam of light in a continuous stream. Blasters fire a pulse of plasma accompanied by a distinct crackle or sound as the bolt leaves the weapon's muzzle. The load rating for energy weapons represents replacing a spent power source. The Ammo rating dictates how many shots can be obtained from the power source before it is depleted. For simplicity, Ammo ratings assume the weapon carries a battery or power pack. For a separate, external source, increase the Ammo rating by ten.

Exotic Weapons

Exotic firearms are ballistic, rather than energy-based, but have a wide variety of different traits to distinguish them from Contemporary Firearms. They represent advancements in ballistics technology, sometimes as a result of unconventional thinking and research, and the availability of suitable materials.

Heavy Weapons

In parallels where combat between vehicles or fortifications is more common, heavy weaponry is used to maximise damage against fortified targets. Disruptors often use heavily armoured soldiers and vehicles in their violent actions, or hold up in secret bunkers behind thick walls of armour. When Valhalla Project agents are sent in to deal with these situations, it takes a special kind of weapon.

Collectively called heavy weapons, these firearms unleash payloads capable of punching through several centimetres of protective materials, levelling everything beyond, or atomising a single target. They are a family of weapons that cross over technological lines, falling into this category specifically if their munitions – whatever they might be – are designed to penetrate a large target and obliterate it. Rockets, plasma packets, and anti-armour tumbler rounds are good examples of what heavy weapons use to bring large targets down.

Most heavy weapon systems are designed to be mounted in some form: to turrets carried by vehicles, or as part of a vehicle's structure. The Vehicles chapter beginning on page 108 deals with such heavy weapon systems in a little more detail, and statistics for example heavy weapons can be found on page 117.

Access to Weapons

Valhalla agents can usually gain access to weapons appropriate to the local parallel through contacts and permanent field officers. The protocol is for agents to avoid using weapons that would be alien to the local parallel; thus, if a parallel has not yet developed (or never will develop) vibro beam technology, a vibro beamer pistol would not be issued and its use *heavily* discouraged if an agent brought in the sidearm from another parallel.

Sometimes agents do need specialised weapons that might ordinarily be frowned upon and, where this is the case, Valhalla Central on Zero-Zero issues such weaponry from its own stores. Agents though, are never in a position to *demand* weapons of a particular kind. A top Valhalla agent might feel most comfortable carrying a Smith and Wesson .44 magnum, but if a parallel has yet to progress beyond the use of muskets, he will be denied the request — or will have to provide an extremely good explanation (usually a Formidable Influence roll) as to why he should be allowed to carry a handgun that can blow an unlucky punk's head clean off.

Armour

Traditional armour is insufficient to stop projectiles fired at close range, and although heavy armour made of plate steel can withstand the impact of a rifle bullet, it is simply too heavy to be of any use save for static personnel.

In parallels contemporaneous with our own, ballistic vests have been developed that afford some protection against firearms. Protecting the chest and abdomen, ballistic vests absorb the impact from projectiles and shrapnel explosions. These vests are made from multiple layers of woven or laminated fibres and are capable of protecting the wearer from small-calibre handgun and shotgun projectiles, and small fragments from explosives such as hand grenades. Metal or ceramic plates can also be incorporated into a ballistic vest, providing additional protection from rifle rounds, and metallic components or tightly-woven fibre layers can give soft armour resistance to stab and slash attacks from knives and similar close-quarter weapons.

Parallels exhibiting significant scientific advancement, such as Zero-Zero and core Disruptor parallels have developed much more sophisticated armour types. Disruptor Pawns wear armour

that is both impact reactive and ablative, offering superior protection against both ballistic and energy weapons. The armour of a Disruptor Pawn is fashioned from graphene integrated with nanotechnology sensors and adapters making it impervious to some high-calibre projectiles and energy weapons. Other parallels have successfully developed personal force field technology that can absorb kinetic and lased energy with ultra-high efficiency, meaning that force fields can be made portable and leave the user invulnerable to most forms of ranged, high-velocity attack. However, personal force fields are energy intensive and require regular recharging. They are also uni-directional, meaning that the user must direct the force field like a physical shield and thus remains vulnerable to strikes from unprotected directions.

All the armour types in the table on page 107 are effective against blades (swords and knives) and ballistic attacks. Disruptor Armour and Force Fields are effective against energy weapons too.

Of course the armour types found in the MYTHRAS rules may also be used for parallels where archaic armour types are still in use or fashionable; and some items of contemporary clothing offer a small amount of protection against blades. A leather jacket, such as a biker's jacket, or Arkwright's own fleece-lined flying jacket (pictured opposite) offers 2 Armour Points with 1 point of ENC, and covers the arms and chest.

Psionics in Combat

Psionic combat, whether between a psychic and non-psychics, or between multiple psychics, operates much in the same way as standard combat. If one considers psionic powers to be a replacement for magic, the following Combat Actions are available:

Activate Psionic Power

This operates in the same way as Cast Magic (MYTHRAS page 91).

Hold Psionic Power

This operates in a similar way to Hold Magic. Once activated, the character can hold a power in temporary check (unless the power has the Instantaneous trait, meaning it takes effect immediately), awaiting the best moment to release it. The power may be held back for as long as the character continues to take this action on his subsequent turns, but allows free use of the Counter Power reaction if pertinent to the held power.

Counter Power

The character can attempt to dismiss or counter an incoming power. This assumes the countering power has a casting time of one Turn, or was prepared in advance and temporarily withheld using the Hold Power action. Successfully intercepting psionic powers in this manner is assumed to negate the entire power, even those with multiple targets or areas of effect.

Most offensive powers can be defended against or resisted with an appropriate skill (Endurance, Evade or Willpower) as listed in it's description. Powers do not impart Special Effects simply because the power itself is of a special nature. If a power is a form of attack, its description will specify if and how armour protects against it.

Firearms Tables

Black Powder Weapon	Damage	Range	Firing Rate	Ammo	Load	Weapon Traits	ENC
Muff Pistol	1d6	5/10/25	1	Single Shot	4 Rounds		-
Flintlock Pistol	1d8	10/20/50	1	Single Shot	4 Rounds		1
Flintlock Pistol, Twin Barrel	1d8	10/20/50	1	2	6 Rounds		2
Flintlock Musket	1d10	15/100/200	1	Single Shot	4 Rounds		3
Flintlock Rifle	2d6	20/200/500	1	Single Shot	4 Rounds		3
Blunderbuss	2d6	5/10/25	1	Single Shot	4 Rounds	Scatter	2

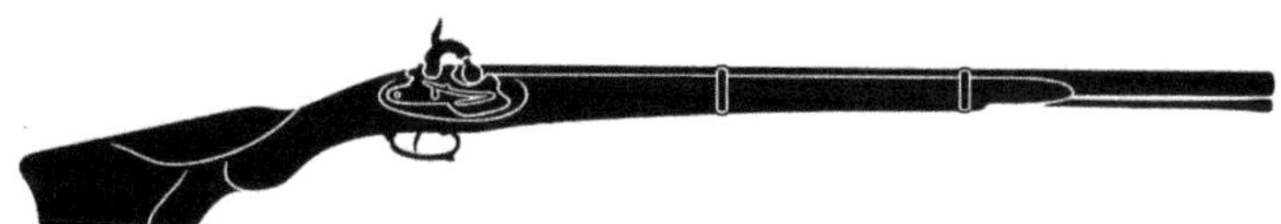

Contemporary Weapon	Damage	Range	Firing Rate	Ammo	Load	Weapon Traits	ENC
.38 Pistol	1d6	50/100/200	1	6-9	3	-	1
9mm Pistol	1d6+1	50/100/200	1	6-9	3	-	1
.45 Pistol	1d8	50/100/200	1	6-9	3	-	1
.357 Pistol	1d8+1	50/100/200	1	6-9	3	-	1
10mm Pistol	1d10	50/100/200	1	6-9	3	-	1
.50 Pistol	1d12	50/100/200	1	6 Box Mag	3	-	2
5.56mm Assault Carbine	2d6-1	500/900/2000	1/3/-	30 Box Mag	3	-	3
5.56mm Assault Rifle	2d6+1	600/1000/3000	1/3/20	30 Box Mag	3	-	3
5.56mm Light Machine Gun	2d6	600/1000/3000	-/-/20	200 Belt	6	-	4
7.62mm Medium Machine Gun	2d8+2	800/1500/4000	-/-/22	50 Drum or 200 Belt	3 Drum, 6 Belt	-	5
7.62mm Sniper Rifle	2d8+4	900/1500/5000	1/-/-	20 Box Mag	3	-	4
.50 Anti-Material Sniper Rifle	2d10+4	1000/2000/6500	1/-/-	10 Box Mag	3	-	6
12 Gauge Combat Shotgun	3d6	20/100/200	1/-/8	8 Box Mag or 32 Drum	3	-	3

Above: Armstrong Siddeley "Royal Albert" Vibro Beamer, found on several Victorian Renaissance Parallels.

Firearms Tables

Energy Weapons	Damage	Range	Firing Rate	Ammo	Load	Weapon Traits	ENC
Blaster Pistol	1d8	10/30/120	1	100	3	Cauterising	1
Blaster Pistol, Heavy*	1d10	7/25/50	1	50	3	Cauterising	1
Blaster Carbine*	2d6	15/50/220	1	50	3	Cauterising, Knockout	2
Blaster Rifle	2d6	30/100/300	1	100	3	Cauterising, Knockout	3
Light Repeating Blaster	2d6	30/100/300	3 shot burst or full auto (up to 25 shots)	25 (250 if connected to backpack generator)	15	Cauterising	7
Disintegrator, Pistol	1d10	8/24/100	1	15	3	Disintegrating	2
Disintergrator, Rifle	2d10	25/75/300	1	10	3	Disintegrating	4
Laser Pistol**	1d6+1	12/36/144	1	50	3	Cauterising, Incendiary, Weakness	1
Laser Carbine**	1d8+2	18/60/300	1	30	3	Cauterising, Incendiary, Weakness	2
Laser Rifle**	1d10+2	40/120/380	1	80 (800 if connected to a backpack generator)	3	Cauterising, Incendiary, Weakness	3
Stun Rifle**	Special	Special	1	20	3	Paralysing**	4
Vibro Beamer****	1d8	10/20/80	1	50	3	Armour Piercing (4), Knockout, Paralysing	

**Blasters are the standard weapon of Disruptor Rooks. Every Pawn Shock Trooper is armed with a Heavy Blaster Pistol and a Blaster Carbine.*

***Lasers can be affected by defensive materials that diffuse, defract or reflect light, such as anti-laser aerosol particles, mist, and mirrors. All and similar will help reduce or even block a visible-light laser. Games Masters should decide on the effectiveness of deterrent and reduce the laser's damage by an appropriate percentage.*

****Stun Rifles produce an energy bubble within a 20-metre arc directly in front of the firer. Do not roll for Hit Location. Victims must succeed in a Hard Endurance roll (unopposed) or be incapacitated until the weapon is deactivated.*

*****Vibro Beamers are close-quarters assault handguns that direct ultra-high-intensity sonic pulses at the target. The sonic pulse ignores up to 4 points of physical armour but cannot penetrate force fields. The weapon can be set to either stun the target (Knockout), paralyse or inflict damage by shattering hard tissue, such as bone and cartilage, and violently shaking soft tissue, causing blood vessels to rupture and nerve endings to shred. In some parallels vibro-beamers are only available in paralysis and/or knockout modes with no capability of inflicting greater damage.*

Firearms Tables

Exotic Weapons	Damage	Range	Firing Rate	Ammo	Load	Weapon Traits	ENC
Fléchette/Needle Gun	1d6	5/15/90	1	80	2	Scatter, Tranquilising	1
Gauss Pistol*	1d12+1	40/80/150	1	12	3	Hollow Point	2
Gauss Rifle*	2d12+2	80/160/300	1/3/-	30	3	Armour Piercing, Hollow Point	4
Snub Pistol	1d6	5/15/90	1	20	2	Frangible	1
Snub Rifle	1d8	10/30/180	1/3/-	50 Drum	3	Frangible	3
Flamer, Hand	1d8	3/10/40	1	8	4	Incendiary	2
Flamer Rifle	2d8	12/36/150	1	20	4	Incendiary	4
Frag Pistol	1d6	10/30/120	1	18	3	Fragmentation	2
Frag Rifle	1d10	15/50/220	1	50	3	Fragmentation	4
Multi-Purpose Pistol**	Special	50/100/200	1	15	3	Variable	2
Multi-Purpose Rifle**	Special	100/400/1200	1/3/-	50 Box	3	Variable	4

** Gauss weapons include an electromagnetic array along the length of the barrel that increases bullet velocity substantially and means that a lower calibre of round can be used to impart significant damage. All Gauss weapons have a power supply in the form of a internal battery that must be replaced after every 50 shots.*

*** Multi-Purpose Weapons use sophisticated computer and ballistics manipulation technology to change the type of the ammunition being fired at the flick of a manual switch (some advanced variants are voice-activated). These weapons can select one of the following Traits to augment their standard ammunition: Armour Piercing, Hollow-Point, Incendiary and Self-Guided. Changing the selection uses the Switch Fire Mode Combat Action.*

Heavy Weapons	Damage	Range	Firing Rate	Ammo	Load	Weapon Traits	ENC
Anti-Armour Rifle	3d10+6	800/1200/2000	1	3 Box Mag	5	Armour Piercing, Mounted	8
Bazooka	5d8+5	200/600/1000	1	Single Shot	4	-	7
Energic Packet Hurler	5d10+10	300/500/1200	1	5 Box Mag	6	Cauterising, Mounted	8
Mini-Missile Pod	10d6	1500/2000/3000	1/3/-	6 Box Mag	8	Mounted, Tracking	7
Plasma Projection Launcher	6d10+12	400/700/1000	1	10 Battery	5	Cauterising, Incendiary	10
Rocket Launcher	4d10+10	500/800/1500	1	2 Box Mag	4	-	9
Tesla Arc Generator	2d6x5	50/75/120	1	25 Battery	10	Ablating, Knockout	10

Armour

Armour	AP	ENC	Locations	Notes
Leather Jacket	2	1	Arms, Chest	What every stylish field agent is wearing in 1981...
Ballistic Vest	4	2	Chest	
Advanced Ballistic Vest	5	3	Chest & Abdomen	Similar to the Ballistic Vest but includes ceramic plates for additional protection.
Advanced Combat Armour	6	4	Full Suit (ENC = 28) including helmet	Battlefield-grade combat armour, highly restricted in availability.
Disruptor Rook Armour	6	3	Full Suit (ENC = 28) including helmet	Helmet contains a respirator, Image Amplification and IR/Low Light imaging. The armour is EMP shielded and includes Psyhic Disruption Circuitry creating the equivalent of an Intensity 2 Mental Shield (see page 61).
Personal Force Field	5	NA	Protects up to 4 locations and is directed in the same way as a shield.	Provides protection for up to 10 minutes before the power cell must be recharged

The Thompson MkII Spitfire Napalm Gun — A typical Disruptor Hand Flamer weapon.

Vehicles

Vehicles in *Luther Arkwright: Roleplaying Across the Parallels* are treated in a semi-abstract fashion. Essentially they are background tools, used to get Characters from A to B, with little need for detailed description or statistics save for the Games Master to note that the agents are now boarding the Hindenburg VI, an airship the size of the Empire State Building, or that the Porsche 961 of parallel 01.17.99 is the fastest steam-clock car in production. On occasion though, Games Masters will require statistics for vehicles when it is necessary to represent them in chases or combat situations.

The rules in this section allow for the representation of most kinds of vehicles, but in an abstracted way that is intended to permit flexibility and enhance storytelling. Starships and space craft are a little different, although they are based on similar principles.

Statistics

All vehicles are described in terms of their Structure, Hull, Speed, Systems and Shields (if present on the parallel).

- Size: All vehicles have one of five Size ratings which determines the value or range of the rest of the characteristics. Due to their larger intrinsic size and the hostile environments of space, starships have their own range of values.
- Hull: Represents Armour Points
- Structure: Represents a vehicle's Hit Points
- Speed: Every vehicle has a basic Speed rating
- Systems: Representing vital components of the vehicle, including the power plant, crew section, and so on.
- Traits: A vehicle may also have 1 or more Traits. Traits, like the Abilities assigned to Creatures in the Mythras rules, or Combat Style Traits, offer an additional game description and advantage, reflecting the vehicle's nature.
- Shields: On parallels with advanced energy manipulation technology, shields may be present that protect the vehicle, but which may ablate under sustained fire.

Hull and Structure

The size and purpose of a vehicle affects the thickness of its hull and resilience of its internal structure. A motorcycle, for example, has a minimal hull, built as it is for speed and agility. A Land Ironclad (a massive, tracked or wheeled armoured behemoth, powered by steam or diesel engines), being a much larger vehicle designed for the battlefield, has a much larger hull.

Whenever a vehicle suffers harm, the incoming damage is reduced by its Hull value. Any remaining damage is subtracted from the vehicle's Structure points and has a percentage chance (equal to the penetrating damage) of affecting a System.

Terrestrial Hulls

Vehicle Size	Civilian Hull Range	Military Hull Range	Structure Range	Example
Small	1-3	4-6	1-20	Motorcycle, Motorcycle and Armoured Sidecar
Medium	1-6	7-9	21-40	Sedan motorcar, Hansom Cab, Steam Stage Coach, Speedboat
Large	4-9	10-12	41-60	Lorry/Truck, Single-Seat Aircraft, Pleasure Cruiser, Tank, Helicopter
Huge	7-12	13-15	61-80	Land Ironclad, Yacht, Airliner
Enormous	10-15	16-18	81-100	Land Leviathan, Dirigible/Airship, Cruise Liner

Starship Hulls

Vehicle Size	Civilian Hull Range	Military Hull Range	Structure Range	Example
Small	4-9	10-12	10-50	Single-Seat Fighter
Medium	7-12	13-15	51-150	Light Freighter, Shuttle Craft
Large	10-15	16-18	151-450	Heavy Freighter, Cruiser
Huge	13-18	19-21	451-1350	Escort Frigate, Light Battle Cruiser
Enormous	16-21	21-24	1351-4050	Generation Ship, Disruptor Heavy Battle Cruiser
Colossal	19-24	24-30	4050-12,110	Orbital Habitat, Battle Station

If the vehicle is ever reduced to zero Structure it is either utterly destroyed, or so badly wrecked it must be scrapped.

Speed

Since the physics of velocity, acceleration, drag and inertia (to name but a few) are complex issues, some simplification is needed and so vehicles are given an abstract speed rating. The Speed characteristic should only be used to see if one vehicle can overtake another; or if in a race to reach an objective, which vehicle will arrive first.

The speed rating represents a vehicle's nominal operational rate. In emergency situations this performance can be increased by one step, at risk of wear or damage to the engines. Although the same table is used for all vehicle types, common sense should be applied so that only vehicles of the same class are compared. For example if a Starship and a sports car both have the same acceleration rate of Rapid, then it should be obvious the spaceship is comparatively faster.

Increasing a vehicle's Speed beyond its standard value is possible on a successful Drive roll. Usually this extra speed is only sustainable for a short period – no more than 1d6 minutes before the vehicle must drop to its standard speed or risk damage to its powerplant. A critical Drive roll allows the period of higher speed to be increased to 1d12 minutes.

A driver can attempt to push a vehicle's speed by 2 steps, but this requires a Herculean Drive roll and the maximum the vehicle can sustain this speed is 1d3 minutes: a critical success will not extend the increased speed's duration.

Speed Rating	Notes
Ponderous	Fastest speed for Enormous vehicles
Sluggish	
Slow	Fastest speed for Huge vehicles
Mediocre	
Gentle	Fastest speed for Large vehicles
Moderate	
Rapid	Fastest speed for Medium vehicles
Fast	
Fleet	Fastest speed for Small vehicles

Systems

Every time a vehicle suffers damage that penetrates its hull, there is a chance that a vital System has been affected. Depending on which system has been hit, the effects of System damage can be catastrophic.

The damage a System can sustain is based purely on the vehicle's size. This is modelled by the number of times it is hit, rather than the actual amount of damage. A single hit on a Small vehicle will instantly destroy that System. It takes two hits to demolish a Medium sized vehicle's Subsystem, three for a Large vehicle, and so on.

Systems that are damaged, but not yet destroyed, suffer a loss in functionality. This is equal to the proportion of current hits to its total capability. Thus an Enormous vehicle hit twice in the Drive would lose 40% of its power (2 hits out of a maximum of 5) and

Size	System Hits
Small	1
Medium	2
Large	3
Huge	4
Enormous	5
Colossal	6

would reduce its Speed rating accordingly. For instance, a Land Ironclad with a Speed of Slow would be reduced to Ponderous.

The specific effect depends on what the Subsystem controls. See the tables on page 111.

Traits

The maximum number of traits a vehicle can have depends on hull size and type:

Size	Terrestrial Vehicle	Spacecraft
Small	1	4
Medium	2	5
Large	3	6
Huge	4	7
Enormous	5	8
Colossal	6	9

Every vehicle has an inherent trait: the travel mode for which it was primarily designed. Therefore aircraft inherently hold the Airborne trait, boats the Seaborne trait, and so on, This inherent trait does not count towards the available number of traits. However, if a vehicle wishes to include a second travel mode — a flying submarine for instance, then the Airborne trait would need to taken as part of its available traits.

Some traits may not be available, depending on the technology level of the parallel; Games Masters must make their own judgement calls as to what traits can be applied.

Airborne

The vehicle is capable of atmospheric flight.

All-Terrain

This Trait must be used with Ground vehicles. The vehicle is capable of traversing inhospitable, difficult and steep terrain, using either tracks, advanced suspension and drive systems, or powerful drive differentials.

Burrowing

The vehicle is designed to burrow and tunnel through the ground. It can achieve a maximum depth equal to its Hull Rating x5 metres.

Camouflaged

The vehicle possesses either camouflage paint or mimetic sensors that allow it to blend with its environment. Attempts to spot the vehicle visually are one grade more difficult.

Cargo

The vehicle is designed specifically to haul cargo rather than passengers. Passenger compartments are kept to a minimum with the rest of the vehicle's usable space being devoted to cargo containment with appropriate sections, tools, and even environmental conditioning (such as freezer sections for transporting perishables). When laden with cargo the vehicle's speed is two steps lower than its hull size would ordinarily allow.

Carrier

The vehicle is designed specifically to carry smaller, lightly-crewed or possibly remotely-controlled vehicles of either a civilian or military nature. Any vehicle possessing this trait must be at least Enormous. The number of small craft carried may vary by mission type and purpose, but can be as few as 10 to as many as the vehicle's Structure rating.

Construction

The vehicle is equipped for heavy construction work. All vehicles with this trait have the All-Terrain Trait too, but speed is two steps lower than their hull size would ordinarily allow. The vehicle is fitted with task-appropriate tools such as crane jibs, digger shovels, dump carts and so on.

EMP Resistant

The vehicle is shielded against electromagnetic pulse attacks.

Enhanced Performance

The vehicle's Speed rating is one step higher than the maximum for its size.

FTL

Spacecraft Only. The craft is fitted with a faster-than-light engine (be this a hyperdrive, warp drive, wormhole generator or similar). The FTL drive has a separate Speed rating which essentially measures the rate at which a starship can cross a single parsec (3.26 light-years, or 31 trillion kilometres, or 19 trillion miles), as follows:

The factor time is for the Games Master to decide, depending on how advanced the parallel's FTL development. *For example, the base factor might be 1 Day, meaning that a ship with a Ponderous FTL drive takes 10 days to complete the journey, whereas a vessel with a Fleet FTL drive completes the trip in 1 day. On another parallel, where FTL*

Terrestrial Vehicle System Damage Table

1d8	System	Partial Damage Result	Total Failure Result
1	Cargo Compartment	An amount of possessions or equipment stored in the hold, proportional to the damage, are destroyed	Everything in the cargo compartment is destroyed
2	Communications	Comms rolls suffer one additional grade of difficulty each time they are damaged	Vehicle can no longer communicate or spoof enemy sensors
3	Controls	Boating, Drive or Pilot rolls suffer one additional grade of difficulty each time they are damaged	Vehicle can no longer be steered or change course
4	Drive/Repulsorlift	Speed is reduced by an amount proportional to the damage	Vehicle can no longer propel itself (or float if supported by a repulsorlift)
5	Pilot/Passengers	A number of passengers proportional to the damage are rendered casualties. Those affected suffer a Major Wound and must succeed in an Endurance roll or be killed instantly	Everyone aboard the vehicle dies
6	Power Core	An additional (powered)subsystem goes off-line each time the power core is hit	Vehicle is destroyed in a disastrous explosion
7	Sensors	Sensor, Navigation and Weapon attack rolls suffer one additional grade of difficulty each time they are damaged	Vehicle is rendered blind
8	Weapons	A number of weapon systems proportional to the damage become inoperative	Vehicle can no longer fire weapons

Starship System Damage Table

1d10	System	Partial Damage Result	Total Failure Result
1	Avionics	Piloting rolls suffer one additional grade of difficulty each time they are damaged	Ship can no longer be steered or change course
2	Communications	Comms rolls suffer one additional grade of difficulty each time they are damaged	Ship can no longer communicate or spoof enemy sensors
3	Crew	A number of crew (and passengers) proportional to the damage are rendered casualties. Those affected suffer a Major Wound and must succeed in an Endurance roll or be killed instantly	Everyone aboard the ship dies in catastrophic atmospheric and life-support failure
4	Hold/Hangar Bay	An amount of cargo or carried vehicles proportional to the damage are destroyed	All ship carried cargo and vehicles are lost
5	Hyperdrive	Hyperdrive speeds are reduced by an amount proportional to the damage	Ship can no longer jump to hyperspace
6	Reactor Core	An additional (powered) Subsystem goes off-line each time the reactor core is hit	Ship is destroyed in a cataclysmic explosion
7	Sensors	Sensor, Astrogation and Weapon attack rolls suffer one additional grade of difficulty each time they are damaged	Ship is rendered blind
8	Shields	Shield strength is reduced by an amount proportional to the damage. Attempts to deflect incoming fire suffer one additional grade of difficulty each time the shields are damaged	Ship can no longer project deflector shields
9	Sublight Drive	Sublight speeds are reduced by an amount proportional to the damage	Ship begins to drift and becomes a sitting duck
10	Weapons	A number of weapon systems proportional to the damage become inoperative	Ship can no longer fire weapons

Speed Rating	Factor to Traverse 1 Parsec
Ponderous	10
Sluggish	8
Slow	7
Mediocre	6
Gentle	5
Moderate	4
Rapid	3
Fast	2
Fleet	1

technology is signficantly less efficient, then the factor time might be measured in months, rather than days.

It is assumed that the ship has fuel reserves to either make a return journey, or a means to refuel at the destination point.

Assume that any size of starship can be fitted with an FTL drive, although, again, this depends on the parallel.

FTL drives cannot be activated within 1.5 Astronomical Units of a star (around 225 million kilometres, or 270 million miles). This means ships must use a sublight drive to move to about the distance of Mars before activating the FTL system.

Ground Vehicle

The vehicle is capable of ground travel.

Hover

The vehicle hovers above the ground either using an air cushion or an anti-gravity repulsor.

Luxurious

The vehicle is designed specifically to carry passengers at a certain level of luxury. Excess cargo space is given over to luxurious passenger accommodations, swimming pools, hot tubs, extra crew to cater to the whims of the passengers, and so forth.

Rails

The vehicle relies on a rail system. Vehicles with this trait can naturally achieve a Speed rating three steps higher than their hull size would ordinarily allow, but are obviously restricted to movement on the rail system only.

Resilient

All systems can withstand one additional hit more than normally determined by Size. This Trait can be stacked — so Resilient 2 indicates that systems can withstand 2 hits more than usual at a cost of two Trait points.

Seaborne

The vehicle is bouyant on water.

Spacecraft

The vehicle is capable of leaving and re-entering the atmosphere, and sustaining flight within an atmosphere. It is sealed against vacuum and shielded against cosmic radiation.

Stealth

Aircraft Only. The vehicle is designed to avoid detection by radar and other long-range sensor systems. Attempts to spot the vehicle using electronic sensors are one grade more difficult.

Submersible

The vehicle is capable of submersing beneath the surface of an ocean to an operating depth of its Hull Rating x10 metres. The collapse depth — the absolute maximum the submersible can reach without being crushed — is 1.5 times its operating depth.

Superior Handling

The vehicle's handling is rated as Easy.

Tractor Beam

Spacecraft Only. The ship is fitted with a tractor beam that can ensnare and draw to it vehicles of two hull steps (or more) than its own. Thus a Huge starship could attract and hold a hull of up to Medium size.

VTOL

Vertical takeoff/landing. This trait is inherent for helicopters and similar vehicles that use a combination of rotors to produce lift. When applied to fixed-wing aircraft it indicates the use of fixed or alignable thrusters to control airborne attitude, ascent and descent.

Walker

The vehicle propels itself using articulated legs. Walker vehicles are capped at the Speed of Gentle, whatever their Size. However, Walkers can be built to heights that would simply be unstable for vehicles equipped with other means of locomotion.

Weaponised

The vehicle has been adapted to accommodate weaponry. The maximum number of weapon systems a vehicle can support is equal to 1/10th of its Structure Points (so a vehicle with 40 Structure could support 4 weapon systems, if a military vehicle or a weaponised civilian vehicle. Weapon systems are discussed on page 117.

Handling and Manoeuvres

Evasive or sudden manoeuvres require a successful Drive/Pilot roll to ensure that the driver or pilot retains control of the vehicle. Most vehicles are designed and built to withstand occasional stresses and strains, but the Games Master may rule that a particular manoeuvre requires a roll at a higher grade of difficulty, depending on how ambitious it is. Failure means that control over the vehicle is lost: roll on the Loss of Control chart.

Note that the Loss of Control Table only applies to terrestrial vehicles. Similar effects can be applied to airborne and space vehicles, but Games Masters will need to adjust the reasoning for the specific effect. For example, an aircraft, rather than skidding, might go into a spin.

Also, a vehicle's inherent handling may have an additional impact on the Drive roll. Handling is either Easy, Standard, Hard, Formidable or Herculean and determines the starting point for the Drive roll when executing a manoeuvre. The difficulty grade for the manoeuvre is then applied to the handling to determine the final difficulty.

For example, a high-performance motorcycle has inbuilt gyro-stabilisers giving it a Handling of Easy. The driver wants to perform a 180 degree skid-turn to evade a pursuer, a manoeuvre the Games Master rates as causing one additional grade of difficulty. The rider must therefore make his Drive roll at Standard rather than Easy. If he had been attempting the same manoeuvre on a non-stabilised motorcycle, the Drive roll would be at Hard.

Superior Handling is a Trait. If a vehicle does not have the trait as part of its description, then the default is Standard handling for any vehicle of size Large and below. Huge and Enormous vehicles inherently have the Handling trait of Formidable and Herculean,

Loss of Control Table

1d100	Result
01-25	Swerve. The loss of control is temporary. Vehicle drops its speed by 1 step for 5 seconds.
26-40	Skid. Driver must fight to keep the vehicle under control. Vehicle drops its speed by 2 steps for 10 seconds.
41-50	Severe Skid. Vehicle ends-up facing in the wrong direction and at a standstill for 15 seconds.
51-60	Roll. Vehicle skids and rolls, sustaining 3d10 damage to its Structure. Occupants must make successful Endurance rolls or sustain 1d10 damage to 1d3 Hit Locations.
61-70	Severe Roll. As above, but vehicle sustains 3d10+10 damage and Occupants receive 1d10 damage even if the Endurance roll succeeds, and 2d10 if it fails.
71-80	Write-Off. As above but the vehicle is reduced to 0 Structure. Occupants sustain same damage as for Severe Roll.
81-90	Explosion. As above but vehicle's fuel system ignites and explodes within 1d20+10 seconds. If unable to get clear, occupants suffer a further 1d6 burn damage to 1d6 locations
91-98	Immediate Explosion. As above but the explosion is immediate.
99-00	Catastrophic Crash. Occupants must successfully roll Endurance or be killed instantly. Damage as for Write-Off is sustained regardless.

respectively, and the Games Master is at liberty to rule that certain manoeuvres are simply impossible to achieve due to the vehicle's size.

Shields

Deflector shields provide an additional layer of protection for those vehicles which can mount them. Shields work slightly differently than the Hull, due to their ablative nature. If incoming damage is equal to or less than the value of the shields, then it is all blocked. If damage exceeds the shield value, then any excess reduces the shield strength by that amount.

For example, a Disruptor Rook troop carrier has an energy shield strength of 12 points.

If the carrier was hit by a laser for 11 damage, it simply does not penetrate and has no additional effect. On the other hand, if the carrier was hit by a blast inflicting 15 damage, the excess three points would drop the shield strength to 9.

Once the strength of a deflector shield has dropped to zero, it collapses. Any remaining damage carries onto the hull.

Weapons

Usually, only military hulls are designed to accommodate weaponry (hard points, ammunition storage, control systems). The 'Weaponised' Trait can be taken for civilian vehicles that may have weapon requirements.

The maximum number of weapon systems a vehicle can support is equal to 1/10th of its Structure Points (so a vehicle with 40 Structure could support 4 weapon systems, if a military vehicle, or a weaponised civilian vehicle).

Weapon systems depend on the Size of the vehicle. The maximum type of weapon system for different Sizes are shown in the tables on page 117.

Sample Vehicles

What follows is a selection of vehicles encompassing different types, technological levels and utilities that can be easily dropped into Arkwright games as needed.

Airship (Helicarrier)

Hull: 17 (Enormous Military), 90 Structure
Speed: Ponderous
Systems: 5
Traits: Airborne, Carrier, VTOL
Shields: None
Weapons: 4 turreted Gatling gun batteries of 2 guns each, 1 Artillery battery

Description: The helicarrier is an enormous aerial vehicle capable of transporting troops, cargo or smaller vehicles (see the picture on page 112 for a good example of this size of vehicle). Featuring huge propellers positioned on outriggers and pylons, the helicarrier can reach altitudes in excess of one kilometer. Their enormous hanger bays and external flight deck can hold up to 90 attack gyrocopters. Helicarriers require a crew in excess of 2,000 sailors, flight crew, pilots and officers.

Armoured Car (Half-Track)

Hull: 12 (Large Military), 55 Structure
Speed: Gentle
Systems: 4
Traits: All-Terrain, Ground Vehicle, Resilient
Shields: None
Weapons: Twin 7.62mm Mounted Machine Guns

Description: The version of the armoured car detailed here is a half-track, with two wheels in front and tank-like treads in the rear, and which allow the vehicle to cross otherwise inaccessible terrain. For a traditional wheeled armored car, simply remove the All-Terrain Trait. An armoured car typically serves as an armored personnel carrier, able to carry a driver, one passenger/gunner, and a squad of up to ten soldiers.

Boat (Speedboat)

Hull: 3 (Medium Civilian), 24 Structure
Speed: Fast
Systems: 3
Traits: Seaborne, Enhanced Performance
Shields: None
Weapons: None

Description: This typical 2-seat speedboat can be found on many different worlds and parallels. What it sacrifices in accommodation it more than makes up for in speed.

Boat (Yacht)

Hull: 10 (Huge Civilian), 75 Structure
Speed: Slow
Systems: 4
Traits: Seaborne, Luxurious
Shields: None
Weapons: None
Description: These pleasure craft range in size from 12 to 50 meters although larger yachts do exist. Designed for pleasure and comfort, yachts are designed for anywhere from 4 to 20 passengers, some even more. They will typically have from 2 to 8 crew.

Boat (Liner)

Hull: 12 (Enormous Civilian), 95 Structure
Speed: Ponderous
Systems: 4
Traits: Seaborne, Luxurious
Shields: None
Weapons: None
Description: Like the fleet of Titanic class vessels of parallel 15.04.12, liners are the most comfortable and luxurious way of moving passengers across the open ocean. They typically feature elegant dining experiences, live entertainment, and a high degree of pampering. Liners are more than capable of carrying 2,000 to 5,000 passengers and crew depending on class, and sometimes even more.

Car (Sedan)

Hull: 4 (Medium Civilian), 25 Structure
Speed: Rapid
Systems: 3
Traits: Ground Vehicle
Shields: None
Weapons: None
Description: The standard 4-door sedan, featuring enough space to comfortably seat a driver and three passengers, or as many as five if they're friendly. Sedans possess an average of .50 square meters of trunk space.

Car (Coupe or Grand Tourer)

Hull: 4 (Medium Civilian), 22 Structure
Speed: Fast
Systems: 3
Traits: Ground Vehicle, Enhanced Performance
Shields: None
Weapons: None
Description: The standard 2-door coupe typically possesses room for a driver and one passenger. Some have room for a single additional passenger in cramped accommodations. They are generally faster and more maneuverable then sedans, but like them possess an average of .50 square meters of trunk space.

Dirigible (Civilian Airship Liner)

Hull: 10 (Enormous Civilian), 85 Structure
Speed: Ponderous
Systems: 5
Traits: Airborne, Luxurious, VTOL
Shields: None
Weapons: None
Description: Similar to the Hindenburg, this class of transcontinental dirigible (and others of its class) is 245 meters in length and requires a crew of 40 to 61. It can typically carry a complement of 50 to 72 passengers in luxury accommodations.

Anna Thames' Chronicle: The Headlong Flight

Hull: 7 (Huge Civilian), 65 Structure
Speed: Slow
Systems: 4
Traits: Airborne, Cargo, Resilient, VTOL, Weaponised
Shields: None
Weapons: Heavy Machine Guns x2 (1-fore and 1-aft)

The Headlong Flight is the personal transcontinental airship of Anna Thames. At 119 meters it is just under half the length of the Hindenburg class dirigible and much older in design. Featuring huge propellers positioned on outriggers, and powered by a pair of Krups diesl powerplants, the Headlong Flight can reach altitudes in excess of one kilometer. With most of its livable space given over to cargo space, the Headlong Flight can still carry a crew of six to eight comfortably.

The airship is at least 30 years old, and the gas bag is patched, mottled, and faded. The gondola carries a half-hearted paint job using greens and browns left over from a locomotive yard, although Anna has tried to brighten things by adding some reds and blues here and there, in what could be considered a jaunty fashion. The engines splutter and clank, and the exhaust is chokingly black when the pistons first start to fire, but the Headlong Flight is still a sturdy vessel and Anna loves her.

Helicopter (Steampunk Gyrocopter)

Hull: 11 (Large Military), 50 Structure
Speed: Mediocre
Systems: 3
Traits: Airborne, Superior Handling, VTOL
Shields: None
Weapons: 1 Gatling gun, 4 rockets
Description: This single seat carrier-based gyrocopter is the mainstay of many steampunk parallels. While not as fast as fixed-wing aircraft, it is more maneuverable and very useful in engaging ground targets and other gyros.

Land Ironclad (Steampunk Tank)

Hull: 15 (Huge Military), 80 Structure
Speed: Sluggish
Systems: 4
Traits: All-Terrain, Ground Vehicle, Resilient
Shields: None
Weapons: 2 Artillery Batteries (turreted), 2 Gatling Batteries (2 guns per battery), 2 Rocket launchers

Description: With their top mounted command bridge and twin stacks belching thick black smoke, these massive weapons of war resemble heavily armoured and tracked land based warships. Mounting two heavy artillery cannons and rocket batteries for long ranged bombardment, and four dual gatling batteries for close defense, land ironclads are one of the most powerful land vehicles in all the Parallels. They typically require a crew of 15 to 25.

Motorcycle

Hull: 2 (Small Civilian), 12 Structure
Speed: Fast
Systems: 3
Traits: Ground Vehicle, Superior Handling
Shields: None
Weapons: None

Description: Motorcycles typically have room for a driver and one passenger. They may be outfitted with a side-car allowing for a third passenger, or to allow a second passenger a more comfortable ride. Adding a sidecar will typically sacrifice the motorcycle's Superior Handling Trait.

Multi-Role Fighter (Twin-Prop Airplane)

Hull: 10 (Large Military), 45 Structure
Speed: Mediocre
Systems: 3
Traits: Airborne, Enhanced Performance
Shields: None
Weapons: 4 nose-mounted Gatling guns (fore), 1 bomb bay (see description)

Description: This twin-seat land-based fighter (similar in type to the De Havilland Mosquito) is well known for its performance and versatility. Its bomb bay is able to carry either two 250 lb. bombs (treat as medium missiles with range 0) or a single torpedo.

Interstellar Freighter (Light High Tech Transport)

Hull: 10 (Medium, Civilian Spaceship), 80 Structure
Speed: Rapid (Parsec Factor of 3)
Systems: 2
Traits: Airborne, Cargo, FTL, Space Craft, VTOL
Shields: None
Weapons: None

Description: This light transport requires a minimum crew of only two, with room for up to four additional passengers. The standard stock version is noted here, however many owners will apply their own "special modifications" such as concealed cargo space, Enhanced Performance or Superior Handling, EMP Resistance, Stealth, and so on.

Vehicle Weapons

Size	Terrestrial	Spacecraft
Small	Light Weapon (eg: Assault Rifle)	Medium Weapon (eg: Machine Gun, Rocket Launcher)
Medium	Medium Weapon (eg: Machine Gun, Rocket Launcher)	Turreted/Heavy Weapon (eg: Heavy Linked Machine Guns, Mini-Guns)
Large	Turreted/Heavy Weapon (eg: Heavy Linked Machine Guns, Mini-Guns)	Weapon Battery (eg: Battlefield Artillery)
Huge	Weapon Battery (eg: Battlefield Artillery)	Advanced Weapons (eg: Missile Systems)
Enormous	Advanced Weapons (eg: Missile Systems)	Spinal Mounted Weapons (one only)
Colossal	Not Applicable	Spinal Mounted Weapons (up to 3)

Sample Vehicle Weapon Systems	Damage	Range	Firing Rate	Ammo	Load	Weapon Traits	ENC
50-inch Cannon	3d6+3	1000/2000/6500	1/10/50	1	5	Fragmentation, Mounted	6
Mini Gun/Gatling Gun	3d6	300/1000/2000	-/20/100	200	4	Mounted	6
Rocket	5d6	5000/20km/60km	1	1	5	Fragmentation	12
Medium Missile/Torpedo	6d10	Max range of 200km	1	1	5	Fragmentation Self-Guided, Mounted,	-
Large Missile/Cruise Missile	6d10+10	Max range of 1000km	1	1	10	Fragmentation Self-Guided, Mounted,	-
Ballistic Missile	10d10+20	Max range of 15,000km	1	1	20	Fragmentation Self-Guided, Mounted,	-
Tactical Nuclear Missile	10d10+50	Max range of 500km	1	1	20	Fragmentation Self-Guided, Mounted,	-
Laser Cannon/Plasma Cannon	4d6	300/1000/2000	-/5/25	500	5	Incendiary, Mounted, Tracking	-
Heavy Laser Cannon/Plasma Cannon	5d6	1000/3000/6000	-/5/25	300	5	Incendiary, Mounted, Tracking	-
Conventional Artillery Battery	5d6+6	Max range of 50km	1	1	5	Fragmentation, Incendiary, Mounted, Tracking	-
Laser/Plasma Artillery Battery	6d6+6	Max range of 50km	-/3/10	10	5	Fragmentation, Incendiary, Mounted, Tracking	-
Spinal Mount Battery	10d6+20	Max range of 20,000km	1	1	10	Incendiary, Tracking	-

Spinal Mount weapons are energy weapons that run the full length of a vessel and are capable of vast amounts of destruction and at typically enormous ranges. This is the sort of weapon a battle station operated by an evil galactic empire might employ against a small, peaceful planet as a demonstration of true power.

W.O.T.A.N & The Disruptors

W.O.T.A.N, the massive supercomputer on Parallel Zero-Zero tracks instabilities across the parallels and helps guide Zero-Zero through computational analysis, is the latest evolution of Marx's discoveries. However, W.O.T.A.N can't work alone. It needs a dedicated group of men and women to interpret the results, maintain the data warehouses and arrays, and take action when it's needed. These brave scientists, technicians, and operators are part of the Valhalla Program.

The World Congress

Zero-Zero is guided by a confederation of scientists, academics, and politicians who form the scientific meritocracy known as the World Congress. They oversee all policies and regulations on Zero-Zero and allocate funding for the Valhalla Program.

The World Congress comprises men and women from cities all over Zero-Zero, staying in near-constant communication with their peers via Terminal complexes. These complexes are massive walls of audio and visual equipment that provide a presence for each and every councilor, not dissimilar to the Trans Parallel Communicators described on page 76. On the rare occasions a face-to-face meeting is preferred, either because of matters of utmost criticality or ceremony, the World Congress building in Aachen, Germania is used.

The Congress is a check and balance for the Valhalla Program. While the Valhalla Program's directive is to prevent the spread of the Disruptors at every turn, the Congress maintains an ethical stance which makes it reluctant to interfere in the destinies of other parallels, especially if it would result in the deaths of numerous innocent people.

Defence Committee

Although war and violence no longer plague Zero-Zero, the ever present threat of inter-dimensional instabilities and the minute risk of Disruptor machinations is recognised. A Defence Committee comprised of politicians, bureaucrats, and scientists is appointed by the World Congress. This committee determines the measures and resources necessary to maintain and ensure Zero-Zero's stability. K-Division is an important arm of the Defence Committee. Its councillors are responsible for monitoring the operations undertaken at Valhalla Nova, studying proposed operations and their risks and reporting back to Defence Division and, when necessary, undertaking personal visits to Valhalla Nova to discuss important projects.

The Valhalla Program

Born of Karl Marx's discovery of the multiverse and the subsequent realization that another force is actively interfering in the development of the other paras, the Valhalla Program is tasked with monitoring the other parallels for Disruptor influence and intervening when necessary. It's this program which recruits and trains the agents who travel from parallel to parallel confronting the Disruptors.

Marx's theories spurred another revolution in science. As scientists and researchers delved into the possibilities presented in a multiverse, a place was needed to provide a workspace. Thus, the first plans for Valhalla Nova were drawn up.

History

The history of the Valhalla Program is inextricably linked with a fateful discovery in 1905, when the Valhalla Nova facility came online and W.O.T.A.N produced its first calculations.

As was predicted by Marx's theories, the parallel earths all have different histories and technologies that diverged at some point from those of their neighbouring parallels. However, the reason behind the divergences was shocking. W.O.T.A.N's analysis revealed that various regimes came to dominate parallel Earths through an unexpected acquisition of advanced technology, espionage, unlikely alliances, and the ability of key people to survive against all odds coupled with the suspicious deaths of individuals and rival powers, even though those powers had successfully opposed them on other parallels. W.O.T.A.N reached the conclusion that a guiding intelligence was at play throughout the continuum to foment war, disease, technological advances, and disasters. W.O.T.A.N theorised, and later confirmed that, agents of this intelligence travel from parallel to parallel to sow the seeds of chaos. These agents were termed, "Disruptors."

In light of these findings, the World Council granted W.O.T.A.N additional processor cycles to devise strategies to combat the threat to Zero-Zero and the Continuum of parallel worlds posed by the Disruptors. The first deficiency W.O.T.A.N determined was a way to combat the Disruptors. As a parallel completely at peace, Zero-Zero lacked any military and police infrastructures, all W.O.T.A.N could do was calculate plans. There was no force to carry them out. First, volunteers from Valhalla Nova were trained in combat techniques, espionage, first-aid, and other skills W.O.T.A.N deemed necessary. These agents of Valhalla began exploring the parallels through vans devised by Valhalla Nova's brilliant engineers. Soon, these agents recruited men and women from other parallels who understood the risk posed by the Disruptors. These agents from other paras are brought to Zero-Zero for training and familiarization with the Program.

Valhalla Nova

The program is headquartered at Valhalla Nova, a massive technological and scientific complex in Zero-Zero's London. Chosen because of its nearness to Greenwich, the prime meridian for calculating time across the world, it was thought that London on Zero-Zero should also serve as a prime meridian of sorts for the multiverse. Located in Planck's Fields, the complex resembles a collection of massive, high-tech ziggurats surmounted by large spheres. Smaller buildings provide dormitories and support services. Massive solar and wind farms line the banks of a pollution free Thames to provide power for Valhalla Nova.

High-speed data trunks connect all the ziggurats, although the most bandwidth is used to connect the Operations Centre with the Marx Facility.

Access to the complex is provided by electric monorails that deposit their riders at stations illuminated by light pillars, decorated in pleasing geometric shapes, and shielded from the elements by transparent roofs. Workers and visitors travel around the complex by conveyor belts, shuttles, and lifts.

The primary structures of Valhalla Nova are:

The Operations Centre

The central and tallest ziggurat in Valhalla Nova. W.O.T.A.N is located in the core of the building and numerous terminals manned by data analysts fill the rooms, pouring over the output constantly to better intercept Disruptor machinations. Even with the miniaturisation of devices, W.O.T.A.N still comprises three entire floors of the ziggurat, surrounded by catwalks and Jeffries tubes to allow engineers access.

The building draws power from the solar panels along the Thames and siphons water directly from the river to provide cooling for W.O.T.A.N and all the terminals. A wall of monitors overlooks the two-storey main data analysis room to provide near-instantaneous communication with the World Congress.

The Rutherford Wing

A smaller ziggurat, the Rutherford Wing was used for further data analysis, but has since been devoted entirely to psi-research. As

Zero-Zero Secularism

Zero-Zero has a completely secular society. Even the game of chess replaces bishops with alchemists. Profanities used by 00:00:00 born operatives generally invoke the names of thinkers and scientists such as Newton, Marx, Dalton and Darwin, though in the aftermath of the FireFrost incident, 'Gotterdammerung!' is an alternative oath used by W.O.T.A.N operatives. German is the preferred language for profanities

such, there are numerous research labs and sleeping quarters for the subjects.

The Curie Wing

The Curie Wing is actually a collection of three smaller ziggurats. They provide medical facilities, dining, entertainment, storage, and residential areas for the engineers, technicians, and analysts who work in the other buildings.

The Marx Facility

The Marx Facility houses a vast library of data on the parallels investigated by the Valhalla Program. It also houses records and artifacts, such as books, optical media, and other archaic forms of data storage from the past of Zero-Zero. The facility also has secure vaults to hold items retrieved from other parallels by agents.

Still other sections of this facility have conference rooms for communication with the World Congress and briefing rooms for agents. Some rooms are reserved for the psychic operatives who can communicate with their alternative selves.

Other Facilities

A sprawling arcology, Valhalla Nova is a self-contained city with an independent infrastructure, but excellent maglev monorail links with the rest of London. Consider it the equivalent of a large university campus. There are leisure facilities, accommodation wings and shops, as well as the restricted and regulated areas where Valhalla's work really takes place.

For game purposes, Characters can find rest and recuperation here should they need to return to Zero-Zero or seek shelter from threats. Many field agents have never visited the complex, remaining on their own parallels, but consider the Characters as part of the select few that have access to Valhalla Nova's facilities as needed — one of the perks of being a chosen Valhalla agent.

Key Personnel

Luther Arkwright

Field Agent

Luther's history has been tied to the Disruptors long before he came to assist the Valhalla Program. Kidnapped and trained by the Disruptors on a para blasted by nuclear war, Luther is the only person W.O.T.A.N has found that can travel from parallel to parallel without the aid of a Van and completely undetected.

Rose Wylde

Field Operative Section Leader

The beautiful and enigmatic Rose Wylde is the most successful Field Operations Section Leader of W.O.T.A.N She has a psychic bond with versions of herself on other parallels. She uses this ability to monitor events across parallels and even pass intelligence to Luther and other agents. She is strong and capable, she can persuasively argue with her superiors and the World Congress and isn't afraid to send agents on suicide missions if it's for the greater good; even though she experiences grief for her decision.

Although each Rose Wylde shares a psychic link, each is also an individual. Each Rose has her own skill set, passions, and dependencies. The Games Master should ensure each Rose is unique. One might be a brutally fierce warrior on a para barely surviving in the wake of annihilation, while another could be a smooth-talking politician in a world ruled by bureaucracy.

Karl Merkel

Valhalla Programme Strategy Division Chief

Karl has the difficult task of maintaining the Valhalla Program's network of agents. Without the aid of W.O.T.A.N, this would be a nigh-impossible task. Keeping track of events as they unfold across a multiverse and directing agents to counter threats takes its toll on a man. Karl truly cares for the agents under his purview, but his demeanor can come across as brusque, especially in times of high stress.

Parsifal C Hackenbush

W.O.T.A.N Programming Supervisor

Parsifal is the bearded senior programmer for W.O.T.A.N He refines the main analytical engines and is the primary point of contact when W.O.T.A.N overheats and is in danger of a meltdown. He handles stress well, and has an excellent working relationship with his other programmers, Rose, and Karl.

W.O.T.A.N

As important a character as any other member of the Valhalla Program, W.O.T.A.N is the cold, calculating heart of Zero-Zero. Without this supercomputer, the Disruptors could run roughshod over the multiverse and no one would be any the wiser. During the 1980s W.O.T.A.N began to develop remarkable powers for self programming and Parsifal Hackenbush determined that the computer was on the brink of developing a form of sapience. In the mid 2000s this becomes a reality with W.O.T.A.N developing not only sapience, but an extensible personality and holographic manifestation based on Odin or W.O.T.A.N of Norse/Anglo Saxon myth.

Other Personnel

Games Masters should feel free to create other Valhalla operatives as needed for their campaign. Section Leaders, Senior Field Agents, scientists, engineers, psychics — all are to be found in the Valhalla Nova arcology.

The Disruptors

The Disruptors emerged from a millennia-long, galaxy-spanning civil war that saw the being known as *the Omega* survive. This being, a carbon based analogue to W.O.T.A.N, seeks to sow chaos and destroy the parallels for a reason known only to itself. It uses the Disruptors to modify and subvert human progress across the parallels for its own ends.

Their origins are shrouded in mystery, but it is known that the Disruptors operate from a hidden base on a parallel unknown to W.O.T.A.N They have also been manipulating the course of human events for much longer than the Valhalla Program has been acting against Disruptor influence.

The Disruptors use the game of chess to describe their ranks. The lowest order are *Pawns*, with *Knights* and *bishops* managing them. *Rooks* are shock troops, designed to spread terror across the paras. The Omega is the king and queen, the source of all that is the Disruptors.

The Disruptor World-Ship

See also the description of the Disruptor Core Parallel on page 127.

The vast Disruptor World-Ship has circled the sun of its parallel for millennia, from even before the days of the civil war that saw FireFrost created. A sprawling, ad-hoc construction, the ship's design owes as much to the Disruptors' adherence to chaos as it does any logical planning.

The ship contains cloning vats to produce more Rooks, training facilities to indoctrinate Knights and bishops recruited from other paras, psychic nerve centers to control the automaton Rooks, and numerous control rooms where bishops maintain contact with the secret societies that have been established across the parallels.

Weapons plants and research laboratories dot the station, laid out in no logical order — simply the order in which they were built. It is here that bishops devise new weapons, both mechanical and chemical, that are supplied to their agents on other parallels to ensure factions loyal to the Disruptors stay in power.

Buried deep in the center of the station is the psychic core of the Disruptors: the Omega. A being so timeless, it might have once been human but has reverted to a fetal state. It has no name, no gender, and no purpose other than to spread discord across the universe in an attempt to bring everything crashing down so that a new order, one of its own devising, is built on the ruins.

The Dark

The Disruptor World-Ship is a terrifying place, but there is a sector roughly the size of Europe where even the Disruptors fear to tread. When the Disruptors first experimented with genetics and bio-manipulation there were numerous missteps. Most unsuccessful by-products were cruelly jettisoned into the void of space. Some, however, were deemed unsuccessful, but had potential future value, usually due to a strong tendency toward violence: something that could be utilised on recalcitrant parallels. These entities were locked away in a prison ward.

Over time, these undesirables grew in number until they posed a serious threat to the Disruptors, should they escape. In a bid to deal with the problem, the Disruptors attempted to open a tunnel to another parallel and transport the entire prison ward through it. Something went wrong and an intense psychic backlash disgorged into the ship, tearing a hole in the fabric between parallels. Numerous entities flooded into the World-Ship. Creatures that can warp the very essence of space-time. These creatures roosted in the prison ward and repulsed several Disruptor attempts to destroy them.

Over the millennia, the creatures, referred to as the Dark, have slowly expanded their area of control. The areas of the World-Ship under their influence have become twisted mockeries of Euclidean geometry and rational science. Large sections are exposed to the vacuum of space. The Disruptors and prisoners not killed in the psychic backlash have warped as well. Very few of them are even vaguely human anymore, adapted to survive in this twisted nightmare.

Rather than purge this contaminated part of the World-Ship, the Disruptors have allowed it to evolve. They see utility in the creatures as possible weapons and the sector as a giant laboratory. They frequently bring Pawns to this parallel and turn them loose in the nightmare to watch what happens. Naturally, the bishops take copious notes.

Disruptor Training Bases

The Disruptors make use of cloning technology to grow new forces. However, they also recruit heavily from other parallels. Not all recruits are willing; Disruptor agents kidnap infants from their cribs and children from bus stops to ship off to training bases. If an adult is recruited, he might not be sent to a training facility but instead left in place, merely thinking he is working for a secret organization native to his world, oblivious that his world is only one of many.

The most advanced training base is the one where a young Luther Arkwright was trained. The only structure on a parallel destroyed by a nuclear war, this base is a large windowless, doorless structure only accessible through shifting parallels. Given the number of Disruptors fielded by the Omega, there are undoubtedly other bases hidden across the parallels. Not all of them need be secreted on destroyed paras, either. Some might be hidden in plain sight, disguised as research labs or even prisons, especially on worlds governed by Disruptor-backed totalitarian regimes.

The training process is vigorous and dangerous. However, a dead or mentally-blasted trainee can easily be replaced with another. Kidnapped infants and young children, as well as the clones, are sedated and raised in nutrient-rich baths, machinery keeping them alive until they're old enough for training.

The most basic instructions are in fighting techniques and the various weapon systems the Disrupters seed across the parallels. At the same time, a cruel streak and a blind obedience to order are drilled into recruits, augmented by drug regimens which sublimate emotions to better prepare a soldier for what it has to do in the future. Bishops watch the recruits closely. Those who demonstrate a deep cruel streak and above average intelligence are pulled aside for further training to become Knights or Bishops. If selected for the honor, a trainee is tested for aptitude and then trained according to those results. Some learn the technical skills to design and build new weapons and equipment. Others train in languages and history to better manipulate other parallels.

Key Personnel

Disruptor Pawn

Martial Disciple

At the bottom rung of the Disruptor organisation are the martial Pawns. These rank-and-file serve as guards, expendable front-line troops, and even weapons practice for the more advanced Disruptors. Many of the Pawns are easy to replace clones. Pawns lack initiative and work best when following orders.

Pawns guard training facilities and are sent to other paras to provide military muscle, if not brains. They frequently serve as occupation forces on other paras if the local powers can't curtail resistance.

Disruptor Pawn

Technological Disciple

Not much higher up the ladder are the technological Pawns, responsible for maintaining the world ship, cloning vats, and the Omega's life support systems.

Some of these Pawns are given the task of monitoring parallels through a bank of terminals on the World-Ship. They don't provide orders, but instead relay information between contacts on the para and Knight and bishops on the World-Ship or other paras.

They wear robes and conical headpieces with built-in communications gear and data read-outs.

Disruptor Rook

Rooks are powerful shock troops encased in ballistic resistant armor carefully designed to trigger deep-seated fears in their targets. Rooks enter a parallel, strike their targets, and leave. They are typically not used as occupation forces.

Rooks are usually armed with laser pistols, but flame-throwers and heavy laser rifles are used if the job requires. The armor resists most firearms in use on other parallels.

They are psychically linked to the Omega (the only psychic waves capable of penetrating their shielded armour), and if the Omega were ever killed or its transmissions interrupted, the Rooks would cease functioning.

Disruptor Knight

Knights are highly intelligent and capable field agents for the Disruptors. They interact with world leaders on other parallels, brokering deals, and devising high-level strategies.

Because of the martial training they were exposed to as recruits, most are also very capable fighters. They are one of the most dangerous foes a Valhalla agent will face, if the Valhalla agents can locate the Knight. These Disruptor agents cover their actions through the use of hirelings, cut-out men, and other deniable assets.

Knights are always recruited from a parallel's military leaders and not clones. The cloning process has never resulted in the mental agility need to be a Knight.

Disruptor Bishop

Bishops are the propaganda and political arm of the Disruptors. Like Knights, they are always recruits, but instead of the military they come from the ranks of politicians, scientists, and religious leaders. Because of their position within a parallel's infrastructure, they have enormous resources on which to draw. Couple that with Disruptor Knights for support, and handlers on the World-Ship, and bishops are truly dangerous adversaries.

Even though many bishops are native to their home para and have been turned by the Disruptors, Valhalla agents shouldn't confuse the fact that the bishops were swayed with bishops being weak-willed. Bishops often side with the Disruptors because of the desire for more power, wealth, or something else that the Disruptors promise them.

The Omega, the Light Bringer

The leader of the Disruptors is an inhuman intellect with such astounding psionic powers that he might only be destroyed by the combined psionic attack of a new breed of humanity supported by the five survivors of the Omega's own race.

It is physically frail, being millennia old. It resides at the centre of the Disruptor World-Ship, invasive, transhumanic machinery keeping it alive. Yet the Omega is not perfect: its massive intellect, while greater than anything humanity has experienced, is divided, watching all the parallels. Subtle maneuvers across multiple paras could escape its notice. It is also prideful,

believing itself to be the sole survivor, and victor of, the ancient civil war. That pride leads it to believe in its own divinity as 'the Light Bringer,' and to possibly overlooking threats.

FireFrost

Not a being, but a device, FireFrost is an ancient weapon that the Disruptors are using to destabilise all the paras. FireFrost, like Arkwright, is unique. It is a singularity in the multiverse currently located in a hidden chamber underneath the Great Pyramid at Giza, in the Egypt of Para 00.72.87. As a unique artifact, it is a source of immense power for the Disruptors, but also a single point of failure. If its two halves are brought together, FireFrost is capable of unleashing powers capable of destablising the very fabric of the multiverse. Its energy is such that even small bursts of its psychic resonance are enough to trigger strange supernatural and Fortean phenomena across the parallels — being responsible for many unexplained events across time and dimensions.

The Five

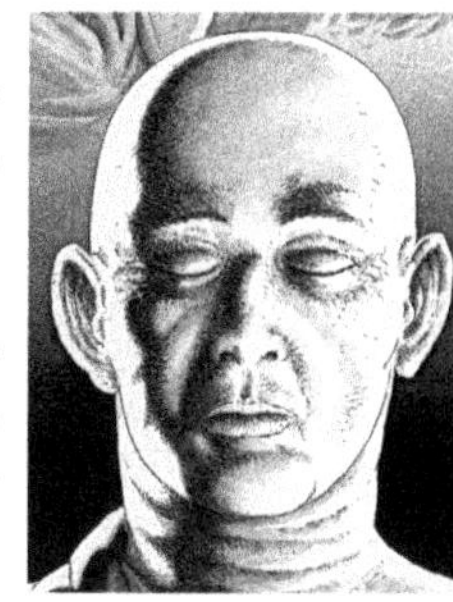

Only five beings survive the civil war against the scientist who becomes the Omega. They hide out of necessity, moving from parallel to parallel, while continuing their resistance to the dictator in surreptitious ways. Their exile denies them access to all the scientific tools they once had. Now, they rely on their psionic powers and an overabundance of caution.

The Five nurture the parallel that develops into Zero-Zero, shielding it from Disruptor notice. They also manipulate human DNA across the parallels to guide the evolution of psychic powers. The crowning achievement of this selection is the birth of Luther Arkwright, the first member of what will become a new human race, *homo novus*.

While Arkwright is indoctrinated to become the ultimate Disruptor agent, the Five use their powers of telepathy to contact him and sow seeds of rebelliousness. Luther escapes the Disruptor training base and returns to his own parallel where the Five guide him to them at their lamasery in Tibet. In the guise of Tibetan monks, the Five train Arkwright to hone his discipline and refine his talents. This provides Luther with so much power he becomes tempting bait in a plan to lure the Omega to expose his location. But Luther is more than just bait, he has the will and ability to confront the Omega. Arkwright's psychic duel with the Light Bringer on the Disruptors' home base allow the Five to accomplish their grand plan at the cost of their own lives. They assist their former student in focusing a powerful psychic attack that annihilates the Omega and splits FireFrost.

The Five are also a source of aid to Valhalla agents. Their assistance comes in the guise of half-remembered dreams and strange waking visions. While they appear to Arkwright as Tibetan monks, they will appear to others in whatever form is most meaningful and easily received.

Parallels

Karl Marx's discovery of multiple Earths in 1882 rocked the scientific community. These Earths are not separated by time or space, they're separated by a dimension, the probability valency. The Earths exist in parallel, most of them occupying the exact same spot, the Core Position, in their respective solar systems. Only a few have been discovered that occupy different points in their orbits around the sun.

Although the Earths share the same Core Position, each Earth has a different history. Some histories are barely divergent from Marx's home Earth, the one he designated 00.00.00, or Zero-Zero. Others might be an Earth where the Roman Empire still holds sway over humanity, Martin Luther never posted his theses, or the Kuomintang win the Chinese Civil War. There are some parallels that are highly divergent, such as where humanity is scrabbling to survive in a post-apocalyptic wasteland, or where humanity never developed. Interestingly, on those parallels, no other creature rose to take humankind's place.

Despite the differences in history, there is an eerie similarity. Cultures, language, and basic human psychology are almost identical across the parallels.

What this means is that a traveler from one parallel to another (or para, for short), can expect to get a feel for how things work very quickly. Although the major societal players and the geo-political topography might be different, the things which make humans human are very much the same.

Designations

Each para has a six digit designator. Using 00.00.00 as the base, most stable parallel, W.O.T.A.N calculates the designator for other Earths based on how divergent they are from Zero-Zero. 00.01.00 and 00.00.01 are considered the least divergent, and therefore the closest to stable.

The further from 00.00.00 that a para is, the more susceptible it is to Disrupter influence and therefore less stable. It's on these more divergent paras that Valhalla agents will be spending many a mission.

Classification

A para's classification is not a scientific calculation based on W.O.T.A.N crunching numbers and calculating an ideal outcome. It's based on the interpretations that Valhalla researchers make of W.O.T.A.N's data and the first-hand accounts of field agents who have visited the parallel.

The classification is usually just a few words that summarise the world. Examples include "stable" for Zero-Zero or "Prussia Ascendant" for 00.72.87, the parallel explored in The Adventures of Luther Arkwright.

Just as it's impossible for a few words to accurately describe the parallel in which you're standing, a classification just imparts the barest of sketches of the world. For example, Prussia Ascendant does little to describe the violent English Civil War that's been raging on 00.72.87 for three centuries.

Indices

Each parallel has three indices, Cultural, Political, and Technological, to further help Valhalla agents understand a parallel's nature.

The Cultural Type represents the dominant culture(s) on the parallel. Although a specific nation's borders can change over time, even to the point of one country disappearing completely or new countries emerging from the smoking ruins of another, cultures tend to persevere for longer. In *Luther Arkwright: Roleplaying Across the Parallels*, the cultures have been divided into twenty large geographical areas.

The Cultural Index

The Cultural Index is a list calculated by W.O.T.A.N of twenty over-arching cultural types that can be found on most parallels.

1. Northern America
2. Central America
3. Southernn America
4. Caribbean
5. Northern Europe
6. Western Europe
7. Southern Europe
8. Eastern Europe
9. Northern Africa
10. Western Africa
11. Central Africa
12. Southern Africa
13. Eastern Africa
14. Western Asia
15. Central Asia
16. Southern Asia
17. Eastern Asia
18. Southeastern Asia
19. Australasia
20. Oceania

The Political Index

This represents the type of government employed by the dominant power on the parallel. Is the nation ruled by a militaristic junta, a byzantine bureaucracy, or maybe an oligarch of academics striving to develop a utopia ruled by reason?

1. Academic
2. Anarchic
3. Artistic
4. Bureaucratic
5. Economic
6. Militaristic
7. Religious

Technological Index

The third index is the Technological Index. W.O.T.A.N calculates the overall level of technology for a parallel. Unlike the Cultural and Political Indices, which can vary from region to region on a given parallel, a Technological level is fairly consistent across a para. One thing a Valhalla agent should be aware of though, is Disruptor influence. A common tactic among Disruptor Knights is to seed a chosen nation with new technology, giving them the edge over their opponents. At the same time, the Disruptors now have their hooks firmly sunk into the government.

1. Pre-Industrial Age
2. Industrial Age
3. Computer Age
4. Nanotechnology Age
5. Spacefaring Age

Moving Between Parallels

Luther Arkwright moves from parallel to parallel under his own psychic power, and more importantly, invisibly to the Disruptors. Most agents do not have that luxury or power. They rely on technology created by the scientists of Zero-Zero to accomplish their missions.

With the exception of Luther Arkwright and powerful psionicists like Rose Wylde, travel between parallels leaves behind a huge energy backlash that can be tracked by both the Disruptors and W.O.T.A.N In other words, once an agent enters a new parallel, he does not want to hang around the entry point for too long: Disruptors will investigate.

One of the first things new agents are trained on is how to properly traverse the parallels. It is not a simple matter of stepping from one to the other. It can be a physically and psychically taxing experience that leaves the unprepared shattered.

Agents of Valhalla

Most Valhalla agents are dependent upon physical means to traverse the parallels. They rely on The Van (see page 77), a massive contraption of metal tubes, control panels, and unimaginably complex internal mechanisms built on a large rectangular body with a pyramidal frame of energy conduits leading to the device's steerage at its apex.

When the trans-parallel portal is opened, the operator must also set the return time. This is a fixed point in space and time that is only available for 144 minutes. The Van consumes vast amounts of multiversal energies, which can have a destabilizing impact on the multiverse and runs the risk of attracting Disruptor attention.

Disruptors

Disruptor Knights and Rooks use devices that resemble The Van. Using these devices, Disruptors rip open the fabric of space-time and travel through to the target parallel. The Disruptors disassemble their pyramid gates and carry them with them, allowing for a tunnel to another parallel to be opened anywhere.

Very few Valhalla agents have stepped foot into a disruptor tunnel and even fewer have returned to detail what it was like. Those

Parallel Lines and Parallel Lives: Optional Rules

In the Luther Arkwright saga, travel between the parallels is limited in nature; in fact, The Van is not even mentioned in the graphic novels and was created by Bryan Talbot for a roleplaying adventure published in Imagine Magazine back in the mid 1980s. Games Masters are quite at liberty to introduce different ways of travelling between planes of existence. Dimensional Gates, matter transporters, dimensional spacecraft and even drugs can be used as the needs of the campaign dictate. Do not hesitate to use different methods — the multiverse is a huge place!

And, given that Characters have myriad versions of themselves, Games Masters are encouraged to make use of the possibilities this offers. If a character dies, there is nothing wrong in having the player continue using another version of themself (perhaps with a slightly different name, different career and different dependency), but one that is conveniently also a Valhalla agent. If a character has the Empathic Link trait, then there is no reason why a new version of Character X does not inherit the previous character's memories and experiences, lending greater continuity to play.

These are, of course, optional suggestions for Games Masters: use them at your discretion.

agents tell of mind-shattering horrors, warping physical and astronomical realities, and absolute terror.

Psychic Connections

Rose Wylde and a few other very specialised agents are psychically aware of their other selves existing on every other parallel. Although each iteration is unique, with its own personality, goals, and life, they are psychically linked. This psycho-empathic tether allows one of these talented agents to feel, sense, and experience what their alternate selves are feeling, sensing, and experiencing. In most cases, this is not a psychic free-for-all. The agent on Zero-Zero can control which iterations it is in contact with at any given time. The only time something is felt by all versions is in the case of massive trauma, like the death of one of the alternate selves. The psychic backlash is immense in these cases and can harm one or more of the linked.

These agents are capable of amazing feats of communication and espionage due to this talent. A message can be transferred instantly and securely to an alternate iteration since it needs to only be thought by the agent on Zero-Zero. Likewise, a critical document on another parallel is seen across the parallels as soon as it's seen at the source. Because of this, they are closely held assets by the Valhalla Project.

Important Parallels

This section provides overviews of a variety of parallels for use in Luther Arkwright campaigns.

Zero-Zero

Designator: 00.00.00
Classification: Stable
Cultural Type: Western Europe
Political Type: Academic
Technological Type: Computer Age

The first parallel of the modern age to become aware of the true nature of reality, Zero-Zero is remarkable in its political, religious and military stability. Entering an age of Enlightenment brought about much earlier than on other parallels, Zero-Zero achieved scientific breakthroughs a good century or so before many of its contemporaries. Scientists such as Karl Marx and John Dalton predicted and then proved the existence of multiple universes, and in 1881 the theory was proved beyond all doubt.

Zero-Zero has achieved a quite astonishing equilibrium. It is a truly secular society with religion having been relegated to the status of a peculiar social curio. Poverty was eradicated in the early 1900s and by 1965 advances in fusion technology brought cheap, clean, safe energy to all.

W.O.T.A.N's development led to worldwide advances in computer intelligence and by 1970, rudimentary artifical intelligences were commonplace, and reasonable degrees of AI sophistication an everyday occurrence by 1980.

Zero-Zero is therefore a highly remarkable version of Earth where rational thought and an ordered, passive attitude prevails. In fact, Zero-Zero is the exact antithesis of the chaos wrought by the Disruptors and, in particular, their own parallel of origin.

Disruptor Core Parallel

Designator: Unknown
Classification: Devoid of Earth
Cultural Type: Uncertain
Political Type: Militaristic
Technological Type: Spacefaring

The Disruptor parallel is unique. It is the only parallel that W.O.T.A.N has predicted to have life, but lack an Earth.

Whether or not there ever was an Earth is unclear. Instead, a massive, decrepit space station floats through the void of space, locked in an orbit around a sun.

Although the place of origin of the Disruptors, and home to the World-Ship, the Disruptors have reached many, many parallels, bringing instability and destruction in their wake. What has been left behind is a parallel that still bears the scars of massive, catastrophic warfare that eradicated entire civilsations and caused the fall of whole planetary systems. The psychic power unleashed in the Disruptor Core Parallel was such that residual waves are still being felt across the multiverse, millennia after the original war. For the Disruptors, it was a pyrrhic victory: their enemies were destroyed, but so was much of their universe. Aside from the World-Ship, it inhabitants, the Omega, and the horrors of the Dark, the Disruptor Core Parallel is devoid of meaningful life; it is a miserable, derelict reality, a temple to meaningless, wanton destruction in pursuit of ultimate power. Proof, if it were needed, of what happens when beings who have mastered the control of reality, lose all sense of reason.

Valley of the Kings

Designator: 02.84.17
Classification: Egypt Ascendant
Cultural Type: Northern African
Political Type: Religious Oligarchy
Technological Type: Industrial Age

The Disruptors first visited this parallel in the 14th century BC. They provided assistance to a young pharaoh, allowing him to seize the throne. As his power grew, fuelled by Disruptor technology, this pharaoh, now known as Akhenaton, threw down the old gods and established worship of a single deity, Aten. Heady with power, he thought he could do the same with the Disruptors – replace their support with his own power; after all they had provided him with powerful weapons – which could be turned back on their creators.

Akhenaton launched a surprise attack on the Disruptors, but was surprised to find the Disruptors ready for him. He was even more surprised by his young son, Tutankhamun, less than ten years old, bearing the weapon that would end Akhenaton's life.

Under Tutankhamum's leadership, the Empire of Kemet spread in all directions, conquering any foe who did not immediately surrender. With the help of Disruptor technology, the pharaohs fought off attempts by Greek warlords to conquer the land. The Egyptians kept the Greeks, Persians, Romans, and other Mediterranean would-be Empires in check, forever altering the face of global politics.

However, as with all mighty empires, the greatest threats frequently come from within. Numerous threats have risen and fallen within Kemet's long history. The Israelites rose up, but were crushed. Alexander the supposedly Great died on the shores of the Nile, his fleet burnt to ash. The Romans tried and failed. One threat, though, has refused to fade into the history books. The trouble began in the late 18th century when a soldier in the pharaoh's army named Napoleon secretly gathered forces within Egypt's territory in Europe and launched a surprise attack on the city of Marseille. The Egyptians expected a quick victory, but Napoleon had solicited the aid of the Mongol Empire who supplied him with intelligence and materiel. The Egyptian forces were beaten back and eventually driven from southern Europe. The resistance started by Napoleon still holds the area to this day, slowly expanding their borders.

In the present day, three world powers hold an uneasy truce. The Empire of Kemet, the Mongol Empire, and the Aztecs have the world divided among themselves, with a few smaller powers such as the Revolutionary State of France carving out small niches for themselves.

The Empire of Kemet

Arguably, the greatest power in the world. Kemet's armies range far and wide and her dirigibles hold uncontested control of the skies. Ruled by Pharaoh Hatshepsut XI, the empire is a melting pot of cultures from across the globe. At its greatest, the early 20th century, the Empire covered all of Africa, the Middle East, the Balkans, Europe west of the Rhine and north of the Loire, and the British Isles. Border struggles with the Mongols and third-column action by the Revolutionary State of France have pushed Kemet west to the Tigris in the Middle East and out of Serbia and Montenegro in the Balkans.

Hatshepsut XI and a cabinet of high priests oversee the Empire's rule from the city of Memphis. The pharaoh is further served by qenbets, provincial governors, who enforce her autocratic will across the whole of the empire. Aided by Disruptor Knights as military aides and Bishops as scientific advisors, the political scene is stable. At least, it is in Memphis and the provincial capitals of Great Zimbabwe, Rouen, London, and Acre. In the outlying areas, furthest from cities, local rulers often take liberties with the laws, only enforcing the ones that serve their personal needs.

The pharaoh is the undisputed head of the Empire's polytheistic religion, she is a deity, seated alongside Thoth and Ra as the primary foci for worship, although the entire pantheon of Egyptian deities is worshipped as the need arises.

Ancient Kemet's survival was tied to the Nile. If the Nile ever failed to flood, the entire empire was in danger of starvation. The Disruptors, in addition to providing military assistance, lent scientific know how to tame the Nile centuries before it happened on other parallels. Because of this, Kemet is a technological marvel. Giant ironclad chariots pulled by diesel engines support the ground troops and dirigibles sporting the royal scarab provide air support and long-range bombing capabilities. A top-secret weapon is under development at the empire's largest military facility on the Isle of Rhodes. This weapon, dubbed Apep, is a last ditch effort to crush the French. It's a class of giant weapons platforms in the shape of the pantheon.

The Disruptors are urging the pharaoh to unleash the new weapons as soon as they are ready. Hatshepsut is more than willing to take their advice. She views their guidance as invaluable, evidenced by the fact that she always has at least two Disruptor Knights by her side. Her two most trusted aides are Ammut, destroyer of the weak, a sadistic weapons master par excellence, and Djet, a depraved genius responsible for the Apep program and several thousand missing men and women. To ensure their value, the Disruptors periodically stage assassination attempts on Hatshepsut that only they can thwart. She is every bit a Pawn in their plans.

As the economy grew after the arrival of the Disruptors, the pharaohs burials became more and more elaborate. In addition to the three pyramids most Valhalla agents are familiar with, hundreds more dot the desert. Rather than stone, these high-tech necropolises are built of glass and iron, manned by hundreds of slaves, and tower over the pyramid of Khufu. Each pharaoh strives to outdo the last, and Hatshepsut XI commenced building her funerary monument when she took the throne thirteen years ago. Provincial leaders and the wealthy also build grand tombs, but are careful that their tombs do not exceed the pomp of the pharaoh's tomb, one of the greatest edifices outside the Nile Valley is the tomb of the former qenbet of London, Percy Shelley.

Travel throughout the empire is by train or horse for the average person. The wealthiest supporters of the pharaoh and her royal court use diesel-powered chariots provided by the Disruptors. A string of impressive fortresses roughly 30 miles apart, known as "The Way of Horus," protect the empire's borders with the Mongol Empire and the French Revolutionary State. While the border with the Mongol Empire is open to any properly documented traveler, the border with the French Revolutionary State is closed and anyone caught crossing it is executed.

The Mongol Empire

Headquartered in Ulan Bator, the Mongol Empire is a loose federation that covers most of Asia, including South East Asia and the Indian subcontinent, and Europe up to the Rhine's east bank. Ruled by Batbayar III, a descendent of the great khans of history, this empire is continually clashing with the more powerful Empire of Kemet.

Unhindered by the pitfalls that hindered the Mongols in other paras, this empire has maintained a long tradition of military and artistic achievement that would be unmatched if not for the Disuptor's influence in Kemet.

Barring a few diesel-powered chariots captured in clashes with Kemet, the Mongols still rely on horse travel in the open expanses of Eastern Europe and Central Asia, and many of their towns in those regions are mobile. The small houses are built on wheels and pulled by horses or oxen. This allows the Mongols extreme flexibility when low on natural resources or in times of war. A Mongol force attacks from out of nowhere and quickly fades away. By the time the slower Kemet army can give chase, the entire Mongol settlement has moved. These skirmishes are sufficient to harry invading forces, but are not sustainable over a long campaign.

Like Kemet, the Mongol Empire is a multi-cultural one. Each region sends multiple delegates to Ulan Bator where they serve the khan as advisors. It's not a peaceful time for the delegates, they jockey for position within the government, trying to make sure that their requests are heard by the khan. Poisonings and stabbings are frequent occurrences between delegates at Ulan Bator. The khan enjoys these squabbles, as they ensure that only the strongest delegates are heard.

The economy is built on two pillars, trade and pillage from raiding. It's not uncommon for one group to raid a neighboring settlement, even though they're part of the same empire. While Ulan Bator frowns on this, the powers that be do little to stop it. However, the favorite raiding target for groups along the western border are the rich towns and cities in the Empire of Kemet.

Without the aid of the Disruptors, the Mongol Empire's military technology has not advanced as far as Kemet's. Warriors carry muskets, repeating rifles, and swords into battle. Horse drawn carriages haul cannons and similar artillery when needed.

The Aztec Nations

On this parallel, the Aztecs rule a massive republic that covers most of the Americas. Governed from New Tenochtitlan by Nahuatl, Chosen of the Gods, the Aztecs have forsaken their bloody past for a life of commerce and prosperity.

However, the Aztecs are not one to pass up a good opportunity. Their warships and dirigibles are painted in red splotches, simulating the blood of sacrifice. Delegates are encouraged to spread the rumours that the republic is more than willing to spill the blood of anyone foolish enough to stand in its way. This posturing is not an empty bluff, however. The republic's soldiers are fierce and skilled fighters, equipped with technology that comes close to rivaling that of Kemet.

When the Republic first came in contact with the Empire of Kemet, they were trounced at the Battle of Hawai'i. However, the Aztecs collected every scrap of materiel and sent spies deep into Kemet. Based on this intelligence, the Republic ramped up its weapons programs and within a century had a fleet of dirigibles capable of crossing either ocean.

However, Disruptor influence ensures that Kemet always has the upper hand, militarily, and the Aztec Republic has ceased pursuing revenge for the Battles of Hawai'i, Tunisia, and Cornwall. Now, they're biding their time, using their dirigible fleet to trade with any willing partner and to smuggle weapons into the French Revolutionary State.

The French Revolutionary State

A recent entrant into the world, it was founded by former Kemet general, Napoleon Bonaparte, after he rebelled against the pharaoh. It stretches across Southern Europe from Marseille to the Sar Mountains in the east. Originally a dictatorship, an elected parliament was added in 1813 and the dictator replaced with an elected Prime Minister in 1821. The current Prime Minister is Javier Mendez who earned his popularity and lost a leg seizing and holding one of the fortresses along the Way of Horus for 48 days before the Kemet forces could oust the revolutionaries.

The French Revolutionary State is sandwiched between the Mediterranean Sea and its greatest foe, the Empire of Kemet. The Way of Horus cuts the French off from any land support, so most trade is conducted over the sea and through the air with Aztec blockade runners. Some trade does arrive overland from Mongols and sympathisers in the Empire of Kemet who are willing to risk running the gauntlet.

Although isolated, the state is holding on to its freedom through tenacity, foreign arms, and a willingness to retreat in the face of overwhelming odds. This tactic lures the larger, less mobile Kemet forces into treacherous mountains or swampy lands where the French can strike like lightning and then retreat in the night.

The French like to joke that their newborn state is more Aztec than the Aztec Republic, but they keep a careful eye on any Aztec delegations. While the aid is helpful now, if the French Revolutionary State is to survive as an independent entity, it does not want any nation meddling in its affairs, even one with a common goal of seeing the Empire of Kemet fall.

The Diamond Age

Designator: 14.03.71
Classification: British Empire Variation
Cultural Type: Northern American
Political Type: Militaristic
Technological Type: Industrial Age

This parallel is classified by W.O.T.A.N as a surviving British Empire variation. Its point of divergence was the emergence of the Confederate States of America as the victor in the American Civil War. From this point onwards, the CSA became a major global power and technologies developed in the war, such as large airships, are still the dominant focus of scientific achievement. The parallel is one that is heavily influenced by the Disruptors.

The nations of 14.03.71 have varying political systems and technologies. Most of the powers are militaristic and to some degree religious, though faiths followed vary. Christianity is dominant in the CSA, but Europe is largely secular although the Catholic church maintains a strong power base in the kingdom of Italia. The level of technology used by the imperial powers is that of the industrial revolution where both steam and fossil fuels are utilised.

Technology

The main form of communication is the telegram and the written and printed word. Pneumatic tubes for delivering documents and small packages are common apparatus in government and commercial buildings. Photography and the cinema are in use for information and entertainment throughout the 'civilised' world. The computers that exist are huge metal structures based on the designs of Charles Babbage.

The principal means of transport throughout most of the world is horse powered. Steamships are the principal means of transporting passengers and cargos, though huge passenger airships accommodate a sizeable amount of well-moneyed travellers. Smaller airships and balloons are used for military, commercial and personal flights. Autogyro devices are being developed by various inventors, and already feature in the military arsenal of the German Empire.

Gas is an important source of power for lighting in the cities and towns in the home nations and colonial capital cities of the great powers.

Politics and Culture

The prevailing ideology is one of Imperialism: powerful nations, whether led by monarchs or presidents, whose wealth and prestige is based on the acquisition of territory and states. The Imperial powers have amassed huge armies and armadas of ships and air vessels, and are constantly engaged in trying to further their mercantile power through expanding their domains. The last full European War was the conflict between France and the German states in the later part of the eighteenth century. Since then the only open warfare between two major modern powers has been the sporadic border wars between Japan and Russia. There is no shortage of sabre rattlers in the 1980s and many rulers and advisors yearn to put their meticulous military plans of conquest into action.

Throughout most of the world, power and wealth rests in the hands of small minorities of aristocrats or industrialists. Many nations have populations of serfs or slaves and even 'enlightened' nations with a pride in their democracy and 'civilization' have far flung Empires of foreign subjects whose labours and resources enrich their colonial masters. Closer to home, the industrial countries have large populations of their own citizens who toil, rot and die in ghettoes and slums. Slavery is still a feature of the CSA and some regions of the 'Indian State' and is also widespread in areas of Ottoman influence. Communism is a political concept that influences some Russian and European individuals and organisations but violent attempts to impose it in France, Spain and Russia have, thus far, failed.

Various branches of Freemasons are widely prevalent throughout North America and Europe and far-flung colonies, where brother masons can hope to get assistance. Some of these lodges are actually composed of members with fierce political ambitions who work against the governments of their native countries. The Disruptors have found these societies to be a useful tool for centuries.

The fashions and culture of the world resemble that of the Late Victorian and the Edwardian periods of most parallels, though the assorted religious beliefs of the parallel have not been eroded as strongly as other post industrial revolution parallels. The theories of Charles Darwin are only taught as a science in some French and German universities. Duelling is a convention that is highly popular in the upper echelons of the CSA and various European nations.

The Confederate States of America

The CSA is a nation which comprises of most the entire area of North America between Canada and Mexico and includes the states of Alaska and Hawaii whilst Mexico and Panama are protectorates held in an iron grip. A huge number of Caribbean and Pacific islands are also under the flag of the CSA, including the former Spanish colonies of Cuba and the Philippines. Moreover, South America is a sphere of influence that is jealously guarded and all the South America regimes and governments rely heavily on the favour of the CSA government and its industrialists.

The key to the CSA's victory in the civil war of the previous century was Disruptor influence. Britain and France were supportive enough of the fledgling Confederacy to form a League of Armed Neutrality and used their navies to prevent an efficient US blockade of Confederate ports. France proved an enthusiastic financial ally in exchange for the CSA's recognition of a French puppet empire being established in Mexico whilst Britain was able to manufacture and sell warships.

The CSA's military triumphed over the USA by the use of superior technology, which fell into their laps through covert Disruptor intervention. Early in the war, the south's generals made efficient use of the primitive machine guns in its arsenals which helped to offset the Union's numbers. Warfare on the parallel suddenly took a quantum leap when the CSA was able to deploy armed airships that were able to bombard and intimidate US armies and garrisons with relative impunity and helped to achieve victory.

Relations with the CSA between both Britain and France soured when the Confederate government reneged on its agreement to emancipate slaves. Instead, the CSA left the decision in the hands of the individual states. France became increasingly hostile after the collapse of the Mexican Empire, where rebellion had been encouraged by the CSA. During this time, the espionage network of the Confederate Secret Service Bureau became an efficient worldwide espionage network.

In 1917, an intercepted communication between the USA and the Mexican Government was deemed sufficiently threatening to prove a 'casus belli' sufficient enough for the CSA to invade and annex Mexico and the last remnant of the USA.

The CSA is distrusted by most of the world's Imperial powers. International opinions are also fuelled by US political activists who operate throughout Europe. The Papacy is viewed in a hostile fashion by the CSA due to its influence in Latin America.

The wealth of the CSA's industrialists is bolstered by the ability of its government to limit imports into Latin America from European nations when they are in competition with North

American goods. The cities of South America are heavily influenced by the CSA's culture. One of the most obvious CSA imports is the fast food chain of General MacAnders which dominates the two Americas. Now that it controls most of the Americas, both militarily and economically, the CSA is eager to undermine the economies of its chief mercantile rivals, Germany and Britain. Currently the CSA is covertly giving her approval and support to an imminent attempt by Argentina to capture some former Spanish colonies in the South Atlantic from Britain.

President Samuel Forrest

President Forrest is the current leader of the CSA. He is actually a Disruptot Bishop who receives his information and instructions via a Disruptor communication terminal that is located in a hidden office. When transmitting, the communicator's screen projects the voice and image of a hooded individual who Forrest believes is a Grand Master of the Freemasons. He is also deluded enough to believe that the current Pope is the herald of the Anti-Christ.

The White Knights of America

The WKA is a paramilitary order formed in 1915 to defend the Confederacy against internal enemies and to 'protect its purity of race and religion'. The members enforce their own brand of bigoted, vigilante law and wear white robes and pointed hoods to protect themselves from reprisals. Their brotherhoods use ritualistic oaths and ceremonies, and use a rank structure with mystical sounding names. Many of its leaders believe that there is a secret upper tier of leadership, a Masonic lodge whose members are privy to magical powers. Besides distrusting and hating people a different race, most of the WKA is also hostile towards the Catholic Church. Colonel Chivington is currently its most prominent leader and is rumoured to have political ambitions.

First Nation Territories

During the American Civil War, the CSA honoured pledges made with the Native American tribes who sided with them. Most of these lands are in the mid-west of the nation. Over the next century these lands became overpopulated with immigrant tribes and violent feuding is common. The habitat, culture, rights and freedoms of most of the population have been eroded and mining and industrial complexes run by CSA industrialists have been installed. In recent years, a resurgence of their old religious beliefs has occurred — including rituals which will, they believe, protect the tribes' warriors against the white men's weapons.

The De la Canne Corporation

During the First American Civil War the New Orleans based De Cannes family made a fortune running armaments through the early blockades. Since then they have prospered and have accumulated a vast fortune based on trade in slaves, coffee, rubber, rum, cotton, opium and tobacco. They have factories and plantations in Florida, South America, the Caribbean and West Africa.

The current heads of the family are Dominic and Dominique de la Canne, a pair of twins, born on a family estate in the Republic of Dominica. The twins are actually gifted psychics who were involved with the voodoo religion from an early age. They are involved with an assortment of cults throughout the countries where this faith is practiced. Already powerful due to their financial might, this has added considerably to their power and influence in various countries where superstitious people fear to cross them. Their involvement in the slave trade and the use of a drug that is used to make their workers compliant is a feature of many of their plantations and factories. The twins are actually two highly competent agents for the Disruptors.

The US Government in Exile

Since losing the brief Second American Civil War, a Government in Exile based in Paris was formed in 1918. Both Italy and Great Britain have allowed the establishment of consulates in their capitals. President Regan, the current leader, is a genial geriatric with romantic notions about liberating the East Coast of America. As a former actor of propaganda films, he has already starred in this role several times.

The Daughters of the Revolution

This paramilitary organisation is comprised of ex-patriot women who are sworn to liberate the USA. They have a presence amongst the resistance movement based in their homeland. They are noted for flamboyant and colourful costumes that commemorate the history of their nation. Inspiration comes from pilgrims, buck-skinned hunters and the uniforms of the both the American revolutionary and civil wars. They are viewed by many as mere propaganda poster-girls, rather than a useful military force, a view which they are keen to rectify.

France

The disastrous war against the German states over a century ago toppled the second French Empire and left provinces of France absorbed by the new German Empire.

The new republic has lasted for over a century now, though various political parties are always simmering to stage coups and uprisings. Paris is both home to various foreign political exiles and small colonies of artists.

Excepting Great Britain, she currently controls the largest overseas Empire with territories in the Caribbean, North and West Africa, South East Asia and the Pacific. France's restored military might and her intention to recover her lost home provinces is a matter of pride to most of its citizens. The French navy is, as yet, the only nation to have received a practical design of submersible, though these craft are still undergoing trials and are protected by a shroud of secrecy.

Stormy Weather

A recent technological advance made by French scientists is still a closely guarded secret. Weather control machines were initially designed to help agriculture in the French Sahara. The project was taken over by the French military who termed these devices as TP cannons, an abbreviation of tempéte porter (stormbringer), though they are still passed off as experimental heliograph or water collection apparatus to hide their true purpose. The machines are currently being tested in remote corners of colonial Africa, and in recent years are actually responsible for several global calamities and increasingly difficult to predict weather patterns. The imminent Jupiter Effect serves to cloak the activities of these experiments and military actions during the coming year.

Germany

Seen by many as the most powerful nation in Europe, the German Empire has colossal military and industrial might, though it still lags behind Britain and France regarding the size of its dominions. The empire expanded considerably in the last century, absorbing Austria and other German-speaking regions, and establishing alliances with many central and eastern European states.

The current ruler is actually the Prince Regent Karl, who is proving to be a vain and ambitious ruler. Born crippled, he is heavily reliant on a scientific exoskeleton to move and stand tall amongst his subjects. His father, Kaiser Rudolph, is a raving madman confined to one of the extravagant castles in Bavaria. Rather than being a victim of consanguinity, as many believe, he was actually driven mad by the activities of a Disruptor agent.

Germany is a leading country in the design and manufacture of arms and munitions and it is famous for its universities and its promotion of all forms of science. Already it has produced world -renowned scientists in the fields of chemistry, physics and astronomy. Medical scientists have made enormous progress and the elite of society are kept alive and active by primitive cybernetics.

The pride of the army and their inventor, Krupp, are two enormous, armour-plated, mechanical war machines that resemble huge iron statues. Inside, they incorporate batteries of artillery and crews of well-drilled gunners and technicians. These machines are able to move like a man, though in a ponderous fashion, and are also armed with a sword that can be swung to attack targets not already obliterated by its guns. The first built, 'Gross Hermann' is a 54-metre colossus based on the statue of the ancient hero who defeated the Roman legions, which stands in the Teutoburg Forest. The second is 'Prinz Karl' which is modelled on its namesake, though it was, at the insistence of the Prince Regent himself, built some ten metres taller than the earlier model. Krupp's other products include magazine-fed howitzers and the maxim machine gun. Also famous are the Golem Guard Regiment, military automatons from a collaboration of design between Krupp's scientific teams and the reclusive scientific genius, Herr Eisenhand.

Another military design that bodes to revolutionise warfare are the gyrocopters that have been developed for the Imperial Luftwaffe. As yet, it is only intended for undertaking reconnaissance missions, though pilots have already started to carry a variety of pistols, flare guns, heavy darts and small bombs.

The greatest potential leap in aviation and warfare comes from the designs and experiments in rocket propulsion from Professor von Braun. A new jet pack incorporates fuel and propulsion units backed with a primitive control mechanism. There is already a unit of 'jagerindenhimmel' who are trained in the use of this device which may also revolutionise warfare. The most ambitious scheme of Braun's scientific team is to design rockets capable of reaching other bodies of the solar system. They have already received encouragement from the Prince Regent, who now dreams of seeing the German Empire place its banners and jackboots on new worlds.

Great Britain

Great Britain has an enormous Empire linked by the largest mercantile fleet in the world. Her Queen Empress, Gloriana II, is a popular monarch who rules through a parliament.

After a Queen Victoria's death from typhus in 1861, the country enjoyed a long Edwardian age of Imperial glory and prosperity. The era was renowned enough to still influence fashion and architecture across the world to the current day.

Britain has considerable pride and faith in her navy, and she has more ironclad battleships than any other two nations combined. Recent developments in warfare, particularly airpower and submersibles will, however, quickly put considerable strain on her ability to rule the waves. Her army is well-trained but relatively small compared with many other Imperial powers. The Royal Sky Force is another small but efficient military arm, its pilots, young, dashing men like Major Arkwright, are the new heroes of the patriotic public.

Traditionally, Britain has avoided military intervention in European squabbles since the time of the First French Empire. During the previous century, she found herself co-operating with the French in various foreign expeditions and the two nations ensured the victory of the CSA. The 'Entente Cordiale' was ended with Britain's reluctance to assist the French in their war against the German states. Officially, the Queen's government is committed to maintaining a balance of power in the world, although her old return to 'Splendid Isolation' is threatened by other powers. Japan and Turkey are her largest perceived threat at the current time, as she is unaware of the impending threat from Argentina. Worse yet for the Empire, her colonies are starting to question the authority of the Mother Country and the unrest and agitation for Home Rule in Ireland is a constant problem. For the moment, it is only the use of the army as an Imperial police force that has kept dissention from breaking out into full scale wars of independence.

Society for Psychical Research

The SPR was founded in 1882 and undertakes investigation into psychic phenomena. It has helped expose various frauds over its history but, its members are still engaged in scientific tests that sometimes provide possible evidence of psychic abilities in individuals or resonances in objects. Needless to say, the findings are monitored by a Disruptor Knight — Doctor Ernst Ruprecht Bastable — who is eager to find new talents for his masters.

Valhalla is countering Doctor Bastable with Ms Rosemary Olivia Wilde, its senior field agent on the parallel. Ms Wilde has been instructed to recruit her own team of psychics to oppose those corrupted by Bastable's efforts, his Disruptor Pawns, and those who have unwittingly fallen into his sphere of influence. Ms Wilde travels the sky lanes of the Empire regularly, searching for likely recruits into her secretive Valhalla cell.

The Kingdom of Italia

Italia is a late starter amongst the great powers and, having no significant empire of her own, she is keen to be on the winning side of a war if able to start one. She nurses a particular ambition to gain possessions in the Mediterranean, especially those held by the Ottoman Empire. Italia has been a consistent critic of the CSA, especially after the cities on the east coast of the USA, along with their Italian-American communities, were absorbed. The anti-Catholic activities of the White Knights of America keep diplomatic tensions continually stoked up.

King Bruno, the titular head of state, is under the thumb of Pope Constantine IV, as the supreme pontiff was once his household confessor, during which period, the holy man gained an intimate knowledge of the monarch's guilty secrets. The pope is served by a widespread church whose churches and missions are used to spread his doctrines into most of the world's nations. Less obvious, though ruthlessly efficient, is the Inquisition, a network of priests and agents devoted to the Vatican. Many of the greatest threats to the pope's power actually come from within Italy itself. The criminal mafia pays lip service to the Church of Rome, but has considerable power, especially in the poorest parts of the country. Worse yet, a powerful secret cabal of Freemasons which incorporates politicians, officials and businessmen seek to enrich themselves through control of the government, the police and the judiciary. Nor can the cardinals themselves be trusted totally, as many scheme to wear the papal crown and enjoy power in the realm of earth before they ascend to heaven. However, the Pope's biggest personal fear is of assassins sent against him by the Ottomans. In the previous year, a Turkish assassin shot and wounded the Pope with several bullets, but failed to kill him. Now the pontiff fears that the Turks have approached The Old Man of the Mountain to ensure that a fresh attempt will succeed.

Japan

From the middle of the previous century, Japan allowed Western influence to bring about rapid change to its level of technology and also converted it from an isolationist, inward-looking feudal nation to a fledgling great power. The Japanese retained an Emperor and the warrior code of *Bushido,* but modernised their military might. The Imperial Air Force was heavily influenced by CSA advisors, whilst Great Britain helped develop Japan's navy. Since the start of the current century, Japan has annexed parts of China and Russia and continues to adopt an aggressive stance towards them. Her good relations with both the CSA and Great Britain are potentially compromised in recent years due to her desire to obtain colonies that will provide raw materials for her industrial might.

Her army is noted for its fanatical devotion and her air and naval arms are equipped with modern vessels. A notable feature of her naval warfare has been the use of fast torpedo boats, some of which have been modified to conduct suicidal ramming operations with their sterns packed with explosives. The military are keen to gain German assistance in producing autogyros and are pressuring the Japanese into making a huge diplomatic effort to build an alliance with Germany. If this is to fail, the obtaining of blueprints and a working aircraft will be accorded the highest priority by the espionage services.

Largely unheeded, some mystics in the Empire are actually trying to steer their country towards forming alliances against the CSA, influenced by visions of destruction shown to them by five saints or Buddhas.

Russia

The Empire of the Czars is an ailing giant weakened by lost wars. The current ruler, Czar Vladimir, is closely related to most of Europe's monarchs. He is a proud, religiously devout, traditionalist who resists any attempts to introduce democracy or national independence within his realm.

The country's economy and government is poorly developed alongside its rivals and her armies and armadas are, whilst vast, poorly equipped and led. Currently the country is trying to stop Turkish and Japanese encroachment on its borders.

Although many of the Czar's subjects are fiercely loyal, others resent their lot and periodically uprisings occur, only to be ruthlessly quashed. The secret police are vigilant against attempts to question or undermine the system and dissidents are sent to colonies and mines in Siberia. Many of these exiles have been freed in recent years by warbands opposed to Imperial rule. The most persistent terrorist threat comes from the successful activist and guerrilla leader, Octobriana.

The Ministry of the Interior is currently developing techniques into controlling the behaviour and thinking of human subjects. To date, these psychological tests, aided by drugs, have achieved debatable results, other than an improvement in interrogation techniques. The Ministry has high hopes that some experimental apparatus can be used to subvert captured dissidents and foreign spies into the service of the Ministry.

Turkey

Bellicose Russian foreign policy encouraged various nations to assist the modernisation of the ailing Ottoman Empire's military during the latter half of the nineteenth century. This allowed her to hang on to her possessions in the Balkans and the Middle East and to consolidate and expand her hold in large parts of Africa. In recent decades, her Empire has expanded into parts of Persia, much to the consternation of Britain and Russia. Turkey aspires to regain control of North Africa and parts of Russia.

The Pasha has become a mere state figurehead, as power now resides with a military elite. Although possessed of considerable military might, the Empire also makes use of the services of The Old Man of the Mountain. The later is a descendant of his namesake, the Syria-based leader of a religious sect which made use of skilled and fanatical assassins. From his mountain fortress, the ancient, vulture-like man operates as an information broker who is not too scrupulous about how he gets what he needs or to whom he hires his services.

The New Cold War

Designator: 13.16.94
Classification: Snowball Earth
Cultural Type: Northern American
Political Type: Anarchic
Technological Type: Industrial Age

Based on an explosion of Disruptor influence that quickly faded to nothing, W.O.T.A.N initially calculated this parallel to be devoid of life. However, subsequent data mining revealed a world where humanity is still clinging to life, although its fingers are slipping over the edge.

When the Disruptors first interfered in this parallel, it was at the pinnacle of the computer age. Megaplexes and arcologies covered the globe and over 90% of the population enjoyed unparalleled security and well-being. Instead of just introducing weapons and fomenting strife, the Disruptors introduced massive terra-forming equipment and encouraged the nations of the world to reshape the landscape to better meet their needs. Even the Disruptors were not prepared for what came next. The terra-forming ran haywire and the planet was plunged into a new ice age that worsened. City after city blinked out of existence as the glaciers spread across the globe. By the time the glaciers stopped, the world as it was known was gone. Handfuls of people banded together to rebuild. Lacking anything to do the Disruptors retreated to monitor this parallel from their World-Ship.

Although the technology is lost, the knowledge is not. Humankind is rebuilding. Only a few hundred years since the last glaciation, society has already reached an early industrial age with ice-clippers carving paths across the ice from settlement to settlement.

The largest settlement, with over 10,000 people is New Toronto, built on the remains of the Montreal-Ottawa-Toronto megaplex. The settlement's leader is Mayor Frode, a massively corpulent man, assisted by a clockwork exoskeleton. More and more people flock to New Toronto when word spreads of the available work and relatively plentiful resources. Yonge ensures the settlement takes in no more people than it can currently care for and defend, his analytical engine calculating probabilities for survival. Those who are turned away are guided by New Toronto ice-explorers to other friendly settlements such as Balt-Wash and Bismark.

As humanity rebuilds, the Disruptors have returned, choosing to bolster the fortunes of North Winds Organisation, a confederation of pirates operating from the Reykjavik ice shelf. Using state-of-the-art ice clippers, the pirates are able to cover most of the globe raiding for months at a time before needing to refuel or empty holds of plunder and slaves. So far, they are avoiding the well-defended New Toronto, but the pirates are becoming bolder.

Valhalla agents can help rebuild society, protect settlements from the pirates, or hunt down Disruptor Pawns across the ice shelves.

Secession

Designator: 01.09.11
Classification: Solar Colonies
Cultural Type: Northern American
Political Type: Bureaucracy
Technological Type: Spacefaring Age

The Disruptors involved themselves in this world at the dawn of the space age, providing enough knowledge to propel several nations to the stars faster than would otherwise have been possible. Then, the Disruptors faded into the shadows to watch how things played out.

As exploration developed, lunar and Martian colonies soon followed. Now that there are thriving colonies in space, the Disruptors re-emerged. They agitated extremist anti-colony groups on Earth, arming them with weapons and fanning the flames of the groups' isolationist policies. As one, the extremists rose up and attacked the governments, which are fighting for their very existence. The ferocity and firepower brought to bear by the terrorists completely overwhelmed the government forces.

As the battles tear across the Earth's surface, the colonies are running out of supplies. They were never self-sufficient and depend on supply ships from Earth to augment what little they can produce locally. If the extremists are not pushed back and the supply lines re-established, the colonies will slowly wither.

Valhalla agents can strike at the extremists to push them back from the space ports or even attempt to resupply the

colonies, with or without the governments' knowledge. However, the warfare is taking its toll on nations across the planet and the agents can help protect citizens from the Disruptor backed forces.

Barbarians at the Gates

Designator: 01.11.43
Classification: Japan Ascendant
Cultural Type: Eastern Asia
Political Type: Militaristic
Technological Type: Nanotechnology Age

When Tokugawa closed Japan, he did so at the behest of the Disruptors. In the intervening centuries between the commencement of Sakoku, the closing, and the arrival of Commodore Perry in 1853, the Disruptors provided Japan with numerous technological upgrades, propelling the island nation through its industrial age.

When the Black Fleet arrived, the Japanese blew it out of the water. Before word could even reach London or Washington, Japanese gun-samurai had besieged Peking and Manila and rockets were falling on Vladivostok.

By the time the European powers could organise enough to make a stand, the governments of China, Russia, and Germany were operating in exile in Reykjavik and the American west coast was under heavy bombardment. A standstill was reached; the Western world consisted of North America east of the Mississippi, South America, Africa, and Europe west of the Meuse. Japan controls everything else.

In the present day, the Japanese Emperor keeps a close on his dominions, accepting fealty from nations his ancestors mercilessly crushed. His vast economy exports goods to his satellite states and even those he did not conquer. His high tech networks keep track of all his loyal citizens, just in case there's a turncoat in the mix.

It transpires there are numerous turncoats. Spies loyal to the other powers, or even just the concept of freedom, have worked within Japan's borders for years. It has surfaced that after 80 years of peace, Japan is once again eyeing those parts of the world it does not own. The Disruptors have introduced new weapons to upgrade Japan's forces and the weapons factories are in full operation.

If something is not done soon, the rest of the world will fall.

Time Slip

Designator: 07.99.54
Classification: Europe In Flames
Cultural Type: Northern Europe
Political Type: Bureaucratic
Technological Type: Industrial Age

Most parallels have the same place in their orbit around the sun. This one is different, it's several hours ahead, which accounts for the high designator. The Disruptors were hard at work bolstering Serbian terrorists to assassinate several world leaders when the meteorite that struck Tunguska in most other paras struck London, obliterating the city. In a matter of moments, the economic capital of the world disappeared and the global economy collapsed. Europe, and much of the world, began backsliding into a near feudal state over the intervening decades.

Even the Disruptors were surprised by this turn of events, but seized the opportunity and in the chaos that followed began propping up warlords to seize control of regions. They even went one step further, experimenting with releasing The Dark into this parallel to see how events play out.

Now, the world is a patchwork of warring, petty kingdoms with the stuff of nightmares prowling the darkness. Strange human-animal hybrids prey on the unsuspecting. Once-men, former humans wracked by radiation try to infiltrate camps to steal supplies and slaves. Large entities comprised of little more than claws, teeth, and hate devour entire caravans. Small worms, no larger than grains of sand, burrow their way into sleepers' brains to re-wire the pathways and turn the victims into homicidal maniacs that are fully aware of what they're doing, but are powerless to stop.

There are some lights in the darkness, though. Sub-Saharan Africa is home to several kingdoms that are attempting to reestablish the rule of law over the rule of might. Recognizing this threat to the global disorder, the Disruptors are re-arming the warlords and declaring a new crusade, one against the Kingdoms of Kenya and Cameroon.

Which Side?

Designator: 00.01.19
Classification: West Vs. East
Cultural Type: Northern America and Europe
Political Type: Militaristic
Technological Type: Computer Age

The differences in this para are subtle. The world is still gripped in the Cold War, a Democratic United Soviet Republic and her allies fighting against the Communist American Socialist Union and its puppet states in Western Europe. The Berlin Wall still stands, patrolled by American troops armed with Disruptor weapons. The Soviets are on high alert because American missiles are spotted in Finland and more American ships are steaming toward the country.

Spies battle for control of neutral cities such as Mexico City and Caracas, hoping to tip the balance of power ever so slightly for their side. Double agents betray their nations for a chance to live the dream in Warsaw or Moscow.

Americans meanwhile, toil to meet quotas and wait in bread lines for their evening rations. However, there are elements in American society led by a shadow government that are attempting to overthrow Regan's politburo and end this stalemate before the world lights up in a nuclear exchange.

Valhalla agents can be called on to help overthrow the despotic regime or merely put out fires caused by the proxy wars being fought in the Philippines, Egypt, and Chile.

Civil War

Designator: 00.04.20
Classification: War of Art
Cultural Type: Southern Europe
Political Type: Artistic
Technological Type: Pre-Industrial

The Disruptor influence on this para began in the Renaissance, quickly unifying the Italian states under the Medici banner. Rather than conquer through warfare, the Medici syndicate spread its rule through the export of art. As the art spread across Europe, heads of states welcomed the Medicis as their overlords, thanks to chemicals released by that art from special Disruptor-designed canisters.

Now, much of Europe is under Italian control without the Italians having to deploy a single soldier. Of course, they did deploy soldiers to enforce their edicts, but it was not necessary. Nations who attempt to attack the Italian Empire soon find their capitals flooded with gifts of Italian art. They quickly realise warfare is not necessary. This is a world dominated by the Catholic Church. The Reformation was crushed by papal armies and Constantinople was reclaimed and restored to its former glory, ranking with Rome, Dublin, Alexandria, and Sao Paolo as the most powerful cities in the world. Islam's spread was halted in Arabia and Egypt's Copts converted to Catholicism.

An anti-art movement spreads among the intelligentsia as people realise what is really causing their beloved homelands to capitulate to the Italians.

Agents can take on the roles of art thieves, trying to liberate cities from the Medici throne or even become vandals, smashing art to expose the Medici's crimes.

For Science

Designator: 00.08.31
Classification: Scientific Utopia
Cultural Type: Central Asia
Political Type: Academic
Technological Type: Computer Age

Every so often unexpected scientific breakthroughs catapult the world ahead by leaps and bounds. One such event occurred in this parallel after the outbreak of a brutal world war. Researchers in Tashkent dealing with the walking wounded and living dead, discovered a means to cure all disease; bacterial, viral, it did not matter. Unfortunately, the scientists did not realise the cost, or that the cure came from the Disruptors.

At first the world rejoiced. Economies exploded as medical costs plummeted. Research could be put toward extending life spans instead of fighting diseases. However, it became apparent that a steady supply of the drug is needed and the materials to synthesise it are rare.

Soon the drug becomes a commodity, trading for high prices. Scientists struggle to come up with alternatives, but it soon becomes apparent that only the best and brightest deserve the cure if humankind is to survive. The scientific elite gather in gleaming cities rising out of vast wastelands that are strip-mined by the unlucky masses deemed 'not eligible.'

In theory the scientists are searching for ways to mass produce the drug, but the Disruptor Pawns in their midst encourage and enable bad experiments and faulty logic, ensuring that the drug supply remains low. Now, the cities are descending into hedonistic pleasure centers, many of the best and brightest deciding to enjoy the long, healthy lives they have because of the broken backs of the leprous poor.

Creating Your Own Parallels

As the Valhalla agents move from para to para, it'll be necessary for the Games Master to create new parallels for agents to visit. Use the following tables to create random parallels or just draw inspiration from them. These tables will help the Games Master get started, but a visit to reference books or online encyclopedias will really help flesh out the world.

Timeline

First, it's necessary to determine when the Disruptors started manipulating history. Although the Disruptors typically become involved once mankind has at least reached the Industrial Age, there's no reason they cannot start modifying things earlier.

The Period Table defines the millennium and century in which the Disruptors being their tweaking of events on a parallel. If, after narrowing it down to a millennium and century, the Games Master wants to determine an actual year, then roll 1d10 and use that value for the year.

Location

Once the time when the Disruptors become involved has been established, it is necessary to determine where on the planet they start interfering. The locations are intentionally vague because a specific country might not exist for a few hundred years.

Once a time and location have been determined, the Games Master can check a reference book or the internet to see what countries exist in the chosen region during that period. He can pick whichever country piques his interest. It does not need to be the biggest country or the one the Games Master knows the most about; just the one that, at that moment, is the most interesting.

The Event

In the worlds of Luther Arkwright, the event is always precipitated by the Disruptors as they start manipulating events to meet their goals. Once a country is chosen, the Games Master should scan their resources for interesting events that occur around that point in time.

One of the Disruptors' favourite pastimes is to prop up faltering regimes, providing means and materiel for that government to stay in power and continue spreading chaos. To determine exactly how the Disruptors do this, consult The Event table.

Astronomical Event

An astronomical event could be as simple as a comet providing a sign of forthcoming catastrophe, spurring a ruler or religion to change their mind concerning a matter of state, or the deadly nature of a major meteor strike on a nation at the crux of some historical event. While the Disruptors lack the capability to

Millenium (1d8)	Result
1	Prehistoric (Roll on Prehistory table)
2	4th Millennium BC
3	3rd Millennium BC
4	2nd Millennium BC
5	1st Millennium BC
6	1st Millennium AD
7	2nd Millennium AD
8	3rd Millennium AD

Century (1d10)	Result
1	10th BC/1st AD
2	9th BC/2nd AD
3	8th BC/3rd AD
4	7th BC/4th AD
5	6th BC/5th AD
6	5th BC/6th AD
7	4th BC/7th AD
8	3rd BC/8th AD
9	2nd BC/9th AD
10	1st BC/10th AD

Prehistory (1d4)	Era
1	Pleistocene
2	Palaeolithic
3	Mesolithic
4	Neolithic

affect astronomical events, they can manipulate how the people respond. A comet streaked across Europe in 1618 near the start of the Thirty Years War. The Disruptors could spread propaganda that the comet is sign the powers should not go to war and over the course of the next century Protestantism is slowly exterminated, first in the German states, then elsewhere.

Battle Outcome Reversed

A simple change to make to any established history, merely search for a major battle and reverse its outcome. Marc Antony winning the Battle of Actium, thus propagating the center of the Roman power to Egypt and forever changing its main focus from Europe to Asia. Many of history's most famous battles have brought about the rise of a dynasty or fall of an empire. This is one of the Disruptors' most popular techniques, either by providing advanced military equipment or techniques. Imagine what the world would be like if the Ottomans had water-cooled machine guns at the Battle of Vienna. The city would have fallen and the Ottomans sweep into Europe.

1D20	Location
1	Northern America
2	Central America
3	South America
4	Caribbean
5	Northern Europe
6	Western Europe
7	Southern Europe
8	Eastern Europe
9	Northern Africa
10	Western Africa
11	Central Africa
12	Southern Africa
13	Eastern Africa
14	Western Asia
15	Central Asia
16	Southern Asia
17	Eastern Asia
18	Southeastern Asia
19	Australasia
20	Oceania

1D20	The Event
1	Astronomical Event
2	Battle Outcome Reversed
3	Climate Change
4	Devastating Weapon
5	Ecological Upset
6	Economic Boom or Bust
7	Geological Disaster
8	Great Leader Dies or Survives
9	Invaluable Resource Discovered
10	Invasion by Neighbours
11	New Philosophy
12	Outside Intervention
13	Plagues and Immunities
14	Political Ideology
15	Racial Genocide
16	Religious Persecution
17	Rulers Overthrown
18	Scientific Breakthrough
19	Technological Crash
20	Unexpected Alliance

Climate Change

What could happen to the chosen region if it became warmer, colder, wetter or dryer? Would it cause widespread famine and migrations of people, or make the nation more bountiful, thus driving a burst of cultural development? South America has seen dozens of small empires rise and fall because of enduring weather changes, and similarly, there is the survival of Norse settlements in the northern Atlantic. This is another situation where the Disruptors can change perception of climate change more easily than affect climate change. However, the Disruptors can introduce technology that starts the Industrial Age early, hastening the Greenhouse Effect. Or, they can use their Pawns to assassinate scientists and critics of climate change, ensuring that remediation and mitigation is hampered or stopped all together.

Devastating Weapon

The development of a radical new military weapon can overthrow the power balance between nations. What would have occurred if Nazi Germany had developed the Atom Bomb first, or if the Songhai Empire of Africa had developed massed gunpowder musketeers before the European nations?

Ecological Upset

Thoughtless transfer of plants or animals can subvert or even overthrow an entire ecosystem, the arrival of mankind to Australia during the Pleistocene being a case in point. Introducing rats or toads can collapse the food chain forcing a nation to war in search of sustenance. Twisting it the other way, imagine a world where humans did not discover the Americas until the 15th Century, leaving the entire continent up for grabs, yet still heaving with huge and deadly megafauna!

Economic Boom or Bust

Collapsing economies are precursors of war or radical social upheaval, whereas prosperity encourages the opposite. Poverty tends to drive nationalism, racism and religious intolerance as people look around themselves for others to blame. The French Revolution, for instance, brought about the rise of Napoleon and his expansionist wars. But what if it had been France which discovered South America and looted its stores of gold, silver and other precious substances? Would the lives of the French peasants have been bolstered by the wealth brought back to their country, thus bringing enlightenment without the need for bloodshed?

Geological Disaster

Volcanic eruptions and mighty earthquakes, including their associated tsunamis, often place tremendous stress on the nations within which they occur. The explosion of Thera brought about the collapse of the Minoans, and soon after the Mycenaean city states. If the volcano had not erupted, perhaps 'Atlantis' would have spurred technology and philosophy to develop a millennium earlier and forged a pan-Mediterranean civilisation to rival that of Rome's. Disruptor technology can cause disasters and they can also warn civilizations that one is coming, allowing a potentially doomed empire to survive.

Great Leader Dies or Survives

What would have happened if Stalin had prematurely died at the end of the Second World War, or Alexander the Great had not died in Babylon, but had gone on to conquer India and perhaps the entire Orient, living on as a tyrant until his 70's? It may seem that generals and politicians are the most influential personages in history, but scientists or religious leaders can have even more influence.

Invaluable Resource Discovered

The discovery of valuable resources and the rush to exploit them have driven much of human history. Precious metals and hydrocarbons have been the cause of many invasions, even in modern times, but the lack of a resource is not the only aspect which can be exploited. Britain once overthrew an entire nation by capitalizing on Opium and creating a drug culture which could only be satisfied via their near monopoly.

Invasion by Neighbours

Although this can be caused by innumerable reasons, an invasion is often catastrophic to a region. Even if the invasion is not military in nature, population displacement can bring famine as local food supplies are overstretched, revolutionise society with newly introduced ideas, cause religious tension as different faiths co-mingle, or simple population surplus can lead to apartheid or slavery.

New Philosophy

A new philosophy can have religious, political or ethical effects. If a national leader suddenly changes religion or decides to introduce a new justice system, it can radically change the course of history. Beneficial examples include women's suffrage, secular government, and social welfare. Negative effects might occur such as the right to use those convicted of capital crimes as human guinea pigs, or enforced social castes.

Outside Intervention

An outside intervention is pretty self-explanatory. Usually this will be a large state or empire coming to the aid, or taking advantage of, a smaller nation, although the unforeseen efforts of a tiny region, association or religion can occur too. Alternate history does not necessarily need to constrain itself to mundane realism, however. Intervention from a parallel plane of existence is very easy to imagine, since it's how the Disruptors operate. Remember, though, that Valhalla agents can have as big an impact on history as the Disruptors.

Plagues and Immunities

Disease often has a dramatic effect on world history, the spread of smallpox devastating the population of the Americas for instance, or European armies laid low by Malaria or Yellow Fever. However, this change need not always be one of susceptibility. Imagine the world if the Disruptors provided smallpox vaccinations to the First Nations of America or provided a cure for the bubonic plague in Medieval Europe?

Political Ideology

The advent or fall of political ideologies has often shaped human history. Communism and Fascism, Republics and Democracies, each time they have been introduced or allowed to grow corrupt the cultural effects have been profound. An alternate history might change what actually happened by preventing the ideology from occurring in the first place, or by changing it entirely. Where might China be today if it its last emperor had not abdicated in 1912, contributing to its military factionalism when it attempted to become a republic?

Religious Persecution

Religious persecution often seems to occur, not only when two culturally different faiths come into contact with one another, but also when a faith suffers an internal schism. Whether driven by the passions of its believers, or cynically utilised by its priesthood as a political tool to garner power, religious persecution can force population exodus, genocide or civil war. However, not all persecution is so harsh, some societies allow pursuit of other faiths at the cost of becoming a second class citizen or paying higher taxes.

Rulers Overthrown

The ruler of a nation, creed or organised religion can be overthrown for a multitude of reasons from war to failing to uphold the tenets of their beliefs. How the ruler is overthrown, and whether they survive to return are vital to consider. If William the Conqueror had failed to defeat the rebellions following his victory at the Battle of Hastings, he could have been deposed, opening the throne of England to one of the surviving Anglo-Saxon earls or Danish invaders.

Scientific Breakthrough

New scientific developments cause radical social, economic or military change. Cures for disease allow population growth, whilst the advent of steam and water power brought about the Industrial Revolution and all the ills and benefits of subsequent urbanization. Not all scientific breakthroughs are necessarily advantageous, as Weapons of Mass Destruction and today's inescapable surveillance state now show, but always incur a major cultural and political effect. Neither does the breakthrough need to be technologically advanced, as a mere copper axe can be a radical development during the Paleolithic.

Technological Crash

Although there are few major technological crashes evidenced in history, they have happened. The ancient classical world was able to achieve the construction of sophisticated clockwork astronomical computers and prototype steam motivation prior to the fall of their respective civilizations. The more modern the period however, the greater the sociological disaster which accompanies such a collapse. A limited nuclear war, uncontrolled spread of a highly lethal disease, or massive weather shifts can have radical effects on the world, and are within the capabilities of the Disruptors.

Unexpected Alliance

An unexpected alliance can produce economic or socio-political stability for a region, or conversely, cause friction among those threatened or jealous of such a union. Whilst a strong union might deter financial or political meddling by others, it could also provoke direct attack if considered too threatening. Other examples could include erstwhile enemy nations suddenly switching sides to ensure their own survival.

Finishing Touches

Once a change has been decided upon, give a little thought to how it affects the larger world. Do not worry about all the socio-political ramifications and what would or would not be accurate. After all, you're not modelling history, you're modelling *alternate* history. The same change in the same location in the same period could have different ramifications in different parallels — and serve as an excellent platform for adventure and consternation for the agents. Just think about what would be fun for the Games Master and the players.

Then, decide how long the Disruptors have been involved before W.O.T.A.N calculates that it is time to intercede. Feel free to roll multiple times on the Change Table to create further deviations from expected history if W.O.T.A.N is slow to recognise the threat and drive the Valhalla Project to act.

The Designator

W.O.T.A.N has a very complex algorithm for calculating each parallel's designator. It is way too long to reproduce here and could attract unwanted Disruptor attention. So, the Games Master should base the designator on how different he thinks the parallel is from the base of 00.00.00. As noted on page 38, *Home Parallels*, birthdays can be a useful source of indication, or simply roll 1d100 for each set of digits to determine a suitable Designation.

BRYAN TALBOT '89

Games Master Resources

This, and the following chapters offer advice on running Luther Arkwright campaigns, provides game statistics for personalities featured in the graphic novels (and others) and rounds out with an introductory scenario for Valhalla Agents.

Arkwright Campaigns

This is a game of alternate histories, not a reproduction of a certain time in Earth's history. The Games Master should work to create an atmosphere that represents the parallel, not try to model everything down to the last detail. There are a few reason for this. First of all, this is a game and it's about fun, not doctoral theses. Second, with Disruptor influence, all bets are off. If the Games Master and players think it would be fun for everyone to be wearing classical Edo fashion, then so be it.

The Games Master can explain all the differences of the new para to the players, but it's experiencing the differences that will make it memorable.

There are several ways to help create the atmosphere.

Remember the Medium 1

Luther Arkwright is a graphic novel character. He is larger than life, capable of superhuman feats and exists in a shadowy, dangerous, hedonistic landscape where larger than life Characters abound. Villains are truly heinous; sex and drugs are ways of life; the fate of the multiverse is at stake. Although one does not necessarily need to lever all these elements into an Arkwright campaign, understanding the graphic novel trope — and the episodic nature of the story will help enormously. Try to view each game session as a 24 page instalment in a weekly or monthly series. Each episode should attempt to:

- Establish a theme or mood (is this episode a little more light-hearted than others? Or is this where the ultraviolence kicks-in?)
- Advance the story a little further towards the final goal
- Reveal something new, and resolve something introduced earlier
- Provide a little more character development and depth
- Provide a challenge for the protagonists
- Engage the audience a little more, and gain greater audience buy-in for the complete story (in this case, the players are the audience).

A Luther Arkwright instalment typically hits three to four of these elements, each episode building towards a conclusion where several story strands, involving separate groups of protagonists, finally come together into a unified whole. Each episode sees the emphasis shift a little. In some episodes there is focus on developing Arkwright's character; in others the focus shifts to the villains. In others the Rude Mechanicals (a Shakespearean term for the supporting cast, such as Harry Fairfax, to provide some comic relief) are allowed to shine. And, at carefully planned intervals, there are bursts of some quite horrific violence, be they duels, shoot-outs, picthed battles, or vicious truncheon beatings. One word on violence in Arkwright games: use it sparingly. There is no need for a gun fight every session — the Characters will simply die at an alarming rate. Instead, combat should occur only when utterly necessary and when there is no other alternative. Gun combat in particular is unflinchingly brutal, and the combat rules in this book reflect that. But be sparing with combat. It should shock and appal; it should not be treated as a 'must have' or an essential component of every scenario.

Remember the Medium 2

Luther Arkwright is part of a very British tradition of counter-culture adventure that evolved in the 1960s and 1970s, primarily through the New Wave of Science Fiction promoted by Michael Moorcock, J G Ballard, Brian *Aldiss* and others; and 'agency' TV shows such as *The Avengers, The Prisoner, Danger Man, Department S, Jason King* and others. Charismatic antiheroes who swagger their way through precarious situations in an exagerated Britain where the soundtrack is by Cream, Pink Floyd and Jimi Hendrix. The outlandish is embraced and the Establishment gleefully rebelled against (even though the protagonists are ultimately working on its side). These times, which actively rebelled against the austerity of the 1950s and the grim threat of the grey Cold War, are reflected amply in Luther Arkwright, even though the original stories take place in the early 1980s. That same atmosphere found in the New Wave novels such as the Jerry Cornelius quartet, deliberately permeates Arkwright. Games Masters are encouraged to read the works of Ballard, Aldiss, Moorcock and Anthony Burgess to get a feel for the both the times and the atmosphere. Or watch shows such as *The Avengers, Sapphire and Steel, Department S*, and *The Prisoner* to get a better idea of Luther Arkwright's roots.

Have Fun With It

It bears repeating one more time. When running a Luther Arkwright campaign, feel free to toss everything but a basic knowledge of history out the window. Want a world where the Wild West still exists, but intermingled with Chinese warlords? Go for it. Do not worry about the repercussions.

Use Names

Once it has been decided where the point of Disruptor influence occurred, use that region's names for most non-player Characters. If it's a world where Rome never fell, then having Roman sounding names helps convey the period. It's more likely that agents will encounter someone named Marcus Aurelius than Benjamin Franklin, so save the less common names for when they'll have the most impact.

The same goes for place names. The Games Master does not have to research what other countries and cities were called by the nation that's the focal point of the change. But if the Games Master can create appropriate sounding place names, it'll help sell the change. Using the Roman example again, call Germany Germania and players will get the hint that things are different.

Use Architectural Features

Every culture puts its own spin on architecture. If the Games Master refers to the Central Pagoda of London or the Kraal of Portland, certain mental images are created. Just like referring to the Eiffel Tower of Jakarta or the Kremlin of Mombasa will spur certain images to set the mood.

Use Retro-Sci-Fi Elements

The Luther Arkwright comic books are a pastiche of numerous different eras. Nominally set in the latter part of the 20th century, motorcycles are rare, a tool of the Disruptors, dirigibles ply the skyways, and Luther himself affects an old British military uniform. Take advantage of the precedent set by the source material. If there's an appealing aesthetic, incorporate it. Old technology works alongside new technology, although having the flashiest technology is often a sign of Disruptor allegiance.

Use Multiple Parallels

The multiverse is a huge place and the Disruptors' plans span all of it. The agents might have to hop from one parallel to another chasing the Disruptors before they can put a stop to whatever it is the Disruptors are planning. The agents might even have to return to the same paras multiple times in order to truly get to the bottom of what's going on. Luther's ability to shift from one para to another without the help of technology greatly facilitated this, and the agents might run into resistance from Zero-Zero regarding all the shifting, but that contention can add to the drama.

Make the Most of a Parallel

Remember that each parallel is an entire Earth, and the Disruptors are an organised force. Resist the temptation to have agents slide into a new parallel each session to experience the latest alternate history. Have missions that span parallels, but require significant investigation on each parallel. The more familiar players become with a given parallel, the more memorable it will be.

Mix Genres

Many role-playing games stick to a single genre. This one is an opportunity to mix-and-match genres. While every mission should have a mix of investigation, interpersonal drama, and action, each parallel can be the embodiment of a genre. Perhaps one parallel requires covert operations on behalf of the Fourth Boer Orange State. Maybe another has the agents going toe-to-toe with Disruptor enhanced super-soldiers trying to crush the Mughal Empire. A third is a slow burn mystery into why children are disappearing from orphanages across Communist Mexico. The Games Master should draw upon all sorts of influences and bring those references to the fore.

A Touch of Magic

The Mythras rules offer five magic systems, of which one, Mysticism, is used in Luther Arkwright. Even though the Arkwright saga is a Science Fiction series, with rational explanations for seemingly supernatural events, there is nothing to prevent a parallel from having access to magical powers such as sorcery or even theism. On some parallels the laws of physics might be different; on others there may be creator deities who grant their followers miracles. On another, extra-dimensional beings might be regarded and venerated as spirits. Used wisely and sparingly, a little magic could lend a whole new aspect to an Arkwright campaign.

Inject a Little Horror

In *Heart of Empire* more than a few horror elements are present; the vampiric nature of Queen Anne and the mutated psychic being of

Victoria's brother, Henry. Do not be afraid to add such elements to a parallel, be they the result of science or the supernatural. Aliens, mutants, monsters, creatures of the Id — everything is usable and nothing should be off limits.

Expand the MacGuffins

FireFrost's activation drives the imperative of the first set of Arkwright's adventures and a similar cataclysm drives *Heart of Empire*. There will be other technologies and devices, either Disruptor-created or hijacked by them for nefarious purposes, that can form the imperative for your own Arkwright campaign. Well-meaning scientists stumble on powerful weapons that fit the need of the Disruptors nicely; an ancient weapon predating FireFrost is suddenly uncovered by a spacefaring parallel. But do not forget less grandiose plot drivers: the Disruptors act subtly and seek to manipulate power bases. Many missions and campaigns can be centred around covertly identifying and breaking Disruptor control so that a parallel can lead its own destiny. What, though, if that destiny might result in something akin to the Holocaust? What if the Disruptors' machinations are actually preventing a greater catastrophe? Valhalla agents might have to make difficult choices and face situations that are morally questionable, even though it would mean a Disruptor defeat...

Read the Graphic Novels

Finally, read the Luther Arkwright graphic novels if you have not already done so. They are readily available and, at the time of writing, have been released in a wonderful Anniversay edition *Arkwright Integral*. There is no substitute and Bryan's masterful artwork and storytelling is an unparalleled (every pun intended) work of graphic novel fiction.

For those who need it, the Arkwright Saga is summarised beginning on page 167.

Personalities

This section provides game statistics for a variety of Characters from the Arkwright stories. Many can be used in scenarios for the players' Characters to interact with, whilst others can be used as templates (or even outright alternate versions) for a whole variety of non-player character types.

A note or two on using Luther Arkwright himself. Arkwright is a very special case; not only is he unique, he is also the epitome of *homo novus* and thus way beyond the capabilities of most player Characters. If Games Masters decide to introduce in their games, he should be a shadowy, spraely used figure. It might be too easy for Arkwright to simply become a deus ex machina, solving the Characters problems if he is allowed too great a role in proceedings. It is therefore recommended that the player Characters only encounter him occasionally. Although based on his adventures, this game is about the Characters' stories, their chronicles, their struggle against the Disruptors. Give them a chance to shine and leave Luther Arkwright as a very occasional guest star.

Luther Arkwright

Arkwright's background is given throughout this book and especially on pages 13 to 14. He is Valhalla's top agent: an extraordinary psychic that has the power to translocate and leave behind no discernible signature alerting others to his presence on a parallel. He is the only one of his kind anywhere in the multiverse and was part of both the Five's attempt to develop *homo novus* and the Disruptors' attempt to create the ultimate warrior.

With his white-blond hair and boyish good looks, Arkwright is engimatic and charming. Before the FireFrost incident he is something of a loose cannon, with a prediliction for casual sex, occasional drug use (even though he conquered serious drug addiction once) and an adversity to creating emotional attachments.

Indeed, this very coldness is what contributes to his to his effectiveness as a Valhalla agent. Arkwright is emotionally detached from reality and therefore able to commit appalling acts of violence, and use other people for his own ends, without suffering any personal consequences. If he cares for anyone, it is for Rose Wylde in many of her incarnations, although he maintains a stream of lovers on many parallels and likely has many illegitimate children.

Arkwright is the most successful and well developed example of *homo novus*. With the ability to translocate, Arkwright is widely travelled across the multiverse. On some parallels he is well known; on others as obscure as anyone else. He has held several important military positions, as a result of his bravery and combat training. Wherever he goes he affects a similar dress; a ceremonial military uniform of some kind, or a crisp, cotton, linen or satin shirt in a blousson style, coupled with leather trousers, boots and a Royal Air Force airman's jacket. Round sunglasses complete the conceit.

He favours three kinds of weapon: a cavalry sabre, a 9mm automatic pistol, and, in parallels where the technology has developed it, a vibrobeamer or its equivalent.

Psychic Powers

Arkwright's powers increase immeasurably after his transfiguration on parallel 00.72.87 during the FireFrost incident. The powers given here are for his 1981, pre-transfiguration abilities. Remember also that Arkwright has been intensively trained by the Disruptors; his psychic talents are therefore far more well-developed than most.

Mysticism

As a result of spending a year with the Five in their remote Himalayan monsatery, Arkwright is a reasonably competent mystic, as reflected in his Mysticism disciplines.

Luther Arkwright	Attributes
STR: 15	**Action Points:** 3
CON: 15	**Damage Modifier:** +1d2
SIZ: 13	**Prana: 18**
DEX: 17	**Tenacity:** 12 **(18-6 for Dependencies)**
INT: 17	**Movement: 6 metres**
POW: 18	**Initiative Bonus:** 17
CHA: 16	**Armour: Leather Jacket (2 points)**

1d20	Hit Location	AP/HP
1 – 3	Right Leg	0/6
4 – 6	Left Leg	0/6
7 – 9	Abdomen	0/7
10 – 12	Chest	2/8
13 – 15	Right Arm	2/5
16 – 18	Left Arm	2/5
19 – 20	Head	0/6

Skills	Passions, Traits & Dependencies
Acrobatics 80%, Athletics 90%, Brawn 28%, Comms 80%, Computers 70%, Conceal 75%, Courtesy 90%, Culture (Various) 55%, Deceit 88%, Demolitions 75%, Electronics 75%, Endurance 70%, Evade 74%, First Aid 72%, Gambling 75%, Influence 80%, Insight 70%, Language (French) 69%, Language (German) 62%, Meditation 80%, Mysticism 55%, Native Language (English), 100%, Oratory 37%, Pilot 48%, Perception 85%, Politics 70%, Science (Multiverse) 58%, Seduction 80%, Sensors 75%, Stealth 84%, Streetwise 75%, Survival 61%, Swim 80%, Willpower 80%	Passions: Love (Rose Wylde) 45%, Loyalty (Valhalla) 75% , Respect (Octobriana) 55% Traits: Psionic, Unique Dependencies: Discipline 65%, Violent 70% Arkwright was addicted to heroin for several years but managed to kick the dependency when he joined the Valhalla Programme. He occasionally uses tobacco and cocaine, but purely recreationally and without risk of dependency.

Psionics & Mysticism	
Attrition 80% (Drain Prana, Evil Eye, Mental Shield) Clairvoyance 84% (Precognition, Psychometry, Sense Danger, Sense Psi) Telekinesis 72% (Focus Force, Shatter) Telepathy 70% (Mind Probe, Thought Implant) Translocate 90% (Shift Parallel)	Transcendental Enlightenment (Astral Projection, Deny Pain, Indomitable)

Combat Style & Weapons	Traits & Notes
Pistol Combat (Ballistic and Energy Handguns) 80% Rifles (Automatic and semi automatic rifles and sub machine guns) 75% Duellist (Duelling Pistols, Cavalry Sabre) 80%	Arkwright favours 9mm automatic pistols and vibrobeamers (technology permitting).

Weapon	Damage	Range	Ammo	Fire Rate/ Load
9mm Pistol	1d6+1	50/100/200	9 (clip)	1/3
Vibrobeamer	1d8	10/20/80	50	1/3
Weapon	**Damage**	**Size/Reach**	**AP/HP**	**Effects**
Sabre	1d8+1d2	M/M	6/12	Bleed, Impale

Rose Wylde

On many, many parallels, Rose Wylde is a highly successful and driven Valhalla agent: often a Senior Field Agent; sometimes an undercover operative; sometimes a contact and provisioner. She is never anything less than loyal, stylish, enigmatic and sensual. Rose possesses an extraordinarily strong empathic link with the vast majority of her selves (a few have no psychic abilities and no link, but they are few) and each version of Rose has almost identical values. She is a passionate defender of multiversal order, hateful of authoritarian regimes, and a staunch defender of personal freedom of expression.

Several Roses have had love affairs with Luther Arkwright, and their personal chemistry is, indeed, very strong; but it is by no means total. On Zero-Zero, Rose has been Karl Merkel's lover, and on 00.72.87, she is involved in an affair with Freda, another Valhalla operative. Although Valhalla protocol discourages inter-operative liaisons, they are not forbidden, and Rose Wyldes have a tendency to form close relationships with working colleagues.

It is likely that Characters in an Arkwright campaign will meet with and get to know several Roses. She is an excellent point of consistency, always well informed, and her empathic link means that she offers a ready connection with Zero-Zero if the Characters ever need it.

Psychic Powers

Although her Empathic Link is her key trait, Rose may also be a skilled Clairvoyant and Telepath. Her powers vary between incarnations; see the Psychic Powers box opposite.

Rose Wylde	Attributes
STR: 11	**Action Points:** 3
CON: 14	**Damage Modifier:** 0
SIZ: 10	**Prana:** 16
DEX: 16	**Tenacity:** 13 (16-3 for Dependencies)
INT: 15	**Movement:** 6 metres
POW: 16	**Initiative Bonus:** 16
CHA: 17	**Armour:** None

1d20	Hit Location	AP/HP
1 – 3	Right Leg	0/5
4 – 6	Left Leg	0/5
7 – 9	Abdomen	0/6
10 – 12	Chest	0/7
13 – 15	Right Arm	0/4
16 – 18	Left Arm	0/4
19 – 20	Head	0/5

Skills	Passions, Traits & Dependencies
Acting 78%, Athletics 46%, Conceal 63%, Comms 30%, Courtesy 64%, Customs (As Needed) 65%*, Dance 55%, Disguise 74%, Endurance 43%, Evade 62%, First Aid 46%, Gambling 42%, Home Parallel 40%, Influence 68%, Insight 72%, Language (English) 54%, Language (German) 34%, Lock Picking 52 %, Oratory 56%, Perception 62%, Politics 36%, Seduction 86%, Sing 33%, Sleight 55%, Stealth 61%, Streetwise 56%, Unarmed 51%, Willpower 71%	Passions: Love (Luther Arkwright) 60%, Loyalty (Valhalla) 80% , Hate (Disruptors) 75% Traits: Psychic, Self Awareness Dependencies: Alcohol 30%, Narcotics 30%, Sex 30%

Psionics	
Clairvoyance 75% (Mental Shield, Sense Danger) Empathy 90% (Empathic Link, Empathic Push, Feel Emotions) Telepathy 70% (Mental Scan, Telepathy)	There is a 90% chance of a Rose Wylde having Psychic abilities. When she does, Empathy is always present, but roll 1d4 to determine if she possess another talent. 1 = None, 2 = Clairvoyance, 3 = Telepathy, 4 = Both

Combat Style & Weapons	Traits & Notes
Pistol Combat (Ballistic and Energy Handguns) 76% Concealed Weapons (Knife, Stilleto) 60%	Rose uses a variety of weapons, but is known to favour the Mauser C96 machine pistol. Her hat pins are usually heavy enough to be used as knives.

Weapon	Damage	Range	Ammo	Fire Rate/ Load
9mm Pistol	1d6+1	50/100/200	10 (clip)	1/3
Weapon	**Damage**	**Size/Reach**	**AP/HP**	**Effects**
Knife/Stilleto	1d3	S/S	2/3	Bleed

Harry Fairfax

Fairfax is a resident of 00.72.87 and a scoundrel of the old area of London known as the Maze. On other parallels Fairfax is member of the landed gentry, but no less scurrilous in his behaviour. The perennial black sheep, Fairfax enjoys drinking, whoring, farting and fighting — not necessarily in that order. He has countless illegitimate offspring and seems to revel in his own debauched nature.

All that said, Harry Fairfax (and several different ones, if the truth be known) is a Valhalla agent, albeit an unwitting one. His knowledge of local politics, the underground Royal Family of 00.72.87 and the mean streets of London Town make him the perfect insurgent. Fairfax is not afraid to get his hands bloody, and if it affords him the opportunity to get revenge on the authoritarian government, even better.

He is no lover of authority at all: anything that interferes with his carousing is guaranteed to earn his resentment. He is therefore an excellent contact on many parallels, where the local version of Rose Wylde tends to act as a controller and minder. He is oblivious to the nature of the Disruptors and their agenda, but he knows there is a bigger picture and little surprises him.

Harry Fairfax	Attributes
STR: 14	**Action Points:** 3
CON: 14	**Damage Modifier:** +1d2
SIZ: 13	**Prana:** 12
DEX: 15	**Tenacity: 8 (-4 for Dependencies)**
INT: 15	**Movement: 6 metres**
POW: 12	**Initiative Bonus:** 15
CHA: 14	**Armour: None**

1d20	Hit Location	AP/HP
1 – 3	Right Leg	0/6
4 – 6	Left Leg	0/6
7 – 9	Abdomen	0/7
10 – 12	Chest	0/8
13 – 15	Right Arm	0/5
16 – 18	Left Arm	0/5
19 – 20	Head	0/6

Skills	Passions, Traits & Dependencies
Athletics 36%, Brawn 54%, Conceal 72%, Culture (The Maze) 80%, Deceit 86%, Demolitions 41%, Endurance 66%, Evade 45%, First Aid 37%, Gambling 90%, Influence 63%, Insight 68%, Mechanisms 80%, Native Language (English), 100%, Perception 74%, Politics 75%, Sleight 77%, Stealth 56%, Streetwise 90%, Survival 75%, Swim 80%, Willpower 80%, Unarmed 68%	Passions: Adore Carousing 90%, Loyalty (Valhalla) 60%, Hate Authority 90% Traits: Deadshot, Fart on Command Dependencies: Alcohol 80%

Combat Style & Weapons	Traits & Notes
Street Brawler (Unarmed, Knife, Brass Knuckles) 85%	Brass knuckles increase unarmed damage by one step.
Low Tech Firearms (Blunderbuss, Bolt Action Rifle, Pistol) 80%	

Weapon	Damage	Range	Ammo	Fire Rate/ Load
.38 Pistol	1d6	50/100/200	6 (revolver)	1/3
.303 Rifle	1d10	100/300/800	20	1/3

Weapon	Damage	Size/Reach	AP/HP	Effects
Knife	1d3+1d2	S/S	2/3	Bleed, Impale
Brass Knuckles	1d4+1d2	T/S	2/1	Stun Location

Octobriana

A fierce Mongol warrior and fighter for Russian liberation, Octobriana is one of Arkwright's many contacts (and lovers) across the multiverse. Tough, single-minded and with seemingly insatiable appetites, Octobriana epitomises the revolutionary zeal in the face of totalitarian regimes.

Octobriana is a multiversal constant. Every version of her across the parallels is engaged in the same attempts to effect revolution in whichever country she has adopted or been born into. Her appearance varies slightly, but the star mark on her forehead (sometimes a tattoo, sometimes warpaint, sometimes a birthmark) is always present, as is her lusty nature, fierce devotion to overthrowing the incumbent regime, and a deep-seated passion for violence.

She also demonstrates some mystical training, and her Mysticism powers are reflected in the character statistics, opposite.

Octobriana	Attributes
STR: 16	**Action Points:** 2
CON: 16	**Damage Modifier:** +1d2
SIZ: 14	**Prana:** 12
DEX: 15	**Tenacity:** 9 (-3 for Dependencies)
INT: 12	**Movement:** 6 metres
POW: 12	**Initiative Bonus:** 14
CHA: 12	**Armour:** None

1d20	Hit Location	AP/HP
1 – 3	Right Leg	0/6
4 – 6	Left Leg	0/6
7 – 9	Abdomen	0/7
10 – 12	Chest	0/8
13 – 15	Right Arm	0/5
16 – 18	Left Arm	0/5
19 – 20	Head	0/6

Skills	Passions, Traits & Dependencies
Athletics 68%, Brawn 60%, Conceal 34%, Culture (Revolutionary Classes) 80%, Deceit 37%, Demolitions 66%, Endurance 71%, Evade 55%, First Aid 55%, Influence 36%, Insight 34%, Language (English) 60%, Meditation 38%, Mysticism 40%, Native Language (Russian) 100%, Lore (Tarot) 90%, Perception 58%, Politics 80%, Ride 90%, Seduction 74%, Stealth 60%, Streetwise 52%, Survival 80%, Swim 30%, Willpower 61%, Unarmed 90%	Passions: Love Sex 90%, Loyalty (Revolutionary Cause) 95%, Hate Bourgeoise 90% Traits: Unshakeable Dependencies: Sex 70%

Mysticism
Mongol Focused Aggression (Awareness, Enhance Damage Modifier, Indomitable, Pain Control)

Combat Style & Weapons	Traits & Notes
Steppes Barbarian (Shortbow, Scimitar. Mounted Combat) 88%	Brass knuckles increase unarmed damage by one step.
Revolutionary Soldier (Pistols, Sub Machine Guns) 84%	

Weapon	Damage	Range	Ammo	Fire Rate/ Load
Uzi 9mm SMG	2d6	600/1000/3000	30 (Clip)	-/-/3, 3
9mm Pistol	1d10	100/300/800	10	1/3

Weapon	Damage	Size/Reach	AP/HP	Effects
Scimitar	1d8+1d2	M/M	4/8	Bleed

Hiram Kowalsky

Hailing from New Amsterdam in the Confederated States of America, Hiram Kowalsky is a hard-smoking, jaded, yet still idealistic reporter for the New Amsterdam Herald. His characteristics presented here can act as a template for any journalist or private investigator.

Kowalsky is dedicated and dogged. His instincts for a story are first-rate and he is deeply interested in socio-political issues. Although not technology averse, he prefers pen, paper and a Remingon manual typewriter to voice recorders and computers. The news is somehow more authentic when the reporter's sweat stains the copy.

Kowalsky has no training in firearms or combat and tries to remain pacifistic.

Hiram Kowalsky	Attributes
STR: 11	**Action Points:** 2
CON: 10	**Damage Modifier:** +0
SIZ: 15	**Prana:** 10
DEX: 12	**Tenacity:** 7 (-3 for Dependencies)
INT: 17	**Movement:** 6 metres
POW: 10	**Initiative Bonus:** 15
CHA: 13	**Armour:** None

1d20	Hit Location	AP/HP
1 – 3	Right Leg	0/5
4 – 6	Left Leg	0/5
7 – 9	Abdomen	0/6
10 – 12	Chest	0/7
13 – 15	Right Arm	0/4
16 – 18	Left Arm	0/4
19 – 20	Head	0/5

Skills	Passions, Traits & Dependencies
Art (Writing) 89%, Athletics 35%, Brawn 44%, Conceal 60%, Culture (New Amsterdam) 90%, Deceit 45%, Drive 75%, Endurance 51%, Evade 32%, First Aid 30%, Influence 68%, Insight 70%, Language (Dutch) 60%, Native Language (English) 100%, Lore (Journalism) 90%, Perception 75%, Politics 90%, Stealth 62%, Streetwise 61%, Swim 30%, Willpower 58%, Unarmed 45%	Passions: Report the Truth 90%, Hate Inequality 80%, Love Intrigue 80% Traits: None Dependencies: Tobacco 60%

Queen Anne Stuart

Sister to the exiled King Charles, Anne is an ambitious monarch-in-waiting and a powerful psychic in her own right. While Charles sets his sights on reclaiming the throne stolen from the Royal Family 300 years before, Anne's sights are set on a greater prize: a British Empire to rival that of the Russo-Prussian Alliance, one that will challenge the supremacy of Rome and one that will bring Europe, India and the Far East firmly under Britannia's benevolent dominion.

Anne achieves all this, but at great cost. She sacrifices Charles to gain the throne. When Arkwright kills Cromwell and his cabinet, she seizes power and ruthlessly expands, using all the methods Cromwell had so adeptly employed (including a Secret Police, spies and dirty tricks), plus some new ones of her own: blackmail, psychic dominance and the taking of hostages from conquered royal houses to ensure obedience.

Her own psychic powers are fuelled by a vampiric need to drain the life force of others. Without doing so, Anne's body quickly emaciates; once renewed with Prana, her sexual appetites are insatiable, a by product of the sheer sexual energy psychic renewal triggers.

There are many such Annes across the multiverse: scheming, ambitious and psionically imbued. On some parallels her ambitions are curtailed by royal protocol, but on many she engineers positions of power for herself and her progeny — just as any good mother, and responsible queen, should.

Psychic Powers

Anne's psychic talents are Attrition and Telepathy: these are summarised opposite. She also suffers from a condition whereby her ability to regenerate Prana is curtailed; as a young woman the condition is slight, but after childbirth her metabolism changes and she can only regain life force by draining it from others. If she does not, she loses one point each from STR and CON every hour until she reaches half her normal levels, as well as regaining no Prana at all.

Her vampiric need has become her driving dependency, accompanied by a voracious sexual appetite. Together they are contributing towards her megalomania, creating a woman who, in later life, is paranoid, cruel, inhumane and self-centred to the point of sociopathy.

Queen Anne Stuart	Attributes
STR: 12	**Action Points:** 3
CON: 14	**Damage Modifier:** 0
SIZ: 10	**Prana:** 16
DEX: 14	**Tenacity:** 6 (-10 for Dependencies)
INT: 18	**Movement:** 6 metres
POW: 16	**Initiative Bonus:** 15
CHA: 15	**Armour:** None

1d20	Hit Location	AP/HP
1 – 3	Right Leg	0/5
4 – 6	Left Leg	0/5
7 – 9	Abdomen	0/6
10 – 12	Chest	0/7
13 – 15	Right Arm	0/4
16 – 18	Left Arm	0/4
19 – 20	Head	0/5

Skills	Passions, Traits & Dependencies
Athletics 44%, Brawn 28%, Courtesy 90%, Culture (Royal Etiquette) 90%, Deceit 90%, Endurance 75%, Evade 30%, First Aid 28%, Influence 110%, Insight 90%, Language (French) 90%, Language (German) 90%, Language (Russian) 80%, Native Language (English), 100%, Lore (Strategy and Tactics) 85%, Oratory 89%, Perception 85%, Politics 90%, Seduction 90%, Stealth 24%, Streetwise 48%, Survival 80%, Willpower 85%, Unarmed 48%	Passions: Rule Britain 110%, Hate Seditionists 95%, Love Children 60% Traits: Psionic, Vampiric Dependencies: Drain Prana 100%, Sex 100% Each point of Prana drained from another directly replenishes 1 point of STR and CON lost to her psychic wasting.

Psionics
Attrition 90% (Drain Prana, Evil Eye, Mental Shield) Telepathy 90% (Mind Probe, Thought Implant)

Combat Style & Weapons	Traits & Notes
Royal Fury (Unarmed) 48%	Brass knuckles increase unarmed damage by one step.
Low Tech Firearms (Bolt Action Rifle, Pistol) 30%	

Weapon	Damage	Range	Ammo	Fire Rate/ Load
.38 Pistol	1d6	50/100/200	6 (revolver)	1/3
.303 Rifle	1d10	100/300/800	20	1/3

Princess Victoria Arkwright-Stuart

The daughter of Luther and Anne, Victoria is much like her father: white-blond hair, a certain imperious detachment, and potent psychic powers. Victoria has not been trained in her talents and so they are raw and unpredictable. She is also under a sustained psionic assault from the creature that her brother, Henry, has now become, resulting in debilitating migraines and nausea that can only be eased through self-pleasuring.

Victoria is something of an architectural and engineering prodigy: at the age of 20 she designed the new Crystal Palace exhibition hall for Hyde Park and oversaw its construction. She is also a phenomenal shot with the English longbow, a natural aptitude for weapons gained from her father, no doubt.

Victoria resents her father's unexplained disappearance and absence from her life. A man venerated by the Britain of 00.72.87 is one she has never known, and until she meets Luther, that resentment borders on hatred. The Princess also exhibits the closeted, bigoted views of an aristocracy utterly insulated from the real world and a Britain that dominates and subjugates its dominions. She is, though, of a progressive frame of mind, keen to learn more of social injustice and understand what drives rebellion. In time her views change and she embraces a republican point of view, dissolving the Empire of Britain and ushering in a new age of democratic rule.

Psychic Powers

Victoria's powers are those of her father, and it is her eventual meeting with him that helps channel them and bring them fully under control.

Victoria Arkwright-Stuart	Attributes
STR: 11	**Action Points:** 3
CON: 12	**Damage Modifier:** 0
SIZ: 11	**Prana:** 18
DEX: 17	**Tenacity:** 6 (-10 for Dependencies)
INT: 18	**Movement:** 6 metres
POW: 18	**Initiative Bonus:** 18
CHA: 16	**Armour:** None

1d20	Hit Location	AP/HP
1 – 3	Right Leg	0/5
4 – 6	Left Leg	0/5
7 – 9	Abdomen	0/6
10 – 12	Chest	0/7
13 – 15	Right Arm	0/4
16 – 18	Left Arm	0/4
19 – 20	Head	0/5

Skills	Passions, Traits & Dependencies
Athletics 52%, Brawn 23%, Courtesy 90%, Culture (Royal Etiquette) 90%, Deceit 31%, Endurance 36%, Evade 44%, Engineering 80%, First Aid 28%, Influence 75%, Insight 45%, Language (French) 90%, Language (German) 90%, Native Language (English), 100%, Lore (Strategy and Tactics) 85%, Oratory 89%, Perception 85%, Politics 90%, Science (Architecture) 70%, Stealth 31%, Willpower 85%, Unarmed 48%	Passions: Love Britain 75%, Love Arkwright 50%, Despise Anne 35% Traits: Deadshot, Psionic Dependencies: Sex 25%

Psionics	
Attrition 36% (Mental Shield) Clairvoyance 36% (Precognition, Psychometry, Sense Danger, Sense Psi) Telekinesis 36% (Focus Force, Shatter) Telepathy 36% (Mind Probe, Thought Implant) Translocate 90% (Levitate, Shift Parallel)	Victoria's powers are nascent, but will grow to be just as powerful as her father's.

Combat Style & Weapons	Traits & Notes
Archery (Longbow) 90%	

Weapon	Damage	Range	Force	Fire Rate/ Load
Longbow	1d8	15/125/250	H	1/2

Disruptor Rook

Armoured head to toe in thick plated protective suits and armed with deadly high-science weaponry, the Rook is the primary shock troop of the Disruptors. They go where the Disruptors need a martial response, and where they want no prisoners taken. Rooks are cold, merciless soldiers that are a perfect example of the way their masters deal with certain problems – with emotionless, faceless, violence. Like their chess piece namesake, Rooks move forward with brute force and eliminate anything in their path.

The Rook's anthropomorphic insectoid styling is more than just a fashion choice. It represents the cloned, drone mentality of the Disruptors' brainwashed troops — the way they can call upon new Rooks whenever they need them. They are not trained as much as fabricated, emerging from the process as one of the many identical tools in the Disruptors' war on order in the multiverse.

Disruptor Rook	Attributes
STR: 20	**Action Points:** 2
CON: 18	**Damage Modifier:** +1d6
SIZ: 18	**Prana:** 12
DEX: 14	**Tenacity:** 12
INT: 8	**Movement: 6 metres**
POW: 12	**Initiative Bonus:** 11
CHA: 6	**Armour: Rook Armour**

1d20	Hit Location	AP/HP
1 – 3	Right Leg	6/8
4 – 6	Left Leg	6/8
7 – 9	Abdomen	6/9
10 – 12	Chest	6/10
13 – 15	Right Arm	6/7
16 – 18	Left Arm	6/7
19 – 20	Head	6/8

Skills	Passions, Traits & Dependencies
Athletics 44%, Brawn 68%, Drive (land vehicle) 52%, Endurance 76%, Evade 68%, Influence 30%, Insight 20%, Mechanisms 32%, Perception 35%, Sensors 34%, Stealth 22%, Unarmed 74%, Willpower 44%	Passions: Obey Commands 100%, Kill Ruthlessley 100% Traits: Nerveless, Null-Psionic Dependencies: None

Combat Style & Weapons	Traits & Notes
Disruptor Energy Weapons (Blasters, Lasers) 85% Disruptor Martial Arts (Unarmed) 80%	Formation Fighting, Skirmishing

Weapon	Damage	Range	Ammo	Fire Rate/ Load
Heavy Blaster	1d10	7/25/50	50	1/3
Blaster Rifle	2d6	30/100/300	100	1/3

Disruptor Pawn

The Disruptors are no fools when it comes to manipulating the multiverse, and one of their primary methods of steering the parallels toward chaos and anarchy is seeding a plot with their own agents. Devoted men and women picked for their ability to be ruthless in whichever way the Disruptors call for. If the mission parameters needed a company brought to its knees, the Pawn will be trained for corporate espionage. If a target is to be assassinated, the Pawn will be a calculated killer. If a revolution-starting terrorist act is the goal, an explosives expert – or a suicide bomber – is precisely what the Pawn can be.

Disruptor Pawns do their best to fit in with their assigned parallel in terms of dress, behaviour and cultural relevance. They are aware Valhalla Project agents will be looking to find them and foil their plans, so they must be careful, but the mission always comes first. If this means self-sacrifice, so be it.

Disruptor Pawn	Attributes
STR: 11	**Action Points:** 3
CON: 12	**Damage Modifier:** +0
SIZ: 13	**Prana:** 12
DEX: 15	**Tenacity:** 12
INT: 12	**Movement:** 6 metres
POW: 12	**Initiative Bonus:** 14
CHA: 10	**Armour:** As Needed

1d20	Hit Location	AP/HP
1 – 3	Right Leg	0/5
4 – 6	Left Leg	0/5
7 – 9	Abdomen	0/6
10 – 12	Chest	0/7
13 – 15	Right Arm	0/4
16 – 18	Left Arm	0/4
19 – 20	Head	0/5

Skills	Passions, Traits & Dependencies
Pawns have a standard 55% rating in skills where they are required to be competent, 75% in skills where they specialise, and 45% in all others.	Passions: Loyalty to Disruptors 90%, Hate Order 90% Traits: Forgettable Features Dependencies: Role Model (Disruptor Knights) 58%

Combat Style & Weapons	Traits & Notes
Firearms (Varies) 55%	

Weapon	Damage	Range	Ammo	Fire Rate/ Load
.38 Pistol	1d6	50/100/200	6 (revolver)	1/3
.303 Rifle	1d10	100/300/800	20	1/3

Disruptor Knight

When a Disruptor agent is successful enough, his or her masters will pour more resources and training into them, transforming them into a higher member of the managing hierarchy. Maintaining the Disruptors' penchant for chessboard analogies, these powerful manipulators within the agency are called Knights – likely for their cunning ability to misdirect and strike with creativity instead of simple brute force.

Disruptor Knights are much like elite Valhalla agents in how they function. They travel the multiverse with their own machinations, plotting and scheming their way through the parallels. They are multi-faceted and multi-talented agents who are not single-minded tools like lower level Disruptors. They are the real movers and shakers in the war against order, and Valhalla agent teams will find that Knights will not be eliminated easily and many become longstanding nemeses instead of simple obstacles.

Disruptor Knight	Attributes
STR: 13	**Action Points:** 3
CON: 16	**Damage Modifier:** +1d2
SIZ: 14	**Prana:** 18
DEX: 14	**Tenacity:** 18
INT: 16	**Movement:** 6 metres
POW: 18	**Initiative Bonus:** 14
CHA: 16	**Armour:** As Needed

1d20	Hit Location	AP/HP
1 – 3	Right Leg	0/5
4 – 6	Left Leg	0/5
7 – 9	Abdomen	0/6
10 – 12	Chest	0/7
13 – 15	Right Arm	0/4
16 – 18	Left Arm	0/4
19 – 20	Head	0/5

Skills	Passions, Traits & Dependencies
Knights have a standard 75% rating in skills where they are required to be competent, 95% in skills where they specialise, and 55% in all others. Games Masters should create bespoke Knights with diverse skills, as needed.	Passions: Loyalty to Disruptors 90%, Contempt for Enemies 90% Traits: Varies, but can be Psychic Dependencies: Authority 58%, Competitive 48%

Combat Style & Weapons	Traits & Notes
Firearms (Varies) 75%	

Weapon	Damage	Range	Ammo	Fire Rate/ Load
Heavy Blaster	1d10	7/25/50	50	1/3
.45 Automatic	1d8	50/100/200	9	1/3

Disruptor Psion

Disruptor Psion	Attributes
STR: 11	**Action Points:** 3
CON: 12	**Damage Modifier:** +0
SIZ: 13	**Prana:** 12
DEX: 15	**Tenacity:** 12
INT: 12	**Movement:** 6 metres
POW: 12	**Initiative Bonus:** 14
CHA: 10	**Armour:** As Needed

1d20	Hit Location	AP/HP
1 – 3	Right Leg	0/5
4 – 6	Left Leg	0/5
7 – 9	Abdomen	0/6
10 – 12	Chest	0/7
13 – 15	Right Arm	0/4
16 – 18	Left Arm	0/4
19 – 20	Head	0/5

Skills	Passions, Traits & Dependencies
Athletics 47%, Brawn 35%, Bureaucracy 32%, Conceal 37%, Customs 50%, Deceit 42%, Endurance 50%, Evade 42%, Influence 46%, Insight 44%, Lore (multiversal theory) 40%, Mechanisms 42%, Perception 50%, Stealth 55%, Unarmed 45%, Willpower 55%	Passions: Loyalty to Disruptors 90%, Hate Order 90% Traits: Psionic Dependencies: Games/Puzzles 44%

Combat Style & Weapons	Traits & Notes
Psions are not expected to use traditional weapons. They rely on Pawn bodyguards and use their psionics in combat.	

The Valhalla Project and W.O.T.A.N are not alone in the multiverse when it comes to monitoring the parallels for truly gifted examples of preternatural abilities. The Disruptors watch out for examples of these powers to appear in someone susceptible to their wiles, scoop them up, and brainwash them into being the perfect supernatural weapons in their war. They become the Psions – and they are truly dangerous entities that pose a serious threat to anyone or anything that stands in the way of the Disruptors' goals.

Disruptor Psions are rarely deployed by their masters; normally only when other means will not be enough to overcome their Valhalla enemies or when their special combination of psychic skills is needed. Unlike Knights or Pawns, the Psions rarely manage to fit into a specific parallel's society; that is not their role. They are mindscape weapons deployed when the Disruptors need the scales decisively tipped in their favour.

Psionics	
Choose 2 Talents, one at 80%, one at 60%, from: Attrition (Drain Prana, Evil Eye, Psychic Wrack) Biokineses (Bioelectric Shock, Body Fortress, Synaptic Puppetry) Clairvoyance (Mental Scan, Mental Shield, Sense Psi) Telekinesis (Focus Force, Psychokinesis, Shatter) Telepathy (Mental Scan, Mind Probe, Thought Implant)	Psions are very carefully deployed, with most remaining on the World-Ship to control agents across the parallels. It is a rare occurrence for a Disruptor Psion to be placed into the field and when this happens, there is usually a bodyguard of 3+1d4 Pawns available at all times.

Valhalla Scientist

The Valhalla Project is a scentific endeavour, with many scientists collecting data and using technology from across the multiverse to help keep order. There are teams of vastly intelligent and well-schooled scientists that operate the devices at the core of the agency as well as designing new pieces of equipment and aiding in the travels around the parallels. Without their staff of scientists, the Valhalla Project would not be able to exist.

Disruptor Scientist	Attributes
STR: 9	**Action Points:** 3
CON: 12	**Damage Modifier:** +0
SIZ: 12	**Prana:** 12
DEX: 15	**Tenacity:** 12
INT: 17	**Movement:** 6 metres
POW: 12	**Initiative Bonus:** 16
CHA: 10	**Armour:** None

1d20	Hit Location	AP/HP
1 – 3	Right Leg	0/5
4 – 6	Left Leg	0/5
7 – 9	Abdomen	0/6
10 – 12	Chest	0/7
13 – 15	Right Arm	0/4
16 – 18	Left Arm	0/4
19 – 20	Head	0/5

Skills	Passions, Traits & Dependencies
Athletics 24%, Brawn 21%, Bureaucracy 58%, Conceal 37%, Customs 48%, Deceit 43%, Endurance 34%, Evade 32%, First Aid 50%, Home Parallel (Zero-Zero) 75%, Influence 48%, Insight 51%, Mechanisms 68%, Native Tongue (English) 100%, Perception 42%, Probabilities 65%, Any three Sciences 75/60/45% Unarmed 24%, Willpower 34%	Passions: Loyalty to Zero-Zero 90%, Hate Chaos 90% Traits: Technical Dependencies: Caffeine 44%

Combat Style & Weapons	Traits & Notes
Firearms (Pistol) 25%	

Weapon	Damage	Range	Ammo	Fire Rate/ Load
.45 Automatic	1d8	50/100/200	9	1/3

Valhalla Psychic

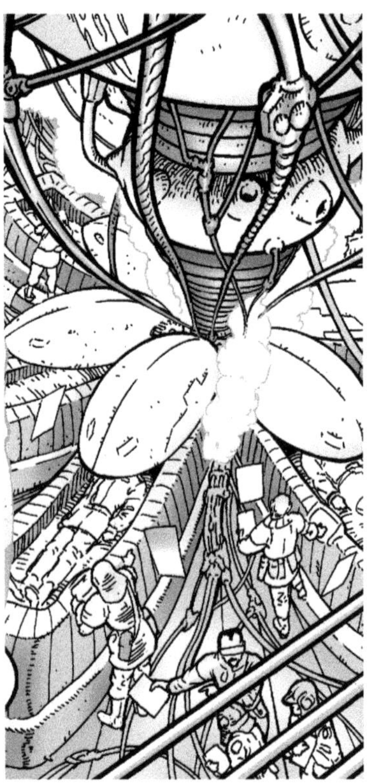

The connection between *homo novus*, psionic abilities and multi-parallelism is well-documented by the experts in the Valhalla Project. The need for those who understand, practice and maintain some mastery over the mental arts is great within the agency. Some of these gifted folk are trained to be field agents, but many psychics are maintained in a more instructional and utilitarian role. Without the Project's psychic staff members, field agents might not be able to maintain contact with Zero-Zero, shift parallels, or pass information between multiversal parallel selves.

Valhalla Psion	Attributes
STR: 11	**Action Points:** 3
CON: 12	**Damage Modifier:** +0
SIZ: 13	**Prana:** 12
DEX: 15	**Tenacity:** 12
INT: 12	**Movement:** 6 metres
POW: 12	**Initiative Bonus:** 14
CHA: 10	**Armour:** As Needed

1d20	Hit Location	AP/HP
1 – 3	Right Leg	0/5
4 – 6	Left Leg	0/5
7 – 9	Abdomen	0/6
10 – 12	Chest	0/7
13 – 15	Right Arm	0/4
16 – 18	Left Arm	0/4
19 – 20	Head	0/5

Skills	Passions, Traits & Dependencies
Athletics 28%, Endurance 44%, Evade 36%, First Aid 37%, Home Parallel (Zero-Zero) 60%, Influence 48%, Insight 42%, Native Tongue (English) 65%, Perception 42%, Probabilities 65%, Stealth 30%, Unarmed 28%, Willpower 50%	Passions: Loyalty to Valhalla 80%, Hate Chaos 60% Traits: Psionic Dependencies: Activity 44%

Psionics	
Choose 2 Talents, one at 60%, one at 40%, from: Clairvoyance (Mental Scan, Precognition, Psychometry) Empathy (Empathic Link, Empathic Push, Feel Emotions) Telepathy (Mental Shield, Mind Probe, Telepathy)	Valhalla has many machines designed to enhance psionic abilities, or to allow psions to use their powers on distant parallels from the relative safety of Valhalla's halls. The so-called Dream Couches mentally interface psions with the multiversal flow, all monitored by W.O.T.A.N, allowing them to watch and influence the Million Spheres.

Combat Style & Weapons	Traits & Notes
Firearms (Pistol) 25%	

Weapon	Damage	Range	Ammo	Fire Rate/ Load
.45 Automatic	1d8	50/100/200	9	1/3

Scenario: On Thin Ice

A surprise move by the Disruptors forces W.O.T.A.N to recalculate the projected stability of parallel 13.16.94. Without immediate intervention, the valency rates will spike and the parallel has a high probability of collapsing. Valhalla agents are hastily summoned to Zero-Zero, briefed, and shunted off to a frozen wasteland.

Introduction

This scenario is designed as an introductory adventure for new Arkwright Characters. As this mission will be many agents' first journey across the parallels, it is somewhat simple in structure; however, it offers plenty of scope for investigation, espionage, negotiation, and even some wholesale destruction.

Cast of Characters

The following are non-player Characters the agents will meet during the mission. Game statistics are provided on pages 163-165.

Althea

Captain of the Sargasso, an ice schooner out of New Toronto.

Dunkirk

Althea's first mate, and secretly a Disruptor Pawn.

Mayor Frode

The clockwork-assisted leader of New Toronto

Conroy

Disruptor Knight

Key Points & Timeline

1. W.O.T.A.N calculates the risk posed to the multiverse by Disruptor activity on para 13.16.94.
2. The agents are sent to the parallel where they see the aftermath of the murders at the drift station.
3. The agents encounter Althea and the Sargasso.
4. The Sargasso arrives in New Toronto where the agents can meet the mayor.
5. Missing hunters and Siberyak-Russo spies cause problems for the agents.
6. The pirates arrive with the bomb.
7. The agents must escape.

Background

Parallel 13.16.94 is an Earth trapped in a new ice age. A catastrophic climate event in this parallel's nineteenth century decimated the population and left cities buried under ice and snow. Humanity slowly clawed its way back and adapted. Although technology was lost, knowledge was not and the world has entered a Neo-Edwardian age.

Those locations already adapted to colder environments recovered faster and the dominant powers are fleets of anarchic pirates operating from the Reykjavik ice shelf — a Siberyak-Russo State in Vladivostok, and the Northern Federation, centered on the city of New Toronto, built on the glacier that covers the original city. The two powers exist in a détente, warily watching each other, but neither side taking any overt action.

The Disruptors are destabilizing the status-quo, utilizing their Pawns as agitators disguised as Siberyak-Russo agents and supplying the pirates with advanced weaponry. Worse yet, a Disruptor Knight, Conroy, has delivered a firebomb to 13.16.94, one with the destructive power to blast through the ice covering the globe and destabilize much of the planet. They plan on detonating it in New Toronto in the midst of a large-scale pirate raid.

W.O.T.A.N has calculated that the Disruptors are planning a big push on this parallel, massing Pawns in the area of Reykjavik: the Characters' task is to stop them.

Agent Briefing

The agents are summoned to a briefing room in Valhalla Nova where Karl Merkel anxiously awaits their arrival. He stands next to a psychic strapped into a Bifrost chair connected to a wall of monitors, waiting for the agents to take their own seats. Once everyone is ready, Karl relays the following information, either directly to the agents or as answers to their questions.

W.O.T.A.N has seen, over the past month, a spike in Disruptor activity on parallel 13.16.94. Prior to that, W.O.T.A.N had calculated this parallel was devoid of life due to a supposed extinction event several centuries ago.

It is unclear what the Disruptors are after, but if activity continues at its current rate, W.O.T.A.N predicts things will come to a head in less than a week. And, if it's something the Disruptors want this badly, then Zero-Zero wants to stop them.

Arms have been shipped across the multiverse by Disruptor Pawns: machine guns and other weapons. The Disruptors also went to great pains to hide the transit of a large item.

The agents need to travel to the parallel, take stock of the situation, and do what they can to stop the Disruptors. To aid the agents, a new piece of equipment, The Van, is made available to them to assist in transitioning to 13.16.94.

Karl flips a lever and the wall of monitors blinks to life. He explains that the agents are seeing para 13.16.94 through the eyes of the psionicist in the Bifrost chair, connecting to her alter-self on the destination parallel. Several important pieces of intelligence are readily available and Karl goes into more detail.

The parallel appears to be an ice age variation. As the agents watch, the psionicist's eyes pan across the horizon. Snow covered ground stretches in all directions. The person appears to be standing at the fore of a vehicle as the falling snow is whipping past at an incredible rate.

At the person's feet is the body of a man, blood pouring from a chest wound. Under his heavy winter clothes, a Disruptor uniform is visible. The monitors go dark and the person in the Bifrost chair lets out a massive sigh.

Karl explains that the body was a Disruptor clone that was caught aboard the *Sargasso*, an ice-schooner. He was caught trying to sabotage the boat and was killed in a struggle before any information could be dragged out of him.

The captain of the schooner, Althea, is the other-self of the psionicist in the chair. Through her, they were able to determine the parallel isn't devoid of life. Unfortunately, the valency between the parallels is high and the connection can only be established for short times, at great cost.

Althea's other-self isn't aware of the multiverse. She only knows that she "loses time" periodically.

Valhalla knows very little about this parallel, so the agents won't have a lot of reliable intelligence to go on.

The agents need to leave as soon as possible. They will be given a short period of time to gather their gear and then assemble at the rapid-transit system where a shuttle will takem to Heathrow Airport: "You're going to Canada," Karl tells them. "The Van is going with you and from there'll you'll shift across the continua to 13.16.94 — Ottawa, to be precise."

Ottawa

The transit from Valhalla Nova to Heathrow takes less than 30 minutes by MAGLEV shuttle. From there, the Characters are escorted through security to a flight chartered by Valhalla that is bound for the Peart-Lee International Airport just outside Ottawa (the area where the psychic from the briefing believed her counterpart to be located). Accompanying the Characters are scientists from the Rutherford wing who are experts in The Van's operation. As The Van cannot move through space, it is necessary to take one of several prototypes to the geographical location corresponding with their destination. The Valhalla project has hired premises in Ottawa, close to the airport, where The Van can be used discreetly.

The flight is aboard a Concordia II, the next generation of supersonic airliners with this particular craft designed for commercial, rather than leisure, use. In three hours the Concordia is in Canadian airspace and taxiing into the Peart-Lee's Lifeson cargo terminal. From there an unremarkable minibus whisks the Characters to the cargo facility nearby, The Van following them in an unmarked truck.

It takes about an hour to unload and prepare The Van (see the description on page 76). The lead technician, Wells, explains that the destination will be pre-set and controlled by the technical team who have accompanied the agents to Ottawa. Wells explains that once the Characters have left The Van when they reach 13.16.94, the device will automatically return to parallel Zero-Zero. "It's too valuable to risk leaving it in an unknown parallel," Wells explains. "So you'll be dropped-off, and then The Van will return to the same coordinates in 60 hours. It will stay there for 30 minutes before automatically flipping back to Zero-Zero. We'll repeat that process at 36-hour intervals in case you miss the first window of opportunity. If you need to get out sooner, find a way to tell Althea that she needs to think the letters Y-Y-Z in rapid succession. Valhalla's Althea will be psychicallymonitoring and she'll get a message to us. We'll send The Van for you immediately, but remember you have to get to the coordinates of your arrival."

The situation understood, the Characters climb into The Van and strap in. Wells wishes them luck and then closes the hatch. A screen shows a countdown for the Shift sequences and, when it decrements to zero, the whole fabric of reality warps and screams as the Characters are transported across the multiverse.

Drift Station

Arriving on this parallel the Characters first encounter a horrific murder scene. A group of New Toronto spies monitoring the Reykjavik pirates were ambushed by Disruptor Pawns, who believed the Torontonian spies overheard their collusion with the pirates to destroy New Toronto.

The agents emerge from The Van to find that, instead of the warm cargo warehouse, there is, instead, several tents on a wind-swept, ice-covered, featureless plain. As the last agent emerges, The Van blinks out of existence with a crackle of electricity.

Three tents and a portable radio antenna are a few metres away, but there is no sign of movement. The agents learn the following as they explore the small camp. Some clues are visible without the need for any skill roll; others will require skill rolls and will indicate as much.

- There are three dead bodies, two women and one men. Each is riddled with bullet holes. Based on the arrangement of the bodies, a successful Perception roll reveals the victims were trying to protect the equipment when shot.
- The names Jackson, Elias, and Gavigan are on the uniforms. Each person has a patch sewn onto their jacket, a maple leaf surrounded by the letters N.T.I.S. This stands for *New Toronto Intelligence and Surveillance*, a branch of the New Toronto militia, but is something the agents cannot know yet.
- An Engineering roll or a Hard Mechanisms roll reveals the equipment in the tents is all monitoring gear, with the exception of portable kerosene heaters. There are oscilloscopes, seismic monitors, and a small radar. It's all constructed of brass and copper with large dials and levers and no printed information.
- A large calendar has a date three weeks ago circled and marked with "Arr." Today is circles and marked with "Dep. Sar."
- Elias, one of the women, clutches several blood-splattered pages ripped from a notebook. The hastily scrawled notes read "<current date>: Chatter picked up from east <obscured text>. Say they have the devi<obscured text>ing tomorrow morning<obscured text>. However, the rest of the notebook is nowhere to be found.
- Several breech-loading rifles are stacked in the corner; they are not loaded.
- A Medicine check reveals the victims were shot by different calibers.
- A successful Perception check uncovers several spent shell casings from 5.56 rounds. A much more advanced weapon than the breech loaders.
- A successful Track roll indicates that four, maybe five booted men approached from the north and continued to the south. These boot prints have deep, well-defined treads versus the crampons the three victims are wearing. Following the tracks to the north for two miles reveal they appeared out of nowhere. To the south, they end about 1,000 feet from the camp at an ice shelf with three east-west furrows scraped onto it. These are the tracks from the skis of the ice schooner they boarded.

After about 20 minutes of searching the murder scene, even if the Characters haven't found all the clues, a successful Perception roll reveals what is initially a faint rumbling and scraping sound coming from the east. As it nears, a faint glow is visible in the distance. In a matter of minutes a 40-metre long schooner, mounted on three large skis and with a large, rumbling engine providing thrust, slows to a stop near the tents. *Sargasso* is etched on her side.

The Sargasso

The ship has a crew of eight, including her captain and first mate. Large-bore guns are mounted fore and aft, with firing arcs capable of covering the front and rear of the ship, but not the sides.

Things can start very badly for the agents. The Sargasso is arriving to pick up the three researchers and their findings, and take them back to New Toronto. The Sargasso is returning from the reconnaissance of the pirate fleet and has, unbeknownst to her captain, picked up a tail.

Strange people at the camp and the carnage immediately place Althea and her crew on-edge and the Games Master is encouraged to portray them as wary and understandably untrusting of the Characters — especially if they mention anything about alternate worlds or other parallels. Althea, Dunkirk, and two other armed crewmen descend to the ground to inspect the camp when the Sargasso comes to a halt. Upon seeing the carnage, Dunkirk advocates for the Characters to be shot where they stand. Insight rolls reveal that while Althea and the two crew members are visibly shaken by what happened to the victims, Dunkirk, the first-mate appears to be faking his disgust.

The crew gathers all the scientific equipment and builds small cairns for the bodies, forcing the Characters to help. By the time the ship is ready to set sail, it is about an hour from sunset.

Althea isn't sure whether or not to trust the agents at this time, so unless the agents are very quick to convince her, Althea has any obvious weapons confiscated and the Characters are hauled on board as prisoners. Although captives, the Sargasso has no brig, so the agents are forced to remain on deck where the crew can keep an eye on them.

Althea

Althea is a weather-beaten woman with dark complexion in her mid-to-late 40s. She's cautious and slow to trust. An old revolver and sabre are on her hip. The agents have to somehow win her over with facts to prove that they're not responsible for the killing. The boot prints and furrows, which Althea recognises as another schooner, are solid evidence in the agents' favour. Helping defend the ship against the *Windswept* in the forthcoming encounter will also help. If the Characters are carrying "exotic" weaponry, it is a strike against them because it denotes them as obvious outsiders. Revealing that Althea is psychically linked with other people across the parallels could go poorly, especially if the agents lead with that: at this stage, it requires a Formidable Influence roll, opposed by Althea's Easy Willpower to successfully convince her of her Zero-Zero counterpart. Successful Courtesy and Influence rolls can also help win her over generally — or at least convince her that the Characters are relatively innocent in all of this.

If the Characters convince her they're on her side, Althea takes them into her confidence. She knows the following information, which she imparts as answers to questions, or part of natural conversation.

- The Sargasso was picking up a science team from the drift station to take them back to New Toronto. She didn't know the people personally. The N.T.I.S. stands for the New Toronto Institute of Science.
- If the Characters have convinced her they're on her side, Althea admits the truth: the dead researchers were spies for the New Toronto Intelligence and Surveillance, tasked with keeping an eye on the pirates, the same thing she was doing.
- The Sargasso is about six hours from New Toronto.
- There was a Siberyak-Russo spy on board the Sargasso that must have been in league with the pirates. They killed him and dumped his body overboard. He was armed with a strange gun, which Dunkirk took. They have the spy's correspondence intended for Vladivostok.

You're Not From Around Here, Are You?

If the agents reveal their mission to Althea, or tell her about her other selves, she will be initially disbelieving. However, the more the agents can explain about the strange weapons or actions of the enemies, the more accepting she'll become. If an agent has psionic powers, they can try to explain Althea's multi-parallel existence. At the Games Master's discretion, the agents can use Althea to pass messages back to Zero-Zero.

The Death of Fenris Allgood

Fenris was a disposable Disruptor Pawn sent to this parallel to create distrust and shatter the detante between the Northern Federation and the Siberyak-Russo State. His mission was to seek employment on a New Toronto ship and leave a trail of evidence that the Siberyak-Rus were spying on New Toronto. The intent was to get New Toronto focused on the far-eastern threat so the Disruptors could strike with the element of surprise.

However, Fenris was too good at being a fake spy and was caught by Althea, captain of the Sargasso. She put the man under guard and questioned him. She was convinced the man was a Siberyak-Russo spy, but Fenris was starting to crack. The other Disruptor on the ship, Dunkirk, was afraid that Fenris would reveal the entire plan, so he took the initiative and executed Fenris on the spot. Only Dunkirk knows the full truth of these events and he's too loyal to the Disruptor cause to ever admit what really transpired. However, there are some clues for the agents to get to the root of the matter.

Beyond the letter in Fenris' quarters, agents can find the Disruptor Pawn's damaged communication device, a small ear bud and mic hidden in the false bottom of a wooden cup. If repaired with a Hard Mechanisms roll, the Characters can listen in on any communications Dunkirk has with Conroy, including Dunkirk confirming that Fenris is dead and Althea thinks the Siberyak-Rus are to blame.

In addition, if Dunkirk rendezvous with the other Disruptors in New Toronto, he brags to his cohorts about his surprise execution of Fenris.

Dunkirk

Dunkirk is Althea's first mate, and a Disruptor Pawn. He's been an ice-sailor his entire life and looks it. He walks with a limp — the result of several accidents on the ice. Althea trusts him implicitly and any betrayal on Dunkirk's part wounds her deeply. Dunkirk is aware of this, so he's waiting for the right moment to strike. Dunkirk is in contact with the Disruptors through a small microphone and receiver he keeps sewn into his elaborately piped great-coat.

Dunkirk parrots the line that the Sargasso was out to pick up scientists. No matter what Althea tells the agents, Dunkirk pretends to be a loyal New Toronto man and toes the line. If questioned about his lack of a reaction to the bodies, he explains that he's used to violence. However, Hard Insight rolls when conversing with Dunkirk reveal that he's being evasive. If the agents push, Dunkirk lashes out — at the very least trying to cmpletely discredit the Characters, and at worst, physically.

The Spy's Note

As Althea has revealed, the Sargasso's crew uncovered a spy aboard their ship. In a brief battle he was killed and his body dumped over the side. To further disguise Disruptor activities, the now-dead Pawn posing as a Siberyak-Russo spy wrote a fake intelligence report and hid it in his bunk.

To ~~Valdi~~ Vladivostok Station Chief. New Toronto forces are weaker than expected. Plans for Operation Brunhilde should commence immediately. Requesting urgent retrieval.

There are three clues in this letter that the Siberyak-Rus might not be behind this.

- Vladivostok is misspelled, struck-through, and re-written.
- The operation code name is in German.
- The letter is in English: why not Russian?

If the Characters bring these concerns to Althea, she is confused, but accepts that something is amiss. She summons Dunkirk and asks for his opinion. The man shrugs noncommitally and remarks that the message is exactly what he'd expect any spy to send; there is nothing unusual he can see. The spy is dead, so what more is there left to say? If challenged, he grows angry and storms from the room, another signal of some form of involvement.

Note that if Dunkirk is seriously challenged over potential or suspected links to the enemy, he has plausible alibis prepared, as most Disruptor Pawns do. He will aim to have the Characters killed though, either using the attack of the *Windswept* as an opportunity, or by sending some of the other Pawns based in New Toronto after the Characters as they make their way around the city.

Windswept

The *Windswept* is a pirate vessel shadowing the *Sargasso*, and crewed by ten pirates, one of them a Disruptor Pawn. It is larger than the *Sargasso*, towering above it, and fitted with a heavy machine gun. The gunner is well protected behind a thick iron shield fitted with a narrow view slit. Although it protects him, it does limit his field of vision drastically. The *Windswept* strikes either as the *Sargasso* is getting underway from the drift station or during that night.

The attack starts with the ship darting in from the south. Successful Perception checks mean the agents hear something coming across the ice and can warn the *Sargasso*. Otherwise, the *Windswept* gets one free round of attacks on Althea's vessel.

Both captains will be using evasive maneuvers to line up shots and avoid being hit. Unless a character has experience on ships, all physical skill checks will be Hard and the Games Master can rule that periodic Athletics checks are necessary to stay upright. The agents can take any role they want in the fight. They can use the large fore and aft guns to attack the *Windswept* or get their weapons from Althea's quarters and attack the enemy crew. A Hard Perception check reveals that Dunkirk, while firing, is way off target.

Two rounds into the fight, the *Windswept* veers close to the *Sargasso* and the pirates use gun-launched grappling hooks to latch on to the *Sargasso's* hull. Once the two ships are entangled, Characters can try to climb the ropes to the *Windswept*, jump from the rail of the *Sargasso* to the *Windswept* and pull themselves aboard, or try to cut through the grappling lines. Anyone who falls while climbing or jumping will need to Evade or be run over by the two ships as the crews battle for their lives.

When the grappling hooks punch through the deck of the *Sargasso*, some pirates provide cover fire with primitive firearms and the heavy machine gun, while others slide down the lines to land on the *Sargasso's* deck and engage in hand-to-hand fighting with sword and pistol. Shooting a pirate sliding on a line requires a Formidable shot. Every pirate except the captain, Bjorn Henson, and the heavy machine gunner boards the *Sargasso* in an attempt to seize the ship.

The *Windswept's* crew will fight to the bitter end: returning in defeat to Reykjavik is a death sentence. If the agents try to capture any of the enemies, Dunkirk will do his best to assassinate captives before they can talk.

If the agents interrogate a pirate, they find he does not know much about the overall mission and is completely unaware of the Disruptors. The pirates do know the following, which they relay with typical pirate bravado.

- The greatest pirate fleet ever assembled is getting ready to set sail for New Toronto, with plans to wipe the city off the face of the earth.
- A new weapon will be unveiled that will make the rest of the world tremble. They don't know anything other than the fact that it's big.

If Althea hears this news, she immediately increases speed for New Toronto to warn the city. If the Windswept is still functional, she'll claim it as the spoils of war and have it lashed to the Sargasso.

New Toronto

Once the Characters arrive in New Toronto, they set the pace of the investigation. These sections are provided in a rough chronological order, but Games Masters must be prepared for the agents to go in any direction.

The settlement of New Toronto is a modern marvel. A city built on ice and encased in a vast, steel wall, it houses over 10,000 residents. It stretches across six square miles of stable ice-shelf and is considered the most modern city in the world. Most streets are tunnels carved through the buildings, and the tunnels have sharp turns. This primitive measure provides some protection from the

That Dunkirk Spirit

Assuming Dunkirk is still alive, the agents might try to follow him from the port. He leads them to Roncevalles Warehouse, which is where he's living along with his fellow conspirators. However, Dunkirk is wily and agents must oppose their Stealth or Track against Dunkirk's Perception to avoid being noticed. If Dunkirk spots them, he'll try to lead them into an ambush. In that case, the agents must oppose their Perception against Dunkirk's Stealth.

bone-chilling straight-line winds that whip in across the Ontario Ice Sheet without warning.

As the Sargasso approaches, the city walls open and Althea slowly guides the ship in. The ship docks at Union Quay and the crew quickly disperses into the city, which is a warren of multi-story buildings leaning against one another for support. Dunkirk immediately announces that he's going to get drunk, but is actually going to warn his fellow Disruptors that Valhalla Agents might be present. If agents want to surreptitiously follow Dunkirk, skip to *The Warehouse* section for more information.

Althea suggests the agents accompany her to see the mayor; she needs to report what has been learned without delay.

The Paper

As the agents walk through the city, moving through one of the large open squares that passes for a public area, a young news-hawker is screaming the headline from the latest issue of the New Sun: "Siberyak Spies to Be Executed!"

If the agents take a look at the paper (the newsboy insists they buy one first. He'll try to convince them that they each need to buy their own copy if they want to read it), they learn that three Siberyak agents are to be hanged at noon. They were caught burying explosives under the city hall, and they will be displayed for the public for 30 minutes before the sentence is carried out, in Dundas Square.

As the agents walk through the streets, the general populace talks about the upcoming hanging. Spies in New Toronto! Who would have imagined it?

A Clockwork Mayor

New Toronto's city hall is the most impressive building on the ice shelf, a repurposing of the upper portion of Old Toronto's CN Tower. The original building was round with a spire rising high into the sky, but iron and steel additions have been grafted on, creating a large, winding series of interconnecting rooms.

The mayor is in the central audience area, surrounded by functionaries. The room is decorated in thick red and white curtains that add a layer of opulence to the otherwise cold, metal room. Mayor Frode is a massive figure: corpulent, thick-faced, and with small, beady eyes. Unable to walk unassisted, his vast bulk is contained in a steel exoskeleton that appears to be clockwork powered.

Frode has a terrible temper and little patience, although he listens to Althea and seems to place high regard on her observations. On her recommendation, depending on how well the Characters have engaged with her aboard the *Sargasso*, Frode listen to the agents and answers any questions. He knows the following information.

- He's never heard of the Disruptors.
- The pirates are a minor threat compared to the danger now posed by the Siberyaks. The spies the New Toronto constabulary have rooted out tried to blow up the city hall. The spies will be executed at noon. They will be placed on public display at 11.30am for the customary beating by rock-filled snowballs.
- Frode is preparing to raise a levy and sail west on Vladivstok. The city has no professional soldiers; any time military action is needed, hunters, trackers, and other similar types form a levy. Occasionally mercenaries from the south are hired.
- The walls of the city are defended by ten cannon, evenly spaced around its circumference.

If Frode can be convinced that the Siberyaks aren't a threat, but are instead a ruse created by the Disruptors and their pirate allies, he'll lend the agents what aid he can.

The Hanging

The hanging takes place in Dundas Square.

The accused spies, all men, are locked into stocks next to the gallows, from 11.30am until noon, at which point they will be hanged, in accordance with city ordnance. The square is crowded with onlookers and snowball throwers. Two men dressed in thick parkas and balaclavas, and armed with muskets, keep the populace at least 10 metres from the spies. Even at this distance, it is obvious that the snow-encased rocks are leaving bruises and tearing skin.

A successful Perception roll reveals that while two of the accused have stony glares, the third is weeping. If the Characters can get close to the spies, perhaps by distracting, bribing, or convincing the guards to let them through, the two who aren't weeping make no response. An Insight roll for the third man, Paul, reveals he is terrified, and not necessarily of the hanging.

He admits he helped plant the bomb, but he, and the other two men were forced into it. They were approached by a well-dressed man who told them that if they didn't plant a bomb in the name of the Siberyak-Russo Federation, their families would be killed in front of them. The same fate awaited any of the three who didn't keep their mouths shut.

The men picked up the bomb from a warehouse at the Chorus Quay. There were six other men present, but not the well-dressed man who made the threat. The one in charge was very rough looking and walked with a pronounced limp. The Characters should be able to equate this description with Dunkirk, Althea's first mate from the Sargasso.

If the agents reach Althea, she can get them an audience with Mayor Frode; or they can go to Frode directly and try to convince him of the plot. If successful, he will stay the execution while he has the New Toronto militia investigate. The men are still guilty of treason, but mitigating circumstances might warrant a lesser punishment.

The Warehouse

This four-story brick building only has windows on the second and higher floors, and most of these are broken. A sign proclaiming it Roncevalles Warehouse hangs above double wooden doors. A smaller man-sized door is at the back of the building. Both doors are locked with simple padlocks and chains. The lock on the double-doors is frozen over, but the one at the rear is free from ice. Several iron ladders allow roof access, which is peppered with filthy sky lights.

One Disruptor Pawn patrols the back alley, but he's more interested in smoking and scratching various sores to keep a close eye on things.

If the agents gain access to the building, they find old crates stacked floor to ceiling. Most of the crates are filled with old knick-knacks and trinkets from before the glaciation. However, in the center of the warehouse the Disruptors are gathering around a portable propane heater to discuss the upcoming attack. The agents will need to use Stealth to get close enough to hear. If Dunkirk is still alive, he leads the conversation. Nearby, are ten wooden crates containing a mixture of laser pistols and laser rifles; clearly weaponry that is at odds with this parallel's technology level.

Eavesdropping on the Disruptor conversation yields the following.

- Someone called Conroy plans to lead the pirate fleet across the ice so that it reaches New Toronto by dawn. They will approach at speed from the east.
- The bomb is carried aboard one of the pirate ships and will be activated near the eastern gate of the city wall. Once it detonates it will breach the wall and start to burn a hole through the ice, the weapon continuing to penetrate the glacier and cut-down through the bedrock. The result will destabilise much of the ice shelf as it burrows through the ice peaking at several thousands of degrees before finally exploding. The result will be an upblast of superheated steam that will completely engulf New Toronto and lead to its collapse into the resulting fissure in the destabilised glacier. The Siberyak-Russo State will then become the dominant world power.
- Conroy has the timer set for five minutes to provide himself and his fellow Disruptors time to escape. The rest of the pirates are simply fodder to keep New Toronto busy.

If the agents charge in, the Disruptors retaliate, trying to create opportunities to flee. They take full advantage of the unstable stacks of crates littered around the warehouse.

If left to their own devices, the Disruptors settle down to sleep in sleeping bags. The Characters can sneak in and loot the weapon crates if they want. Several Disruptors are light sleepers, so Stealth rolls will be necessary. If awoken, the Disruptors take a combat round to realise what is happening, providing the agents with one round of free action.

The Disruptors do everything in their power to avoid capture. However, if the agents manage to take one alive, he'll confess the plans, adding the following details:

- Conroy is a high ranking Disruptor who was sent here to destabilize the parallel. The captured Disruptor Pawn doesn't have information on the over-arching plan.
- Conroy will arrive on the *Memento Mori*, which is the ice ship carrying the bomb.

The Battle for New Toronto

If the agents take the information to Frode, he starts mobilising hunters to defend the walls. Most of New Toronto's fleet are lightly armed transports, so Frode would like to avoid a battle on the open ice. But Althea is amenable to using the *Sargasso* to sail against the pirate fleet.

This battle can play out in many ways, so only guide lines are provided. Let the agents take the lead; they are probably the most skilled and best-armed combatants New Toronto has on their side.

Unless the agents sail out to meet the incoming fleet, ten pirate ships descend on and surround New Toronto, assailing its walls with heavy machine gun fire. The Games Master is encouraged to use the heavy machine guns narratively unless agents directly challenge them. The guns can tear across the walls, ripping large holes, blasting away defenders, and exploding fuel barrels. The pirate flagship, the *Memento Mori* sails right up to the east gate and drops the bomb before retreating back to the east.

Pirates fire grappling hooks from deck-mounted guns and start scaling the wall. Dunkirk and his fellow Disruptors in the city will attack from the rear in an attempt to assassinate as many defenders as possible. The agents should see New Toronto men fall from the walls as any Disruptors blast their way across the rampart.

The *Memento Mori* has a crew of 20 pirates plus Conroy. They will fight to protect Conroy, who, for his part, would like nothing more than to kill some fresh Valhalla Project recruits.

The bomb can be disarmed. It has a countdown timer of 5 minutes. It takes three successful hard Mechanism checks to disarm. Each check takes 30 seconds, but failure reduces the clock by 1 minute (so a failed check technically removes 1:30 from the timer).

Conclusion

If the agents are successful in stopping Conroy from destroying New Toronto and burning a hole through the ice shelf, they still have to make it back to The Van by the appointed time. Althea will gladly provide them passage aboard on the *Sargasso*. If they can do that, they're greeted back on Zero-Zero as heroes for a job well done. Althea and Frode could prove to be useful contacts and both Dunkirk and Conroy, if they survive, are a nasty foes.

NPC Statistics

Althea

Captain of the *Sargasso* and one of the more powerful people in New Toronto. Althea is a tall, dark complexioned woman with weather-beaten skin and an unassuming demeanor. She will be wary of the agents at first, but if they can win her over, they'll have a steadfast companion for life.

Althea is not aware of the fact that she's psychically linked to other Altheas across the parallels. She only knows that she's been "losing time" recently. Those blackouts correspond to the times when the Althea on Zero-Zero taps into this Althea's senses. If Althea accepts the fact that she exists on numerous planes of existence at the same time, she will begin mastering the necessary skills to communicate psychically across the parallels without interrupting her consciousness.

Althea	Attributes
STR: 15	**Action Points:** 3
CON: 14	**Damage Modifier:** +1d2
SIZ: 12	**Prana:** 12
DEX: 12	**Tenacity:** 12
INT: 15	**Movement:** 6 metres
POW: 12	**Initiative Bonus:** 11
CHA: 11	**Armour:** Thick Parka with Hood

1d20	Hit Location	AP/HP
1 – 3	Right Leg	0/6
4 – 6	Left Leg	0/6
7 – 9	Abdomen	2/7
10 – 12	Chest	2/8
13 – 15	Right Arm	2/5
16 – 18	Left Arm	2/5
19 – 20	Head	2/6

Skills	Passions, Traits & Dependencies
Athletics 65%, Brawn 45%, Commerce 37%, Endurance 45%, Evade 30%, Locale (New Toronto and environs) 60%, Navigation 60%, Perception 60%, Seamanship 70%, Survival 45%, Stealth 62%, Unarmed 47%, Willpower 30%	Passions: Loyalty to New Toronto 65%, Loyalty to Crew 70%, Hate Pirates 55% Traits: None Dependencies: Tobacco 30%

Combat Style & Weapons	Traits & Notes
Ice Buccaneer Skirmisher (Pistol, Knife, Ice Pick) 65%	Skirmisher Trait

Weapon	Damage	Range	Ammo	Fire Rate/ Load
.38 Pistol	1d6	50/100/200	6 (revolver)	1/3

Weapon	Damage	Size/Reach	AP/HP	Effects
Knife	1d3+1d2	S/S	2/3	Bleed, Impale
Ice Pick	1d4+1d2	S/S	2/3	Impale

Dunkirk

Dunkirk is an unpleasant man: crass and cantankerous. His thick stubble covers a pock-marked face. He is never without his great coat, which has a Disruptor transmitter hidden inside.

Although native to this parallel, he is loyal only to the Disruptors. They have offered him power which he knows he could never find any other way. He walks with a pronounced limp from numerous sailing accidents.

Dunkirk	Attributes
STR: 11	**Action Points:** 3
CON: 12	**Damage Modifier:** +0
SIZ: 13	**Prana:** 12
DEX: 15	**Tenacity:** 12
INT: 13	**Movement:** 6 metres
POW: 12	**Initiative Bonus:** 13
CHA: 12	**Armour:** Padded Great Coat

1d20	Hit Location	AP/HP
1 – 3	Right Leg	0/5
4 – 6	Left Leg	0/3
7 – 9	Abdomen	1/6
10 – 12	Chest	1/7
13 – 15	Right Arm	1/4
16 – 18	Left Arm	1/4
19 – 20	Head	0/6

Skills	Passions, Traits & Dependencies
Athletics 26%, Brawn 24%, Conceal 34%, Deceit 45%, Endurance 32%, Evade 32%, First Aid 28%, Forgery 42%, Influence 34%, Insight 40%, Mechanisms 37%, Perception 35%, Stealth 38%, Streetwise 52%, Survival 22%, Unarmed 36%, Willpower 32%	Passions: Lust for Power 60%, Loyalty to Disruptors 80% Traits: None Dependencies: Role Model (Disruptor Knights) 48%

Combat Style & Weapons	Traits & Notes
Advanced Firearms (Blasters) 36%, Assassin (Knife, Garrotte) 39%, Ice Buccaneer Skirmisher (Pistol, Knife, Ice Pick) 44%	Skirmisher Trait for the Buccaneer style. Dunkirk only uses his blaster when alone or in the company of other disruptors

Weapon	Damage	Range	Ammo	Fire Rate/ Load
Heavy Blaster	1d10	7/25/50	50	1/3
.45 Automatic	1d8	50/100/200	9	1/3

Weapon	Damage	Size/Reach	AP/HP	Effects
Knife	1d3	S/S	2/3	Bleed, Impale
Ice Pick	1d4	S/S	2/3	Impale

Conroy

Conroy is the Disruptor Knight charged with leading the operation against New Toronto. Tall, beguiling and suave, he has no qualms about throwing the entire pirate force at his enemies and watching them die on the city's walls. All he wants to do is get close enough to set off his bomb.

Conroy's speech is very precise; he shuns contractions and slang, considering profanity vulgar and distasteful.

Conroy	Attributes
STR: 13	**Action Points:** 3
CON: 16	**Damage Modifier:** +1d2
SIZ: 14	**Prana:** 18
DEX: 14	**Tenacity:** 18
INT: 16	**Movement: 6 metres**
POW: 18	**Initiative Bonus:** 17
CHA: 16	**Armour: Ballistic Jacket**

1d20	Hit Location	AP/HP
1 – 3	Right Leg	0/6
4 – 6	Left Leg	0/6
7 – 9	Abdomen	4/7
10 – 12	Chest	4/8
13 – 15	Right Arm	4/5
16 – 18	Left Arm	4/5
19 – 20	Head	0/6

Skills	Passions, Traits & Dependencies
Athletics 40%, Brawn 37%, Conceal 54%, Customs 75%, Deceit 72%, Drive (land vehicle) 41%, Endurance 40%, Evade 34%, First Aid 35%, Forgery 52%, Influence 53%, Insight 44%, Linguistics (3 local languages) 48%, Lore (multiversal theory) 56%, Mechanisms 50%, Perception 44%, Probabilities 45%, Stealth 40%, Streetwise 44%, Survival 28%, Unarmed 47%, Willpower 46%	Passions: Contempt for Enemies 68%, Loyalty to Disruptors 85% Traits: Psychic Dependencies: Competitive 48%

Psionics	
Attrition 44% (Drain Prana, Infliction, Sap Vigour) Translocation 38% (Mental Shield, Shift Parallel)	Conroy is a talented Disruptor psychic. He uses his powers sparingly, and always to personal advantage. If things are going awry, he simply leaves the parallel entirely.

Combat Style & Weapons	Traits & Notes
Advanced Firearms (Blasters) 36%, Assassin (Knife, Garrotte) 39%, Ice Buchaneer Skirmisher (Pistol, Knife, Ice Pick) 44%	Skirmisher Trait for the Buchaneer style. Dunkirk only uses his blaster when alone or in the company of other disruptors

Weapon	Damage	Range	Ammo	Fire Rate/ Load
Heavy Blaster	1d10	7/25/50	50	1/3
.45 Automatic	1d8	50/100/200	9	1/3

Weapon	Damage	Size/Reach	AP/HP	Effects
Knife	1d3	S/S	2/3	Bleed, Impale
Ice Pick	1d4	S/S	2/3	Impale

Pirates

A typical set of rough types from Iceland and the Siberian wastes. They lack finesse, manners and subtlety, but have ruthlessness and viciousness in spades.

Attributes	1d20	Hit Location	AP/HP
Action Points: 2	1 – 3	Right Leg	0/6
Damage Modifier: 0	4 – 6	Left Leg	0/6
Prana: 10	7 – 9	Abdomen	2/7
Tenacity: 10	10 – 12	Chest	2/8
Movement: 6 metres	13 – 15	Right Arm	2/5
Initiative Bonus: 11	16 – 18	Left Arm	2/5
Armour: Thick Parka	19 – 20	Head	0/6

Skills	Passions, Traits & Dependencies
Athletics 38%, Brawn 25%, Endurance 36%, Evade 28%, Locale (13.16.94) 40%, Perception 41%, Survival 31%, Unarmed 38%, Willpower 19%, Stealth 39%	Passions: Love Wealth 75%

Combat Style & Weapons	Traits & Notes
Ice Pirate (Pistol, Knife, Ice Pick)	

Weapon	Damage	Range	Ammo	Fire Rate/ Load
.45 Automatic	1d8	50/100/200	9	1/3

Weapon	Damage	Size/Reach	AP/HP	Effects
Knife	1d3	S/S	2/3	Bleed, Impale
Ice Pick	1d4	S/S	2/3	Impale

Mayor Frode

Mayor Frode is an immense, corpulent man, ruddy of complexion, with reddish hair and small, intense, beady eyes. His mass is such that he cannot move without considerable aid, and so the engineers of New Toronto have fashioned for him a clockwork exoskeleton that encases his bulk and allows him to amble around with a stiff clanking and whirring motion, as long as the springs in the joints remained wound. He has a pair of long-suffering lackies who are responsible for winding the springs with a set of large keys.

Frode is very loyal to New Toronto and the Northern Federation, but he loathes the Siberyak-Russo passionately and is easily moved to support anyone who can convince him that the eastern bloc is responsible for seditious activity.

Althea	Attributes
STR: 12	**Action Points:** 2
CON: 10	**Damage Modifier:** +0
SIZ: 21	**Prana:** 10
DEX: 8	**Tenacity:** 10
INT: 15	**Movement:** 2 metres
POW: 10	**Initiative Bonus:** 8
CHA: 13	**Armour:** Steel Exoskeleton

1d20	Hit Location	AP/HP
1 – 3	Right Leg	4/6
4 – 6	Left Leg	4/6
7 – 9	Abdomen	4/7
10 – 12	Chest	4/8
13 – 15	Right Arm	4/5
16 – 18	Left Arm	4/5
19 – 20	Head	0/6

Skills	Passions, Traits & Dependencies
Athletics 12%, Brawn 32%, Commerce 80%, Endurance 66%, Evade 20%, Influence 75%, Locale (New Toronto and environs) 80%, Oratory 65%, Perception 60%, Politics 80%, Unarmed 30%, Willpower 60%	Passions: Loyalty to New Toronto 90%, Hate Siberyak-Russo State 90% Traits: Unshakeable Dependencies: Food 85%

Combat Style & Weapons	Traits & Notes
None	Frode is too large to move fast enough for combat.

The Sargasso

Hull: 10 (Huge Civilian), 75 Structure

Speed: Slow

Systems: 4

Traits: Ice Skies, Cargo, Resilient

Shields: None

Weapons: 2 x Large Bore Machine Guns

Description: The Sargasso has a crew of eight, including her captain and first mate. Large-bore guns are mounted fore and aft, with firing arcs capable of covering the front and rear of the ship, but not the sides.

Weapons	Damage	Range	Firing Rate
Large Bore Machine Gun	3d6	300/1000/2000	-/20/100

The Windswept

Hull: 12 (Huge Civilian), 80 Structure

Speed: Slow

Systems: 4

Traits: Ice Skies, Cargo, Superior Handling

Shields: None

Weapons: 1 x 50mm cannon

Description: The Windswept has a crew of ten, including her captain and first mate. The 50mm cannon is housed behind a protective iron shield that offers 100% cover for the gunner and has the equivalent of 6 Armour Points.

Weapons	Damage	Range	Firing Rate
50mm Cannon	3d6+3	1000/2000/6500	1/10/50

Warehouse Floor Plan

1 Packing Crate = 1.5m³

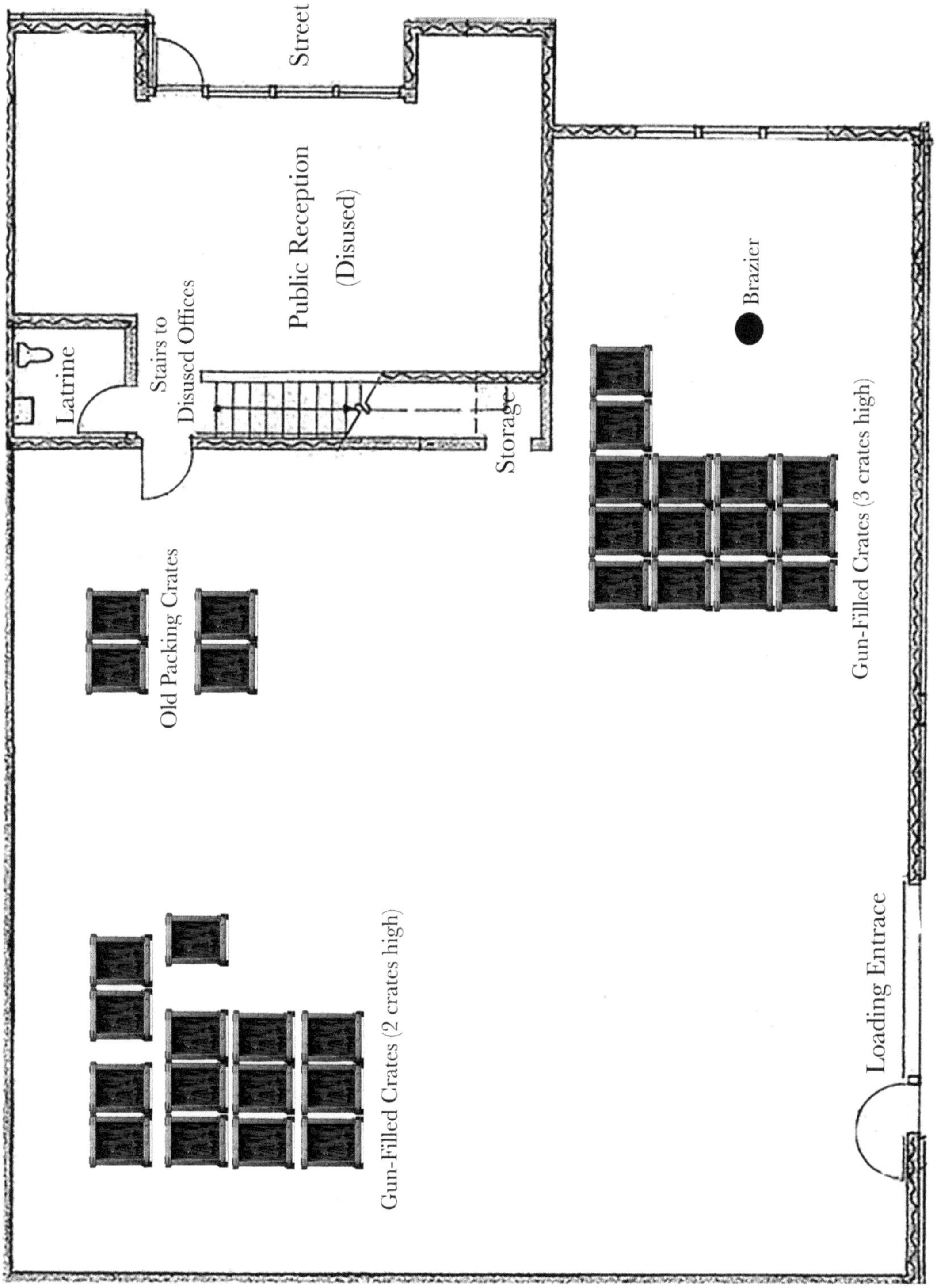

The Arkwright Saga

In this chapter we have summarised the two parts of the Arkwright Saga. There is, of course, no substitute for reading Bryan Talbot's masterpiece, but for those unfamiliar with the two graphic novels — and those who have read them and simply require a quick refresher — this chapter offers a quick primer.

The Adventures of Luther Arkwright

Luther Arkwright is first introduced in this nine part eponymous series, first published by Valkyrie Press in 1987. It concerns the discovery and hunt for FireFrost and takes place on several parallels but with the focus on 00.72.87, a world where the Restoration of the British Monarchy never took place, Oliver Cromwell's bloodline still controls a Puritan Britain, and the great imperial houses of Europe await their chance to seize power.

The story begins on the 22 of September 1984, in the Hyde Park, London, of Para 00.38.56, an alternative Earth where a Victorian style British Empire is the dominant world power. Arkwright, wearing the uniform of the 10th Prince of Wales Own Hussars, is waiting by the Albert Memorial for a contact. A boy scout arrives with a message from his contact, Rose Wylde, summoning him to a meeting at the Crystal Palace.

Inside the Great Exhibition Hall Arkwright and Rose are attacked by a pair of assassins; Arkwright's psychic powers alert him to the presence of Disruptor agents, a split second before the killers unleash an assault with napalm guns, starting a fire. Arkwright and Rose despatch both assassins in a brief gun fight, but the fire started by the napalm is soon raging out of control. As the Crystal Palace burns, Arkwright and Rose make a hasty escape.

In the safety of Rose's apartment, Arkwright uses her Trans-Parallel Communicator to contact Zero-Zero; he is recalled

immediately to Valhalla Nova, such is the gravity of the situation he has created in 00.38.56. He uses his inate powers to translocate between this parallel and Zero-Zero.

Arkwright learns from Zero-Zero that the Disruptors have discovered and taken control of FireFrost, a potent and almost mythological alien doomsday device, and activated the weapon. W.O.T.A.N is monitoring increased instances of entropy, and these entropic effects, it predicts, will continue, increasing until the Earth, solar system and galaxy and all its parallel counterparts, are destroyed. W.O.T.A.N has plotted a mitigating strategy: the *Ragnarok Equation*; a course of action designed to draw out the Disruptor's shock troops in such numbers that W.O.T.A.N will be able to trace them back to their parallel of origin. Arkwright will then follow the signature, locate FireFrost and attempt its deactivation.

Arkwright translocates to 00.72.87, a parallel he knows well. It is also the parallel on which FireFrost originally fell to Earth, and where the Disruptors recovered it in 1975: the perfect place to start W.O.T.A.N's plan.

In St. Petersburg Arkwright helps broker a treaty between Russia, under Czar Nicholas, and Greater Prussia — the greatest power on this parallel — to aid a rebel army in Britain in overthrowing their government. Britain is ruled by the fascist parliamentarian dictatorship of Lord Protector Nathaniel Cromwell, a direct descendant of Oliver. Cromwell. He and his inner cabinet are Disruptor agents, taking orders from the 'Holy Power' that has sustained the regime for centuries. The rebel army Arkwright's Russo-Prussian alliance intends to support are the Royalists, in hiding for 300 years. The self-styled Charles III, descendant of Charles I, is the pretender king of the Royalists and Czar Nicholas' nephew.

The Prussians arrive for the signing in the vast helicarrier *Siegfried*. Arkwright identifies and kills, through the use of his psionics, a Disruptor agent hidden within the Prussian high command. The alliance between Russia, Greater Prussia and Charles III's government in exile is sealed and a declaration of war made against the Cromwellian regime.

During his time in St. Petersburg Arkwright also contacts Octobriana, another Zero-Zero agent, to discuss a planned revolution in Russia, which will take place while the Russian nobility is occupied, fighting the war against the Puritans.

Heading to London, Arkwright makes contact with the Rose Wylde of this parallel. Rose, and her sidekick Freda, are undercover agents in the Puritan regime, gathering intelligence for the Royalists. After discussing the progress of their plans Arkwright makes his way into the Royalist enclave of London to meet with one of King Charles' operatives, Harry Fairfax. This ghetto is known as the Maze; enclosed by the London Wall, it contains most of the old city of London which, unlike most other Londons, did not suffer a Great Fire in 1666. It is a decaying slum where London's dissenting and dispossessed Royalist population has been forced to live for well over three hundred years. Once in the Maze, Arkwright makes contact with Fairfax at a sleazy crowded tavern called The Hilton. After using his psychic powers to perform an 'exorcism', Arkwright and Fairfax spend the night at a safe house, intending to meet with the King the following morning.

In the meantime the Disruptors have informed Cromwell that Arkwright is active on this parallel and has been observed in St. Petersburg. Cromwell and his cabinet are expecting a Royalist revolt, and have the the Maze under close surveillance.

Arkwright and Fairfax make their way through the Maze to the Royalist headquarters, a large town house enclosed by a walled courtyard. Arkwright senses the Puritan surveillance unit almost as soon as they arrive and he sends Fairfax and a group of Royalists to kill Cromwell's surveillance agents. Before dying, the surveillance team contacts their superiors, confirming the message that Arkwright has arrived in England. Cromwell orders a raid on the Royalist base, to be led by General Standish, Cromwell's right-hand man. Standish sends a division of elite Puritan motorcycle troops from the Westminster Barracks to spearhead the assault on the Maze.

At the Royalist headquarters Arkwright is granted an audience with King Charles, Princess Anne and assorted nobility. The King signs the treaty, sealing the pact with Russia and Prussia, and accepts a substantial war loan that Arkwright has brought with him. Arkwright learns that Princess Anne, the king's formidable and clever sister, is heavily pregnant. She and Arkwright were formerly lovers and there is no doubt the children (for she carries twins) are his.

During his meeting with Anne, Arkwright has been experiencing a growing unease: a warning of the Puritan attack. As the Puritan motorcycles burst into the Maze, the horror of its innocent inhabitants sends an unmistakable signal through the psychic ether. Arkwright is suddenly aware of the attack and orders the alarm to be sounded. Arkwright instructs the King and Princess Anne to flee the headquarters — something King Charles resists. In order to get the King to agree to leave, Arkwright has to psychically implant an overwhelming fear of death in Charles' mind, forcing him to flee to safety.

Arkwright joins the Royalist defence. Despite the Disruptor supplied superior weapons the Puritans use, the Royalists can win — but only if they can hold until their forces, scattered across the Maze, can group and outflank the attackers. As Arkwright coordinates this strategy, Princess Anne, herself a psychic, uses her own powers to send Charles into battle, overriding Arkwright's implanted command. The King rushes from the headquarters mere seconds after an explosion buries Harry Fairfax under a section of wall, despite Arkwight's shouted warnings. Arkwright turns to see the King, making a heroic, but futile charge, cut down by machine gun fire.

A Puritan soldier takes aim as a shocked Arkwright finds himself standing over the King's corpse, stunned by this sudden turn of events. Arkwright realises his peril too late and fails to avoid the sniper. He is struck in the head and falls to the ground, unconscious.

In the aftermath of the Battle of the Maze a badly injured Fairfax drags himself from beneath the large timber beam which saved his life in the collapse of the building. He sees Arkwright's body being dragged away by Puritan troops, then makes his escape through one of the breaches in the wall surrounding the headquarters.

To celebrate the defeat over the Royalists, Cromwell addresses a huge crowd at a Nuremburg-style rally held in Westminster Square. Unbeknown to him, two of his Cabinet Ministers, Whitelaw and Compton, are hatching a plot to rid themselves of Cromwell, whom they see as a depraved tyrant. They intend to assume control after assassinating Cromwell and those closest to him, by planting a bomb in the Cabinet Office. Whitelaw and Compton believe themselves free agents in this, but the the bomb plot is being orchestrated by the Disruptors, who consider that Cromwell has outlived his usefulness, but can still be made into an effective martyr.

On Zero-Zero W.O.T.A.N is beginning to malfunction, leading to the worrying conclusion that the hypercomputer may not be able to accurately locate the Disruptor's parallel of origin when Arkwright draws them out. For all its vast computing power, W.O.T.A.N failed to factor-in that it too will be affected by FireFrost.

Meanwhile, on 00.72.87, Arkwright is badly injured, but living. Interred at the Dissident Detention Centre at Westminster, he has been subjected to brutal torture. To resist, Arkwright has slipped into a coma-like state and, as his interrogators resume their questioning, he begins to return to his own mind-space. He manages to achieves a trance state in which he undergoes a mystical rebirth. Arkwright's psyche changes profoundly, undergoing a form of enlightenment akin to that of the Five who mentored him years before. He becomes more powerful; able to perceive the totality of the Multiverse and, as he achieves this perfect state of being, his body dies — fulfilling many premonitions Arkwright has had of his own death.

Czar Nicholas and Archduke Frederick have mobilised their forces and are converging on England. Despite the treaty with Charles, they intend to seize Britain after aiding the Royalist revolution, a plan motivated by Krupp, a Disruptor Bishop controlling a Prussian Lodge and exercising great influence in the Prussian court and government. The Disruptors intend Britain to fragment into areas of Puritan and Royalist loyalty, fighting a bloody guerrilla war against the Prussian and Russian occupiers; who will themselves be manipulated into conflict, causing a Eurasian war plunging the world into utter chaos.

In his cell, Arkwright's transformation is complete; he is reborn — emerging from a symbolic death and rebirth as *homo novus*; the next step of human evolution. His rebirth unleashed violent psionic energy, tearing through his cell and driving his interrogators mad. Struggling to control his perception of reality, and to master his enhanced powers, Arkwright uses a newfound power of Intangibility and walks unhindered from his cell. He escapes unhindered from Westminster and makes his way slowly to Aldershot and the Royalist encampment, where he meets Princess Anne, now the queen-in-waiting.

Although disorientated by his rebirth Arkwright unintentionally uses his psychometry to perceive Anne's true nature and intentions. Anne forced her brother to his death so that she could assume power. Like Arkwright she is possessed of psionic abilities — the Holy Power of the Royal Line as she believes it to be. Anne knew Arkwright to be a powerful psychic from the moment they met and the pregnancy is completely contrived; all part of her greater plan. She is carrying twins, a boy and a girl, and it is her intention that Arkwright rule by her side, their children — no doubt powerful psychics themselves — will help in the forging of a British Empire. That night Arkwright wanders the Royalist camp, discovering Fairfax, who is dying from his injuries. Arkwright uses his new powers to cure Fairfax — another astounding revelation of *homo novus*.

Events on Para 00.72.87 are now building to a head. Arkwright returns to London, meeting Rose in Westminster Abbey. She has brought a valise of equipment, including his vibrobeamer and a flare gun. Arkwright intends to assassinate Cromwell and his entire cabinet, removing the Disruptor Elite with a single stroke. Once this is done he will signal the Royalists with the flare gun — the sign for the Royalists and their allies to advance on London. Taking his goodbye from Rose, Arkwright ascends to the roof of the Abbey, standing opposite the building in which the Puritan cabinet is meeting. Arkwright climbs onto the parapet and launches himself towards the window.

Inside the cabinet room things are not going well for Whitelaw and Compton. Cromwell has received word of the Royalist advance on London. He is elated, seeing his chance to crush the Monarchists decisively. With only two minutes before the Whitelaw and Compton's bomb explodes, Cromwell refuses permission for anyone to leave the cabinet room and embarks on a rant about how the Holy Ones (the name by which the Disruptors are known to the Elite) will protect the Puritan regime if if it is seriously threatened.

Outside, Arkwright glides between the buildings, kept aloft by psychic force. He smashes through the window and methodically executes the Disruptor Elite of Cromwell's cabinet. He has slowed down their perception of time and is moving with (what appears to them) incredible speed. In the carnage, the case containing the bomb is knocked to one side, falling open. By the time Arkwright succeeds in killing Cromwell there are just seventy-two seconds left before it detonates; however Arkwright has collapsed, the psionic defences of the Disruptor Elite having ravaged his tenacity and drained his life force. As he lies helpless on the floor, the seconds tick by.

Elsewhere the joint Prussian and Russia command centre is established at a mansion in Greenwich. The planned betrayal of the Royalists, Operation Overlord, is discussed. At the same time, as the Royalist army advances, Princess Anne is going into labour.

On Zero-Zero the problems with W.O.T.A.N continue, with parts of Valhalla Nova being destroyed by unleashed entropic energy — the result of FireFrost's activation and impending detonation.

At Westminster Cromwell's secretary comes into the Cabinet room. As she stares in shock at the carnage, Arkwright recovers his senses and pins her to the table. He drains her Prana, channelling her life force to restore his own. Revived, he staggers to the window and fires the flare gun, signalling for the Royalists to attack. Puritan guards, alerted by the sound of the assassination, arrive in the cabinet room. They have barely time to take stock of the situation when the bomb detonates. Arkwright has gone.

The Royalist army advances through London, initially meeting stiff resistance that begins to crumble as it becomes apparent that the Puritan chain of command has failed. No longer receiving orders from Westminster, the Government Command Centre has fallen into chaos, lending the advantage to the Royalists and their Russo-Prussian allies.

Rose enters the battle at the head of her brigade of female warriors, the Daughters of Albion, leading them into battle — a massed sisterhood of valkyries with Rose herself dressed as Britannia, complete with sword and shield.

Meanwhile, Queen Anne begins to give birth as around her the Battle for London rages. The Puritan air force appears, using their biplanes to strafe the Royalists ground forces. In turn they are driven from the skies by the appearance of the Prussian helicarriers and their fleets of one-man auto gyros. As battle rages, storm-clouds gather over London; the storm threatens to break, with thunder, lightning, gun fire and the cries of battle competing for sensory attention. The Puritans are being decimated and retreat, which soon turns into a chaotic rout.

Anne gives birth. The newborn twins are held up to the crowd while, in the thunderclouds, psychic visions manifest, triggered by the growing entropy of FireFrost and Anne's own powers being unleashed with the birth of her children. Arkwright moves calmly through the battle, waiting for the Disruptors to make their move.

On Zero-Zero W.O.T.A.N begins to register a trans parallel gate forming, but before the computer can track the source of the signature, it suffers a complete breakdown of its sensors.

In London, on the Thames Embankment, space itself distorts as the trans parallel gateway opens and an army of Disruptor Rooks streams forth. The plan has succeeded; the Disruptors have exposed themselves as Arkwright hoped, but with W.O.T.A.N compromised, the plan may be doomed to failure.

The Rooks attack the Royalist and Russian infantry, decimating them with energy weapons. Arkwright, sensing their materialisation, rushes to the scene. He is too late to save Rose, who is killed by a burst of four laser pulses: the shock of her death is felt by her Alternate Selves across numerous parallels, transmitted to every version of Rose through the shared Empathic Link.

Arkwright prepares to track the Disruptors to their base. No longer needing W.O.T.A.N, he reaches out with his vastly enhanced psychometry, locating the source of the Rook's trans parallel gate, and translocates, reappearing aboard the vast, decaying hulk of the World-Ship that is the Disruptor base.

He evades the Rooks using the trans parallel gate and makes his way into the heart of the hulk. Passing by the vast lines of clone vats where the Rooks are created, and through a vast hall of Trans Parallel Communicators where orders are issued to the Disruptor Bishops across the multiverse. Finally Arkwright reaches the centre of the complex, discovering FireFrost and the

Bringer of Light. The ancient alien uses illusions in an attempt to distract Arkwright, appearing first as a white-bearded, robed and god-like figure. Arkwright is unfooled and launches a psychic attack of his own on the *real* presence he detects deep within the ancient machines at the very core of the space station.

The Bringer of Light attempts a further deception, appearing as one of the Five to Arkwright, but Luther sees through the ruse and uncovers the withered alien at the heart of the World-Ship: a shrivelled, sexless thing, kept alive by machines, psionic energy and sheer force of will. As they battle, Arkwright is hit and hideously wounded by an ancient energy weapon built into the defensive machinery surrounding the alien. Ignoring the injury to his physical body Arkwright continues the fight in Astral form. He is losing the battle when the *real* Five, sacrificing themselves, merge into a single vibration — a bolt of focused, psychic energy which is directed by Arkwright, destroying the Bringer of Light.

Arkwright physically dies once more, but is sustained by the raw force of the psionic matrix permeating the multiverse. He is almost lost to the totality of creation; yet, submitting to destiny, he returns to his current plane of existence. Arkwright splits FireFrost with a single thought and returns to his body, which he psionically reconstructs, and leaves the Disruptor parallel as the World-Ship explodes.

Equilibrium is restored across the parallels with FireFrost's sundering, and the death of the Disruptors' driving force. On 00.72.87 the Battle for London comes to an abrupt halt as the Rooks flounder and fall, cut off from the alien will that motivated them.

On Zero-Zero the continuum monitor has been jury-rigged by Parsifal and his team, and a small blip is registered as the Disruptor World-Ship explodes. In space, the two halves of FireFrost are dragged away from each other, disappearing into infinity.

Arkwright returns to 00.72.87. In London the Prussian and Russian chiefs of staff are celebrating the turn of events and, in a celebratory mood, are about to give the command to attack the Royalists. Arkwright prevents this final treachery, poisoning the Russo-Prussian high command with nerve agent. Their treachery, which Arkwright always suspected, becoming their doom.

Arkwright wanders through the aftermath of the battle, eventually meeting Fairfax. He witnesses cruelties inflicted by the Royalists every bit as bad as those inflicted by the Puritans. In the days that follow, Anne is crowned Queen of Great Britain and Arkwright attends Rose's funeral before departing 00.72.87. He translocates to 00.38.56, where he joins the Rose of that parallel at her house on the Whitby coastline. There he renounces violence, throwing his vibro-beamer into the sea, his adventures done.

So end the Adventures of Luther Arkwright; but the tale is not yet over... for there are children.

Heart of Empire

Heart of Empire is set almost exclusively on 00.72.87, some 23 years after the Battle for London. It focuses on Victoria, Arkwright's daughter by Queen Anne, her growing psychic abilities, and a further cataclysm — this one not of the Disruptors' making — that once again threatens the multiverse.

In Rome, the depraved monk Barberini (possessed himself of psychic powers, and unfraid of using them for personal gratification), is summoned to the Vatican by the dying Pope. He is ordered to travel to England as the Papal Envoy and ask Empress Anne to render the British Empire unto the Catholic Church. If she refuses, Barberini is to kill both her and her daughter Victoria. Barberini is most loyal to the Holy Father and vows to undertake the mission at all costs; however, something is amiss. Enjoying a plate of pasta before heading for London a strange, five-limbed swirling pattern appears in his meal, clearly an omen of some kind.

In London, Princess Victoria wanders Hyde Park incognito. She has come to oversee the building of the Crystal Palace, an edifice she designed to host the Great Exhibition of 2007. As she wanders, she encounters republican sympathisers disseminating copies of 'Perfidious Albion', a pamphlet promoting the republican cause and challenging the monarchy's divine right to rule. The pamphlet is written by one Gabriel Shelley and something draws Victoria to its author, even though she abhors the message it contains. The poet who gives her the pamphlet remarks on the physical similarities Victoria shares with Shelley.

Aboard the skyship Titanic, Hiram Kowalski and his assistant Angela return to London from New Amsterdam. Kowalski

finds London much changed: gone are the Puritan trappings of Cromwell's day, and its place is a mixture of neo-Regency flamboyance, Art Deco stylings, and grand constructions celebrating the heart of the British Empire.

Returning to the Imperial Palace, Victoria is assailed by courtiers demanding her approval for preparations for the grand masque and a new painting of the glorious victory at the Battle for London. Struck by one of her intensifying migraines, Victoria loses her temper with her courtiers, but is reminded that Doctor Dee, the astrologer and phsyician, is still part of the court, at work in its basement. She leaves her courtiers behind to squabble and descends to Doctor Dee's basement laboratory. Dee prepares potions that help keep Victoria's migraines under control and reminisces of the terrorist attack, eighteen years before, resulting in the death of Victoria's twin brother, Prince Henry. The Queen slaughtered the terrorists herself, but Henry could not be saved from gun shot wounds, despite Dee's best efforts. Henry's death affected Anne deeply and, in Dee's estmation, drove her mad. In fact, Dee believes Victoria has a greater destiny to fulfil; a variety of astrological and numerological factors are coming into alignment, forming a conjunction in five days' time, on Victory Day, which is also Victoria's twenty-third birthday. To help with the accumulations of orgone energy Victoria appears to be suffering, Dee gives her a clockwork device capable of helping unleash the pent-up forces: a *tantric stimulator*. He also conducts a ritual sacrifice to check on his predictions for the fateful conjunction. The cat's blood and entrails form a similar design to the one Barberini witnessed in his plate of spaghetti...

And, as Doctor Dee puzzles over the guts of a dead cat, and Victoria puzzles over both her new toy and the name of Gabriel Shelley, Barberini himself arrives in London at the Lambeth International Railway terminal.

On Zero-Zero the ageing Rose Wilde returns to Valhalla Nova to be greeted by her old chief, Karl Merkel. Both of them have been called back to Valhalla but are unaware why; the only way to discover the truth is to speak with W.O.T.A.N itself, at the Planck Fields section of the arcology.

During a tour of London on 00.72.87, Kowalsky and Angela are horrified to discover that the carefully stage-managed opulence and prosperity of the city barely disguises the continued practice of slavery, something the British Empire has refused to outlaw, much to Kowalski and Angela's abhorrence. Nevertheless, they head towards the imperial seat, Windsor Castle, and hopefully an audience with the Empress herself.

Yet, the Empress's courtiers have plans of their own. Led by Mister Strickland, the immense man known as the Bermondsey Giant, various councillors and advisers to the Empress are preparing a direct challenge to her rule. Their plotting coincides with the arrivals of Kowalski, Angela and the new Papal Envoy; it has also been noticed by Eugene Kray, the Duke of Northumberland and head of Anne's Secret Police. Kray stops short of making an arrest of Mister Strickland as Queen Anne, Empress and living goddess, makes her grand entrance into the throng, flanked by her elite bodyguard, the Daughters of Albion.

Queen Anne announces that the Japanese Empire has surrendered to British Imperial forces in the Far East, further extending her exalted reach. As Victoria is meant to provide an official welcome to the hostages sent by Japan, the Japanese Emperor's sons, her migraine strikes once more, causing a fit of violent vomiting that brings the ceremony to an abrupt close — although not before Barberini's request for an immediate audience is rejected by the Empress, and further incurring the Papal Envoy's wrath.

In the grounds of Windsor Castle, Victoria encounters more 'guests' of the Empress, young hostages of the royal houses Britain has conquered. Victoria is popular with the young royals, but a tantrum by Prince Krishnan of India is too much for her and she storms away from the gathering to seek solitude.

In her antechambers, Queen Anne is divested of her royal magnificence — an elaborate charade to mask the frail and ageing wretch beneath the trappings of empire. The emaciated queen summons Mister Strickland where she reveals to the horrified giant that his schemes with the other nobles of court were not as secret as he'd believed. Strickland, held in Anne's psionic grip, is powerless as the queen reveals that others of 'holy power' have been born twenty three years ago, and shows off her collection of relics, collected from various victims through the years. Anne uses the Bermondsey Giant, draining his Prana in a sadistic embrace that reduces his immense body to dust. Invigorated and renewed, Queen Anne's body becomes youthful once more; a temporary respite from her true, skeletal state.

Touring London, Kowalsky and Angela run into Maurice Williams, the poet and polemiscist who gave Victoria a copy of 'Perfidious Albion' and hinted at her likeness to Gabriel Shelley. Williams wants exposure for the republican cause in New Amsterdam and invites the two journalists to a meeting in Alsatia where, he claims, both Shelley and Victoria will be present. Despite the dangers of Alsatia — a dump containing 'thieves' dens, illicit taverns, brothels and gambling joints, dog fights and ratting pits', Kowalsky agrees to go.

In Doctor Dee's dungeon, Victoria has resolved to attend the meeting where Gabriel Shelley will be present, despite Dee's protestations. Victoria tells Dee that she has determined that Harry Fairfax, hero of the Battle for London, is still alive and living in Notting Hill. Victoria is seeking answers to her past: who Arkwright was, and why he disappeared. Dee though, is more interested in

Victoria's migraines and their significance. He has determined that she is not simply undergoing some form of illness or affliction, but is under a sustained psychic assault — but what is the source?

Above ground, Eugene Kray prepares himself both for an official portrait and his intended role as head of a post-royalist empire. Kray, far from being loyal to Queen Anne, has plans of his own and had intended to install Victoria as a puppet queen in Anne's place. Kray plans to have Anne assassinated by well-placed marksmen as she opens the Great Exhibition, following-up the murder with a lightning strike by his shock troops. To mask his intentions Kray is manipulating the republicans into a riot which will conveniently allow his troops to assume control without a whiff of treason being traceable to himself.

On Zero-Zero, Rose is introduced to a much-changed W.O.T.A.N. The computer has evolved into a true AI with full voice synthesis and holographic representation of Odin. W.O.T.A.N has identified an interference vortex (the pattern witnessed by Barberini and Dee) emanating from parellel 00.72.87. Psychic energy has been leaching from the parallel for 23 years but has suddenly increased at an exponential rate. W.O.T.A.N has calculated that only three days remain before the energy arc reaches catastrophic levels, leaving Valhalla little time to prepare a strategic counterpoint to the event.

Victoria, meanwhile, in the middle of an orgone release, is interrupted by sounds outside her suite. From the balcony she witnesses prisoners being herded to Saint George's chapel and this brings back memories of her brother Henry, before his death. The two children explored the chapel, admiring the victory portraits of Rose Wylde, Harry Fairfax, and Rose's Britannia armour from the Battle for London. Her memories build into a psychic fugue and Victoria witnesses some form of terrible explosion before regaining her senses and having to resort to Dee's elixir for her migraine.

In the round tower of the Imperial Palace, the rejuvenated Queen Anne decides o offer clemency to the treacherous nobles who had sided with Mister Strickland — despite them having undergone a powerful beating and several hours suspended by their ankles from meathooks. Afterwards, she grants Barberini his audience: the monk demands that Britain submit to Rome's power only for Anne to angrily reject the idea, reminding Barberini that Britain suffers Rome and not the other way around. Preparing to strike with a concealed dagger in his crucifix, Barberini is prevented from Cunning Plan B as others, namely Eugene Kray, arrive for their own audience; a royal assassination will simply have to wait. The Queen hears reports of actions against the empire's enemies and also receives a copy of a satirical pamphlet. A cartoon depicting her as an immense sow, squashing the world, causes Anne to fly into a rage and order Kray to send his Anti-Terrorist Squad to crush the perpetrators of the offending magazine — something Kary relishes the opportunity to do.

Victoria visits the shrine raised to her father, Luther Arkwright, where she curses his memory for the fate she now endures. Her brother murdered, her governess, Diana, driven mad; Harry Fairfax banished; the distraught young woman declares her hatred for her father's abandonment and, with a sudden release of psychic power that mirrors Arkwright's own, she destroys a statue of her father through a single blast of uncontrolled psychic energy. Afterward, Victoria heads to Notting Hill, and the crumbling pile known as Witherslack Hall, the seat of the Fairfax family. There, riddled with disease, is 'Uncle' Harry, a foul-mouthed alcoholic who has lost none of his Maze-born charm. Victoria questions him about her father and his sudden disappearance but learns nothing concrete — save that Fairfax has many illegitimate children (the Bastards of Fairfax) residing in the slums of Alsatia, which is where Victoria is heading herself, and the appointment with Gabriel Shelley.

Victoria enters Alsatia via the old underground railway network and makes her way to the tavern known as The Cockpit, in Shoe Lane. There, Gabriel Shelley — who bears as astonishing resemblance to both Victoria and Arkwright, spurs a crowd to rebellion, decrying the 1% who own 99% of the world's wealth. Without, Kray's Anti-Terrorist Thugs prepare to mete out their own particular brand of East-End justice, and, gaining entry to the tavern, launch attacks with knives, guns and grenades. Shelley proves to be as martially

adept as Luther Arkwright ever was, despatching several of the ATG thugs with their own weapons. Kowalsky and Angela, there to document proceedings, assist in the fight, and Victoria, who has remained in the shadows, offers her own defence, forcing a hand-grenade down the throat of one of Kray's murderers and hurling him through the window. Shelley watches in wry amusement even though Victoria is, herself, astonished at the violence she has just committed.

Queen Anne also mourns Luther's absence and confesses to his portrait of her reliance on opium and absinthe to sustain her will. Yet the Queen, even in her cups, is still wily. Her intelligence network send news via a messenger hawk that Barberini has taken refuge in a convent in Baker Street (where he is busy corrupting the holy sisters, two at a time). Anne vows that the Papal Envoy will be damned for whatever treachery he plans and goes to seek a blessed corruption of her own with three of her Irish Guardsmen.

In Alsatia, Victoria, Shelley, Angela and Kowalsky discuss the precarious political climate. Shelley claims that, while he promotes a republican government, he remains committed to the arts and science, and has no hopes for personal power. He remarks on the corruption in the royal household and Eugene Kray's own ambitions, something both Kowalsky and Victoria find shocking. Finally, talk turns to Shelley's own lineage and he reveals that he, like Victoria, is 23, was born a bastard to an East-End whore. The chemistry between Victoria and Shelley generates a powerful field of psycho-sexual energy that affects even Kowalsky and Angela. And, as Queen Anne tests the regimental strength of the Irish Guards' columns, Victoria, Shelley and Ophelia; Kowalsky and Angela, find their own resolves tested and needs satiated.

The next morning, Victoria learns from Shelley that they are not alone in being... different. He too suffers the migraines Victoria experiences and knows of many others, all of a similar age, that share the same thing. Shelley knows that humanity is entering a new phase of development: stronger, faster, psychically gifted. Shelley gives Victoria some vials of a psychoactive drug he has developed which can help control her migraines. He also reveals that he was once a boy soldier in Queen Anne's army who saw the horrors the British Empire was inflicting on the world, hence his republican views. Angered by the psychic visions Shelley communicates, and troubled by the presence of a statue to liberty Shelley has been constructing, Victoria leaves Alsatia, troubled by thoughts of an impending massacre.

On Zero-Zero, Rose and the other Valhalla personnel have been trying to locate Arkwright, the only person capable of understanding and stopping the Interference Vortex W.O.T.A.N has been tracking. Exhausted from the efforts, Rose is called to a meeting where W.O.T.A.N has sought the permission of the World Council to launch a pre-emptive strike against parallel 00.72.87, to prevent the Inteference Vortex from spreading across the multiverse.

In 00.72.87 Kowalsky and Angela, their romance blooming, find they need to seek sanctuary. Inter-racial relations are illegal in Queen Anne's Britain and, having been found in flagrante at their hotel, the two have no option but to seek safety in Alsatia. Arranging their safe passage is Harry Fairfax — or rather, the Bastards of Fairfax; and, as one of Harry's boys meets the two, Angie chooses the moment to reveal that she works for the CIA.

Victoria, meanwhile, visits Bethlehem Asylum, intending to see Diana, her old governess. Driven mad after the assassination attempt that claimed Prince Henry's life, Diana has been committed to the asylum for over a decade and her mind is all but broken. Victoria uses a psychic connection to see into her mind but gains little of relevance. Still, appalled at the conditions of the asylum, she decides to have Diana moved to a place of safety and to confront her mother over everything that has been troubling her recently.

Someone else keen on an audience with the queen is Barberini, but his attempt is once again thwarted with the news that the queen wants him returned to Rome immediately. Furious, Barberini decides that they will all die that night. The Queen has heard of Victoria's attendance at the Alsatia rally; in her own spate of fury Queen Anne gives Eugene Kray absolute control over the armed forces to quell any uprising taking place at the Britannia Square demonstration. The Queen also reinforces her requirements that certain prisoners be taken to St. George's Chapel, as usual. However, when wondering precisely *why* prisoners are taken there, neither Kray nor his 2iC, Stanley, can remember.

Victoria, adamant to see her mother, is denied a direct audience and so gains access to Queen Anne's boudoir via old secret tunnels. Emerging through a concealed door, she discovers her mother and several Irish Guardsmen undergoing a kind of kit inspection that no princess of the realm should ever witness her mother and queen performing. Angered, migraine building, she storms to her rooms and quaffs one of the psychotropic vials Shelley gave to her. The hallucinations build quickly: Victoria flees the palace and staggers into London, her senses overloaded by garish visions, sounds, mockery and all manner of drug-induced terrors. These experiences build to a point where Victoria sees the face of Rose Wylde — and is, in reality, the Rose of Zero-Zero attempting to make empathic contact across the multiverse. Victoria finds herself cornered by neo-Puritan skinhead thugs who have less than puritanical plans for the princess. Assaulted and threatened, Victoria lashes out physically and, finally, psionically, the wrack powerful enough to blast the thugs into messy, bone-broken smears. The release of energy also does something else: Victoria translocates, leaving 00.72.87 and materialising in the war-torn ruins of 01.69.05 London.

Kowalsky and Angela, safe in Alsatia, discuss her reasons for being in London. The CIA is concerned at the number of people who go missing from London's streets, especially a number of American diplomats who, Angie thinks, have been targeted by Kray's secret police. While talking, Kowalsky recognises Professor Helmut Lang, a defector from the collapsed Prussian Empire who has been devising some form of firework contraption in Hyde Park that will be used to open the Great Exhibition. Deciding to still cover the demonstration in Britannia Square, the two prepare for a long and chilly night.

Victoria regains consciousness on 01.69.05 to find her clothes and migraine gone. The psychic pressure she has dealt with for as long as she can recall has lifted and the release is palpable. She finds herself in a storeroom and when she goes in search of her clothes, discovers that not only is there a considerable gathering of people outside, but there is also a version of Rose Wylde. Clothing herself in a handy Union jack flag, Rose takes Victoria to the next shock of the past few minutes: her father, Luther Arkwright. Luther, seemingly ageless and affecting the dress of a Buddhist monk, is clearly delighted to see his daughter, although Victoria, distraught and angry, is less so.

On Zero-Zero W.O.T.A.N is preparing the counterstrike. Assembling psionically gifted humans, *homo novus* examples, a special apparatus has been prepared to siphon psionic energy and use it to help the Valhalla psychics to trace the instability on 00.72.87 and counter it. There is no doubt the young psychics can trace the source, but countering it is another matter; already the multiverse is undergoing similar instabilities to those of 23 years earlier, as FireFrost was reactivated.

Eugene Kray and his policemen discover the carnage left behind when Victoria abruptly translocated. Part of her cloak has been left behind and the label stitched inside confirms, to Kray, that both belong to the Princess Royal and that she must be in league with Shelley's Leveller terrorists. Kray orders for Victoria to be shot on sight.

Victoria and Luther finally have a chance to become acquainted. Arkwright explains much of his own nature and experience, the nature of the multiverse, and what this means for both homo sapiens and *homo novus*. Despite having become free from ego and mundane concerns, Arkwright nevertheless probes Victoria's mind and discovers the psychic turmoil she has experienced and pinpoints how much relates to St George's Chapel. Agreeing to help her get to the bottom of this psychic trauma, Arkwright translocates them both to 00.72.87, materialising in Witherslack Hall where Fairfax is both surprised and delighted to see his old friend return. Arkwright once again cures Fairfax's ailments, restoring him to both youth and flatulence. Renewed and invigorated, Fairfax is more than willing help father and daughter.

Kowalsky and Angela come across an inebriated Professor Lang. While talking, they witness one of Kray's sinister unmarked police vans load a group of street revellers violently into its cargo bay. In his cups, Lang reveals that his firework device is actually no such thing. The machine he has been designing for the opening of the Great Exhibition is a bomb, designed to test Lang's theories regarding nuclear chain reactions. A disbelieving Angela and Kowalsky leave the old drunk to his rambling.

Across town, in Notting Hill, the Arkwrights and Fairfx do a little window shopping to get Luther his trademark ensemble (floppy shirt, leather trousers and a pair of circle-rimmed sunglasses). Victoria gets a new cloak and a domino mask — disguises are vital as both are easily recognisable on London's streets. Barberini, meanwhile, prepares to pay the Queen a visit. Shedding his filthy monk's habit he arms himself for a murder spree, with duel pistols, copious amounts of ammunition and a fetching spiked codpiece.

Arkwright, Victoria and Fairfax head for Alsatia and the Rat's Castle inn. Nelly, the landlady, greets Fairfax warmly and agrees to help the small group infiltrate St George's Chapel. Arkwright lets Fairfax spend time with old drinking friends before a strategy discussion. Barberini is ahead of them though. albeit unwittingly. En-route to fulfill the orders of the Holy Father, he passes by St George's Chapel as the revellers, rounded-up by Kray's secret Police, are hurried inside the chapel. Barberini experiences a huge psychic surge and blacks out for several hours.

As dawn breaks and he recovers his senses, the Papal Envoy scales the walls of the Royal Palace, gains entry to its hallowed halls, and proceeds to massacre the Irish Guard who act as sentries for the Royal apartments. Sir Kenneth, the Queen's diminutive secretary, discovers Barberini and his butchery and attempts to raise the alarm, but is slain, leaving the mad monk to further carnage. Barberni carves his way into the Queen's private chambers and empties his pistols into the Queen and a pair of Irish Guardsmen who have, coincidentally, just emptied their own. Despite horrific wounds, and to Barberini's shock, Queen Anne survives the assault.

At the Rat's Castle, Kowalsky and Angela have sought refuge and encountered Arkwright. Luther has spent the night teaching Victoria how to master her growing psychic talents, and she uses these to gain some insight into Angela's mind, questioning her own ingrained prejudices and learning something of Angela's fate. Arkwright is struck with a sense of imminent catastrophe and, with Nelly, Fairfax and Victoria, they leave the inn for St George's chapel, using the old underground carriage system to move beneath the city.

At Hyde Park, Doctor Dee and Professor Lang survey the device the latter has built for the exhibition opening ceremony. Lang explains the principles of his nuclear fission device, and even the old astrologer begins to grasp the enormity of what Lang has built.

Arkwright, Victoria, Fairfax and Nelly gain entry to the Royal Palace en route to St George's chapel and come across the carnage Barberini has wrought. Arkwright warily steps into Queen Anne's boudoir to find Barberini's severed head and entrails adorning the bed post — a grisly trophy and unconventional bedstead notch. Anne, drained of psychic energy, is dying but she reveals to Luther that their son, Henry, still lives in St George's Chapel. She considers him the 'elect of God', and tells Arkwright that, even though the assassin's bullet killed the young prince, she used her own powers to bring him back to life. Unfortunately the damaged brain of the young prince could not hold the psychic energy and what was revived was not a small boy, but a terrible, malleable monster that drove the Lady Diana mad. The creature lived and grew, but required constant psychic energy, in ever more quantities, to keep itself alive. Anne's best effort to control it failed and so, confined to St George's Chapel, it has been fed with the psychic energy of those caused to disappear by Eugene Kray's secret police. Having brokered her shameful secret, Queen Anne, Empress of the Great British Empire, dies in Luther's arms.

On Zero-Zero W.O.T.A.N has deduced that the psychic instability centred on 00.72.87 is sapient in origin. The AI attempts to contain the mounting psychic power but its own circuits blow, compromising Valhalla's ability to neutralise the threat.

Shelley leads the Levellers to Britannia Square for the planned demonstration. Kray and his forces wait secretly for them to arrive, planning an attack of their own.

Above St George's Chapel the psychic power of the monster within builds, manifesting as the tentacular stormclouds design that many have witnessed in recent days. Sir Joshua Hirst, the court artist, attempts to stop Arkwright and Victoria from entering the chapel; Victoria reads his mind and learns that Hirst is part of Kray's plan to overthrow the monarchy and seize power for himself. She also learns of the planned ambush of Shelley's demonstrators in Britannia Square. She resolves to stop Kray by leading the militia against the Secret Police and Kray's thugs, while Arkwright deals with what St George's Chapel contains

Henry Arkwright Stuart is an immense, blood-red, organic mass resembling something from the nightmares of Lovecraft and Giger. Its writhing, tentacular form seizes and absorbs Arkwright. Its psychic powers are now so strong that it exerts an influence across the parallels affecting even Zero-Zero where the *homo novus* psychics of Valhalla are the only ones able to maintain an effective barrier against imminent collapse. Arkwright and the thing that was once his son enter psionic battle and even Arkwright is overwhelmed by the power his progeny has developed. Deep within, Henry's young psychic imprint still survives and Arkwright reaches out to communicate with it.

Elsewhere, battle rages. At the Royal Palace the Irish Guards, roused to the carnage wrought by Barberini open fire on Fairfax and Nelly, who wait for Arkwright to finish his business in the chapel. At Britannia Square, Kray orders his own forces to crush Shelley's peaceful demonstration. Fairfax and his team are out of ammunition and at the mercy of the Household Guard when Victoria, clad in the uniform last worn by Rose Wylde at the Battle for London, appears to take command. The Household Guard ceases its assault at their new Queen's command and Victoria goes to the chapel to help her father.

Victoria is repulsed at the sight of the monstrosity that was once Henry and enter physical battle with the creature, just as, in Britannia Square, Kray's forces batter and bludgeon the demonstrators into submission, injuring Ophelia, Shelley's paramour, and riling Shelley to arms.

On Zero-Zero, the defences of the *homo novus* psychics fails as Henry's energy overwhelms the psychic fabric of the multiverse. The young psionics die in their amplifiers and only Rose Wylde has any chance of stopping the overload that threatens to destabilise the cosmos.

Carnage of its own reigns in Britannia Square. Angela Russ falls to the bullets and batons of Kray's forces and even Kowalsky, a man of peace, takes up arms of his own.

Arkwright and Victoria formulate a plan to deal with the creature. While it drains Victoria of prana, Arkwright channels the latent power of the psychic web permeating the multiverse to act as a back-flow and cause a temporary lapse in its destructive rage. Fairfax enters the chapel as the two manage to hold the creature in check, and the residual memories of Fairfax and others successfully give the monster reason to pause.

Such a pause is also enough for Rose's own assault to break through and reach Arkwright and Victoria. With the creature confused, and the combined psychic talents of all three, the realisation that Professor Lang has a nuclear bomb in Hyde Park triggers the final part of the plan. Arkwright, Victoria and Rose translocate the creature to the base of the atomic pile driver just as it prepares to drop its payload to mark the opening of the Great Exhibition; then the creature and bomb are shunted to an uninhabited parallel, rather than have it detonate in Hyde Park . The resulting explosion destroys the creature and ends its psychic assault.

Victoria levitates to Britannia Square, where the rebellion fights a running battle with Kray's troops. At the sight of Britannia herself descending from the skies, all fighting stops long enough for Victoria to kill Kray, Stanley and his henchmen with arrows, bringing an end to the plot to overthrow the monarchy. Yet, in a way, they are successful, because Victoria herself announces the dissolution of the Empire and relinquishes the crown, making Britain a republic. Victoria names Britain the Democratic State of Albion, handing power to the democratic process. Victoria becomes Albion's ambassador with a remit to see the world, and Arkwright bids his daughter farewell as she and Diana, her sanity restored with the creature's death, take to the skies in an ornithopter to begin their peace mission. Kowalsky and Angela have the true story of the Heart of Empire written, and Arkwright and Victoria vow to meet again some time.

Once more, the Arkwrights have saved the multiverse.

Appendix

Here in the appendix we present a miscellany of information for both Games Masters and players aimed at helping both to get the most from Luther Arkwright campaigns. Luther Arkwright draws on a rich tradition of homage and is openly influenced by many different sources of fantastic fiction. This chapter helps to identify and use some of these sources. It is not exhaustive, but it does offer a wide range of media for ideas and inspiration.

Television, Film and Radio

During the 1950s and 1970s British television, film and radio created some of the most memorable and compelling Science Fiction and fantasy of the period, often on a shoestring budget. Incredibly, some of these are still broadcast today, and are fondly remembered.

Quatermass

Nigel Kneale's series involving Professor Bernard Quatermass encompassed radio, television and film. At one point the television series was the most watched programme of the 1950s, being beaten only by Queen Elizabeth's coronation. This was in the dawn of public television and for a Science Fiction series to achieve such ratings was quite incredible. The Quatermass series encompasses alien invasion, psionics, powerful forces harvesting humans, ancient memories leading to demonic-like behaviour and terrible physical transformations. The film of *Quatermass and the Pit* remains a classic, and all the Quatermass stories can easily be adapted to form the core of Arkwright scenarios or campaigns.

Doctor Who

Needing no introduction, Arkwright owes an enormous debt to the Time Lord who travels in a 1960s Police Telephone Box. While Arkwright is far more grounded, *Doctor Who* set many precedents for adventures in alternate histories with an enigmatic central character who confronts fiendish enemies and thwarts plots that intend to wipe out the Earth/Solar System/Galaxy. While *Doctor Who* remains a family show, many of its stories have been particularly dark of theme and mature in storytelling approach. And one of the Doctors, David Tennant, has played Luther in the Big Finish audio production of Luther Arkwright's adventures. Their destinies seem to be intertwined.

Adam Adamant Lives!

Created by the team responsible for *Doctor Who*, An Edwardian adventurer is frozen in time and emerges into the Swinging Sixties. Gerald Harper's caped, sword-stick wielding hero is almost perfect as an example of a Valhalla agent getting to grips with an unfamiliar world.

The Avengers

Not to be confused with the superhero team, *The Avengers* began as a dark revenge drama but evolved into a bright, eclectic, fun, pseudo spy series. John Steed, a debonair agent of the British Government, usually accompanied by a deft female sidekick such as Cathy Gale or Emma Peel, thwarted the plots of mad scientists, megalomaniacs, sinister robots and all manner of fiendish adversaries. *The Avengers*' influence on Arkwright simply cannot be underestimated.

Sapphire and Steel

Transdimensional investigators that appear to be the physical manifestations of the heavy elements tackle supernatural inconsistencies and breaches in the space-time continuum that lead to all kinds of sinister and disturbing anomalies. Steel is cold and ruthless; Sapphire is charming and beautiful. The plots are complex, ingenious, compelling and showcase many of the traits one finds in the Arkwright saga: time paradoxes, hyper-intelligent beings manipulating the dimensions; nursery rhymes and contextual memories physically manifesting to terrify a pair of young children. Unmissable.

The Final Programme

The cinematic adaptation of Michael Moorcock's Jerry Cornelius novel, *The Final Programme* is not an especially good film, but it does have its charms, not least in presenting an enigmatic antihero in Cornelius, and the very template for Luther Arkwright. The film is a confusing mess, but it's sheer style and attitude compensates for some (but not all) of its problems.

Books

Arkwright draws on several very strong literary sources. It is impossible to list them all, but here are some of the best.

The Cornelius Chronicles

Michael Moorcock introduced Jerry Cornelius in four seminal novels: *The Final Programme, A Cure for Cancer, The Condition of Muzak* and *The English Assassin*. Designed to be read in any order, Cornelius adopts different forms and personalities in each book, with continuity provided in the form of a recurring cast of Characters and the backdrop of civilisation on the brink of decay, destruction, or entropic disintegration. The novels are a social commentary, a political diatribe, a strange, psychedelic fairy tale and a way of testing, pushing and dissembling the narrative form. Cornelius and Arkwright are brothers; the latter could not exist without the former, and the adventures of Jerry Cornelius convey the strange, unreal atmosphere that permeated Britain in the late 1960s and early 1970s, and still resonates in Luther Arkwright.

Oswald Bastable

Another Moorcock creation, Oswald Bastable is an early 20th Century soldier who is thrown through several alternate Earths that are perfect examples of Arkwrightian parallels. The novels - *A Nomad of the Time Streams, The Land Ironclads* and *The Steel Tsar* are must-reads for any Arkwright fan.

The Diamond Age

Neal Stephenson's novel gives us an alternate late 20th Century where nanotechnology and artifical intelligence have reached new heights, yet the world has divided into curious cultural archetypes reflecting bygone eras. Thus we have the neo-Victorian European enclave pitted against a Chinese empire modelled on pre-Revolutionary imperial tropes. Into this mix is an AI disguised as a children's book that guides a young girl from the slums of the east to the high society of the west. An intriguing premise that would make a perfect Arkwrightian parallel.

Flashman

Whilst not Science Fiction or fantasy, George Macdonald Fraser's stories of Harry Flashman — bully, rogue, gambler, womaniser and self-confessed coward — are wonderful romps through Victorian history and simply drip with atmosphere, colourful Characters and plot hooks.

The Works of Jules Verne and H G Wells

The grandfathers of Science Fiction should never be ignored as a source of inspiration for Arkwright ideas and campaigns. Verne's *20,000 Leagues Under the Sea* and Wells' *War of the Worlds* are exemplary tales of man's reaction to science, otherworldly threats and the nature of the human condition (themes that frequently recur in Bryan Talbot's work). Imagine a parallel where the Martians stil rule the world in their war machines, opposed by an underwater freedom fighter network established by Captain Nemo...

H P Lovecraft and the Call of Cthulhu Roleplaying game

There are many Lovecraftian themes to be found in Arkwright: an uncaring universe; incredibly powerful psychic beings, and monsters of uncontrolled appetites. The Cthulhu Mythos is a rich source of ideas for Arkwright campaigns and, with a little work, many of the scenarios, campaign books and source books for Chaosium's marvellous *Call of Cthulhu* roleplaying game are compatible with *Luther Arkwright: Roleplaying Across the Parallels*.

A Clockwork Orange

The classic dystopian novel of an intelligent, disaffected youth and how society tries to cure his ills, Anthony Burgess' novel is, once again, an example of the strange atmosphere found in post-war Britain. While only indirectly an influence on Luther Arkwright, it is nevertheless a relative: an alternate Britain where young droogs commit terrible atrocities to a Beethoven soundtrack; where milk is laced with mood-altering drugs, and where the state attempts to use aggressive reversion therapy to cure the very problems it has created. It is almost a parallel where Arkwright would take direct action against the government.

J G Ballard and Christopher Priest

British authors who came to prominence in the New Wave of British Science Fiction, both Ballard and Priest are adept are creating dream-like, often nightmarish alternate worlds where little can be trusted or the very landscape is a threat. Chris Priest's books feature parallel worlds heavily, particularly his *Dream Archepelago* series and *The Adjacent*; but he also deals with paranormal abilities — strikingly so in *The Glamour*.

J G Ballard's work is intense, personal and hallucinogenic. His 'world' novels (*The Drowning World, The Burning World* and *The Crystal World*) provide different views of a post-apocalyptic world that would make for superb backdrops to Arkwright campaigns.

Iain Banks

Famous for *The Wasp Factory* and the *The Culture*, Banks has also dabbled with alternate Earths and parallel dimensions, most notably in *Transitions*, where a secretive agency polices the myriad dimensions and includes some almost direct analogues of Rose Wylde and Arkwright; indeed, *Transitions* is required reading for any Arkwright enthusiast. Like Ballard and Priest, Banks' stories often have a dream-like quality, and many of his non-Science Fiction novels would make for intriguing Luther Arkwright plots or backdrops.

Graphic Novels

The Arkwright Saga has influenced many graphic novels and emerged at a time where the graphic novel medium was beginning to break out from the 'for kids' ghetto. These contemporaries of Bryan Talbot's work are worth investigating.

V for Vendetta

Alan Moore's underrated masterpiece is a perfect parallel for Luther Arkwright games. In a totalitarian London, a masked vigilante wages war against the corrupt government. Indeed, *V for Vendetta* was written four years after Luther Arkwright, and there is a shared atmosphere and depth to the writing that makes them utterly complementary.

The League of Extraordinary Gentlemen

Another work by Alan Moore, the *League of Extraordinary Gentlemen* (ignore the risible film) imagines an alternate Victorian Britain where the great literary adventurers of the day are engaged by a shady government representative to battle an infamous criminal mastermind. So it is that Alan Quartermain, Mina Murray, Doctor Jekyll, Hawley Griffin (the original Invisible Man) and Captain Nemo battle Fu Manchu — surely a Disruptor Knight if ever there was one. In later adventures they come face to face with the Martian invasion of H G Wells' *War of the Worlds*.

Planetary

Influenced by Arkwright, Moorcock and many of the sources listed here, Warren Ellis's engaging series tells of a small organisation dedicated to uncovering the Secret History of the World, which leads them to discover alternate worlds, ships that sail between them, Lovecraftian horrors, 1950s experiments gone wrong and the dark side of superheroics. In one playtest game run by one of this sourcebook's authors, Luther Arkwright became a member of Planetary, recruited for his abilities to shift across the multiversal Bleed.

Index

Luther Arkwright

ROLEPLAYING ACROSS THE PARALLELS

Characteristics

STR	CON	SIZ	DEX	INT	POW	CHA	Luck Points

Attributes

Action Points	Damage Mod	Exp. Mod	Healing Rate	Move Rate	Prana Points	Strike Rank	Tenacity Points

Character Information

Player

Character — Parallel Designator

Sociological Type — Level of Development

Social Class — Career

Age — Gender — Handedness

Frame — Height — Weight

Description

Passions

___%

___%

___%

___%

Dependencies & Traits

___%

___%

Traits:

Hit Locations

1d20	Location	AP / HP	Armour Type	ENC
01-03	Right Leg	/		
04-06	Left Leg	/		
07-09	Abdomen	/		
10-12	Chest	/		
13-15	Right Arm	/		
16-18	Left Arm	/		
19-20	Head	/		

Weapons

Weapon Type	Damage	Fire Rate	Range	Ammo	Traits (Size/Reach for Melee Weapons)	Load

Standard Skills

Skill	Characteristics	%
Athletics	STR+DEX	___%
Brawn	STR+SIZ	___%
Conceal	DEX+POW	___%
Customs	INT x2	___%
Dance	DEX+CHA	___%
Deceit	INT+CHA	___%
Drive	DEX+POW	___%
Endurance	CON x2	___%
Evade	DEX x2	___%
First Aid	INT+DEX	___%
Home Parallel	INT x2	___%
Influence	CHA x2	___%
Insight	INT+POW	___%
Native Tongue	INT+CHA	___%
Perception	INT+POW	___%
Ride	DEX+POW	___%
Sing	POW+CHA	___%
Stealth	INT+DEX	___%
Swim	STR+DEX	___%
Unarmed	STR+DEX	___%
Willpower	POW x2	___%

Professional Skills

Skill	Characteristics	%
		___%
		___%
		___%
		___%
		___%
		___%
		___%
		___%
		___%
		___%

Fatigue

Current Level	State	Skill	Move	Strike Rank	Action Points	Recovery
○	Fresh	-	-	-	-	-
○	Winded	Hard	-	-	-	15 mins
○	Tired	Hard	-1m	-	-	3 hours
○	Wearied	Form	-2m	-2	-	6 hours
○	Exhausted	Form	Half	-4	-1	12 hours
○	Debilitated	Herc	Half	-6	-2	18 hours
○	Incapacitated	Herc	None	-8	-3	24 hours
○	Semi-Conscious	Hope	No Activity Possible			36 hours
○	Comatose	No Activity Possible				48 hours
○	Dead					Never

Sciences

Science	Characteristics	%
	INT x2	___%
	INT x2	___%

Combat Styles

Style	%	Weapons	Traits
Unarmed	___%		
	___%		
	___%		
	___%		

Skill Grades

Grade	Modifier
Automatic	No Roll Needed
Very Easy	Double
Easy	Increase by Half
Standard	-
Hard	Reduce by 1/3
Formidable	Reduce by 1/2
Herculean	Reduce to 1/10
Hopeless	No Attempt Poss

Other Languages

Language	Characteristics	%
	INT+CHA	____%
	INT+CHA	____%
	INT+CHA	____%
	INT+CHA	____%

Equipment

Item	Enc

Money/Wealth/Property

Description

Character

Name	Career

Notes

Psionic Talents and Powers

Talent	%	Intensity	Powers

Allies, Enemies, Friends

Name	A, E or F

Valhalla History/Parallels Visited

Family

Name	Relationship

Special Events & Mental Stability

What Happened?

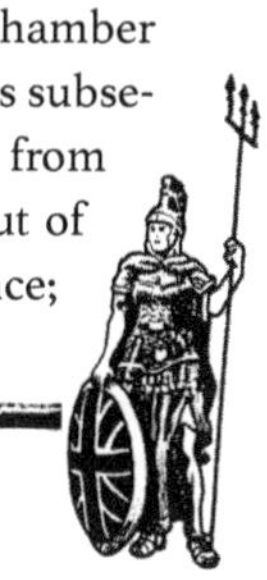

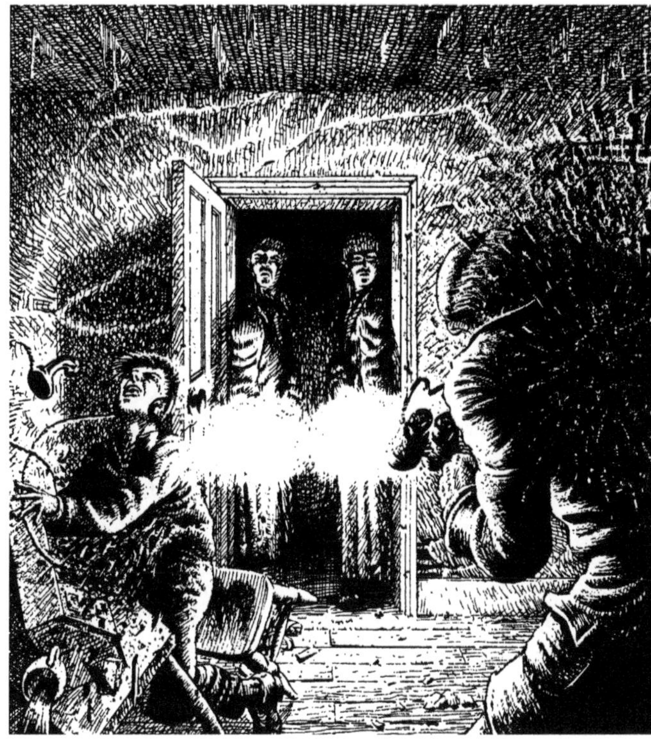

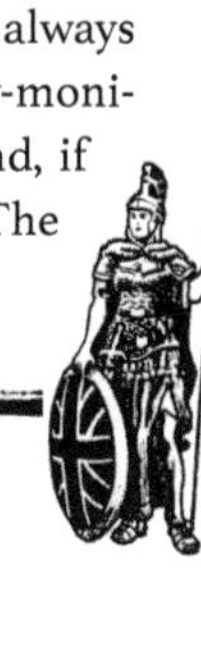

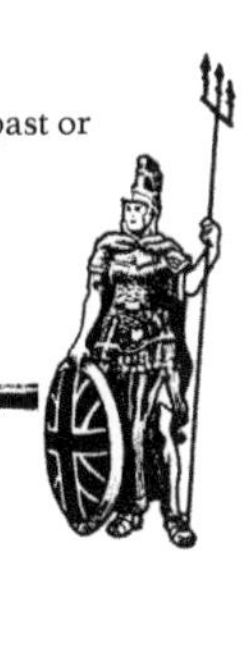

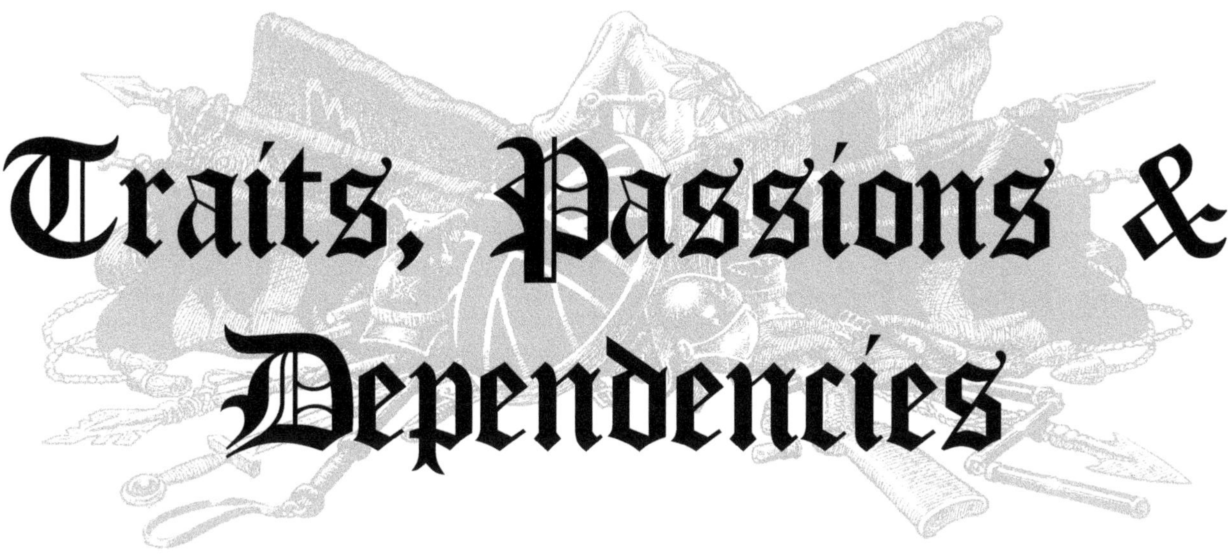

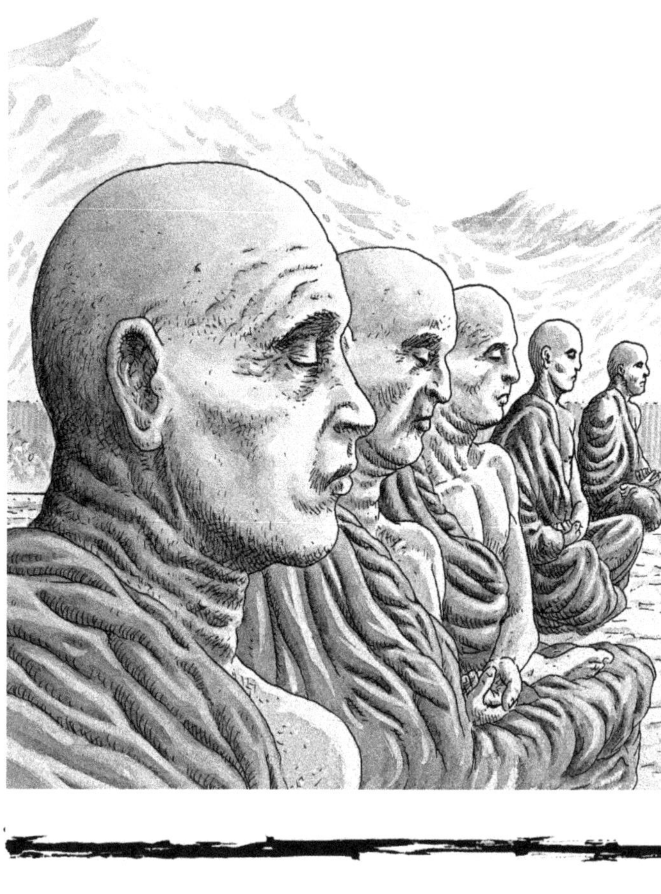

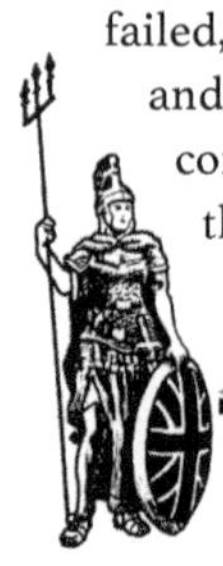

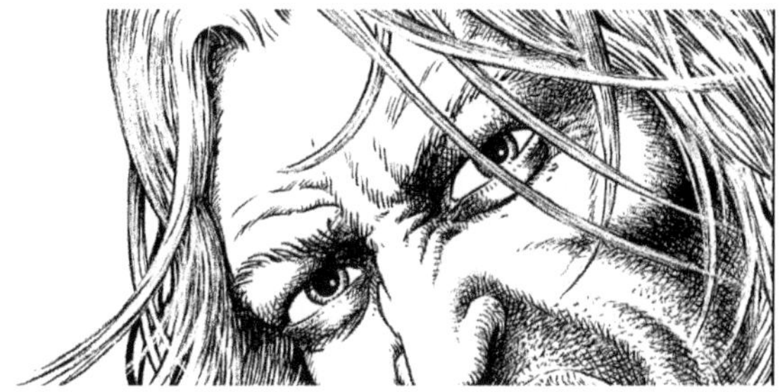

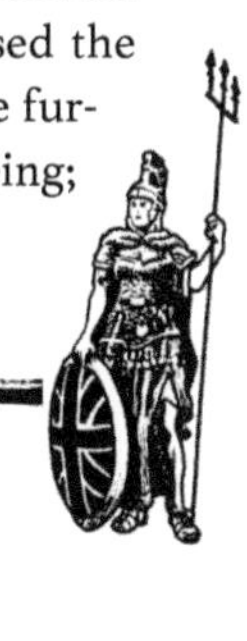

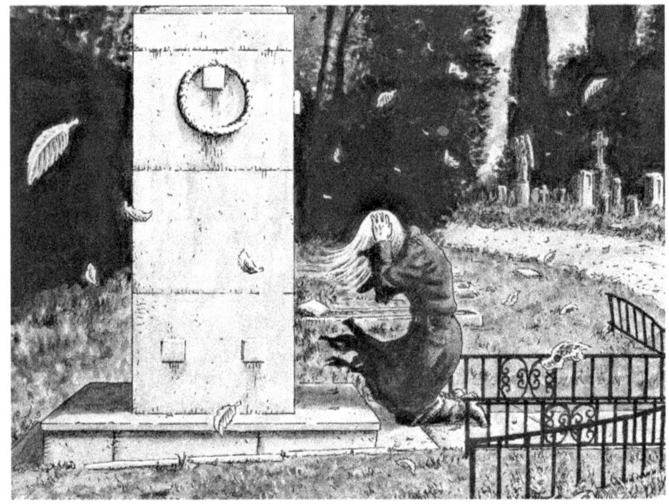

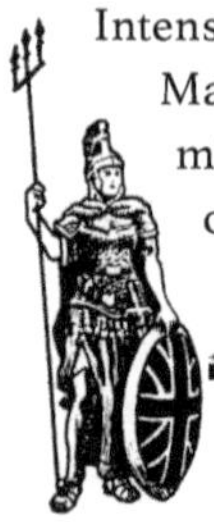

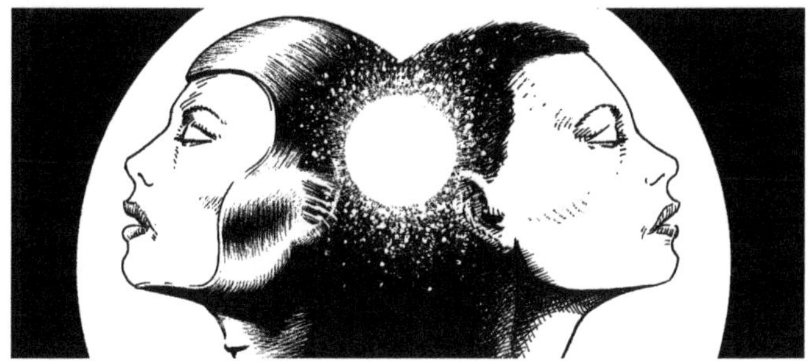

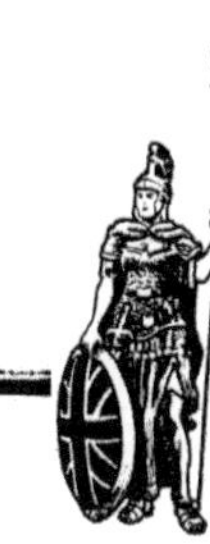

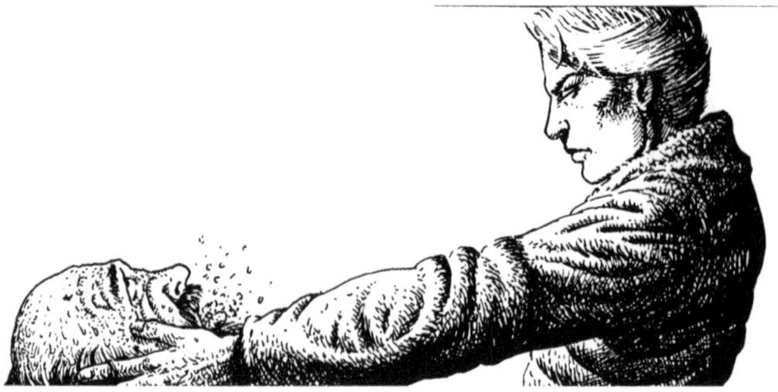

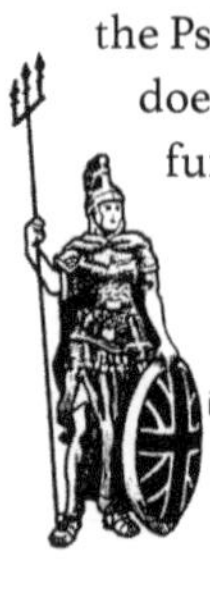

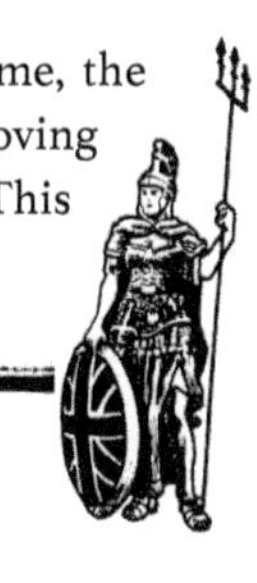

Step 1: Concept Table

1d100	Sociological Type					
	Academic	Artistic	Bureaucratic	Lawless	Manufacturing	Militaristic
01-10	Weapon or Armour	Industrial Tool	Travel Aid	Social Interaction Tool	Weapon or Armour	Personal Equipment
11-20	Industrial Tool	Travel Aid	Industrial Tool	Medical Tool	Travel Aid	Industrial Tool
21-40	Travel Aid	Personal Equipment	Personal Equipment	Weapon or Armour	Personal Equipment	Medical Tool
41-70	Personal Equipment	Social Interaction Tool	Medical Tool	Personal Equipment	Industrial Tool	Weapon or Armour
71-85	Social Interaction Tool	Unique Device	Social Interaction Tool	Travel Aid	Medical Tool	Travel Aid
86-95	Medical Tool	Medical Tool	Weapon or Armour	Industrial Tool	Social Interaction Tool	Social Interaction Device
96-00	Unique Device	Weapon or Armour	Unique Device	Unique Device	Unique Device	Unique Device

Step 2: Technology Base Table

1d100	Parallel Type					
	Steam Age	Industrial Age	Electronics Age	Computer Age	Nanotech Age	Spacefaring Age
01-10	Psionicology and Multiversal Theory	Psionicology and Multiversal Theory	Psionicology and Multiversal Theory	Xeno Science	Xeno Science	Steampunk/ Clockpunk
11-20	Alchemy, Biomancy and Chemistry	Steampunk/ Clockpunk	Psionicology and Multiversal Theory	Xeno Science	Steampunk/ Clockpunk	Alchemy, Biomancy and Chemistry
21-30	Alchemy, Biomancy and Chemistry	Steampunk/ Clockpunk	Steampunk/ Clockpunk	Steampunk/ Clockpunk	Alchemy, Biomancy and Chemistry	Computers, High-Sci and Nanotech
31-40	Steampunk/ Clockpunk	Steampunk/ Clockpunk	Steampunk/ Clockpunk	Computers, High-Sci and Nanotech	Alchemy, Biomancy and Chemistry	Computers, High-Sci and Nanotech
41-50	Steampunk/ Clockpunk	Steampunk/ Clockpunk	Computers, High-Sci and Nanotech	Computers, High-Sci and Nanotech	Computers, High-Sci and Nanotech	Computers, High-Sci and Nanotech
51-60	Steampunk/ Clockpunk	Steampunk/ Clockpunk	Alchemy, Biomancy and Chemistry	Alchemy, Biomancy and Chemistry	Computers, High-Sci and Nanotech	Computers, High-Sci and Nanotech
61-70	Transhumanism	Alchemy, Biomancy and Chemistry	Transhumanism	Alchemy, Biomancy and Chemistry	Computers, High-Sci and Nanotech	Transhumanism
71-80	Transhumanism	Alchemy, Biomancy and Chemistry	Transhumanism	Transhumanism	Transhumanism	Xeno Science
81-90	Xeno Science	Computers, High-Sci and Nanotech	Transhumanism	Psionicology and Multiversal Theory	Transhumanism	Xeno Science
91-00	Computers, High-Sci and Nanotech	Xeno Science	Xeno Science	Psionicology and Multiversal Theory	Psionicology and Multiversal Theory	Psionicology and Multiversal Theory

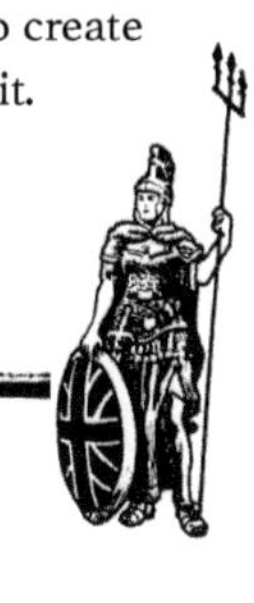

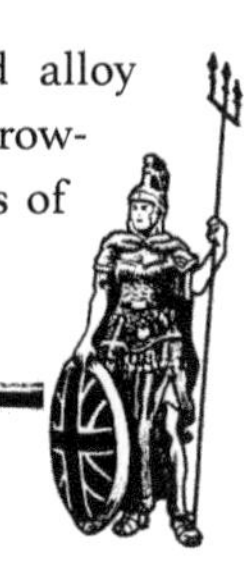

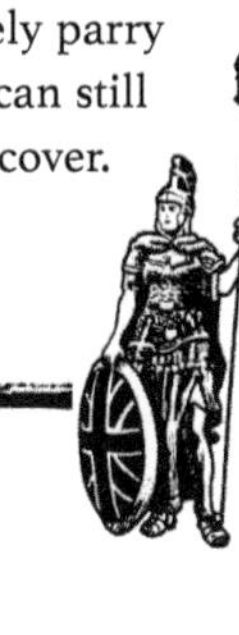

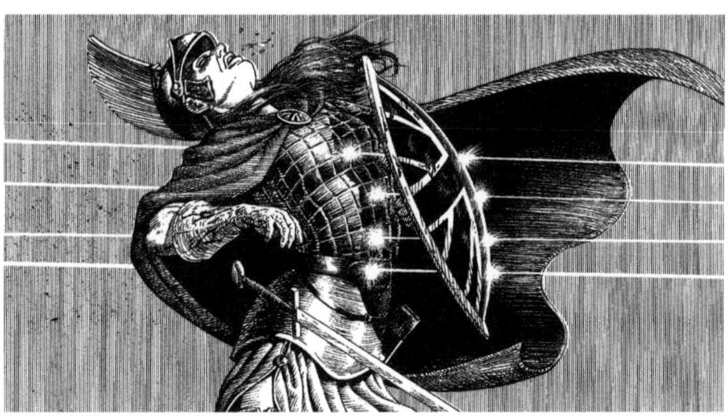

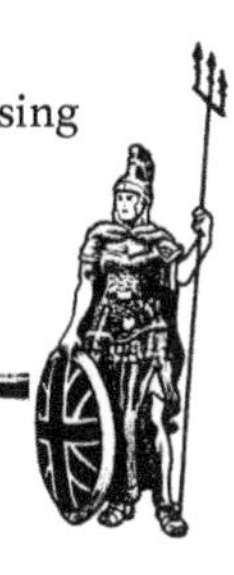

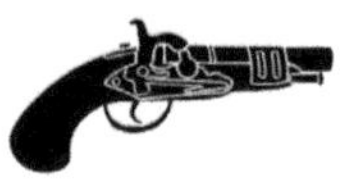
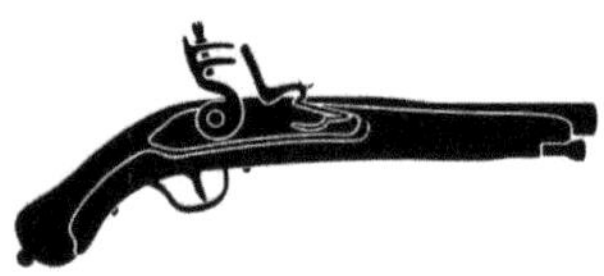
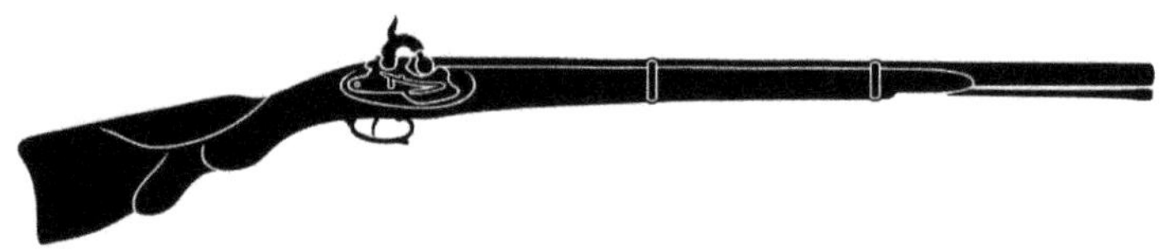

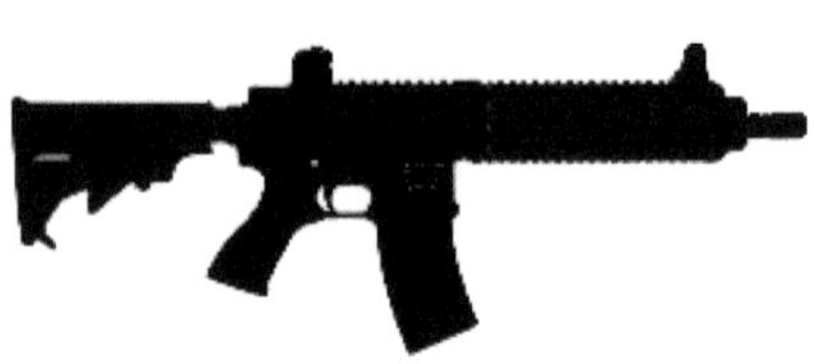
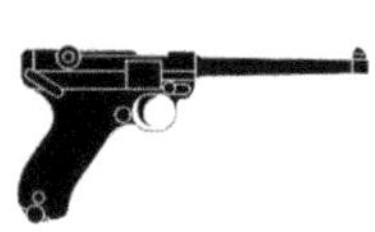
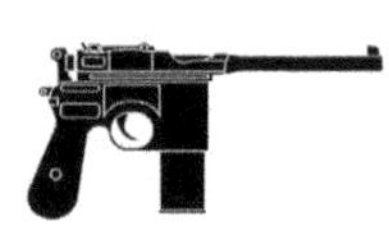
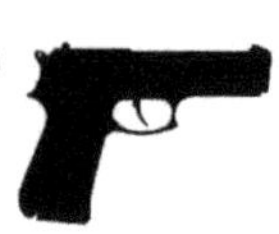
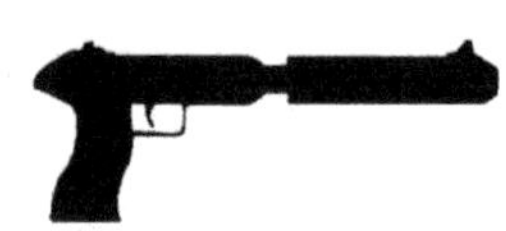

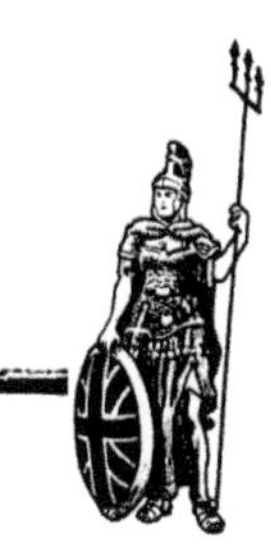

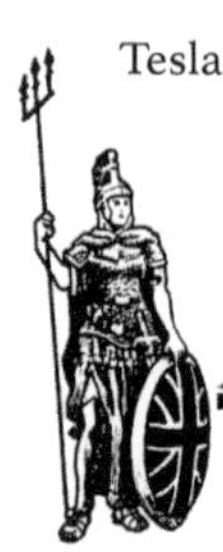

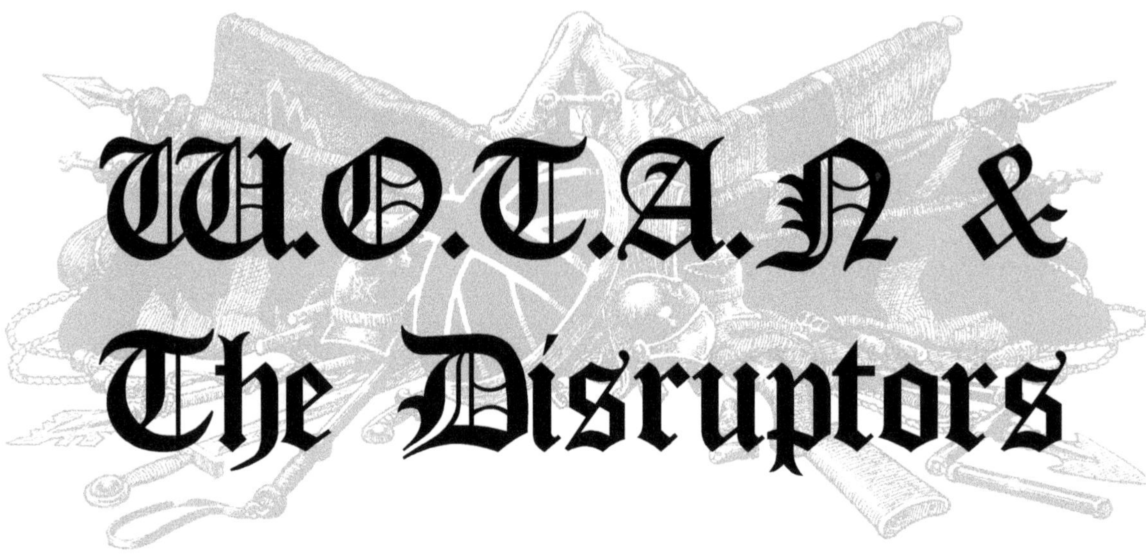

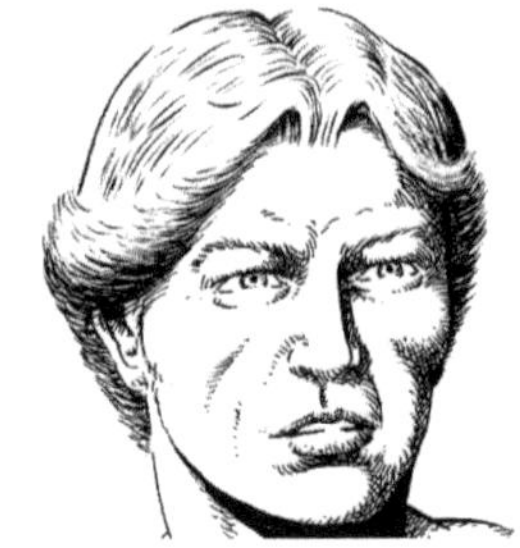

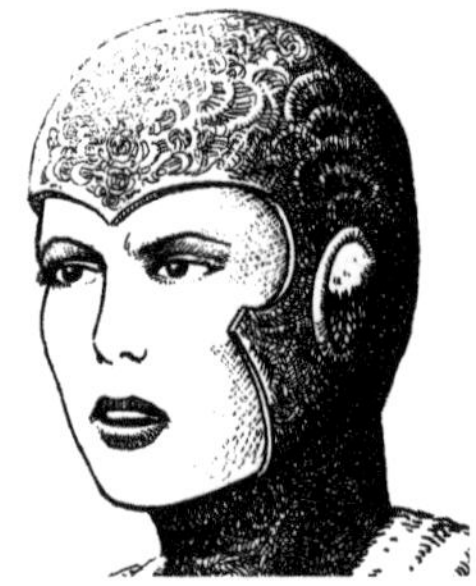

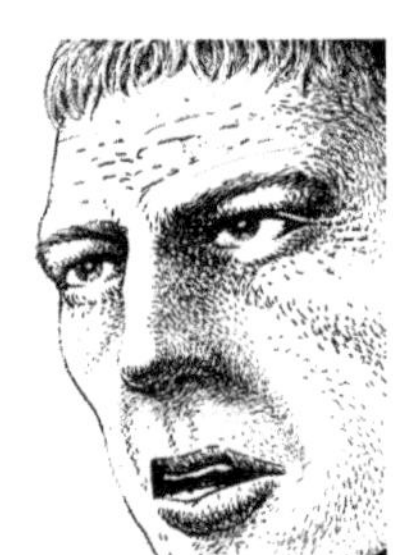

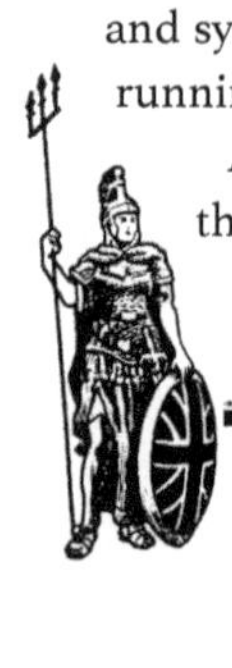

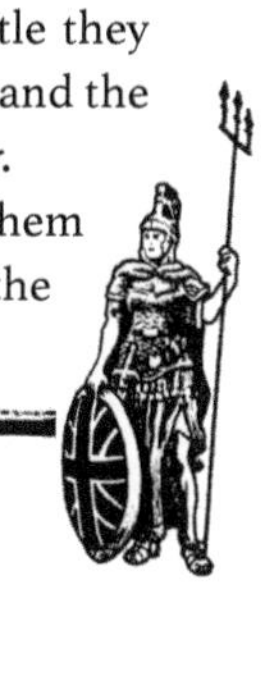

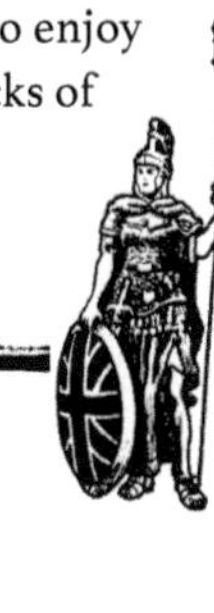

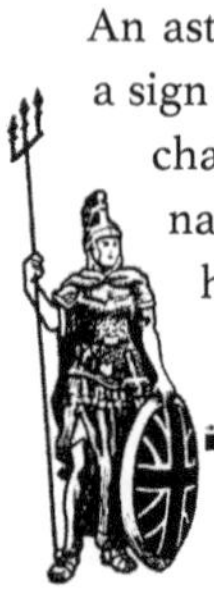

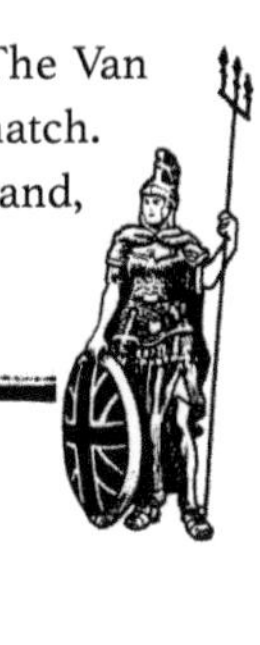

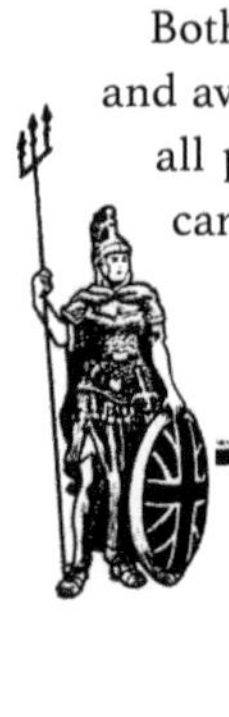

www.ingramcontent.com/pod-product-compliance
Ingram Content Group UK Ltd.
Pitfield, Milton Keynes, MK11 3LW, UK
UKHW051931100926
8556IPUK00022B/1478

9 781911 471073